The Visual Tcl Handbook

David H. Young

Prentice Hall P T R
Upper Saddle River, New Jersey 07458
http://www.prenhall.com

Library of Congress Cataloging-in-Publication Data

Young, David (David H.), 1952-
    The Visual Tcl Handbook / David Young.
      p. cm.
    Includes index.
    ISBN 0-13-461674-X (paper)
    1.Graphical user interfaces (Computer systems)   2. Visual Tcl (Computer program language).
I. Title.
QA76.9.U83Y68 1997
005.13'3—dc20   96–17226
                                     CIP

Editorial/Production Supervision: *Joe Czerwinski*
Acquisitions Editor: *Mark L. Taub*
Manufacturing Buyer: *Alexis R. Heydt*
Cover Design Director: *Jerry Votta*
Cover Illustration: *Marjory Dressler*
Cover Design: *Design Source*
Composition: *Thurn & Taxis*

 © 1997 by Prentice Hall P T R
Prentice-Hall, Inc.
A Division of Simon & Schuster
Upper Saddle River, NJ 07458

The publisher offers discounts on this book when ordered in bulk quantities.
For more information, contact:
    Corporate Sales Department
    Prentice Hall P T R
    One Lake Street
    Upper Saddle River, NJ 07458
    Phone: 800-382-3419
    Fax: 201-236-7141, e-mail: corpsales@prenhall.com

Printed in the United States of America
10   9   8   7   6   5   4   3   2   1

ISBN 0-13-461674-X

Prentice-Hall International (UK) Limited, *London*
Prentice-Hall of Australia Pty. Limited, *Sydney*
Prentice-Hall Canada Inc., *Toronto*
Prentice-Hall Hispanoamericana, S.A., *Mexico*
Prentice-Hall of India Private Limited, *New Delhi*
Prentice-Hall of Japan, Inc., *Tokyo*
Simon & Schuster Asia Pte. Ltd., *Singapore*
Editora Prentice-Hall do Brasil, Ltda., *Rio de Janeiro*

To my daughter Amanda, the real reason I wrote this book.

Contents

Part I: Introductions

Part II: Essential Tcl

Part IV: Command Pages

List of Figures

List of Tables

Preface

Just add Tcl...

By 1992, I had successfully weaned myself of programming in C and was ready to start acting like a real engineering manager. Managers should not do programming. They should spend their time giving reviews, fighting for resources, and enabling their folks to accomplish great feats (and meet a deadline or two!). At the time, we at SCO (The Santa Cruz Operation, Inc.) were implementing a graphical user interface (GUI) development technology we affectionately called the *widget server*. The widget server was the brainchild of Andy Schloss, Louie Boczek, and Susan DeTar, designed with the purpose of enshrouding SCO UNIX systems management with an OSF/Motif interface for the X environment. The widget server supported Motif programming by extending the conventional UNIX shell. As cool as it was to generate "instant" Motif "applets" around UNIX commands, few engineers were interested in doing it with less-than-glamorous shell scripting.

Then Mark Diekhans entered the picture. As codeveloper of the UNIX environment-specific TclX extensions, along with Karl Lehenbauer, Mark eventually made the suggestion that we try this cool scripting command language from UC Berkeley, developed by a professor whose name is one of the most mispronounced in the industry (next to Linux). John Ousterhout's name is pronounced /OH-stir-howt/ (according to his personal WWW page). So, to make a very long story short, we gave Tcl a shot and now, four years later, the technology formerly known as the *widget server* has been rechristened *Visual Tcl* and is available on ten UNIX platforms.

As the new manager of the widget server development group back in 1992, I thought I should develop at least a general notion of what it was like to program with this new language. My first, rather lofty goal was to create a "Motif wrapper" around the old BSD network utility rwho ("remote who"). A few hours later, I had a very useful Motif application up and running, monitoring virtually the entire SCO network of logged-in users. My status as a nonprogramming engineering manager had evaporated within only a few hours. With this book, I hope you will learn what I did—that with Tcl I could take on projects for which I felt I had neither the time nor the bandwidth, and be effective.

As evidenced by their demonstration of a new graphical "GUI Builder" at the SCO Forum conference in August 1995, SCO continues to enhance the feature set of Visual Tcl. To monitor the newsworthy events of the evolution of Visual Tcl, be sure to check out the official SCO Visual Tcl home page at:

```
http://www.sco.com/Products/vtcl/vtcl.html
```

SCO has trademarked this new language as *SCO Visual Tcl*. In this book, we will refer to it simply as *Visual Tcl*.

Strategy and style

Although Visual Tcl is ideal for a wide range of application development, many of the examples and discussions in this book are targeted at people who manage computers, such as system administrators and self-empowered users. UNIX administrators are usually the last folks to get access to tools, such as GUI scripting, that represent current technology trends and could make their lives easier (and more fun!). With that in mind, in addition to including a CD-ROM of Visual Tcl ported to ten flavors of UNIX (attached at the back of this book), I've made extensive use of UNIX administration-related examples to convey how Visual Tcl can be used to implement solutions in short order. Many of these examples represent simple tasks carried out by UNIX system administrators or experienced users who know their way around UNIX.

The goals behind the design of Visual Tcl were motivated by the demand for the rapid development of graphical systems management. As we will discuss in Chapter 1, *Modern Scripting*, much of the reason for the rise in scripting popularity is being driven by the need for flexibility and rapid development in the systems management environment.

This book focuses on examples that illustrate the most commonly used commands. Hoping to give novice readers the "biggest bang for their buck," I have focused on the basic value of each command as it is introduced. I avoid documenting every available option for the command. Instead, I try to use a narrative writing style to walk you through the introductory process of learning a new language. When you are ready to dive into greater detail regarding specific commands, the complete Visual Tcl command language and associated options are available in Part IV, *Command Pages*. This section is based on the man pages acquired from different contributors, including UC Berkeley, SCO, and the creators of TclX—the Tcl library that gives Visual Tcl its UNIX flavor.

This book was written with the assumption that the reader is familiar with at least one programming language, ranging from simple UNIX shell scripting to C, or just about any high-level language such as Pascal.

One last note about style. Dan Heller's style of writing, as found in *the Motif Programming Manual,* volume 6 (O'Reilly & Associates, Inc.), has had a major influence on me. He was the first author I encountered who took something as dry as the X/Motif programming language and explained it in a book that I enjoy cracking open on a regular basis. I hope I've come close to making *The Visual Tcl Handbook* as enjoyable to read.

Why Visual Tcl?

The success of the Tcl language is largely due to the power of its X window development extension called the *Tk toolkit*. Tk is wonderfully crafted and highly diversified in its features, capabilities, and adaptability. Tcl/Tk is one of the languages I love to work with. So, with the availability of Tk, why should you and I be interested in Visual Tcl?

A complete UNIX product

Visual Tcl is a fully supported product, highly focused on leveraging the capabilities of the UNIX server environment. The base language supports a satisfyingly full range of UNIX access commands that control processes and manipulate the UNIX file system. Standard commands supporting enhanced debugging capabilities and built-in TCP/IP access have been added to make it a valid development option for conducting a wide range of projects.

Visual Tcl is fully supported by SCO as part of its cross-platform SCO Premier Motif product, as well as its SCO OpenServer Release 5 operating system. In fact, Visual Tcl is the core implementation language of SCO's graphical and character-oriented systems management environment. Visual Tcl is the only graphical widget-rendering Tcl-based scripting language that ships fully supported and exposed in a mainstream UNIX operating system. Soon, SCO will ship Visual Tcl as the native GUI scripting language for UnixWare.

Designed for the system administrator profile

The Visual Tcl language was expressly designed to be a powerful, easy-to-use GUI development tool for the system administrator "in the trenches," as well as for the developers of graphical systems administration solutions. The widget-building commands of Visual Tcl support default behavior that requires the shortest of learning curves. By taking advantage of standard Motif dialogs, in many cases only one command is required to build, for instance, a file selection box. Conversely, the large number of command options leaves lots of room for customization and greater control over design issues.

Based on the standard OSF/Motif language

Although Tk has become more compliant with the Motif look and feel, it's still very different under the covers. The Visual Tcl display server is built on top of the OSF/Motif library. The Visual Tcl language leverages OSF/Motif conventions and semantics, such as the control of Motif widget resources. The Visual Tcl language is designed to present a single layer of control that insulates the developer from the details of the underlying X library.

For Motif developers, Visual Tcl is ideal for complementing their larger C/Motif applications with the "glue" of Visual Tcl scripts. The Motif developer can apply the same geometry management principles to both Visual Tcl scripts and compiled Motif applications.

Standard Motif Widgets

One of SCO's goals for Visual Tcl is to open up the display server API so that third-party widgets can be added. Supporting the Motif API will make it possible to extend Visual Tcl with the large base of commercially available widget sets.

The use of standard Motif widgets reduces programming effort. Instead of having to craft commonly needed complex dialogs from scratch, novice developers can gain a consistent look and feel by taking advantage of standard Motif dialogs.

Policy and widgets for rapid development

By building on top of a moderate amount of built-in policy in the form of default behavior and the leveraging of OSF/Motif widgets, Visual Tcl supports a level of rapid development that is faster than developing with Tk. There are extensions to Tk that provide "mega-widgets," such as file selection boxes; however, as these are non-Tk features, the burden is on you, the developer, to link these extensions with your development system. Also, if control at the X11 level is key to your development project, Tk may be the appropriate choice.

The Drawn List widget for high-volume data representation

There are a number of widgets that SCO added to the base OSF Motif 1.2 widget set. In addition to combo box and spin button widgets, SCO added the "Drawn List" widget that features the ability to incorporate pixmaps in a column-based list widget, similar to the hierarchical file manager widget in Microsoft's Windows 3.1.

The Drawn List widget gives Visual Tcl the ability to represent a tremendous amount of data in a modest amount of graphical real estate. Arranged hierarchically, the user can view data by expanding or collapsing list items.

An architecture for multiple GUI development...

As you will discover in the Chapter 3, *Run-Time Environment*, Visual Tcl incorporates a client-server architecture, separating the Motif-rendering display server from the interpreter. There are a number of benefits to this, including enhanced performance and support for "GUI independence." In fact, the SCO OpenServer version of Visual Tcl supports two types of user interface "look and feel," namely, X-based Motif and a curses-based character version of Motif called *Charm*. Support for a Microsoft Windows display server is key to SCO's future systems management plans as well.

... and thin client Windows development

SCO is planning to release a Microsoft Windows-based Visual Tcl interpreter in order to support management of SCO server products from the Windows environment. Visual Tcl's client-server architecture will be linked over the network, supporting Windows-based graphical display servers driven by Visual Tcl scripts executing on UNIX servers. This design strategy supports the growing trend toward "thin client" application design, reducing the "application footprint" on desktop environments by shifting the functional part of the application to the remote server. This topic is discussed in more detail in Chapter 1, *Modern Scripting*.

Visual Tcl was not designed to compete with Tk. Instead, it was designed to put the benefits of Motif development in the hands of people who want to take advantage of GUI development but who, until now, have not been able to handle the cost and time-consuming impact of learning GUI development.

If you are a Tcl novice or Tk expert

The Visual Tcl Handbook focuses primarily on the TclX and Vt extensions provided in Visual Tcl. This is done somewhat at the expense of going into extensive detail about the base Tcl language itself. Most of the fundamental Tcl topics are addressed, so that if you are new to Tcl, you will do just fine when you start some serious development with the overall language. If you want to learn more about the fine points of the base Tcl language, you will probably want to consider acquiring one or two books that focus more painstakingly on the base Tcl language itself, such as Brent Welch's *Introduction to Tcl/Tk Programming*. Keep in mind that the entire Tcl language, version 7.3, is documented in the *Command Pages* section of this book.

If you are already a Tk/Tcl programmer and have not worked with the extensions of the TclX library, this book provides an introduction to many of the key features.

Organization

The organization of this book is based on major sections that focus on background and architecture, Tcl and TclX basics, GUI concepts, programming with Visual Tcl, and, finally, the entire Visual Tcl language in man page format. Here are some details about each part and the chapters they contain.

Part I: Introductions

These three chapters address the role of scripting today, introducing Visual Tcl. Its architecture and Tcl components are reviewed in detail. Finally, a step-by-step exercise that builds a "graphical who" application is provided to give you a flavor of Visual Tcl programming before diving into the details.

Part II: Essential Tcl

Essential Tcl covers the broad spectrum on non-GUI building commands contributed by the base Tcl language and the TclX command set that gives Visual Tcl its UNIX server flavor. Special attention is given to the parsing principles and syntax rules of the Tcl interpreter, intended to help the reader avoid the typical pitfalls of those new to Tcl development.

Part III: Visual Tcl

After a brief overview of OSF/Motif, this section covers Visual Tcl concepts such as how callback procedures receive user input information from the graphical display server. The five Visual Tcl option classes are discussed as major Vt commands are reviewed, including those for building custom dialogs, graphical hierarchical lists, and pulldown menus. A Rolodex application is described and used to illustrate common concepts of Visual Tcl programming. The complete Rolodex application is made available on the CD-ROM. This section is wrapped up with a discussion of how to apply a design strategy to the development of interfaces for the configuration of your application.

Part IV: Command Pages

This part is divided into three sections, providing man pages for the nongraphical Tcl and TclX commands, the graphical Vt commands, and the Vx extensions, which add another level of ease of use to the Visual Tcl language.

Conventions

Code Fragments

There are many code fragments in this book, many of which are contained in the CD-ROM at the back of this book.

```
# Code fragments will look like this:
set bookTitle "The Visual Tcl Handbook"
```

Visual Tcl commands that appear in code fragments or normal paragraph text will be identified with the typeface Courier bold, such as the variable-assigning **set** command above.

Output

Text generated by the execution of a Visual Tcl command is prefaced with the ➡ symbol, followed by the output text in Courier fixed font. In the book, we make extensive use of the **echo** command to write the contents of a variable to stdout. For Tcl programmers, this is a TclX command that is roughly equivalent to the **puts** stdout command. The statement below combines the **echo** command with the string stored in the variable `bookTitle` from the statement above.

```
echo "This book is called $bookTitle"
```

results in the following output.

➡ `This book is called The Visual Tcl Handbook`

Tasks

Tasks are identified like this. Depending on the context, they are either suggested exercises for the reader or attempts to illustrate a concept or use of a command by following a suggested task.

Hints and tips boxes

> **Hint, tips, and clarification boxes ...**
>
> ... are bordered boxes that look like this. Their purpose is to point out some subtle uses or characteristics of Visual Tcl, to pass along neat tricks, or to highlight uses of particularly useful commands. The font used here is Helvetica-Narrow, ideal for squeezing a lot of information into a tiny little box.

Font conventions

- **bold Courier**   Visual Tcl commands

- *italicized Courier*   Variables or arguments passed to Visual Tcl commands

- plain Courier   Procedures and callbacks

- plain Times   Normal book text

- Helvetica-Narrow   Hints and tips boxes

Command syntax

The *conventions* listed in Table 1 are used to identify required and optional arguments to Visual Tcl commands. We have attempted to use self-descriptive argument names wherever possible (such as *fileName* to indicate that the argument requires the name of a file).

Table 1   Conventions for specifying command arguments

★	Indicates that the command is contributed by the TclX library. This is provided for those who want to write portable code for environments where Visual Tcl and TclX are not available.
varName	A user-defined variable name for pass-by-reference. Applies to any variable of the form *<object>Name*. Examples of other self-describing variable names are *fileName*, *listName*, and *arrayName*.
var	A generic name for a user-defined variable.
arg	A catch-all reference to an argument.
body	A Tcl script of one or more Tcl commands.
expr	An expression that combines values with one or more operators, such as `$varName == "done" or "$amount > 1.00"`
test	An expression used to test a condition, as in a flow of control command.
list	A list of items, such as `{apples oranges peaches olallieberries}` When the command is invoked, *list* may also be represented by a variable where $ substitution is performed, such as **llength** $myList
[*arg*]	Square brackets indicate that the argument is optional. *arg* may be either a user-created value (italicized) or a predefined command option (nonitalicized)
string	A user-provided string in quotes, such as *"The UNIX System"*. May be a variable, such as *$title*, containing a quoted string.

Command arguments that are italicized imply that the user determines the argument's value. Arguments like *test* and *body* will always be italicized, since the actual argument is created by the user. Nonitalicized arguments imply that a keyword known to the command is to be provided as an option, such as compare in the following command:

string compare *string1* *string2*

UNIX-isms and other details

All of the examples used throughout the book were created with SCO OpenServer Release 5 version of SCO Visual Tcl 1.0. Most of the examples were tested on the Solaris port of SCO Visual Tcl to verify their portability. The Rolodex example that is used to illustrate the use of most of the Visual Tcl graphical Vt commands has been written to be highly portable. The examples scattered throughout the book that utilize UNIX system commands are based on SCO OpenServer Release 5 and may, therefore, require "tweaking" to run on your favorite UNIX platform.

Visual Tcl on CD-ROM

SCO Visual Tcl 1.0 is a core component of the SCO OpenServer Release 5 family of operating systems. If you own or have access to these servers, then you already have access to Visual Tcl. In fact, you also have access to many, many scripts that were written in Visual Tcl as part of the SCO OpenServer native systems management environment called *SCOadmin*. Many of the SCOadmin application scripts are located in

```
/opt/K/SCO/Unix/5.0.0Cl/sa
```

SCO also provides a kit of SCOadmin tools and demonstration Visual Tcl scripting that enable you to write applications even faster than with raw Visual Tcl. It is downloadable via anonymous ftp from

```
ftp.sco.com:/TLS/tls575.custom     (tools and doc)
ftp.sco.com:/TLS/tls575.ltr        (cover letter, install info)
```

and should be useful for you even if you are not an SCO OpenServer customer. This kit has not been ported to non-SCO platforms, so treat it simply as a learning tool.

The CD-ROM enclosed in the back of this book contains the complete binary ports of SCO Visual Tcl 1.0 to ten UNIX platforms, including SCO Open Desktop. SCO requires that you purchase SCO Premier Motif in order to enjoy full support of Visual Tcl. SCO Visual Tcl 1.0 for the following platforms is provided on the CD-ROM.

✔ SunSoft **SunOS** 4.1.2 (For SPARC)	✔ HP **HP-UX** 9.0.1
✔ SunSoft **Solaris** 2.1 (For SPARC)	✔ IBM **AIX** 3.2.5
✔ SunSoft **Solaris** 2.1 (For Intel)	✔ SGI **IRIX** 5.0.2
✔ Digital Unix (**OSF/1**) 3.0 (For Alpha)	✔ SCO **Open Desktop** 3.0
✔ SCO **UnixWare** 2.01	✔ Sequent **DYNIX**/ptx 4.0.3

Visual Tcl Handbook Web Page

The capability of the Web, and Prentice Hall's support. has given me the opportunity to continue the evolution of this book with *The Visual Tcl Handbook* Home Page. This page can be accessed at the URL:

```
http://www/prenhall.com/young
```

My goal is to make this home page a place where I can further explore topics that I was able to only graze over in the book, as well as offer timely information of Visual Tcl-related developments. Topics areas will include:

Hints and Tips

e.g., Development issues with Charm
Expanded examples of passing variable information to callbacks

Errata

List of errors encountered in the book.

Enhancements of book discussions

Topics that might require further explanation are covered here. These topics go beyond the simple hints and tips.

Examples

A collection of examples sent to me from Visual Tcl users.

Rolodex Demo

My hope is to evolve the book's rolodex example with enhanced functionality as well as bug fixes.

Visual Tcl News and Thoughts

Late-breaking news related to Visual Tcl will appear here, as well as any help announcements that might point to recently-identified bugs.

If there is a topic that isn't addressed in this book, be sure to check the home page. If it isn't there either, send e-mail to me at david@inforef.com and we will do what we can to add it to the page.

Credits

Heller, Dan. 1991. *Motif Programming Manual.* Sebastopol, CA: O'Reilly & Associates, Inc.

Ousterhout, John K. 1994. *Tcl and the Tk toolkit.* Reading, MA: Addison-Wesley Publishing Company.

Welch, Brent. 1995. *Practical Programming in Tcl and Tk.* Upper Saddle River, NJ: Prentice Hall PTR.

Acknowledgments

Having the opportunity to publicly thank the people who support you is the best part of writing a book. Besides introducing Tcl to SCO, Mark Diekhans gave me the support and upbeat attention I needed as he patiently explained to me the subtleties of Tcl. People along the way who gave me the vital support I needed to keep the faith were led by Mike Shelton, who was the most supportive executive I've ever known. Other SCO management folks like Ron Rasmussen and Lorie Goudie have always supported me as friend and colleague.

A very special thank you is reserved for Ralf Holighaus of NetCS Informationstechnik GmbH. Ralf inspired the entirety of Chapter 22, *Design issues for configuration scripts*. No matter how wonderful a GUI-building language may be, it isn't worth much without good advice on user interface design. Ralf's wonderful Visual Tcl presentation at SCO Forum 95 inspired me to include his observations in this book.

The folks of the SCO Cambridge engineering team, particularly Olaf von Bremen and Zibi Perlin, made Visual Tcl a multiplatform reality as a component of the SCO Premier Motif CD-ROM, much of it through their own time and perseverance. Thanks Olaf! I hope this makes your efforts even more rewarding. I owe Olaf and Zibi, and the management team of Chris Scheybeler and Michelle Fearn, a great deal for supporting someone on the other side of the world who wanted to write a book.

Thanks to Michael "Hops" Hopkirk for his technical advice and inspiring vision for the next generation of Visual Tcl; also his SCO engineering partners, Shawn McMurdo, Mary Toscano, Susan DeTar, Bob Davis, and Donna Moore, representing the Visual Tcl development team, past and present. Thanks also to Wing Eng, Hops's predecessor, for making that great midcourse redesign that turned Visual Tcl language into a truly unique solution for those who have been reticent to move into graphical development. The entire engineering team poured their hearts into a project that had them swimming against the popular current.

Thanks to other former SCO colleagues Ron Record (of Skunkware fame), Chris Ratcliffe, Dion Johnson, and Brett Matesen. I thank them for going out of their way to help me when I, and Visual Tcl, needed it.

Thanks to Mark Taub of Prentice Hall, the editor who gave me just enough rope to write this book, I appreciate his faith, confidence, and patience.

Thanks to Michael O'Brien of Go Ahead Software. Michael's satisfying experience with using Tcl in his systems management product was particularly inspiring and gave me a number of ideas for examples in the book. Michael's inspiring comment to me was that he knew that Tcl was the way to go when he saw that just about every Can I do this? question posted to comp.lang.tcl was answered with a "yes."

Thanks to the gang of seven, Jean-Pierre Radley, Jerry Heyman, Fulko Hew, Bob Stockler, John 'tms' Navarra, Bueds Marc, and Tom Podnar, for their detailed reviews of the Tcl/TclX chapters. I appreciate their patience as I slid down the learning curve.

Thanks to Joe Moss for providing his *Tcl Language Usage Questions and Answers* Web page, http://route.psg.com/tcl.html, which gave me lots of ideas for example code.

Thanks to my start-up brothers of The Information Refinery, Inc., Paul Morgan, Michael Browder, and John Marco. Imagine trying to write a book and start a new company at the same time.

Thanks to my life friend Gale Frances for supporting a friend through the long haul; and to Lynne Hughes for her inspirational e-mail and miraculous love that pulled me through that last few months. And to Janet Young, thanks for being so supportive and helping me to find the time to wrap this book up.

Finally, like all fathers who have dreams, I did this book for my daughter Amanda and hope that it will inspire her to latch onto opportunities that turn dreams into rewarding accomplishments.

PART I

Introductions

Modern Scripting

✔ The popularity of GUI scripting
✔ Scripting in the distributed environment
✔ Introducing Visual Tcl
✔ Comparing Visual Tcl with other scripting languages

Thanks to the amazing computing power of inexpensive, multimedia-capable computers, as well as the always-increasing need for flexibility within the distributed computing environment, scripting languages are carving out a sizable niche in software development circles. This chapter postulates why and where scripting is exploiting old and new niches in the evolutionary landscape. Thanks to evolving application architectures like three-tier computing and distributed objects described in this chapter, new opportunities for leveraging the benefits of script-based development are becoming available. With a special focus on the needs of the systems administration computing niche, we introduce Visual Tcl for X window programming using the OSF/Motif standard. A brief survey of its origins, features, and strengths are presented. Relating Visual Tcl to other scripting languages, a short comparison with Tk and the Windowing KornShell is provided.

Scripting today

The cover pages of technical language journals, previously dominated by the excitement of object-oriented programming, have recently had to make room for the equally hot topic of run-time interpreter language development, commonly referred to as *scripting*. While extremely promising, the industry-wide adoption of object technology faces a long, uphill battle. Object-oriented languages require significant changes in development planning and practices. No matter how wonderful the promise, developers tend to stick to the tools that have served them well. Languages such as C++ and Smalltalk are fine for large-scale, long-haul, highly focused development projects. But for development conditions that demand

- rapid turnaround,
- cross-platform portability,
- customer-specific customization,
- regular reworking to accommodate dynamic conditions, and
- solutions delivered by individuals or small teams, such as system administrators,

object-oriented languages have yet to offer an environment that can match the flexibility and broad applicability of scripting-based development.

Historically, scripting languages have served as that little bit of glue that guides computers through operating system boot up (e.g., the DOS `autoexec.bat`) or performs essential configuration chores in low-resolution video conditions using simple prompts for equally simple answers, such as `y` for yes, `n` for no, or `q` for quit. While scripting has long served as the native tool for building effective custom solutions on top of powerful UNIX system and network utilities, a significant gap had grown between the standard scripting look and feel of character-based prompts and the more flexible, easier-to-use flow of C-based GUIs. Perceived by UNIX system vendors, the storm clouds on the horizon labeled *NT* represent a new class of server that raises customer expectations for well-integrated graphical interfaces in the server environment. Even veteran UNIX engineers are wondering if, for job security reasons, it might not be a good idea to at least casually crack open a book and see what Microsoft Visual Basic programming is all about.

Thanks to a new generation of very high-level languages (VHLLs) supporting GUI development scripting technologies popularized by UC Berkeley's Tcl/Tk and, indeed, Microsoft Visual Basic, there is little excuse for script-based development to provide solutions that, when well designed, are any less easy to use than are today's graphical desktop applications. The feasibility of these tools has been made possible by the well-documented leaps of everyday computing power, as well as by new design architectures that have been greatly influenced by computing on the network.

These and other powerful scripting languages are presenting general applications developers, systems administrators, and developers of administrative tools with the ability they need today to

- rapidly automate and improve the usability of management tasks utilizing the same underlying tools they have used for years,
- create highly usable interfaces that reduce the customer's need to hire a stable of technical gurus, and
- greatly reduce the pain and logs of support calls traditionally generated during software and hardware installation and configuration steps.

Compiled applications benefit as well by the growing roles that can be taken on by scripting. Graphical applications embedded with an interpreter feature the ability to be tailored and automated from user-written scripts. The company's resident power user uses the application's script-based command language to build a library of tools that simplify daily tasks and incorporate the company's standard practices, policies, and procedures. Reducing tasks to a few simple steps frees users to focus on the work they are hired to do instead of drowning in feature-rich applications about which they need little knowledge.

Using a modern scripting language, graphical dialogs are quickly prototyped for evaluation in a human factors lab. Better than hand-drawn sketches, user interface designs that are scripted to emulate the functionality that occurs when a button is pushed or a menu item is selected improve lab evaluation feedback. Once the design is frozen, the GUI portion of compiled construction can begin with a high degree of confidence that the potential for last-minute reconstruction has been minimized.

Many application tasks and features that do not require high performance characteristics can be crafted simply with a GUI scripting language, making the application much easier to get up and running as well as to maintain. The end result is that your main application can focus on core features and can be easier to maintain and evolve during its product cycle.

Scripting and systems management

So far, most of the graphical scripting craze has been isolated to the desktop environment. Today there is a growing class of scripting languages and technologies addressing the needs of the server environment, most notably served by the UNIX operating system. The relatively new scenario of small departmental clusters of desktop PCs served by large-capacity UNIX application, file, and Internet servers is beginning to take hold. Users in these environments are enjoying centralized resources and services, as well as new cooperative computing capability popularized by products like Lotus Notes.

Despite all of the advantages of the decentralized approach to departmental computing, there are a number of old issues that remain. Most notably, organizations are finding that they still need to maintain a stable of UNIX gurus nearby to troubleshoot common system management situations. The fact is that the practice of linking computers in networks is not yet at the cookie-cutter stage of distributed computing evolution. Corporate networks, and the policies and procedures by which they are governed, reflect an organization's unique identity, attitude, and need for innovation. A one-size-fits-all architecture and management infrastructure will never be a reality. Networks demand flexibility, and management tools must support the ability to adapt to unique issues that occur specific to particular customer needs.

Much of the popularity of UNIX is based on its ability to adapt to virtually any imaginable variation of network configuration. UNIX's powerful set of command line utilities, ranging from who to netstat, as well as commands supporting NFS and remote login, are part of the traditional UNIX TCP/IP arsenal. A new class of native UNIX operating system VHLLs such as Visual Tcl is the key to moving UNIX into the modern server era without abandoning its inherently flexible strengths. Visual Tcl preserves the flexibility of UNIX commands in the process of making them safe and easy to use by users who are less technical than are typical network administrators.

Figure 1–1   Three-tier computing scenario

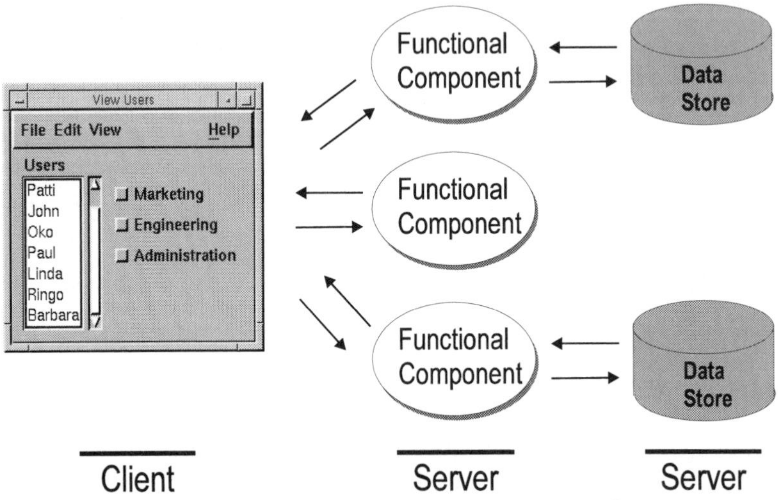

Thin clients, three-tiered computing, and distributed objects

There are new strategies for application design being forged by the forces of distributed computing represented in the popular press by organizations such as the Object Management Group (OMG), Microsoft, major database vendors, and 4GL development toolmakers. These strategies define new approaches to the structure of applications, creating new opportunities for a VHLL such as Visual Tcl to play a major role.

As part of its common object request broker architecture (CORBA), the OMG has defined an object request broker (ORB), that acts like a network telephone switchboard, dispatching requests and responses between application clients and one or more functional objects that provide useful services such as data storage, video rendering, spreadsheet calculation, and so on. In principle, the user has no idea that the application they are using is actually a "virtual application" spread all over the network.

Script-based graphical dialogs are ideal for this type of distributed computing "framework." As functional objects (sometimes referred to as *business objects)* are updated with new capabilities, dialogs can be easily reworked to present new information.

Another view of distributed computing, referred to as *three-tier computing*, defines applications in terms of clear-cut functional roles. Three-tier computing separates the dialog portion of an application from the functional component (Figure 1–1). The first tier component, the dialog, presents the GUI to the user, collecting and presenting data and options. The second tier functional component represents the application's decision-making ability, sometimes referred to as its *business knowledge*. The third tier is characterized by high-powered databases that store information about the state of the functional component. In the distributed world, the functional component may be scattered over a substantial number of servers in a large corporation.

Three-tier computing is one of a number of application architectures that supports the notion of *thin clients*. Thin clients are created by separating an application's front-end dialog from its back-end functional component. The thin client component is left on the desktop system, while the larger functional component is located on a server system.

One of the promises of distributed computing is that it provides businesses with the ability to distribute software in a manner that takes full advantage of the computing power of their network environment. By designing applications so that the compute-intensive functional portion can be located on a powerful server system and accessed by desktop users running thin clients, more efficient use of computing and staff resources can be achieved. For example, thin clients make it easier for system administrators to focus on maintaining the health of the relatively smaller number of servers supporting the functional and database components. Desktop support issues are reduced because there are fewer things that can go wrong, such as running out of disk space. Consider the traditional headache of software distribution and version control when conventional applications, predictably labeled *fat clients*, are scattered all over the enterprise. Once again, thin clients present yet another opportunity for GUI-building scripting to take care of the dialog portion of new-age applications, leaving the performance-sensitive functional components for lower-level compiled languages such as C++.

...And it's fun, too

The joy of programming should not be casually discounted. Internal support departments tend to be the whipping boy of most organizations because they are so visible and easy to single out. Easily accessible GUI tools like Visual Tcl empower system administrators to expand their work experience and build tools that benefit the company in the process. Having fun in the process of development addresses an essential element of team morale, especially when it is applied to departments that are responsible for corporate backbone functions, such as network and systems administration.

Fun and innovation feed off of one another. The subject of this book, Visual Tcl, spawned numerous development projects at SCO that would otherwise never have seen the light of day. The development of SCO's graphical management product for the OSF Distributed Computing Environment (DCE) was the direct result of the availability of Visual Tcl. Engineers were able to use its rapid development capability to design and demonstrate their product ideas to upper management. There is nothing like tangible, demonstrable functionality to boost the confidence of product decision-makers.

Introducing Visual Tcl

Visual Tcl is a very high-level language and run-time environment for the development of tools and applications for the X Window environment. Based on the OSF/Motif standard for GUI look and feel, Visual Tcl scripting is ideal for the development of:

- Motif wrappers around UNIX commands,
- small-to-medium sized productivity applications (or applets), and
- graphical installation and configuration tools.

SCO developed Visual Tcl with the purpose of putting a Motif interface on top of its systems management application suite. Rather than hire more X/Motif engineers, SCO set out to find a way to provide its expert systems management engineers with the means to build Motif applications without drowning in the details of GUI development.

Another design goal acknowledged the reality that a large proportion of system administrators must perform tasks in the character terminal environment. Anybody who is knee-deep in UNIX systems administration responsibilities knows that character terminals are still prevalent throughout many businesses. Therefore, Visual Tcl was designed to support application development in the X and non-X environments. This feature makes it possible for a developer to create a single application that can be rendered in X/Motif as well as in what SCO calls *Character Motif*. As it turns out, there are a number of derivative benefits worth considering. First, only one source tree is required for two distinctly different supported environments. Secondly, because Visual Tcl supports the Motif widget concept in both environments, a single version of the documentation of Visual Tcl applications is possible. By preserving a consistent look and feel between the X and non-X environments, the need for explaining differences in the use of the application is minimized.

Requiring only a minimum number of environment-specific changes, a script developed in the X/Motif environment would "just run" in the dumb terminal character environment. Though this book only modestly addresses the Character Motif aspect of Visual Tcl programming, it is this multi-look-and-feel support that SCO is taking advantage of to eventually add Microsoft Windows support to Visual Tcl.

This is made possible by the Visual Tcl client/server architecture, separating the extended Tcl interpreter client from a display server. This design turns out to have been a serendipitous decision. The ability of Visual Tcl to serve multiple client applications gives it some unique properties as compared to other scripting languages of note, such as Tk and dtksh, discussed below. Chapter 3, *Run-Time Environment*, will address the Visual Tcl architecture in greater detail.

Getting productive with Visual Tcl

The first thing that struck me about Visual Tcl and the public-domain Tcl language upon which it is based was how quickly I could develop something useful, whether it was just manipulating some data or prototyping some interfaces to toy with application ideas. The subsections that follow cover a few reasons for Tcl's popularity and utility, as well as the added value that Visual Tcl brings to developers. In order to make the discussion as meaningful as possible, some Tcl concepts are introduced that will be more fully explained later in the book.

Designed to manipulate data easily

By virtue of its Tcl heritage and language extensions, Visual Tcl supports an impressive set of commonly needed data-manipulating commands. Combined with an extensive set of UNIX access commands, development time is spent on solving problems directly, as opposed to diverting a large portion of time to developing commands for supporting development.

Lists provide a useful means for viewing and organizing things. In the world of systems management, lists typically consist of:

- users
- machines
- processes

- installed applications
- media devices
- system log files

- IP addresses
- print jobs
- file systems

As a VHLL, Visual Tcl provides a comprehensive set of commands that know how to manipulate lists. Tasks that

- match items in a list
- remove duplicate items in a list
- insert or delete a range of items
- sort items

are carried out with single lines of code using the Visual Tcl language.

Suppose you want to create a simple data structure for storing data, using the tried-and-true metaphor of pushing and removing lunch trays from a stack in a cafeteria. There is no need to craft the background routines that manage and manipulate a stack data structure, since they are already provided as an inherent feature of the base Visual Tcl language. Visual Tcl provides two commands, **lvarpush** and **lvarpop**, for pushing and popping data.

As an illustration, suppose we have a list of things to do, stored as a Tcl list in a variable that we will call `thingsToDo`. The list in this variable may already contain three items that we promised ourselves we would do earlier, such as

```
{{Call doctor}
{Write letter to editor}
{Start jogging}}
```

where "`Start jogging`" occupies the bottom of the stack. Suppose we want to add another thing to do, namely, pay the phone bill, which needs to be done as soon as the opportunity presents itself.

```
lvarpush thingsToDo "Pay the phone bill"
```

Our list, which we are treating as a stack, now takes on the following appearance.

```
{{Pay the phone bill}
 {Call doctor}
 {Write letter to editor}
 {Start jogging}}
```

Later in the day, when we finally have time to check in with our list, we can perform the following to extract the most recently stored item.

lvarpop thingsToDo

➡ Pay the phone bill

lvarpop "pops" the topmost item from our stack. Not only are we reminded of the last task we put in our list, but the list has been trimmed back to its original three tasks that we will get to another day. That's it. No linked lists to build. No searching for that old data structures book you remember loaning to the guy down the hall. These are the kinds of native language tools that are characteristic of a VHLL. Visual Tcl represents the evolution of a high-level language that addresses most of the problem-solving you will ever need to confront in the process of application development.

This is a simple example of how some very powerful commands in Visual Tcl can save you a great deal of programming time.

Full UNIX development environment

When you think about C versus shell scripting development, you may think about what C and supporting C libraries provide, such as

- tracking I/O activity on a pipe
- locking and unlocking data files
- executing and forking subprocesses
- sockets programming

Visual Tcl provides this functionality and more, using commands and concepts that will be familiar to veteran UNIX/C developers. The comprehensive nature of Visual Tcl programming makes it ideal for prototyping nongraphical as well as graphical components of C development.

High-volume data support

Management applications are commonly required to work with huge amounts of data. The challenge to GUI designers is to present data in a format that makes it easy for the user to locate the necessary information. Going beyond the OSF/Motif 1.2 toolkit widget set, SCO added the Drawn List widget, a very flexible, list-oriented widget that supports the ability to combine columns of intermingled text and pixmaps. The Visual Tcl

VtDrawnList command also provides graphics primitives for representing data in a hierarchical format similar to the Windows File Manager control (Figure 1–2).

Figure 1–2   Visual Tcl's DrawnList widget for hierarchical data representation

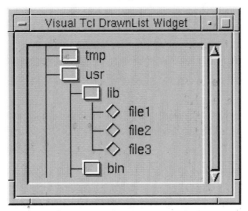

Consistent-looking, easy-to-build user dialogs

Visual Tcl supports many of the standard OSF/Motif user interface elements, such as the *file selection box*. This readily recognizable dialog (Figure 1–3) for selecting files and directories is constructed of at least three push buttons, two lists with adjoining vertical and horizontal scrollbars, three labels, and two text widgets. In addition to its visual elements, this dialog also takes care of retrieving and listing files and directories as well as providing a filtering mechanism to expedite the user's search for a particular file.

Use of backslash character:

All of the examples in this book use the \ character so that each option of a Vt command occurs on its only line. The backslash character tells the Visual Tcl interpreter that the current line continues on the next line. Liberal use of this feature is recommended, particularly as subsequent examples use more and more options. Keeping one option per line makes editing much easier (and keeps code looking very clean).

Rather than having to craft a file selection dialog from scratch, a single call to the Visual Tcl command **VtFileSelectionDialog**

```
VtFileSelectionDialog $form.filesel \
        -filter "/usr/bin/X11/*" \
        -title "X11 applications"
```

with a small number of command line options will display a full-featured Motif file selection dialog, ensuring consistency with the way other file selection boxes appear in other Motif applications. Not only is the programmer relieved of having to construct a lot of code, they are also spared the time it takes to consider what it takes to design this dialog from scratch.

Figure 1–3   Standard Motif FileSelection dialog

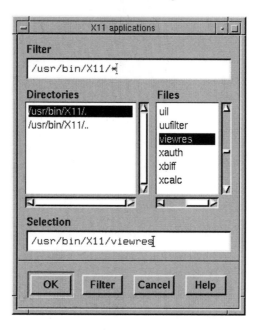

When Visual Tcl is not the solution

During the development phase of Visual Tcl, SCO chose to strike a balance between ease of use and access to Motif capabilities. Also, as a pragmatic consideration, SCO prioritized the number of widgets that Visual Tcl 1.0 would support. As you will discover in the reading of this book, most of the widgets you will ever need are supported. The list of Visual Tcl 1.0 unsupported widgets include:

- drawing area
- arrow button
- paned window

Visual Tcl and other scripting technologies

Visual Tcl represents a unique approach to constructing graphical tools and applications. To understand where it fits in the larger scheme of software development options, some simple comparisons with other well-known GUI scripting technologies are presented below.

Tk

Developed by John Ousterhout while at the University of California, the Tk toolkit is the X11-based Tcl extension for user interface development. Tk is probably the real reason Tcl has enjoyed the popularity that it has. Visual Tcl builds on a number of Tk concepts, most notably its widget-naming convention, described later in Chapter 10, *Visual Tcl Concepts*.

Some of the ways that Visual Tcl is distinguished from Tk are highlighted in the following points.

- Visual Tcl is based on OSF/Motif 1.2. Tk is built on X11.
- Visual Tcl supports a client/server architecture, separating the interpreter from the graphical interface-building functions. Tk is a single binary that interprets scripts and renders graphical interfaces from within a single executing process.
- Visual Tcl is focused on the UNIX server, offering an extensive set of UNIX-specific commands. Tk is a more portable product, requiring that the developer use a development system to link any system-specific extensions, such as the TclX Tcl extension that provides Visual Tcl with its native access to the UNIX environment.
- Both Tk and the Visual Tcl run-time environment are freely available. Visual Tcl source code is not in the public domain. It is a technology supported by SCO. Tk is in the public domain and is supported by a cooperative relationship between the Tk community and John Ousterhout.
- Tk gives the developer more control of the user interface environment. In order to support a very low learning curve and rapid development, Visual Tcl provides control over most of the user interface elements that you will need in most development projects.

For more about Tk, see *Practical Programming in Tcl and Tk* by Brent Welch (Prentice Hall).

The Desktop KornShell (dtksh)

dtksh, formerly known as the *Windowing Korn Shell*, is an extension of the Korn shell environment with Xt and Xm (OSF/Motif) function calls. The comparison is fairly straightforward.

- Both Visual Tcl and dtksh support the OSF/Motif look and feel.
- dtksh is a straight mapping of the entire X11, Xt, and Motif Xm libraries. Visual Tcl provides a layer of abstraction above the Xm and Xt intrinsics.
- Visual Tcl is based on the Tcl language. dtksh is based on Korn shell.

The key to Visual Tcl is Tcl. Tcl is the base language that supports the set of features that makes Visual Tcl an ideal environment of Motif programming. The development of GUI applications requires a level of robustness that probably goes beyond the capability of typical UNIX shell programming. The Tcl community is producing a great number of extensions to the language that Visual Tcl developers will be able to take advantage of. Although dtksh is extensible, there is little evidence that it will enjoy the same abundance of contributions.

A Quick Start

✔ Develop a Motif wrapper around the UNIX who command
✔ Review simple elements of Visual Tcl scripting
✔ Create a simple procedure and callback

*T*he goal of this chapter is to give you a brief but meaningful flavor of the Visual Tcl language by writing a simple Motif wrapper around a well-known UNIX command. First we will compose a simple version of a "graphical who" application (or applet), then rework it a bit to illustrate the use of procedures and event callbacks. In the process of writing this applet, we will introduce a number of features of the Visual Tcl language, all of which will receive detailed treatment in subsequent chapters.

The UNIX who command

System administrators and many users in the multiuser UNIX environment have come to rely on the UNIX who command at one time or another. Typing who at a UNIX shell prompt might yield lines of output such as:

➡
```
carolyn   tty02 May 10 19:26
amanda    ttyp1 May 10 18:01
andrew    ttyp2 May 9 09:50
```

From this example, one might determine that either Andrew forgot to log off the previous evening or he is fast asleep at his desk. Another user of who might have the goal of determining if Amanda has logged in yet before heading over to her office.

In order to execute who in the X11 graphical environment, users need access to an xterm in order to get access to a UNIX shell prompt. An administrator might have the goal of migrating users away from their dependency on the UNIX shell prompt by providing graphical front-ends or Motif wrappers around useful, commonly used UNIX commands. Using Visual Tcl, our administrator can accomplish this very quickly. With the goal of liberating users from the UNIX shell prompt, our administrator might set out to accomplish the following task:

TASK   *Write a Visual Tcl script that displays the list of users currently logged on the system.*

The Graphical Who program

The code that follows is a file containing a complete Visual Tcl application that provides a simple graphical interface for the output of the who command. Each line of code is preceded by a number that we will use to walk through this applet line by line.

```
1:    #! /bin/vtcl
2:    set progTitle "Graphical Who"
3:    # Establish Visual Tcl Server Connection
4:    set appRoot [VtOpen gwho]
5:    set mainForm [VtXformDialog $appRoot.mainForm \
          -title $progTitle \
          ]
6:    set listW [VtList $mainForm.listW \
          -itemList [split [exec /bin/who] \n] \
          -scrollBar True \
          -rightSide FORM \
          -bottomSide FORM \
          -font monoBoldFont \
          ]
7:    VtShow $mainForm
8:    VtMainLoop
```

The result of this program has the following appearance (Figure 2–1).

Figure 2–1   The Graphical Who user/interface

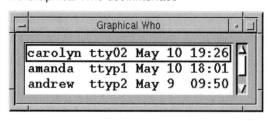

Let's walk through the code.

```
#! /bin/vtcl
```

Line 1 contains non-Visual Tcl code. The #! is a special character sequence that instructs the kernel to execute the named program, /bin/vtcl. The user's current shell (e.g., sh, ksh, or csh) is completely bypassed. /bin/vtcl is the Visual Tcl interpreter required to process the rest of the file's contents.

Coding conventions—variable and procedure names

In this book, we'll use the following naming conventions:

Variables will start with a lowercase letter. Any "words" that are imbedded in the rest of the name will start with an uppercase letter (e.g., userName, myProg).

Procedures (discussed later) will use the same convention, except that the name will start with an uppercase letter (e.g., BuildUserList, OpenTarFile).

Be sure to check the README file included in the CD-ROM. The pathname of the vtcl program varies, depending on the UNIX system.

```
set progTitle "Graphical Who"
```

Line 2 illustrates the Tcl **set** command for storing values in a variable. Here we are storing the string "Graphical Who" in the variable progTitle. If we had not placed quotes around the two words, we would have received an error about attempting to assign more than one word to a variable. The quotes inform the Visual Tcl interpreter to treat multiple words as a single string. Quotes would not have been necessary for a single word, since the interpreter views everything as a string.

Line 2 is also an example of a Tcl script. Tcl defines a *script* as "one or more Tcl commands." A *script file*, on the other hand, is a file containing one or more scripts. To avoid confusion, whenever we are referring to a file containing a script or scripts, we will refer to it as a *script file*.

```
# Establish Visual Tcl Server Connection
```

Line 3 contains the Tcl comment command, **#**. Yes, it is a command. *Tcl treats the first word of any line as a command.* Processing line 3, Tcl simply passes the words, or *arguments*, that follow the # character to the **#** command as a list of parameters. The function of the **#** command is to simply throw these arguments away.

```
set appRoot [VtOpen gwho]
```

As the line 3 comment hints, line 4 opens a connection with the Visual Tcl display server via the Visual Tcl command **VtOpen**, representing our first encounter with one of the interface-building *Vt commands* of the Visual Tcl language. Mentioned in the previous chapter, the Visual Tcl run-time environment makes use of a display server to display, or *render*, graphical elements called *widgets*. Widgets are objects you are probably used to seeing on an application, such as push buttons, labels, and scrollable lists. Because the **VtOpen** command is enclosed in square brackets, [ ], Tcl parsing rules dictate that it is executed first. The use of square brackets for command substitution is roughly analogous to the use of grave quotes in conventional UNIX shell programming. In this case, the **VtOpen** command is, therefore, executed before the **set** command. This is an example of *command substitution*, which will be discussed in detail in Chapter 4, *Parsing Tcl Commands*. The result returned by **VtOpen** is stored in the variable appRoot for later use.

The string gwho was included as a required parameter to the **VtOpen** command. This user-defined string can be used to reference the Graphical Who applet from an X resource file, such as .Xdefaults. This feature is discussed at length in *Visual Tcl Concepts*.

```
set mainForm [VtFormDialog $appRoot.mainForm \
    -title $progTitle \
    ]
```

Line 5 is where the script begins to construct the GUI. **VtFormDialog** instructs the Visual Tcl display server to create a form-based dialog to be enclosed within the window manager's window frame. -title is an example of a Vt command option. The -title option specifies the string to be placed in the title bar at the top of the window frame. Recall from line 2 that the string "Graphical Who" is stored in the variable progTitle and will, therefore, appear in the title bar. The $ symbol performs Tcl *variable substitution*, which directs the interpreter to reveal the contents of the variable.

The form we have just created is referred to as the *main window* of our program from which all tasks and activities supported by Graphical Who are launched. The name of the form widget is returned by **VtFormDialog** and stored in the variable mainForm.

```
set listW [VtList $mainForm.listW \
    -itemList [split [exec /bin/who] \n ]\
    -scrollBar True \
    -rightSide FORM \
    -bottomSide FORM \
    -font monoBoldFont
    ]
```

Line 6 is where we interact with the UNIX who command. The **VtList** command creates a *list* widget that will contain the list of users returned from the execution of the who command. Observe that there are a number of command substitutions taking place.

Commands within square brackets are executed first via command substitution, beginning with the most deeply nested set of square brackets. In this case, [**exec** /bin/who] is executed first. The **exec** command invokes /bin/who as a UNIX subprocess, waiting for its completion. **exec** returns the output of /bin/who as a string that is passed to the Tcl **split** command, which reworks the string into a list of strings. Lists are a fundamental Tcl data structure addressed in detail in Chapter 6, *Data Structures*. As indicated by the \n symbol, **split** has been instructed to break the strings up wherever a new line occurs in the output returned by the who command. The massaged output is then finally passed to the **VtList** command via the -itemList option, which inserts it into the list widget. Reviewing the order of command execution:

1. **exec** executes the /bin/who UNIX command, returning its output as a single string.

2. **split** divides the string into a list of strings. Each substring is determined on the occurrence of new lines that are treated as delimiters. **split** returns the list of strings.

The -rightSide and -bottomSide options deal with *geometry management*, as discussed in Chapter 13, *Geometry Management*. These options are instructing the Visual Tcl display server to *attach* the right and bottom sides of the list widget to the main dialog's outer right and bottom edges. By default, Visual Tcl attaches the top and left sides of the first widget created in a form to its left and top edges. This can be overridden when more control is desired. With these attachments, if the user of Graphical Who were to enlarge the form by clicking and dragging the lower right-hand corner of the window, the list widget would stretch with it. Without the attachments, the size of the list widget would remain unaffected. You might try this if you have this applet up and running. Delete the two options to see the change in behavior when you try to stretch the window again.

The -font option is instructing the list widget to use a nonproportional font represented by monoBoldFont. Visual Tcl provides a set of predefined fonts for easy reference. It is also possible to specify an alternative font via a number of methods we will discuss in Chapter 10, *Visual Tcl Concepts*. A nonproportional font assures us that the rows of information will align nicely. This example could easily be improved to handle more attractive proportional fonts by using the column support in the Drawn List widget described in Chapter 30, *Lists*.

VtShow $mainForm

Line 7 uses the **VtShow** command to tell the Visual Tcl display server to show (*realize*) the main dialog of our program. Up until this point, the widget construction process has been conducted entirely in conventional memory, invisible to the Graphical Who user.

VtMainLoop

Line 8 causes the Visual Tcl interpreter to enter an *event* loop represented by the **VtMainLoop** command. Visual Tcl is an event-driven programming environment. Once the program enters the main loop it waits for events that might be caused by the push of a Quit button or the selection of an item in a list widget. In the case of our example program, we have not (yet) specified that any code be executed if an event occurs.

Having created and saved our script as a file (e.g., /u/amanda/bin/gwho), we can now perform the following last bit of work back at the UNIX shell prompt, making it an executable program with the UNIX chmod program.

```
chmod +x gwho
```

Adding a procedure: GetUserList

Procedures are compact chunks of code typically focused on carrying out a specific task. Thoughtfully designed, a procedure encapsulates a useful function that can be used over and over again when added to a Visual Tcl *package library* for reuse, as discussed in Chapter 7, *Flow and Development*. Appending a line to a file, extracting a word from a string, or retrieving a list of network nodes are examples of tasks that a procedure might fulfill.

Line 6 from our Graphical Who example could be made much more readable by removing the embedded **exec** and **split** commands and inserting them into a more manageable procedure. This bit of code can be reworked to form a procedure that retrieves and returns the list of users for use by our list widget.

```
proc GetUserList {} {
      set whoList [exec /bin/who]
      set splitWhoList [split $whoList \n]
      return $splitWhoList
}
```

The Tcl **proc** command defines a procedure. As indicated by the first argument to **proc**, we have decided to name the procedure GetUserList. The second argument, {}, is reserved for indicating the supported arguments to a procedure. As you can see, GetUserList will not require any arguments. Now the steps for retrieving the user list from the who command are made more clear, providing an easier way to inspect and debug our code. Additionally, we can now more easily add Visual Tcl commands for additional parsing of the output string from who, such as removing the TTY and time information and saving only the user names. (See *Tasks to Consider*, below.)

As we reviewed earlier, the data returned by the who command is stored in the whoList variable as one long string with any number of embedded new lines. The **split** command splits the string into a list of string items, the contents of each item representing the characters found between each new line (\n) character. Thus, if there are two users returned by who, there will be two items in our list. If you are curious about the content of splitWhoList, insert the single line of code:

```
echo "splitWhoList contains: $splitWhoList"
```

just above the **return** command in the procedure. After performing variable substitution on $splitWhoList, the Tcl **echo** command will write the string to stdout in your xterm.

➡ splitWhoList contains: {andrew tty02 May 10} {amanda tty03 May 10}

This list contains two items, each containing a string of words inside curly braces, { }. The list data structure is the focus of many Visual Tcl commands, making it very easy to manage and manipulate a large amount of data with a robust set of list commands, including sorting, deleting, inserting, and dozens of other manipulations.

Now that it is written, the GetUserList procedure can be invoked just like any Tcl command. Reworking Line 6 of our original example to incorporate GetUserList results in the simplified call to **VtList**:

```
set listW [VtList $mainForm.listW \
        -itemList [GetUserList] \
        -scrollBar True \
        -rightSide FORM \
        -bottomSide FORM \
        -font monoBoldFont \
        ]
```

Adding a callback: `ShowUserInfoCB`

Callbacks are procedures that link the widgets in your application's user interface to functional code. In the event-driven environment of Visual Tcl, callbacks are invoked when a user action generates some kind of event, such as

- the push of a push button widget
- dragging the cursor over a widget
- single clicking on a list item
- double-clicking on a list item
- exiting a text field

For Graphical Who, we will add a callback ShowUserInfoCB that will be invoked when an event is generated by the user's selection of an item in the list widget. Our callback will support the task:

Perform the UNIX "finger" command on a selected user.   `TASK`

The callback that represents this task is as follows:

```
1. proc ShowUserInfoCB {cbs} {
2.        # fetch essential widget event information
3.        set dialog [keylget cbs dialog]
```

```
4.        set value  [keylget cbs value]
5.        # extract the selected user's name
6.        set userInfo [join $value]
7.        set userName [lindex $userInfo 0]
8.        # execute finger and display info in a dialog
9.        set fingerInfo [exec finger $userName]
10.       set infoD [VtInformationDialog $dialog.infoDialog \
                -ok \
                -message $fingerInfo \
              ]
11.       VtShow $infoD
          }
```

You may have already noticed that this callback looks just like a procedure. There is really no distinction between a procedure and a callback except in how they are invoked. If a procedure is invoked by an event, rather than by the internal execution of the application, then it is a callback. In this book, we will use the convention of appending the letters "CB" to the end of a procedure name that is intended to function as a callback.

In order to link the callback procedure to the list widget, we must rework line 6 one more time.

```
set listW [VtList $mainForm.listW \
        -itemList [GetUserList] \
        -scrollBar True \
        -rightSide FORM \
        -bottomSide FORM \
        -font monoBoldFont \
        -callback ShowUserInfoCB \
        ]
```

Here we have expanded the call to **VtList** to include a new option, -callback, that associates the callback with the list widget and *registers* our callback with the display server. This callback will now be invoked when the user selects an item from the list.

```
proc ShowUserInfoCB {cbs} {...
```

Taking a look at the design of the new callback, line 1 creates the callback (procedure) and indicates, inside the curly braces, that the callback will expect a single argument, cbs. cbs is a naming convention we will use throughout the book to indicate the argument that is passed to all callbacks. Motif developers will recognize our naming convention as standing for *callback structure*. cbs will receive a special Visual Tcl list called a *keyed list*. Covered in great detail in Chapter 6, *Data Structures*, a keyed list is a list that contains sublists of keys with associated values. An example of a keyed list might look like

```
{{name Amanda} {home {Santa Cruz}} {school Gateway}}
```

In this example, name, home, and school are keys. Amanda, Santa Cruz, and Gateway are their respective associated values. There are special Visual Tcl commands, such as **keylget**, that are used to add and extract data from a keyed list.

```
set personInfo {{name Amanda} {home {Santa Cruz}}}
echo "My daughter's home is [keylget personInfo home]"
```
➡ My daughter's home is Santa Cruz

When an event is detected, the display server sends the name of the callback procedure back to the Visual Tcl interpreter for execution. Along with the callback name, the display server also sends a keyed list containing essential information associated with the event and the widget associated with the event. This is the keyed list that is represented by the cbs argument. All event callbacks will receive a keyed list containing the minimum set of keys listed in the table below.

Table 2–1   Minimum callback keys

key	meaning of the key's associated value
widget	name of the widget that is associated with the event that invoked the callback
dialog	name of the parent widget that contains the widget
value	information generated by the event, such as the item in the list widget selected by the user

There may be other keys and associated values, depending on the type of widget associated with the callback.

```
set widget [keylget cbs widget]
set dialog [keylget cbs dialog]
set value  [keylget cbs value]
```

As described by the comment on line 2, lines 3 and 4 use the **keylget** command to extract the information associated with the event that invoked the callback, i.e., the user's selection of an item in the list widget. The variable dialog is assigned the name of the form widget containing the list widget, and the variable value receives the actual list item selected by the user. The widget's name, indexed in cbs by the widget key, is not required in our callback.

```
set userInfo [lvarpop value]
set userName [lindex $userInfo 0]
```

Lines 6 and 7 simply massage the selected list item information in order to extract the user's name. Assuming the user selected the first item in the list widget shown in Figure 2–1, userInfo contains the value

```
carolyn tty02 May 10 19:26
```

The value returned by a list widget is a list containing one or more lists. That may seem wasteful until you think about the fact that it is possible for a user to select more than one item in a Motif list. However, for our example, we are using the default behavior of **VtList**, which is to allow the user to select only one item. We have chosen **lvarpop** to view the list of lists as a stack and "pop" the first item off the stack. The value saved in userInfo is the only item in the list, representing the list item selected by the user.

Index:	0	1	2	3	4
Item:	carolyn	tty02	May	10	19:26

This makes it possible to use the **lindex** command to retrieve the first item in the extracted list, which will be the name of the selected user. Tcl indexes items in lists beginning with 0, true to Tcl's C heritage. In this case, the 0 item is the user's name, carolyn.

```
set fingerInfo [exec finger $userName]
```

Line 9 executes the UNIX finger command, as a UNIX subprocess, on the selected user, storing the string result in the variable fingerInfo.

```
set infoD [VtInformationDialog $dialog.infoDialog \
        -ok \
        -message $fingerInfo \
]
VtShow $infoD
```

Lines 10 and 11 take the raw output from finger and display it via a Motif *Information Dialog*, one of the six standard, precanned Motif message dialogs supported by Visual Tcl. The six message dialogs reviewed in Chapter 14, *Dialogs*, are:

- Message
- Information
- Question
- Working
- Error
- Warning

Message dialogs automatically display three buttons located at the bottom of the form: OK, Cancel, and Help. The -ok option indicates that only the OK button on the dialog will be displayed to the user. Unless overridden, the default behavior of the OK button in these dialogs is to simply destroy the dialog. In the code, **VtInformationDialog** returns the name of this new dialog, which is then used by **VtShow** to actually render the dialog on the user's screen.

Guidelines for placement of Tcl code and procedures in your scripts

There is a subtle but essential relationship between **VtMainLoop** and the placement of the rest of your application's code. Tcl scripting can be unnervingly flexible and accommodating to whatever your style of code organization may be. However, as you organize your code, be sure to remember that **VtMainLoop** is a kind of `while 1` command that loops forever, waiting for input from the user (e.g., a mouse click on a button). That means that the thread of execution never extends past the location of the **VtMainLoop** command. Placing procedures or procedures acting as callbacks after **VtMainLoop** will generate an "unknown command" error.

The following organization should ensure that you never run into this problem. It recommends simply that you place your procedures before the **VtOpen** call, treating the code between **VtOpen** and **VtMainLoop** as the "main" body.

```
#!/bin/vtcl
# procedure or callback
proc FooA {} {
}
# procedure or callback
proc FooB {} {
}
set app [VtOpen demo]
# Other Tcl code
VtMainLoop
```

Now when the user selects a user from the Graphical Who list widget, they will see an information dialog that looks something like:

Figure 2–2 An Information Dialog containing the raw output of the UNIX finger command

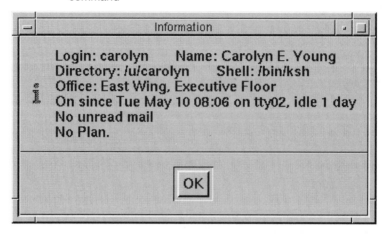

Tasks To Consider

You've probably already thought of some functionality you could add to this little script. Here are some ideas that you might consider after having learned more about Visual Tcl.

TASK   *Replace* who *with the network* rwho *command.*

TASK   *Process the output so that only the user name is displayed*

TASK   *Remove duplicate lists of the same user (see* **lrmdups** *command)*

TASK   *Add a Motif label that indicates the total number of users found.*

Storing useful procedures and callbacks:

Visual Tcl supports "package libraries," which provide a mechanism for building your own libraries of useful function calls. Visual Tcl generates an index file associated with your library to provide a significant performance enhancement during function calls. See Chapter 7, *Flow and Development*, for more on package libraries.

Run-Time Environment

✔ Components of the Visual Tcl Language: Tcl, TclX, and Vt
✔ The Visual Tcl Client/Server Architecture

*G*raphical user interface development challenges the ability of conventional shell scripting to handle the demands of event-driven programming. The standard commands of the Visual Tcl language and its architecture have been constructed both to maximize the capability of scripting for the GUI environment and to leverage the capabilities of the UNIX server. The first half of this chapter will first review the heritage of the Tcl language and then introduce the Visual Tcl language extensions and their special properties, as symbolized in Figure 3–1. The second half focuses on the design of the run-time environment. Visual Tcl is more than a simple interpreter. In fact, the interpreter is only half of the story in a client-server architecture. Performance, resource management, and GUI independence are all affected by this unique architecture.

Figure 3–1   Core functional components of Visual Tcl

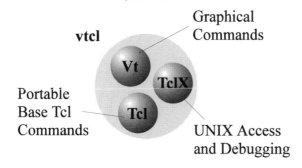

The Visual Tcl language

The Visual Tcl command language is a superset of the popular public-domain command language called *Tcl*. Built expressly for the development of GUI applications for the UNIX server environment, Visual Tcl is the composite of three command libraries represented by

1. the base Tcl Library, including the Tcl interpreter and the portable Tcl command language, version 7.3,

2. the UNIX access TclX library, and

3. the GUI-building library called *Vt*.

The sections that follow review the unique contributions of each of these command libraries, beginning with the base Tcl language itself. Keep in mind that the capabilities that each of the libraries provides are standard features of the Visual Tcl language.

Terminology explanation: "Tcl" and "Visual Tcl"

The look and feel of the syntax and semantics of Visual Tcl are derived from the Tcl language and run-time environment. Visual Tcl leverages the Tcl interpreter and its capability for adding new commands in order to provide the additional support for UNIX access and Motif development that distinguishes it from other graphical user interface scripting languages.

Because so much of the principles, such as parsing and command execution, of the Tcl language show through the layers, it is impossible to describe Visual Tcl without referring to Tcl mechanisms such as the Tcl interpreter. To call it the *Visual Tcl interpreter* might imply that the Visual Tcl interpreter is somehow different from the standard Tcl interpreter, which is not the case. Therefore, we make extensive use of "Tcl" terminology in order to (1) minimize conceptual confusion distinguishing Tcl from Visual Tcl, and (2) reinforce the notion that Visual Tcl is built with the same industry-standard language environment that supports Tk, Expect, and many other popular Tcl extensions.

The Tcl language

Tcl, or *Tool Command Language*, was developed by John Ousterhout at the University of California at Berkeley. Tcl's inherent strengths include its C-like language that becomes a particularly nice feature when moving back and forth between the compiled and scripting environment in your daily work. Tcl incorporates common high-level language concepts such as pass-by-reference procedure arguments and data structures such as arrays. Its ability to handle strings such as those captured from the standard output of executed UNIX commands, like who and ps, makes it extremely easy to manipulate collected data with a few lines of code, turning it into a format that can be redisplayed within a graphical dialog.

The Tcl list data structure provides the data "anvil" used by a wide array of built-in Tcl commands to manipulate data for sorting, searching, replacing, popping, pushing, and so on. The details of Tcl list, array, and flow control commands are addressed in Chapter 6, *Data Structures*, and Chapter 7, *Flow and Development*, with an extensive per-command description in the *Command Pages* section at the end of this book.

Despite its extensive set of commands, Tcl is very easy to learn. By starting with just a handful of Tcl commands, anyone with shell scripting experience can quickly conjure up a useful application. Part of Tcl's ease of use is based on the historical reluctance of Ousterhout to define a syntax that challenges the supported character set of modern keyboards. Using the KornShell for comparison, instead of using built-in variable names such as the $@ variable for examining command line arguments, Tcl uses the C-like, somewhat self-descriptive variable name argv. Common tasks such as fetching the length of a KornShell array is achieved by

```
${#arrayName[*]}
```

whereas the equivalent "noun-verb" command approach of Tcl is

```
array size arrayName
```

Having indulged in a little scripting religion, the fact is that there are a lot of great scripting languages, such as KornShell, Perl, and JavaScript, each with its own set of merits and reasons for success. Tcl's natural language commands and syntax have earned it a huge user base.

The extensible Tcl foundation

John Ousterhout's original goal for developing the Tcl language was to serve as a standard, highly portable, embeddable command language that can be extended with commands that deliver functionality provided by its host application.

Embedding refers to the notion of adding new functionality to a host application. As an embeddable command language, Tcl can be used to extend the capabilities of its host application to provide its users with a scripting interface. *Extensibility* refers to the ability to take functions that are a part of the host application's feature and make them available as extensions of the Tcl language.

Figure 3–2   An SNMP management application extended with Tcl

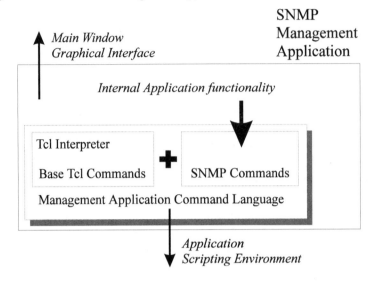

The concept of macro-driven business applications was popularized by the macro language found in the spreadsheet application Lotus 1-2-3, giving users the ability to automate complex tasks that could then be initiated with a single keystroke or mouse click. Another example is provided by WordBasic language found in the popular word processor used to write this book, MS Word. Tcl is differentiated from these macro languages by the fact that it was designed to be portable to an unlimited range of applications and operating system platforms. Tcl is referred to as a *command language* to differentiate it from typical application macro languages that have historically supported a reduced set of programming functionality.

Using Tcl to provide applications with greater customization capabilities is limited only by the imagination. Figure 3–2 illustrates how an SNMP[*] management application might be embedded and extended with Tcl commands in order to present a scripting interface for behind-the-scenes interactions. One could also incorporate a public-domain Internet newsreader with the Tcl interpreter and create Tcl scripts that perform agent-like activities. A "news agent" Tcl script might search for specific incoming news postings and generate e-mail that is sent to certain individuals when a particular subject title is encountered. All of this could be easily performed in the background, bypassing the need for user intervention.

---

[*] SNMP (Simple Network Management by Protocol) is the official management protocol of the Internet.

Practical scripting limits—A Tcl-to-C migration strategy

Visual Tcl is a monotyped language that views the world as one long string. Datatype checking is addressed through the eye of individual

Tcl commands. The Tcl interpreter acts as an efficient match-maker. With each command it encounters in a script, the interpreter finds an associated command procedure written in C to process the arguments associated with the command. In addition to providing the advertised functionality of the command, the command procedure enforces its own set of demands and constructs on the command's arguments. If the command procedure was expecting a "4" instead of a "four," it is up to the procedure to determine how it should react. The interpreter itself performs no checking of this type.

At some point when analyzing the language to select for developing an application, the question of size and performance is evaluated. Scripting may provide the flexibility you are seeking, but will it perform at the minimum required speed? And at what point does the lack of robust datatype checking threaten the maintainability of the code?

Of course, there are no well-known guidelines to offer you. Issues of performance and robustness should be balanced against the benefits of rapid development and flexible design environment.

There is, however, an intermediate solution that brings relief when performance is a key issue. As introduced in this chapter, the Tcl interpreter is designed to be extended with support for new compiled, C-based commands. If a particular portion of a Tcl script is causing a performance bottleneck (see the use of Tcl commands **time** and **profile** in Chapter 7, *Flow and Development),* significant performance gains can be made by rewriting the time-consuming script as a C function command procedure. Once linked with the Tcl interpreter the new command should help with your performance fine tuning. There are also some commercial solutions available, such as Tcl compilers, that should be considered in your evaluation.

Like the tail wagging the dog, Tcl has gained wide acceptance based on its own merits as a stand-alone, high-level programming language rather than as a means to enhance existing applications. Modern tools are being written exclusively in Tcl, taking advantage of its extensible interpreter to enhance the language with commands that address specific problems. Powerful extensions such as Tk and Expect have driven Tcl's widespread use well past its more modest, intended role as a simple command language for laboratory applications. There are many private extensions written for in-house tools, such as test harness environments and manufacturing monitoring applications. There is also a long list of public-domain Tcl language extensions that provide commands to reflect particular application domains, including:

- SNMP for network management
- SQL Databases
- VRML language extensions

Many of these extensions are available from numerous ftp sites, including:

```
ftp.neosoft.com
```

The TclX library for UNIX access

As might be expected of any portable language, the base Tcl commands steer clear of operating system-specific dependencies. Visual Tcl, on the other hand, was written for the UNIX server environment in order to support systems management development. The public-domain TclX command extensions library gives Visual Tcl its UNIX flavor, as well as other Tcl enhancements that make it a robust development tool. Developed by Mark Diekhans and Karl Lehenbauer, TclX is a collection of commands and Tcl procedures that add extended functionality to the existing Tcl command set, including support for POSIX system calls. The general categories of TclX commands are listed in Table 3–1.

Over time, some of the more portable commands and data structures, such as associative arrays, have found their way from TclX into the base Tcl language.

Table 3–1 Categories of TclX extensions

• General commands	• Help facility
• UNIX system access	• File I/O commands
• TCP/IP server access	• File scanning commands
• Math commands	• List manipulation commands
• Debugging and development commands	• String and character manipulation commands
• XPG/3 message catalog commands	• Keyed lists

TclX for expanded file handling

Many of the TclX commands simply enhance the functionality of existing base Tcl language commands. For example, the standard Tcl file I/O commands include:

```
close, eof, file, flush, gets, glob, open, puts, read,
seek, tell
```

TclX adds the file I/O commands:

```
bsearch, chgrp, chmod, chown, chroot, copyfile, dup,
echo, fcntl, flock, for_file, for_recursive_glob,
frename, fstat, funlock, link, mkdir, pipe, read_file,
readdir, recursive_glob, rmdir, select, server_info,
server_open, sync, unlink, write_file
```

If you have UNIX C language development experience, you probably recognize many of these commands as C Library functions, such as **fcntl**, **seek**, and **select**, as well as a number of UNIX system access commands, including **chgrp** and **chown**. TclX makes it possible to build scripts that can take advantage of standard TCP/IP sockets programming, represented by the **server_open** and **server_info** commands. With these two commands, you could develop a personalized Visual Tcl Internet newsreader.

Avoiding the overhead of subprocess execution

In general, if you think you need to use the **exec** command to execute a UNIX command, there is a good chance that the command has been made available through the TclX library. Besides offering a full development stable of I/O control, the TclX library greatly improves application performance, since the overhead of forking and executing a separate UNIX process is eliminated. For example, the following two-code fragments are functionally equivalent.

```
set date [exec /bin/date]
set date [fmtclock [getclock]]
```

However, the second version uses two TclX commands that are linked into the Tcl interpreter and, therefore, avoid the same overhead of dealing with forked subprocesses.

Keeping your scripts portable

Throughout the book, including *Essential Tcl* , and the *Commands* pages, an attempt has been made to clearly identify TclX versus the base Tcl commands. Vt commands are automatically identified by their **vt** prefix. This feature is provided in the event you are using this book as a reference from which to build portable Tcl applications.

Convenience commands

Within the TclX extensions is a class of commands that serve as "convenience commands," such as **read_file**, **for_file**, and **write_file**. Each command reduces the need to repeatedly construct multiple lines of common file operations. In the case of having to

1. open a file,
2. loop through the file's contents, reading each record of the file, and
3. close the file,

you can instead simply pass the name of the file to

1. **read_file**

and get a string of the file's entire contents. These commands are, in a number of cases, simply Tcl procedures that encapsulate a set of Tcl commands and are made available via a TclX library mechanism called a *package library*. Package libraries are discussed in Chapter 29, *Package Library*. Over time, many of these commands will probably be rewritten as C functions and added to the Tcl interpreter.

TclX: the *X* stands for "eXtended"

A common misunderstanding is that TclX is an extension library that features graphical capabilities. In Visual Tcl, it is the Vt library that provides its graphical commands. The *X* in TclX refers to the fact that TclX commands represent a set of general extensions to the existing Tcl language.

Keyed lists and debugging commands

The complete list of TclX commands is addressed in Part II, *Essential Tcl*. Two more important TclX extensions to look for address data structure enhancement, as well as enhanced Tcl debugging capability.

Keyed Lists   A keyed list is a special Visual Tcl list data structure that provides data organizing functionality reminiscent of a "C struct." Providing storage for arbitrary groups of name-value pairs, keyed lists can be used to organize categories of information, such as personnel information (e.g., names, addresses, phone numbers). TclX provides four commands dedicated to manipulating keyed lists.

cmdtrace   TclX provides the level of debugging capability essential to a full development environment like Visual Tcl. One particular command, **cmdtrace**, provides the ability to follow the flow of execution, examining the contents of variables and procedure parameters, in addition to invoking other procedures when certain events occur, such as the modification of a variable's contents.

Vt for GUI construction

The Visual Tcl language provides a set of commands that support OSF/Motif development in an event-driven programming model. In traditional scripting, the script determines the direction the application takes, presenting the user every now and then with a list of limited choices. Event-driven design, discussed in detail in Chapter 9, *Motif and Visual Tcl*, allows the user to control the flow of execution by deciding which buttons to push or items to select.

Widgets are the building blocks of GUIs: buttons, forms, text fields, pulldown menus, and dialogs are all widgets or aggregates of widgets that present the user with representations of things they probably associate with real-life objects, such as a light switch on the kitchen wall. Vt commands create, organize, and control these widgets. By taking advantage of a standard GUI library provided by the OSF/Motif toolkit, Vt commands can be used to create simple precanned dialogs or complex, custom-designed dialogs unique to your application. Chapter 10, *Visual Tcl Concepts*, provides an overview of the key Motif concepts that you will need to quickly grasp Vt command usage.

A scripting language for GUI-independent development

There is no doubt that the assortment of widget-building Vt commands were heavily influenced by the OSF/Motif view of GUI programming. In some cases, there are command options that are provided exclusively for Motif programming, such as -xmArgs, an option that can be used when there is no support for a particular Motif Xm resource, such as the *x* or *y* location in a RowColumn widget. (If you are new to Motif programming, Chapter 9, *Motif and Visual Tcl*, will provide the explanation of Xm and other Motif terminology that you will need for background information.)

However, as you will soon see, Visual Tcl supports an architecture that was designed for GUI-independent development. This means that the script you develop for the X/Motif environment should, with a modest amount of tweaking, simply "just run" in another environment such as Microsoft Windows. This is a realistic expectation, given the commonality of many windowing interface elements, found in both the UNIX X environments and the Microsoft Windows environments. In fact, the OSF/Motif toolkit emulates the Microsoft Common User Access (CUA) specification.

Character Motif, or Charm, is SCO's mapping of the Motif library using the curses library for the character or dumb terminal environment. Charm is the technology used by a special version of Visual Tcl for the character environment.

At the time of this writing, Visual Tcl provides support for OSF/Motif development on ten UNIX platforms. Support for the Windows environment will be made available later in 1996.

Extending the Visual Tcl language

The Visual Tcl language doesn't have to stop at the Tcl, TclX and Vt command libraries. Armed with a C compiler, any developer can extend the Visual Tcl interpreter environment for any number of motivations, including

1. improving performance,
2. leveraging many of the publicly available extensions,
3. achieving code protection (using compilation to move the details of how your application performs sensitive tasks from Tcl to the C level), as well as
4. presenting extensions as very high-level functions, making it conceptually easy for customers to work with.

See Brent Welch's *Practical Programming in Tcl and Tk* for a discussion of how to extend the Tcl interpreter. The files required to extend Visual Tcl are included on the CD-ROM of this book.

Figure 3–3   Visual Tcl = Tcl Interpreter + extensions

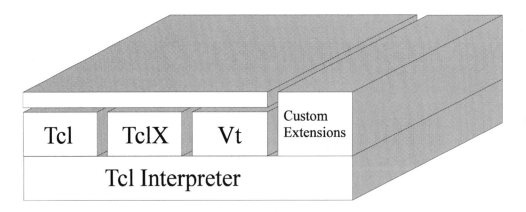

The Visual Tcl client/server architecture

Unlike graphical CAD/CAM tools that are operated on hardware specifically purchased for supporting high-resolution, high-performance computing, systems administration tools must be prepared to support the widest range of operating environments sprinkled around a business environment. Environments in which administrators must operate range from beefy, high-resolution servers to Windows desktops and dumb character terminals dialed in from homes or remote offices.

The challenge facing administration tool developers is to provide their products in all of these environments. Visual Tcl was designed expressly to meet this need by supporting user interface design for the X/Motif environment while simultaneously supporting tool development for the still-huge installed base of legacy 80×24 character terminals.

Separate source trees for different environments is a nightmare. Redundant development as well as long-term maintenance issues are things to avoid. These same issues confront publication departments, which have little desire to build separate documentation source trees to parallel the character and Motif versions of administration tools.

Figure 3–4   Visual Tcl client and server library

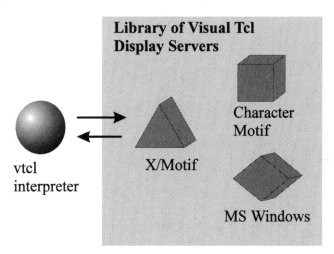

The Visual Tcl run-time environment represents a client/server model, chosen to make it possible to plug in different user interface rendering technologies as illustrated in Figure 3–4. The current list of display servers supports OSF/Motif for the X environment and Charm (discussed in the previous section) for the dumb terminal environment. Eventually, a display server supporting Microsoft Windows for the desktop environment will be supported as well. The CD-ROM in this book contains the UNIX OSF/Motif display server for ten versions of the UNIX operating system. (See *Preface* for the complete list.) Charm is currently available only on the SCO OpenServer platform.

Visual Tcl components

There are two major components of the Visual Tcl run-time environment:

client
> The client, `vtcl`, is a special application that has been embedded with the Tcl interpreter as well as extended with the command libraries that, together, define the Visual Tcl API. The client processes Visual Tcl scripts.

server
> The Visual Tcl display server `xm_vtcld` represents the server. The display server provides GUI-building services to the client by performing the actual construction and rendering of the user interface. The client is informed by the server of user actions, such as the selection of a push-button menu item.

Routes taken by Visual Tcl commands

During the processing of a Visual Tcl script, the client's Tcl interpreter takes each command and its arguments and turns them over to the actual C function or Tcl procedure responsible for carrying out their advertised functionality. The interpreter has no significant run-time role beyond this match-making function. This process is explained in great detail in Chapter 4, *Parsing Tcl Commands*.

Each command within the Visual Tcl language requires access to different resources, depending on its functionality. Most Tcl commands carry out their functionality within the interpreter client process space, such as manipulating a list data structure in core memory. Other Tcl commands, such as many of the TclX extensions, access the UNIX environment to get details about the file system or processes in execution. The user interface building commands of the Vt library generate instructions that are sent to the display server (which performs the real widget-building). The paths that these commands take within the client server environment are illustrated in Figure 3–5. A few typical commands, and the resources routes they take, are shown below.

```
set listName   "Files in /tmp"      ────► Access internal Tcl data structures
VtLabel app.label -label $listName  ────► Access Visual Tcl Display Server
set fileList [readdir /tmp]          ────► Access UNIX system
VtList app.list -itemList $fileList ────► Access Visual Tcl Display Server
```

Figure 3–5   The interactive components of the Visual Tcl environment

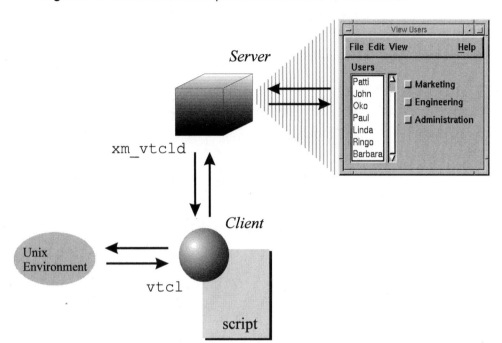

Client/Server interactions in a Visual Tcl session

Let's examine how the client and server components work together by following their interactions during the execution of a simple Visual Tcl application. Keeping things simple, the script below will display a simple push button widget that terminates the application when pushed.

```
proc ExitCB {cbs} {
        VtClose
        exit 0
}
set rootName [VtOpen Demo]
```

```
set pushB [VtPushButton $rootName.pushB \
    -label "Goodbye" \
    -callback ExitCB \
    ]
VtShow $pushB
VtMainLoop
```

Normal Tcl processing begins as soon as the script file is loaded into the interpreter. (We typically use a script file as an example, but it is also possible to invoke vtcl as an interactive shell, typing in one command after another.) First the procedure ExitCB is created with the Tcl **proc** command. Although it contains a script with a Vt command, **VtClose**, it is not yet invoked. The GUI-building magic begins when the interpreter encounters the **VtOpen** command.

Establishing a connection

VtOpen attempts to establish a connection with the display server. The display server runs as a UNIX daemon process. If the process representing the display server cannot be located, **VtOpen** loads the display server daemon into memory, then repeats its attempt to establish a connection. The communication between the client and server occurs via a named pipe. The successful completion of the **VtOpen** request returns the *root name* of the widget tree that will provide the basis for all widget naming used by the subsequent Vt commands. Widget naming is addressed in Chapter 10, *Visual Tcl Concepts*.

Storing callback information

With the client-server connection established, the command **VtPushButton** issues a request to the display server to create a push button widget. Included in the request is the name of the ExitCB Tcl procedure identified as a *callback*. The callback's name and other details about the push button are stored in the memory of the display server.

The last two Vt commands request the display server to display the push button using **VtShow** and to place the script into an event-driven execution environment with **VtMainLoop**.

A message from the display server

VtMainLoop is one of the few Vt commands that does not initiate a message to the display server. Instead, it "listens" for incoming messages *from* the display server. User-generated events result in messages initiated by the display server. In this example, the "push" of the push button by the point and click of the user's mouse is perceived as an event. The display server immediately sends a message to the client with information about the event that just occurred. Included in the message is the name of the callback, ExitCB. **VtMainLoop** directs the interpreter to immediately process ExitCB.

Disconnecting from the display server

Two terminating commands occur during the execution of the ExitCB callback procedure. First, **VtClose** disconnects the connection to the display server by sending a farewell message to the server and closing the client's file descriptor. The server, having received the message from **VtClose**, performs all necessary housekeeping to free up the internal data structures that were allocated for the client-server session. Back in the client, the Tcl **exit** command terminates the client interpreter, returning a 0 return code to the UNIX shell environment, representing a successful completion.

Performance, event loops, and multiclient support

When you come into the office in the morning, log in, then fire up your first Visual Tcl application of the day, it appears before you in the startup time that is typical of most X/Motif applications. This assumes that the initial Motif dialog of your application is average in size and complexity. From that point on and until you log off, all subsequent invocations of Visual Tcl applications will result in a marked increase in user interface rendering performance. Why? Because once that first application uses **VtOpen** to spawn the display server daemon, the daemon remains in memory, eliminating the overhead of repeated display server startup. Its internal data structures are already initialized and ready to go.

Display server allocation

A single display server is executed per real TTY per user. If you run a Visual Tcl application as yourself, then use the UNIX su command to become the root superuser to start another Visual Tcl application, there will be two display server daemons in memory. The maximum process lifetime of a display server daemon is the period of time starting from the first execution of a Visual Tcl script to the end of your login session.

Supporting multiple clients

The display server was designed to provide GUI rendering services to more than one vtcl client simultaneously, illustrated in Figure 3–6. Each client represents a single Visual Tcl application, operating as though it owns the entire display server. Each client provides its application script with its own event loop waiting for events to be sent down the pipe from the display server, causing the associated callback to be executed. The actions of each application occur in complete isolation, having no impact on the other's behavior unless there are so many executing that the performance of the display server begins to retard.

Figure 3–6   Visual Tcl Client/Server Architecture

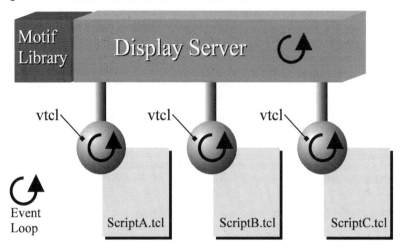

The upper limit of hosted applications varies with the computing power of the host machine as well as with the type of application that is executing. If an application is running a fast loop that barks out lots of GUI-building Vt commands, it may negatively impact the display server's ability to keep in step with all of its clients. For the most part, however, Visual Tcl applications and GUI-based applications, in general, are usually written to present dialogs that spend most of their time waiting for user input.

Working with an interface-rendering daemon

In the Visual Tcl client/server configuration, it is the display server that is the real X/Motif application. The client has absolutely no linked-in Xlib capability. It simply knows how to instruct the display server to perform GUI-rendering activities. This design has a direct effect to keep in mind when you are adjusting the X resources associated with your application.

In the X environment, you can control the use of resource attributes, such as the background color of a push button widget, in a particular application. The granularity of a resource value can range from affecting all push buttons created by any application in your environment to affecting a particular push button in a particular dialog in a particular application.

When you change a resource in a resource file, such as the .Xdefaults file located in your home directory, you must restart your application to see the effect of the resource change. However, for a Visual Tcl application, you must keep in mind that the actual application from the X environment's point of view is the display server. Since all of the Xlib functions that reference the X environment for resource information are in the display server and not in your script or in the interpreter, the display server must be restarted for the resource change to take effect.

Restarting the display server daemon is something you will want to consider carefully. Since the display server might be serving other Visual Tcl clients, killing the daemon will close down those other clients as well. Any pending data will not be written to disk, so there is the potential that your work will be lost. The effect of this is limited to the display server that is associated with your login session, thus not affecting other Visual Tcl users in a multiuser UNIX environment.

Stopping the display server without requiring your log out can be performed with the UNIX `kill` command or from a Visual Tcl interpreter session using **VtQuitServer**. You can enter interactive session with the `vtcl` command, discussed in Chapter 4, *Parsing Tcl Commands*, by typing `vtcl` at the UNIX command prompt. Having done that, type:

```
VtOpen fred
VtQuitServer
```

VtOpen establishes the `vtcl` client connection with the display server. **VtQuitServer** then shuts down the server. When you invoke your Visual Tcl script, the display server will be launched, and any resource changes should take effect.

Summary of the Visual Tcl architecture

The Visual Tcl run-time environment is composed of two executable binaries, or applications. The first application is the Visual Tcl interpreter (vtcl). Its role is to process Visual Tcl scripts. Vt commands that are encountered in these scripts generate instructions that are sent across a named pipe to the second application, the Visual Tcl display server. It is the display server that has the ability to construct and render the X/Motif widgets that the user sees. This client/server model supports script development that is GUI-independent and achieves excellent performance, thanks to the benefits of its in-memory display server.

There are distinctive characteristics of the Visual Tcl run-time environment that are worth remembering as you develop your applications.

- In order to support GUI-independent development, the interpreter contains no user interface-rendering code. It relies entirely on the display server to render graphical user interfaces.
- Multiple `vtcl` interpreters, running simultaneously, can be supported by a single display server.
- For changes in X resources to take effect in Visual Tcl applications, the display server must be stopped and restarted.

PART II

Essential Tcl

Parsing Tcl Commands

✔ Command parsing and execution

✔ Executing via interactive shell or as a loadable file

✔ Variable, backslash, and command substitution

✔ Tcl quoting and substitution

✔ The ten Tcl syntax rules

*T*he Tcl Internet newsgroup *comp.lang.tcl* is filled with postings from perplexed users, asking questions that can be answered easily with a few key concepts of how the Tcl interpreter processes a Tcl script. The goal of this chapter is to provide a level of conceptual comfort that will help you avoid common perception pitfalls and confidently perform fundamental Tcl programming.

Leveraging its view of the world as a string, the power of Tcl is its infinite flexibility for solving problems. There is very little that you cannot achieve with Tcl, especially with the TclX and Vt extensions of Visual Tcl. To take full advantage of the capabilities that Visual Tcl offers requires a reasonable understanding of what Tcl does behind the scenes to process the commands and procedures of your script. Quoting and substitution are Tcl mechanisms for adapting scripting to the event-driven environment of GUI development. Our discussion of Tcl syntax and parsing is boiled down to ten rules listed at the end of this chapter.

Visual Tcl is an enhancement of the standard Tcl environment. Throughout this chapter, references to *Tcl* in lieu of *Visual Tcl* imply that the functionality described is a feature of the base Tcl library that provides the Visual Tcl foundation.

Visual Tcl execution environments

A great way to learn any new language is to work with examples that accompany the introduction of new concepts and commands. Visual Tcl provides two approaches to experimenting with the many examples scattered throughout this book: the interactive shell and file-based execution.

The **vtcl** interactive shell

The Visual Tcl interactive shell provides an environment that is great for learning, debugging, or experimenting with bits of vtcl code. To enter the interactive shell, type

```
vtcl
```

at the UNIX prompt. You will see a vtcl shell prompt

```
vtcl>
```

representing a Visual Tcl shell session. The interpreter is now ready to process your Visual Tcl commands. Type in the following two commands and view the result:

```
vtcl>set message "Welcome to Visual Tcl" <RETURN>
vtcl>echo $message
```

➡ Welcome to Visual Tcl

A command that returns a string will display the result on the next line without a vtcl> prompt in front of it.

```
vtcl>llength {Dorothy Wizard {Cowardly Lion} Scarecrow}
```

➡ 4
```
vtcl>
```

This feature is particularly useful when you're not sure if you are using a command correctly, how to use one of its options, or how its result might be formatted. To end your vtcl shell session, type

exit

vtcl acts much like a normal UNIX shell, passing on to the UNIX environment commands that are not recognized as part of the Visual Tcl language. For instance, you can use vi to edit a file from the tcl> prompt. Command pass-through can be turned off by executing the following inside the vtcl shell.

```
vtcl
vtcl>set auto_noexec 1
```

The majority of examples that are scattered throughout the remainder of this book are written to be executed from inside a file. Examples that are illustrated within the vtcl interactive shell are prefixed with the `vtcl` shell prompt.

As an executable file

Using the interactive shell is fine for working with simple examples. However, for more complex Tcl programming, particularly when you are developing user interfaces with the Vt command extensions, you will want to open a file, add your code, then execute the file. To execute your scripted file, simply type the following at the UNIX shell prompt.

```
vtcl filename
```

where `filename` is the name of the file containing your script. Another way to execute your script file is to turn it into an executable. This requires taking two steps at the UNIX command prompt:

`chmod 755 filename`   Change the file permissions to make it executable.

`#!/bin/vtcl`   Place this string on the first line of your Visual Tcl script. This will instruct the UNIX shell to pass the remaining file contents to `/bin/vtcl`.

Remember!

Check with the CD-ROM README file regarding the actual location of the `vtcl` binary of the version of UNIX that you are working with.

You can now execute your script by simply typing the name of the file.

Evaluating Tcl commands

In *Run-Time Environment*, we established that the original goal driving the design of Tcl was to provide compiled applications with the ability to support a standard scripting command language. Once embedded in the host application, the command language could then be extended with additional commands representing the particular functionality supported by the application. For instance, a host spreadsheet application extended with Tcl might feature Tcl commands like `CalculateCell` or `PrintCellRange`.

`vtcl`, the Visual Tcl client interpreter, is a host application embedded with version 7.3 of the Tcl interpreter. The command language has been extended with TclX and Visual Tcl's special user interface-building abilities. Taking full advantage of its Tcl heritage, the Visual Tcl command language inherits all of the principles of Tcl command processing.

A near-grammarless language for extensibility

From a high-level view, Tcl command processing can be broken into two phases. The Tcl interpreter uses this two-step approach to process *all commands*.

Parsing Phase

The interpreter applies its simple set of parsing rules in order to identify a *command name* and all associated arguments. If necessary, *command*, *variable*, and *backslash substitutions* are performed before parsing of the current command is completed.

Execution Phase

Having identified and collected the command name and its arguments, the interpreter looks for a command function that is associated with the command. The command function performs the command's advertised functionality, accepting the arguments passed to the command in the script.

The command processing steps taken by the interpreter reflect the absence of significant built-in language grammar characteristics of languages such as C or Pascal, where commands such as *if* and *while* are reserved keywords that have special meaning to the compiler. **if**, **while**, **getclock**, **VtPushButton**, and **server_open** are commands that represent a portion of the core Visual Tcl language, all inherited from one of the three Tcl command libraries, Tcl, TclX, or Vt. To the interpreter, these are simply names of commands that it must process. The interpreter has no special knowledge of a command's heritage, function, or the number of expected command arguments. Individual command traits are of no interest to the Tcl interpreter.

An interpreter mechanism with no prejudicial treatment of any of its commands makes the ideal extensible environment. Adding new commands represents a plug-and-play process, requiring no reworking of the interpreter's internal mechanism.

Elements of scripts: words and commands

To the Tcl interpreter, the world is one long *string* of ASCII characters. In the form of a text-based *script file*, a Visual Tcl program is a single string consisting of *commands* separated by *semicolons* and *newlines*. Each command contains one or more *words*, delimited by spaces. One might view commands and words as sentences. Therefore, "command" and "command sentence" are used interchangeably throughout the book.

In the Tcl script below, a single command is terminated by an invisible newline located at the end of the sentence. The interpreter identifies the first word in a command sentence as a *command name*. Therefore, **set** is the command name. **set** is used to assign a value to a Tcl variable. The words that follow, machineName and Scorpion, are arguments for the **set** command.

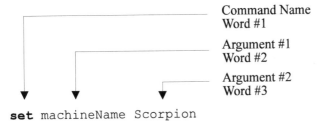

Command Name
Word #1

Argument #1
Word #2

Argument #2
Word #3

```
set machineName Scorpion
```

If desired, semicolons can be used to put multiple commands on a single line. The script below contains two commands separated by a semicolon.

```
set i 0; set j 0
```

A *script* versus a *script file*

A *Tcl script* is defined as "one or more Tcl commands." This can cause confusion for folks who use the term *script* to refer to a file that contains a scripting language. Just remember that when you encounter a reference to a "Tcl script," it minimally means "a single Tcl command." To make things easier, this book will use the phrase *script file* when referring to a file containing a Tcl script.

The parsing phase

When a script is loaded into memory, the Tcl interpreter marches through the code, line by line, decomposing each line into words.

```
set message "This machine belongs to Leland"
```

The line above is a command that assigns a string to a variable named message. This command is terminated by an invisible newline, \n. The interpreter views this command as a sentence of three words.

1. **set**
2. message
3. "This machine belongs to Leland"

The first word is treated as a command name. The remaining two words, or arguments, will be passed to the **set** command name during the execution phase. So far, neither word has significance. To the interpreter, these arguments are simply words.

Double quotes are used to convince the interpreter that one or more words should be treated as a single word. The same effect can be accomplished with braces, { }, or with backslashes, \. This process is referred to as *quoting*.

```
"This machine belongs to Leland"
{This machine belongs to Leland}
This\ machine\ belongs\ to\ Leland
```

In these particular examples, each approach to quoting instructs the interpreter that this long string is a single word. As we will learn later, these different types of quoting cause different behavior during Tcl parsing.

The execution phase

At this point, our working example has been simply parsed into a command name and its associated arguments.

```
command name:          set
argument #1:           message
argument #2:           This machine belongs to Leland
```

With all the components of the command in hand, it's time to execute the function represented by the **set** command. To begin the execution phase, the interpreter checks for the existence of a *command function* that is associated with the command name. A command function is a compiled C function that has been linked to the interpreter using a set of published Tcl C functions that support the extension of the interpreter environment.

If the interpreter is unable to locate an associated command function, it then searches predefined locations, including the current script, for a Tcl *procedure* of the same name. Procedures are Tcl scripts that typically perform well-defined tasks, such as GetData or SendPing. Continuing with Tcl's minimal grammar, not even the concept of a procedure has special meaning to the interpreter. Defining a procedure, therefore, requires the use of the **proc** command. The **proc** command takes a number of arguments that form what looks very much like a C function.

```
proc GetData {filename} {
        set fd [open $filename r]
        . . .
}
```

To the Tcl interpreter, there is no distinction between a command name referring to a linked-in command function and a procedure containing a Tcl script.

Continuing with our example, the interpreter locates a command function that represents the functionality of the **set** command name, turning execution control over to the procedure. At this point, the words representing the command name and its arguments take on meaning. It is up to the command function to carry out the function of the **set** command, applying its own set of rules and functionality to its associated arguments. In the case of **set**, the first argument is a variable name. The second argument is the value to assign to the variable name. As a consequence, it is not until the execution phase that potential errors, such as incorrect number of allowable arguments, are detected and made known to the interpreter.

Processing of our example is completed as the **set** command function assigns the value of the second argument, This machine belongs to Leland, to the first argument, message. Finally, the function returns with a return code, informing the Tcl interpreter of a successful completion of the command execution.

Enforcing command syntax

Command functions and procedures enforce the syntax expected by a Tcl command, such as minimum or maximum number of expected arguments, supported options, and/or the required data type of an individual argument. The following Tcl script illustrates how a command carries out "type checking" on its arguments.

```
set value 0
incr value
echo $value
```

➡ 1

In this Tcl script, the first command sets the variable value to 0. The Tcl command **incr** takes the contents of value and increments it by the default value of 1 to generate the result, 1. Suppose value had been set to "Tuesday." The following would have resulted.

```
set value Tuesday
incr value
```

➡ Error: expected integer but got "Tuesday"

This error output is generated by the command function for the command **incr**, and not by the Tcl interpreter. The return code of the command function informs the interpreter of the error, causing the interpreter to halt command processing and return control to the UNIX shell. Errors represent a class of Tcl *exceptions* presented in *Tcl procedures.*

Making that conceptual hurdle!

Most programmers are coming from a programming language that is grammar-rich. It is a natural tendency to make the mistake of projecting past experience onto Tcl. Just keep telling yourself, "Everything is a string," "Command names are the first word in a string," and "The interpreter doesn't know a thing about a command." You'll find that you can answer most of your own questions when you're getting unexpected results from your Tcl code. Reviewing key points about the Tcl interpreter:

1. The first word in a command is always the command name.

2. There is no built-in Tcl interpreter knowledge of command names.

3. The Tcl interpreter performs no checking of the validity of the type of arguments or of the required number of arguments prior to command execution. To the interpreter, everything is a string.

4. The command function performs its own checking on argument and type argument count.

Substitution rules!

Substitution is a major feature of Tcl that provides a great deal of flexibility to your coding strategies. Three types of substitution are supported:

- variable substitution
- command substitution
- backslash substitution

Variable and command substitution represent a kind of "late binding" of information to the command currently under evaluation by the Tcl interpreter. Backslash substitution provides the ability to insert Tcl special characters, such as $ and \, into commands as literal characters.

The interpreter performs all substitutions *before* parsing the command into its final command name and arguments. Up-to-the-minute information can be calculated or gathered from the environment and inserted anywhere in the arguments of a command string. As we will discuss later in the book, you can even use substitution to build the command name "on the fly!" Carefully crafted code can take advantage of substitution to reduce the number of lines in a procedure without reducing the readability of the procedure's intended function.

Variable substitution

Building on the example used earlier, we will use variable substitution to add a little more flexibility to our variable assignment code.

```
set userName Leland
set message "This machine belongs to $userName"
```

We have restructured the single Tcl command into two commands in order to separate the potentially volatile portion, the user's name, from the portion of the string that is likely to remain unchanged. The first command assigns the string Leland to the variable userName.

Quoting single words

For single words there is no difference resulting from the use or nonuse of double quotes. The following two statements are functionality equivalent. All the quotes are doing is telling the interpreter to treat the enclosed string as a single word. Since it's not a multiple word to begin with, nothing is gained.

```
set userName Leland
set userName "Leland"
```

However, this will not always be true, as in the case of Tcl expressions, using operators to compare strings, which is discussed later in Chapter 7, *Flow and Development*.

In our revised working example, the interpreter encounters the dollar-sign symbol, $, in the second command sentence. This symbol is a Tcl special character that signals the interpreter to perform variable substitution on the adjoining variable name. The string $userName is replaced with the contents of the userName variable. All of this takes place before the interpreter completes its parsing of the command. Examining the contents of message reveals that variable substitution has been successfully carried out.

```
echo $message
```

➡ This machine belongs to Leland

Tcl substitution never alters the word boundaries of the command in which it occurs. In other words, if a command sentence contains four words, there will still be four words, no matter how many occurrences of variable substitution take place. This applies to command and backslash substitution as well.

Command substitution

Using square brackets, Tcl commands can be inserted and executed within command sentences. During the parsing phase, the interpreter scans the current command sentence for embedded square brackets. Within the brackets, the interpreter conducts full command parsing and execution, eventually replacing the brackets and the enclosed command with the string returned by the command. In keeping with Tcl command execution mechanism, the embedded command can represent a command function that is implemented as a C function or as a script-based Tcl procedure.

Let's use command substitution to increase the flexibility of our working script by accessing the UNIX environment in order to determine the user's name.

```
set userName [id user]
set message "This machine belongs to $userName"
```
➡ `This machine belongs to carolyn`

The TclX **id** command provides the ability to set, get, and convert user, group, and process ID information. The `user` argument is a supported **id** subcommand that instructs **id** to return the user ID of the person executing the current script. Adhering to substitution rules, the interpreter evaluates the bracketed command first. The entire command string and its enclosing square brackets is then replaced by the command's results in the form of a single word. Having successfully removed the remaining hard-coded data (i.e., the user's name), we now have a very portable script!

If we choose, we can reorganize our example by embedding the **id** command directly into the long string, economizing our Tcl script from two lines to one.

```
set message "This machine belongs to [id user]"
```

The result from [**id** user] becomes a part of the string, which is then assigned by the **set** command to `message`.

Commands inside the brackets are treated exactly the same as stand-alone command lines. The amount of command substitution nesting that you perform is limited only by how readable you would like your code to appear to others who may be asked to perform maintenance chores, including your future self.

The interpreter prioritizes command substitutions by dealing with the most deeply nested brackets first. Moving up nested depths, each embedded command is evaluated one by one. To illustrate nested command substitution, let's modify our example to incorporate a couple of hypothetical Tcl procedures. `GetUserName` performs a lookup of a user's name based on a required argument that represents the user's machine. In order to provide the machine's name, we will use a second hypothetical Tcl procedure, `GetMachineName`, that returns the name of the machine.

```
set message "This machine belongs to [GetUserName [GetMachineName]]"
```

$ and set for accessing variables

The **set** command displays two personalities, depending on the number of arguments it receives. When a single argument is passed to the **set** command, it returns the value stored in the variable named by the argument. Combining this feature with command substitution produces functionality roughly equivalent to the variable substitution command. The two **echo** scripts below produce the same output string.

```
set dateToday "21 Feb 96"
echo "Today is [set dateToday]"
```

➡ Today is 21 Feb 96

```
echo "Today is $dateToday"
```

➡ Today is 21 Feb 96

There are subtle but important differences, depending on which approach you use. These issues are covered in the next chapter.

Backslash substitution

Backslash substitution provides per-character control when influencing Tcl evaluation. It is used to accomplish two things:

1. Insert special characters in commands.
2. Prevent Tcl interpreter from evaluating substitution characters, such as $ and [.

When the interpreter encounters a backslash character, \, it performs backslash substitution on the immediately following character. If the backslash-character sequence is one identified in Table 4–1, the sequence is replaced by the associated item, such as a backspace for \b or a tab for \t. If the backslash sequence is not one of those listed in

Table 4–1, the sequence of the backslash and the character is replaced with the character. The result is that the special character has received the treatment of any normal character.

Backslash substitution becomes extremely useful when dealing with special Tcl characters that happen to have real-world significance as well. For example, when you need to use the dollar character to convey a message to your paying customer:

```
set costLabel "Please pay \$1.25 for this service."
```

Earlier in this chapter, and shown in the example below, we used backslash substitution to convince the interpreter that the multiple word sequence was to be treated as one long word. By using the backslash-space sequence, we substituted the word-delimiting whitespaces for space characters.

```
set message This\ machine\ belongs\ to\ Leland
```

Table 4–1   Special Backslash Sequences

Backslash Sequence	Description
\a	Audible alert (bell) (0x7)
\b	Backspace (0x8)
\f	Form feed (0xc)
\n	Newline (0xa)
\r	Carriage-return (0xd)
\t	Tab (0x9)
\v	Vertical tab (0xb)
\<newline>Space	Replace newline and all following whitespace with single space
\\	Backslash (\)
\ooo	One to three digits 000 give the octal value of a character
\xhh	Hexadecimal digits hh give the hexadecimal value of the character (any number of digits may be present)

The use of backslash sequences can make Tcl output more readable when displayed to a user. For example, you might use the newline sequence to break a long string into a set of easy-to-read fragments. This will be shown to be very useful in Motif dialogs like warning message dialogs.

```
set message "Your file cannot be saved due to:\n\t-\
    insufficient file space, or\n\t- your read-only\
    permissions."
echo $message
```

➡ Your file cannot be saved due to:
    - insufficient file space, or
    - your read-only permissions.

Using \ to handle long strings and Tcl scripts in your script file

Sometimes you will want to assign a very long string to a variable. You could simply allow the string to wrap around your script file; however, it doesn't have a very nice appearance in the midst of your well-structured, regularly indented code.

The \<newline> sequence has the nice attribute of allowing you to (1) continue a string onto a new line and (2) indent the string without inheriting all the leading whitespaces and tabs. The following example will result in a single word with only one whitespace between the first on and the following and.

```
set message "There are days that go on\
    and on and on and on..."
```

\ is also handy for continuing your Tcl script commands onto the next line. With Vt commands, you will find that putting individual options on separate lines helps make your script easier to read and rework. Options can be easily added or removed from the following Vt statement:

```
VtLabel $app.label \
    -label "Welcome to Visual Tcl" \
    -font largeBoldFont \
    -rightSide FORM \
    -bottomSide FORM
```

CAUTION: For Vt commands, be sure that you don't insert a space or tab *after* the \ character. Otherwise, you'll catch an assortment of error messages from the Tcl interpreter, depending on where and in which command the spurious postslash character occurred. If you are using the UNIX vi editor, use of the

```
:set list
```

command is a nice way to locate unwanted backslash-space sequences. For non-Vt commands, this is not an issue.

Curly braces, double quotes, and substitution

Much of the construction of a Tcl script is an exercise in controlling where and when substitution is performed. As it turns out, this is an essential feature of Tcl that makes it the perfect language for support of event-driven Motif development. The need for *deferring* substitution will become more obvious as you incorporate graphical interfaces that incrementally build UNIX commands to be executed at some future point.

Quoting is the process of preventing the interpreter from interpreting Tcl special characters, such as $ or [. Tcl supports three different styles of quoting, described briefly in Table 4–2.

Table 4–2   Quoting characters

Character	Character name	Action
{}	curly braces	Disable almost all special characters
""	double quotes	Disable word and command separators
\	backslash substitution	Disable $, [, {, and other characters not found in Table 4–1

One way to approach quoting and the decision of which quoting characters to use is to ask questions like "Which kinds of substitution do curly braces allow?" Earlier, we hinted that there might be issues to consider in deciding when to use braces versus double quotes to instruct the interpreter to treat a string of words as a single word. If we had used braces instead of double quotes, we would have encountered the following effect.

```
set userName Leland
set message {This machine belongs to $userName}
echo $message
```

➡   This machine belongs to $userName

The output demonstrates that variable substitution has been prevented. So, the use of double quotes instead of curly braces was based on the need to

1.   disable space word separators in order to instruct the interpreter to treat the sentence as one word, yet

2.   allow for the variable substitution to be carried out.

Deferring evaluation

Typical UNIX system administration shell scripts lead the user through a highly directed, carefully constructed series of character-based questions and options. A well-designed graphical application, on the other hand, provides the user with the flexibility to enter data and to select from a palette of options at different places at different times. Assisted by context-sensitive help, the user can scan all the available options before making decisions. The user simply directs the mouse focus to whatever available options he or she pleases. Not until the user is finished with the task is the OK button pressed to generate the command—with selected options—that is eventually executed. The design challenge of flexible graphical systems administration tools is how to generate a conventional UNIX command from the flexible interface of a Motif dialog.

Deferring evaluation is ideal for generating UNIX commands within an event-driven execution environment. The complement of substitution-preventing curly braces and the Tcl **eval** command provides essential tools for constructing and controlling the execution of a UNIX command. As the user selects options and enters data, the application methodically constructs a command to be executed when the OK button at the bottom of the dialog is finally pushed.

Returning to our working example, let's suppose the userName variable has not yet been set. Perhaps the by-product of a text field widget is to gather the user's name and set the userName variable. Suppose, however, that the user goes ahead and clicks on the OK button to indicate (mistakenly) that the task is done, having neglected to enter a user name. Since the **set** command has not been called to create the userName variable, the command

```
set message "This machine belongs to $userName"
```

would generate an error due to the nonexistence of the userName variable. To avoid this situation, we could rework the command to appear as

```
set cmd {set message "This machine belongs to
$userName"}
```

Note that the second **set** command inside the string is not executed, since it is not the first word of the command sentence Furthermore, the curly braces prevent variable substitution of the nonexistent userName. Later, when the user Carolyn has entered her name, causing the userName variable to be created and assigned, the script can then evaluate the command stored in the cmd variable. Just to make sure that the userName variable has indeed been set, we can check for its existence, using the Tcl **info** command.

```
if {[info exists userName]} {
    eval $cmd
    echo $message
}
```

➡ This machine belongs to Carolyn

The **eval** command, using its format listed in Table 4–3, directs the Tcl interpreter to evaluate its arguments as a normal Tcl command. In this case, the contents of cmd are evaluated, causing variable substitution to be safely performed on userName before the string is assigned to message.

Table 4–3 Tcl evaluation command

```
eval arg [arg ...]
```

Having worked through this small example, it may have occurred to you how this mechanism can be used to create strings of preprepared UNIX commands for execution at some future time. Using the UNIX dd command as an example:

```
set ddCmd {system "dd if=$inFile of=$outFile}
```

Here we have set up a command that uses the Tcl **system** command to eventually invoke the UNIX dd command (which does a byte-by-byte copy of a file to another file). Once the user has provided enough information to apply the two variable substitutions, the command can be executed using **eval**. Other uses of deferred evaluation will appear later in the book.

Test your Tcl command evaluation knowledge! What's wrong with this script?

Now that we've addressed everything from parsing to quoting, take a look at the following code and see if you can figure out what's wrong with this script. In this script, the **while** command tests the expression to determine if variable count contains a value less than ten. It reads "while the value in count is less than ten..." and **while** will keep processing the script until the test returns a 0, representing a "false" condition and the fact that count now contains a value of ten or greater.

```
while $count < 10 {
    # add 1 to count with incr
    incr count
}
```

The problem is that this loop never terminates because the test never returns 0. Why? Because curly braces are not being used to defer evaluation of the test expression. Normally, **while** gets the test in its preevaluated form so that it can apply the expression as a test to decide if looping should continue. Because there are no braces, the interpreter evaluates the expression before it is passed to the **while** command.

```
while 1 {
    # add 1 to count with incr
    incr count
}
```

Since the test is now always true (i.e., non-zero), count is going to become quite large indeed, eventually causing an overflow condition. This situation is eliminated by the use of curly braces below.

```
while {$count < 10} {
    # add 1 to count with incr
    incr count
}
```

Comments

The **#** character is a special-case command, representing one of the few grammar elements built into the interpreter. If the first nonblank character in a Tcl command is a **#**, then all subsequent words are discarded. All of this is done by the interpreter, without the use of an evaluation phase command function. The obvious result is that fewer steps are taken during the command parsing of comments.

```
# the next line is an example script
set verboseMode 0; # run in non-verbose mode
```

The first command in the example above is a comment that is discarded by the interpreter. The second line contains two commands separated by a semicolon. The second command is a comment that explains the first command. If we had neglected to separate the **set** and **#** commands with a semicolon, an error would have been generated by the **set** command, complaining of "too many arguments."

Although the interpreter saves a few cycles processing comments as special-case commands, you might want to consider removing comments that are repeatedly processed in your script. Keep in mind that comments inside loops are evaluated with each iteration. If performance is a consideration, comments inside loops should be removed.

Backslash substitution can be used for comments that run greater than the width of your file and must be continued on the next line.

```
# This is an example of a comment that \
   flows to the next line.
```

Balancing braces, even in comments

The use of comments is not as benign as one might expect. The fact is that the interpreter parses braces that may be commented out. This is the direct result of the interpreter focused on evaluating commands as words first, then getting to the handling of the command name. If there is an imbalance, an error will result. The following code results in a Tcl error, "missing close-brace."

```
if {$flag == 1} {
# if {$flag == 2} {
   echo "Flag set"
}
```

The correct way to handle this is to think in terms of keeping braces balanced, even though they are "commented out."

```
if {$flag == 1} {
# if {$flag == 2} {

   echo "Flag set"
#}
}
```

Reviewing Tcl syntax

Having described most of the grammar and command evaluation processes of Tcl, here is a summary of ten Tcl syntax rules. Rule 7 addresses variables and arrays, discussed in Chapter 6, *Data Structures*.

1. A Tcl script is a string containing one or more commands. Semicolons and newlines are command separators *unless quoted*. Close brackets are command terminators during command substitution *unless quoted*.

2. A command is evaluated in two steps. First the Tcl interpreter breaks the command into words and performs substitutions. These substitutions are performed the same way for all commands.

    The first word is used to locate a command function to carry out the command, then all of the words of the command are passed as arguments to the command procedure.

    The command function is free to interpret each of its word arguments (e.g., as an integer, a variable name, or a Tcl script). Different commands interpret words differently.

3. Words of a command are separated by whitespace (except for newlines, which are command separators).

4. If the first character of a word is a double-quote character, ", the word is terminated by the next double-quote character. If semicolons, close brackets, or whitespace characters (including newlines) appear between the quotes, they are treated as ordinary characters and included in the word. Command substitution, variable substitution, and backslash substitution are performed on the characters between the quotes. The double quotes are not retained as part of the word.

5. If the first character of a word is an open brace, {, the word is terminated by the matching close brace, }. Braces nest within the word. For each open brace there must be a close brace. Matching braces are not required if a brace has been backslash-quoted.

    No substitutions are performed on the characters between the braces, except for backslash-newline substitutions, described below. There is no special interpretation of semicolons, newlines, close brackets, or whitespaces.

    The word will consist of exactly the characters between the outer braces, not including the braces themselves.

6. If a word contains an open bracket, [, Tcl performs command substitution. To do this, it invokes the Tcl interpreter recursively to process the characters following the open bracket as a Tcl script. The script may contain any number of commands and must be terminated by a close bracket,].

The result of the script (i.e., the result of its last command) is substituted into the word in place of the brackets and all the characters between them. There may be any number of command substitutions in a single word. Command substitution is not performed on words enclosed in braces.

7. If a word contains a dollar sign, $, then Tcl performs *variable substitution*. The dollar sign and the following characters are replaced in the word by the value of a variable. Variable substitution may take any of the following forms:

`$name`	`name` is the name of a scalar variable; the name is terminated by any character that is not a letter, digit, or underscore.
`$name(index)`	`name` gives the name of an array variable and `index` gives the name of an element within that array. `name` must contain only letters, digits, and underscores. Command substitutions, variable substitutions, and backslash substitutions are performed on the characters of `index`.
`${name}`	`name` is the name of a scalar variable. It may contain any characters whatsoever except for close braces.

There may be any number of variable substitutions in a single word. Variable substitution is not performed on words enclosed in braces.

8. If a backslash, \, appears within a word, *backslash substitution* occurs. In all cases except those described in Table 4–1, the backslash is dropped, and the following character is treated as an ordinary character and included in the word. This allows characters such as double quotes, close brackets, and dollar signs to be included in words without triggering special processing. Table 4–1 describes the backslash sequences that are handled specially, along with the value that replaces each sequence.

    Backslash substitution is not performed on words enclosed in braces, except for the backslash-newline sequence, in which a single space character replaces the backslash, newline, and all whitespace after the newline. This backslash sequence is unique in that it is replaced in a separate pre-pass before the command is actually parsed. This means that it will be replaced even when it occurs between braces, and the resulting space will be treated as a word separator if it is not in braces or quotes.

9. If a hash character, #, appears at a point where Tcl is expecting the first character of the first word of a command, then the hash character and the characters that follow it, up to and including the next newline, are treated as a comment and ignored. This "comment character" has significance only when it appears at the beginning of a command.

10. Each character is processed exactly once by the Tcl interpreter as part of creating the words of a command. For example, if variable substitution occurs, no further substitutions are performed on the value of the variable; the value is inserted into the word verbatim. If command substitution occurs, the nested command is processed entirely by the recursive call to the Tcl interpreter; no substitutions are performed before making the recursive call, and no additional substitutions are performed on the result of the nested script.

11. Substitutions do not affect the word boundaries of a command. For example, during variable substitution, the entire value of the variable becomes part of a single word, even if the variable's value contains spaces.

Tcl Procedures

✔ Procedures
✔ Variable scope
✔ Exceptions, errors, and stack unwinds

Tcl does not differentiate between commands and procedures. To the script invoking a command, there is no structural hint that the command is implemented as a C command function or as a Tcl script in the form of a procedure. This feature makes it possible to transparently migrate commands from Tcl procedures to C functions without impacting your Tcl script.

For writing bulletproof scripts and procedures, Tcl provides extensive error handling that allows you to trace quickly the origin of problematic code. Errors can be intercepted, examined, and processed in a manner that makes Tcl an ideal run-time language for the unforgiving demands of the graphical desktop environment.

Procedures

Well-defined programming tasks are typically organized as reusable scripts called *Tcl procedures*. A Tcl procedure is a command representing a Tcl script rather than a C function. Since procedures are not a part of the native Tcl grammar, they must be created with the **proc** command. Here are some examples of task-oriented Tcl procedure names that we might create.

GetNextUID   Fetch the next available UID (to create a new user
                          account)

OpenTmpFile	Open a temporary file for writing
MakeDateStamp	Generate a date stamp to associate with some data
PostErrorMessage	Post an error message, using a Motif dialog

Procedures are invoked just like Tcl commands. The **proc** command registers procedures with the Tcl interpreter command table. When the name of a Tcl procedure is invoked as a command, Tcl executes the script that was registered by **proc**. The **proc** command supports the following syntax.

proc *name args body*

There are three arguments passed to the **proc** command: the name of the procedure, the argument list, and the body of the procedure, containing one or more Tcl scripts. Later, when the **proc** command is actually executed by its command function, the script commands found in the *body* argument are then processed one by one.

```
proc EchoHometown {name place} {
        # begin script...
        echo "Name is $name"
        echo "Hometown is $place"
        # ...end script
}
```

This example procedure, EchoHometown, simply writes two strings to the UNIX shell, using the **echo** command. EchoHometown has been defined with the **proc** command to require two arguments. Invoked with fewer or more than two arguments will cause **proc** to generate an error message. The quoting power of curly braces instructs the interpreter to treat the body of the Tcl script as one long word argument, even though it contains multiple lines of commands.

Table 5–1   Commands supporting procedures and commands

global	*varName [varName ...]*
proc	*name args body*
rename	*oldName newName*
return	*[-code code] [-errorinfo info] [-errorcode code] [string]*
uplevel	*[level] arg [arg ...]*
upvar	*[level] otherVar myVar [otherVar myVar ...]*

To invoke the procedure, we type the following:

```
EchoHometown John "San Francisco"
```

➡ Name is John
   Hometown is San Francisco

Errors that occur inside a Tcl procedure cause termination of the procedure script. The error generated by the script is passed back from the **proc** command to the interpreter. Anything that terminates a Tcl script is called an *exception*. Exceptions are discussed in detail later in this chapter.

Default procedure argument values

Tcl supports the ability to specify default values for procedure arguments. When using the **proc** command to define a procedure, each argument and its default value can be supplied as a quoted list of two words. In the example below, memorySize is the name of the first argument, and its default value is 8MB.

```
proc EchoConfiguration {{memorySize 8MB} {diskSize 512MB}} {
        echo "Memory:\t\t$memorySize"
        echo "Disk Capacity:\t$diskSize"
}
```

Because we have specified default values, invoking EchoConfiguration with fewer than the number of the expected arguments avoids an error condition. Supplying one or two values would override the corresponding default values.

```
EchoConfiguration 16MB
```

➡ Memory: 16MB
Disk Capacity: 512MB

If you define a procedure to use default values for fewer than the total number of specified arguments, the defaulted arguments must be organized to occur at the end of the procedure's argument list.

Returning values from procedures: `return`

The Tcl **return** command is used to return values from a procedure. **return** is another example of a Tcl exception, since it causes the termination of the procedure's script. The example below uses **return** to return a string of characters converted to uppercase.

```
proc ConvertToCaps {string} {
        # capitalize all lowercase alpha characters
        set convertedString [translit a-z A-Z $string]
        return $convertedString
}
```

The script that invokes ConvertToCaps might look like

```
echo "There is something [ConvertToCaps "seriously wrong!"]"
```

➡ There is something SERIOUSLY WRONG!

The **return** command supports additional functionality for returning more detailed information to the calling command. These options are discussed later in this chapter.

Accessing global variables: `global`

All variables inside the body of a procedure have *local scope*. They exist only during the lifetime of the executing procedure. Unlike C functions, Tcl does not support the notion of a static local variable that can be preserved from one procedure invocation to the next. Variables that lie *outside* the procedure are in the *global scope* and are unknown to the Tcl script inside the procedure, unless explicitly registered using the **global** command.

```
set verboseMode 1

proc CheckForVerboseMode {} {
    global verboseMode
    if {$verboseMode == 1} {
        echo "Running in verbose mode"
    }
}
```

Variables that are created outside of a procedure's scope are global, such as verboseMode in the example above. Using the **global** command makes verboseMode accessible from within the procedure.

Call-by-reference: `upvar`

Extensive use of global variables to circumvent the inherent variable scoping of procedures can lead to a mess of bug-causing side effects. Good programming practice leverages the use of *call-by-reference* procedure arguments to update variables, controlling the flow of data to and from procedures.

By default, arguments passed to a Tcl procedure are *call-by-value* in nature. Procedure arguments are treated as values rather than as variable names containing values. The following examples invoke a procedure with different forms of an argument. We will assume that we have created AddUserName, a Tcl procedure that requires a single argument.

```
set name Amanda
AddUserName name          ok, but you'll just get "name" and not "Amanda"
AddUserName $name         ok
AddUserName Amanda        ok
AddUserName "Amanda"      ok, though quotes in this case are unnecessary
```

Tcl supports call-by-reference procedure arguments with the **upvar** command, solely created for use inside a Tcl procedure. Outside of a procedure, **upvar** has no meaning.

In the example procedure below, **upvar** is used to indicate that itemList is a pass-by-reference argument. RemoveDuplicateItems accepts a variable containing a list of items. It removes any redundant items, producing two results:

1. a return value containing the number of items removed, and

2. an updated list variable with redundant items removed.

```
proc RemoveDuplicateItems {itemList} {
     upvar $itemList tmpList

     # save the length of the old list
     set oldListLength [llength $tmpList]

     # remove the duplicate items with
     # the TclX lrmdups command
     set tmpList [lrmdups $tmpList]

     # get new length, and return the difference
     set newListLength [llength $tmpList]

     # use expr to evaluate an arithmetic expression
     return [expr {$oldListLength - $newListLength}]
}
```

upvar assigns an alias name to the name of the pass-by-reference procedure argument. Manipulating the alias is the only way to achieve a pass-by-reference effect. In RemoveDuplicateItems, tmpList is the alias for the argument itemList. Observe that itemList is never directly referenced after the **upvar** command.

RemoveDuplicateItems is invoked below, passing the name of a variable that contains a list of machines named after planets. Note that the variable machineList, below, is passed to the procedure without using $ substitution, since it is the variable that is to be updated with the list of redundant items removed.

```
set machineList {Jupiter Mars Mars Venus Saturn Venus}
set count [RemoveDuplicateItems machineList]
echo "$count duplicate machine names were removed"
echo "the machine list is: $machineList"
```

➡ 2 duplicate machine names were removed
   the machine list is: Jupiter Mars Saturn Venus

These commands are introduced in RemoveDuplicateItems, to be discussed in subsequent chapters:

llength	returns the number of items in a Tcl list
lrmdups	removes redundant items in a Tcl list
expr	evaluates expressions such as arithmetic operations

Extending a procedure's influence: `uplevel`

The Tcl name space is viewed as a *call stack* containing multiple *levels*. With each invocation of a procedure, you move up the stack. Your Tcl script's initial position within a stack is at level 0. When you invoke a procedure, the variables in the scope of the procedure exist within level 1. Invoking another procedure within the procedure creates level 2, and so on.

With **uplevel**, you can place the execution of a procedure's script anywhere in the name space of your Tcl script environment. Rather than control access to variables in other variable name spaces, **uplevel** provides a procedure with the ability to execute a script in other variable scopes. It does this by moving the script up the call stack to the desired level, where it can be evaluated by the interpreter in the context of the variables that exist at that level.

```
set globalVar "Hello"

proc Procedure1 {} {
      set proc1Var "there!"
      Procedure2
      echo $proc1Var
}
proc Procedure2 {} {
      # execute script at top of procedure stack
      uplevel #0 set globalVar bye!
      # execute script one procedure level up
      uplevel #1 set proc1Var Good
}
Procedure1
echo $globalVar
```

➡ Good
   bye!

This example features two procedures, one invoking the other. The most deeply nested procedure, `Procedure2`, uses the **uplevel** command to execute the script

```
set globalVar bye!
```

in the global name space, two levels up the procedure calling stack, with

```
uplevel #0 set globalVar bye!
```

The use of # means that the numeric argument is absolute. #0 means level 0, which is the global space. Instead of using #0, the command could have been written as

```
uplevel 2 set globalVar bye!
```

meaning "move two levels up the stack." Continuing with the example, `Procedure2` then sends the script **set** proc1Var Good one level up to the scope of its parent procedure, `Procedure1`, where it is executed. The end result is that the two variables in name spaces outside `Procedure2` are updated to deliver a different message when printed to `stdout` with the **echo** command.

Create a new version of the **for_file** *command. The new command,* `TASK`
`safe_for_file`, *should check for the existence of the file before attempting to read it. To view the original* **for_file** *command, enter the* `vtcl` *interactive shell and type* **showproc** `for_file`

```
proc safe_for_file {var filename body} {
    upvar $var line
    # check for the existence of the file
    if {[info exists $filename]} {
        set fp [open $filename r]
    } else {
        error "File $filename does not exist"
    }
    while {[gets $fp line] >= 0} {
        uplevel $body
    }
    close $fp
}
```

Using **uplevel** makes it easy to build your own class of wrapper commands that enhance the robustness of an existing Tcl command. The TclX **for_file** convenience command loops through a file, returning each line it reads one at a time. Our enhanced procedure, `safe_for_file`, adds a check for the existence of the file before attempting to open it.

rename removes a procedure from the Tcl command table. For instance, you could replace the **for_file** command, implemented as a procedure, with the `safe_for_file` procedure. This is accomplished with the following command sequence.

```
rename for_file ""
rename save_for_file for_file
```

First, **for_file** must be removed from the execution environment. Then, `safe_for_file` can be turned into the new **for_file**, at least for the lifetime of the current `vtcl` interpreter session.

Variable length argument list: `args`

For situations when you want your procedure to support any number of arguments, ranging from none to many, Tcl provides the keyword `args` variable. As with the case of default argument values, if you decide to mix required arguments with an optional number of additional arguments, your procedure should list the `args` keyword last in the argument list.

```
proc DoSomething {name args} {
      echo Name is $name
      echo The remaining arguments are:
      foreach arg $args}
echo $arg
}
```

The following procedure adds one or more machines to a global list variable, called machineList.

```
proc BuildMachineList args {
      global machineList
      foreach machine $args {
         lappend machineList $machine
      }
}

BuildMachineList Jupiter Mars Venus
```

Expected and unexpected exceptions

One by one, the Tcl interpreter processes commands as long as the command function returns a 0 to the interpreter, signaling the successful completion of the command. The value that is returned by a command function is internal to the interaction between it and the interpreter. A nonzero result causes Tcl to abort the execution of the script. Any script-terminating effect is called a *Tcl exception*.

An exception's effect may terminate an entire application or it may simply cause a simple loop to return to the top of a looping command, where processing continues. Inside a procedure, the **return** command causes an exception that terminates the procedure's script, returning execution flow to the point that the procedure was invoked. Reviewed in Chapter 7, *Flow and Development*, **break** and **continue** are other examples of exceptions that terminate scripts in limited, but useful ways.

Table 5–2   Error processing commands

catch *script* [*varName*]
error *message* [*info*] [*code*]

An *error* is a Tcl exception that terminates an entire script file. When a command encounters an error condition, the command issues an error message, and the interpreter terminates the Tcl script and the Tcl session containing the script.

The following example illustrates the results of the incorrect use of the **sleep** command, causing the termination of a script.

```
sleep five
```

➡ Error: expected unsigned integer, but got "five"

In this script, the intended use of **sleep** is to cause the script to sleep for 5 seconds. However, expecting an integer, **sleep** sees the unfamiliar argument five, causing it to give up.

In a few paragraphs, we see how the termination of a Tcl script can be prevented with the **catch** command. The use of **catch** is critical to ensuring that graphical Visual Tcl applications don't simply "go away" when an error condition occurs.

Diagnosing errors with stack unwinds

An error may occur deep inside a set of nested Tcl scripts. For example, an error may occur in the script of a procedure that was invoked by another procedure. To help the developer track the sequence of Tcl statements that might have led to the error, Tcl "unwinds" the error stack, writing diagnostic information to stderr.

```
proc OpenTmpFile {fileName} {
        set fd [open $fileName w]
        return $fd
}
proc StampTmpFile {fileName} {
        set fd [OpenTmpFile $fileName]
        puts $fd [fmtclock [getclock]]
        close $fd
}
StampTmpFile /tmpp/stamp
```

The script above initializes a file by opening it for writing, then places a date stamp inside. The script is written to carry out the following sequence of steps:

1. StampTmpFile invokes the OpenTmpFile procedure to stamp the file contained in fileName

2. OpenTmpFile uses the Tcl **open** command to open the file for writing.

3. OpenTmpFile returns the file descriptor of the opened file to StampTmpFile.

4. StampTmpFile uses the Tcl command **puts** to write the current date, generated by **getclock** and formatted by **fmtclock**, to the open file.

5. Having been stamped, the file is closed with the Tcl **close** command.

Due to the presence on an extra *p* in /tmpp, an error is encountered during the attempt to open the file for writing. The following error message is written to stderr by the Tcl interpreter.

```
Error: couldn't open "/tmpp/stamp": No such file or
directory
couldn't open "/tmpp/stamp": No such file or directory
        while executing
"open /tmpp/stamp w"
        invoked from within
"set fd [open /tmpp/stamp w]..."
        (procedure "OpenTmpFile" line 2)
        invoked from within
"OpenTmpFile"
        invoked from within
"set fd [OpenTmpFile $fileName]..."
        (procedure "StampTmpFile" line 2)
        invoked from within
"StampTmpFile"
        (file "f8" line 10)
```

This output represents the unwinding of the execution stack that led to the error that occurred inside the call to OpenTmpFile. Starting from the bottom, you can see the commands and procedure calls representing the path of execution that led to the occurrence of the error.

You can prevent stack unwinds by invoking vtcl with the -n option. This can be done at the top of your executable file, as well as at the UNIX command prompt.

```
#! /bin/vtcl -n
```

Intercepting exceptions with the catch command

The example of the stack unwind, above, is obviously very useful during the development phase of your application. However, output as chaotic-appearing as this is the last thing you want a user to see, especially a user who has no programming experience and, in a graphical environment, no idea that they are running a Tcl script. Stack unwinds will never be seen by the user who launches your graphical application by double-clicking on a desktop icon. Instead, the application simply disappears. This is an unacceptable situation.

The good news is that Tcl supports a powerful exception-handling command called **catch**. For Visual Tcl programming, **catch** can be used to intercept error messages and display them via a graphical Motif dialog. The stack unwind above could have been prevented with the following modification to the script.

```
proc OpenTmpFile {fileName} {
        set rc [catch {open $fileName w} fd ]
        if {$rc == 0} {
            return $fd
        } else {
            echo "We could not open $fileName. Try again. \
                \nThe system error said, \"$fd\""
        }
}
OpenTmpFile /tmpp/stamp
```

➡ We could not open /tmpp/stamp. Try again.
The system error said, "couldn't open "/tmpp/stamp": No
such file or directory"

When successful, the **open** command returns a string representing the file descriptor. When not successful, it returns an error message. **catch** intercepts any string returned by its Tcl script argument (in this case, **open**), and stores it in its second argument, represented by fd. If the return code is good, fd will receive the file descriptor. If not, fd will receive the error message. **catch** itself returns a numeric code representing the success or failure of its executed script.

Exception return codes

The possible integer values returned by the **catch** command are Tcl-generated values. It is a common misunderstanding that **catch** returns the exit code value returned by the command that generated the error, such as **open** in the OpenTmpFile example. The values that are potentially returned by **catch** are:

0 When command(s) inside the **catch** script executes without error.
1 When command(s) inside the **catch** script has generated an error condition
2 When the **return** command was executed inside the **catch** script.
3 When the **break** command was executed inside the **catch** script.
4 When the **continue** command was executed inside the **catch** script.

Clearly, checking for 0 and 1 is the best way to determine the result of a **catch**-enshrouded command. **return**, **break**, and **continue** are examples of nonerror Tcl exceptions.

It is also possible for **catch** to return a value other than 0 through 4. Using the **return** command, a script may specify any value, for example:

return -code 15 $returnString

In fact, it's also possible to store information in the built-in errorInfo variable, discussed below.

return -code 15 -errorinfo $traceInfo

Built-in Tcl error variables

errorCode and errorInfo are built-in global Tcl variables that are updated when an error exception occurs. errorInfo will contain the stack trace. If your script uses **catch** to intercept an error exception, you can set up your own debugging environment to examine the contents of errorInfo or provide an alternate method for passing along error details to your users, such as writing the error information to a file.

If we had used **catch** to intercept the error generated by the **sleep** command in our earlier example, it might have looked like the following:

```
set rc [catch {sleep five}]
if {$rc == 1} {
        echo errorCode:$errorCode
        echo errorInfo:$errorInfo
}
```
➡ errorCode:NONE
```
errorInfo:expected unsigned integer but got "five"
while executing
"sleep five"
```

The value NONE indicates that the error was not generated during the execution of a POSIX call. If an error occurs and the Tcl command is implemented by command functions using POSIX calls, the contents of errorCode will contain a list of three items. The OpenTmpFile example generates an error from the **open** call, which makes use of POSIX commands to open a file. If we had examined the contents of errorCode when the **open** failed to open the nonexistent file, we would have seen:

```
POSIX ENOENT {No such file or directory}
```

POSIX indicates that the error occurred during the execution of a POSIX system call. ENOENT is the POSIX name for the error, and the third item is a human-readable message explaining the error. Other supported keywords that may appear in errorCode are

ARITH	When arithmetic errors occur, such as dividing by zero.
CHILDSTATUS	When a child process has exited with a nonzero result.
CHILDKILLED	When a child process has exited due to a signal.
CHILDSUSP	When a child process been suspended due to a signal.

Generating errors with the `error` command

The **error** command gives your script the ability to generate a Tcl error if a condition exists that merits a stack unwind, followed by termination of the program in execution.

```
...
if {($debugOn == 1) && (![info exists userName])} {
      error "This script needs debugging!"
}
```

Use of the **error** command should be considered carefully when developing an application for execution in the graphical environment. Not only is there a good chance that your application may be executed via an icon, but consider that one of the goals of a GUI environment is to make it easier for users to control applications. In the example above, we have created an assertion statement that verifies the existence of the variable `userInfo` when debugging is turned on.

Data Structures

✔ Simple variables
✔ Associative arrays
✔ Strings
✔ Lists
✔ Keyed lists
✔ Built-in variables

*T*he Tcl language, extended with the TclX command library, provides the data-handling engine that propels graphical Visual Tcl applications. Together, these nongraphical commands represent a very high-level language for retrieving, manipulating, and storing data, complementary of the equally easy-to-use Vt interface-building commands.

The *Visual Tcl Handbook* focuses primarily on the features that go beyond standard Tcl programming. It is, however, impossible to explain Visual Tcl without addressing many of the commands and data structures found in base Tcl. More than enough basic Tcl is featured in order to get you started writing serious Visual Tcl applications. This chapter introduces each Tcl and TclX command in table format, highlighting the use of selected commands with simple examples. As you experiment with these examples, you can explore each command's expanded features by referring to their detailed descriptions in Part IV, *Command Pages*. To gain a greater working knowledge of the finer points of Tcl programming, you may want to consider acquiring one of the two Tcl introductory books listed in the preface of this book.

Tasks, echo, and—soon—widgets

As we survey the bulk of the nongraphical Tcl and TclX commands, this book takes a "hands-on" approach, making heavy use of examples to illustrate the uses and subtleties of many Visual Tcl commands. In many cases, we will use suggested tasks and explore how they might be carried out:

TASK *Sort a list of users found on the department server named* bigben. *Assume that the procedure* GetUserNames *returns a list of users currently logged on to the machine named as an argument.*

```
set userList [GetUserNames bigben]
echo "presorted list:\t$userList"
echo "sorted list:\t$[lsort $userList]"
```

➡ presorted list: Ann Randy Beatrice Alex
   sorted list: Alex Ann Beatrice Randy

We make extensive use of the **echo** command to show the results of many examples. Where it helps to draw a mental picture, we'll use fictitious procedures that are quite possible to implement as a deferred exercise.

Many of these examples can be easily reworked to incorporate the use of widget-building Vt commands to display their output. This will become apparent in subsequent chapters. For example, using the **VtList** command for building a Motif list widget, we can use the results of our sorted list from above:

```
VtList $root.listW \
      -itemList $sortedUserList
```

➡
```
┌─────────────┬─┐
│ Alex        │▲│
│ Anne        │ │
│ Beatrice    │▼│
└─────────────┴─┘
```

Command-driven data structure

In keeping with the highly dynamic nature of the Tcl language, Visual Tcl data structures are simply strings that acquire structural meaning, depending on the command that operates on them. Just as the Tcl interpreter treats the first word of every line of script as a command name, the **lvarpop** command (as we'll soon see), interprets the first item in a list to be the top of a stack. To the **lindex** command, a list is simply a set of items that are referenced, beginning with the number 0.

Commands like **lvarpop** and **lindex** project their own sense of organization and meaning onto the Tcl list structure, enforcing behavior and attributes that mimic different data structures found in many programming languages, such as sets and linked lists.

Variable names are simply strings that the **set** command identifies as variables. The variable substitution command, **$**, takes the complementary view of interpreting the appended string as the name of a variable.

In a sense, the Tcl command mechanism is similar to object-oriented programming, where a data structure such as a list is an object, as viewed and manipulated by its member functions. However, it is very much unlike object-oriented programming, in that there's nothing preventing a script from directly editing a list and corrupting its structure. The flexibility of Tcl is what gives it the power to solve many problems with relatively little coding. The flip side of this capability is that the Tcl developer must be aware of the behavior and characteristics of fundamental Tcl commands and structures.

The rest of this chapter conducts a survey of Visual Tcl data structures, introducing the commands that provide supporting operations. With each data structure and functional discussion, a listing of the supporting commands is provided.

Simple variables

Tcl variables support a liberal naming convention. There is virtually no limit to the variety of characters you can use. To maximize the readability of your code, it is best to adopt a consistent naming convention for variable names and procedures throughout your application. Examples of legal variable names include:

```
userName
username
user_Name
"her 2nd user name"
USERNAME
user#1
```

Clearly, this list reinforces the world-as-a-string view of Tcl. Variable names are context-sensitive and may contain spaces and other special characters requiring quoting. The following illustrates a completely legitimate operation:

```
set "her 2nd user name" Young
echo Her 2nd name is: ${her 2nd user name}
```

➡ Her 2nd name is: Young

Imagine seeing code like this through the eyes of a first-year programmer inheriting maintenance responsibilities! Just about any string will work, as long as you know how and when to use quoting or backslash substitution to create and reference the variable name.

This example also illustrates the unbalanced treatment of Tcl variable names. A Tcl variable name containing special characters like # and ! is treated differently, depending on when it is created with the **set** command and when it is dereferenced with **$** substitution.

Clearly, Tcl supports the ability to create a variable out of just about any character combination. However, unless you have special needs, work with a consistent, easy-to-understand naming convention. Restricting your naming convention to letters, digits, and underscores will go a long way to improve your ability to produce bug-free Tcl scripts.

Table 6–1   Variable Commands

---

set *varName* [*value*]

unset *varName* [*varName varName ...*]

Just as variables can be created, they can be destroyed as well. The **unset** command removes variables from your script's name space. This is particularly handy in preventing bugs by identifying scripts that are trying to access data that should not be around any longer.

TASK   *Use the* **unset** *command to destroy variables that will no longer be used in a script:*

```
unset user#1 user#2 user#3
```

Accessing variables with $ substitution or the set command

The **$** variable substitution command has no problem with variable names composed of any combination of `a-z`, `A-Z`, `0-9`, and `_` characters. So, even though the **set** command may not complain when you create a variable with a name like `user#1`, when you perform variable substitution on that variable, you will be forced to take advantage of quoting to do so. For example,

```
echo "The first user is: ${user#1}"
```

is one way to access `user#1` without getting an error message stating that "variable `user` does not exist." Curly brace quoting is required to prevent special character evaluation.

Accessing variables with $ substitution or the `set` command (cont.)

There is a way to dereference a variable containing ! and # without having to use quoting. When called with only one argument, the **set** command returns the value contained in a variable named by that argument. Taking advantage of this feature, the same example can be implemented without the need for quoting with braces.

```
echo "The first user is: [set user#1]"
```

Using **set** to access the contents of a variable is useful when your script needs to access the contents of a variable name inside another variable.

```
set greeting "Good morning"
set var greeting
echo $$var
```

➡ `$greeting`

Using two $ substitution characters only gets us half-way. Combining $ and **set** or using **set** twice will give us the result we are looking for

```
echo [set $var]
```

or

```
echo [set [set var]]
```

➡ `Good morning`

Quoting for embedded variable substitution

The mechanism of quoting also makes it possible to perform variable substitution in the midst of a word of consecutive characters without changing the name of the variable. For example,

```
set middle fragil
set name super${middle}istic
echo $name
```

➡ `superfragilistic`

The curly braces are used to delimit the name of the variable associated with the $ substitution character. If we had not used the curly braces, a Tcl error would have been generated:

```
set name super$middleistic
```

➡ `Error: can't read "middleistic": no such variable`

$middle and ${middle} are forms for variable substitution that are functionally equivalent. It's how and where they are used within a string that reveals their functional distinction.

Creating variable names at run-time!

Every now and then you may want to take advantage of variable substitution to build your variable names on the fly.

```
set i 0
foreach flower {rose carnation tulip} {
  incr i
  set flower$i $flower
}
```

In this example using the looping **foreach** command, three new variables, `flower1`, `flower2`, and `flower3` are created. Among other benefits, this approach to self-modifying code gives you the ability to build a series of graphical widgets, such as push buttons, without having to type a lot of redundant code. The advantage of this approach will become more clear when we construct the "Rolodex Program."

Associative arrays

Tcl is commonly called upon to work with real-world data represented by computers, people, buildings, and other common objects. Tcl associative arrays are ideal for organizing information using indexing that supports the use of meaningful naming, such as printer names or names of devices associated with a computer. The example below uses a Tcl array to store lists of users who are currently logged on servers in a network. Rather than using numbers, the indexes that reference the elements of the array networkUsers are the names of the machines Jupiter, Mars, and Mercury.

```
set networkUsers(Jupiter) {Jane Jack Andy Amanda}
set networkUsers(Mars) {Carol Bob Ted Alice}
set networkUsers(Mercury) {Hank Linda Ron Mary}
```

Table 6–2   Array Commands

	array *option arrayName* [*arg arg ...*]
★	**for_array_keys** *var array_name code*

Arrays are also useful for internal Tcl scripting purposes, such as storing options provided by a user to an application, as the UNIX dd command:

```
set ddOptions(if) /tmp/inputFile
set ddOptions(of) /tmp/outputFile
set ddOptions(ibs) 1024
set ddOptions(obs) 1024
set ddOptions(seek) 0
set ddOptions(conv) ASCII
```

or for creating templates of default values that might be used to create new users:

```
set userTemplate(useridMin) 1000
set userTemplate(defaultgid) group
set userTemplate(homeDirRoot) /u
set userTemplate(mailDirectory) /usr/spool/mail
```

Elements in an array are accessed very much like simple Tcl variables. To create an array, simply use **set** to create the first element. Then reference the name of the array using the same or other index names.

```
set birthDays(Gale) "30 July"
set personName Mark
set birthDays($personName) "24 Dec"
echo Mark's birthday is $birthDays(Mark).
```

➡ Mark's birthday is 24 Dec.

Manipulating arrays with **array**

The array data structure is supported by convenient commands that make it easy to manipulate, traverse, and investigate the information stored in an array. Although the list of array-related commands shown in Table 6–2 is short, the number of supported subcommands is large. The structure of Tcl commands is divided into two styles of format. One style supports single commands that provide very specific functions, such as **llength**, the command that returns the length of a Tcl list. **array**, on the other hand, is an example of a single Tcl command that supports a large number of related subcommands using a noun-verb format. For example, two of the six verb options that are supported by **array** are:

array names *arrayName*	Returns the names of the array elements.
array size *arrayName*	Returns the number of array elements.

```
echo "There are [array size networkUsers] servers."
echo "The servers are: [array names networkUsers]"
```

➡ There are 3 servers.
   The servers are: Mercury Mars Jupiter

For extremely large arrays, the **array** command supports a set of verb subcommands that enhance fast element searches. However, in the majority of cases, you most likely examine the contents of an array using code that is typified by the following example.

```
foreach index [array name networkUsers] {
    set nameList $networkUsers($index)
    if {[lmatch -exact $nameList "Alice"] != {}} {
        echo "Alice is on $index!"
        break
    }
}
```

➡ Alice is on Mars!

In the example above, the list-looping **foreach** command processes the array networkUsers, one element at a time. The **array** name subcommand provides the list of all index names found in networkUsers. One by one, each element is searched for a list containing the item Alice. **lmatch** is the list command for finding items in a list. It returns the one or more matched items as a list. If **lmatch** fails to detect a match, then an empty list, represented by {}, is returned. Because we are using the **break** command to terminate the **foreach** script, the search terminates as soon as a match is found.

Example tasks

TASK

PingNode *is a fictitious procedure that tests for the on-line presence of nodes on a network.* unreachableNodes *is an array where each element represents a node that failed the* PingNode *test. Use the* **unset** *command to remove elements that, when pinged again, are able to respond.*

```
if {[PingNode "Barney"] == "OK"} {
    unset unreachableNodes(Barney)
}
```

TASK

Use the **for_array_keys** *command to extract all the keys from the array* unreachableNodes.

```
echo "Unable to reach the following machines:"
for_array_keys node unreachableNodes {
    echo $node
}
```

Multidimensional arrays

Tcl supports one-dimensional arrays. However, the flexibility of string-based naming makes it possible to create the illusion of multidimensional arrays. The example below builds a two-dimensional array using two loops, one nested in the other. The first index is the car manufacturer and the second is the car model, identified by its configuration of doors. GetCarModels is a fictitious procedure that returns a list of car model names that support the current door configuration.

```
foreach i {Chrysler Pontiac Buick} {
        foreach j {twodoor fourdoor hatchback stationwagon} {
            set carModels($i,$j) [GetCarModels $i $j]
        }
}
```

The illusion of a two-dimensional array is made possible by the ability to use virtually any string as an element's name. For example, you could use the notation of i:j. To access a element within a two-dimensional array simply requires that you stick with the element naming convention you used to create the array. The example below fetches car model information from the array we just constructed.

```
echo "Pontiac offers the following hatchback models:\n\
        $carModels(Pontiac,hatchback)"
```

Element names of arrays reflect the same conventions of naming variables. Arrays require only a single argument inside the parentheses.

Arrays and index names

The following name will generate a Tcl error.

```
set carModel(Pontiac, hatchback) {tuck&roll}
```

➡ Error: wrong # args: should be "set varName ?newValue?"

At first, you might think that Tcl arrays do not allow spaces in array index names. However, the error message is generated by the **set** command, the result of the space character following the comma, causing the Tcl interpreter to pass three arguments, instead of two. Applying what we have learned about Tcl quoting solves this situation.

```
set "carModels(Pontiac, hatchback)" {tuck&roll}
```

or

Arrays and index names (cont.)

```
set indexName "Pontiac, hatchback"
set carModels($indexName) {tuck&roll}
```

If you are not convinced that `carModel` has been recognized as an array, then listing the current index names should convince you. The index name containing the space is highlighted in bold. Note that the interpreter automatically applied brace quoting in order to represent the index as a single word.

```
echo [array names carModels]
```

➡ Chrysler,fourdoor Pontiac,stationwagon
Buick,stationwagon Chrysler,hatchback
Chrysler,stationwagon Pontiac,twodoor Buick,twodoor
Pontiac,fourdoor Buick,fourdoor
{Pontiac, hatchback} Pontiac,hatchback
Buick,hatchback Chrysler,twodoor

Accessing arrays inside procedures

Using arrays to pass a large volume of related information to procedures is a useful practice. Unfortunately, Tcl does not recognize arrays as first-class variables, due to the underlying implementation of arrays, which we will not explore here. For instance, you cannot pass an array as a call-by-value argument. If you attempt to pass the name of an array variable as a procedure argument, there is no apparent problem. However, the first time the procedure script attempts to index the argument's name as an array, a "`variable isn't an array`" error will result. Also, you cannot return an array using the **return** command. However, all is not lost. There are two approaches to passing array variables to procedures:

1. use of the **global** command or
2. as a call-by-reference variable using **upvar**.

Use of the **upvar** command to support pass-by-reference is illustrated below.

```
# A procedure erases the contents of an array
proc eraseArrayContents {arrayName} {
        upvar $arrayName myArray
        foreach element [array names myArray] {
           set myArray($element) {}
        }
}

# erase the contents of the carModels array
eraseArrayContents carModels
```

The use of **global** or **upvar** will compensate for the inability to use **return**.

As a general guideline, use the **global** approach when the array contains constant values that are not meant to change after array initialization, such as the default options for an application. Use the **upvar** approach when the array is to be modified.

Tcl lists

Tcl's popularity within the system administration community rests largely on its powerful capacity for manipulating chunks of information, such as the kind of information that might be returned by a UNIX command. Tcl makes it conceptually easy to view and manipulate data in the form of simple lists. Lists are things that people use everyday. Little struggle is required to understand data as lists within the context of a programming language.

Visual Tcl supports two views of a list: the basic Tcl list and the TclX keyed list. The distinction between Tcl lists and keyed lists is made on the basis of how commands interpret and apply structure to the basic list data structure. First, we will address standard Tcl lists.

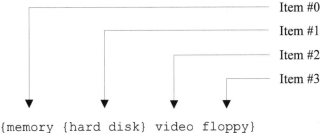

```
{memory {hard disk} video floppy}
```

Lists represent a set of 0 or more items that are indexed beginning with the number 0, as shown above. A null or empty list is represented by two curly braces with nothing in between:

```
{}
```

Curly braces are used to quote lists for different purposes. Curly braces can be used to give the structure needed to treat items as a single word. For example, braces are used to identify {hard disk} as one word in the list above. Or braces might be used to simply organize related sets of data within a larger disk, such as some possible memory size values or floppy sizes.

```
{memory {4MB 8MB 12MB 16MB} video floppy {5.25" 3.5"}}
```

Spaces are required to separate list items, including lists within lists. The following list will generate an error from any list-manipulating command,

┌─────── No space
│
▼

```
{Mars Earth {water land}{plants animals fungi} Venus}
```

due to the absence of a space separating the two nested lists.

Table 6–3 contains the list of Visual Tcl commands that are specifically designed to perform general list operations.

Table 6–3 List Commands

	concat [*arg arg ...*]
★	**intersect** *lista listb*
★	**intersect3** *lista listb*
	join *list* [*joinString*]
	lappend *varName* [*value value ...*]
★	**lassign** *list var* [*var ...*]
★	**lempty** *list*
	lindex *list index*
	linsert *list index element* [*element element ...*]
	list [*arg arg ...*]
	llength *list*
★	**lmatch** [*mode*] *list pattern*
	lrange *list first last*
	lreplace *list first last* [*element ...*]
★	**lrmdups** *list*
	lsearch [*mode*] *list pattern*
	lsort [*switches*] *list*
★	**lvarcat** *listName string* [*string ...*]
★	**lvarpop** *listName* [*indexExpr*] [*string*]
★	**lvarpush** *listName string* [*indexExpr*]
	split *string* [*splitChars*]
★	**union** *lista listb*

List-building strategies

There are multiple approaches available for constructing lists in Tcl. Your list-building strategy will be influenced by a number of possible issues:

1. Is the list static?
2. Is the list going to change during execution via substitution?
3. Is the list to be constructed by merging multiple lists?
4. Is the list going to grow with new items?

Let's take a look at five methods for constructing lists.

Command/Method	Highlighted feature
`list`	Returns its arguments as a list. Guarantees correctly formed lists
`lappend`	Appends one or more items to an existing list. Can be used to create a list from scratch. Guarantees correctly formed lists.
`concat`	Concatenates multiple lists into a single list. The effect eliminates one level of list structure.
`" "`	Usually for handcrafting a list that may be altered via substitution during execution.
`{ }`	Usually for handcrafting a list that is meant to remain unaltered by substitution during execution.

Your application will commonly utilize static lists representing data that never change, such as the length of the 12 individual months in a leap year:

```
set leapYearMonths {31 29 31 30 31 30 31 31 30 31 30 31}
```

Curly braces are ideal for this type of list, since issues of substitution are irrelevant. It is the script developer's responsibility to make sure that the list is a correctly formed list.

In the case of scripts that must modify list data, there are a number of options. Suppose we choose to make one list of months and simply update the contents of the item representing February, depending on whether or not it is a leap year.

```
set yearMonths {31 $days 31 30 31 30 31 31 30 31 30 31}
```

Now we have the problem of not being able to update $days, due to the brace quoting. To allow substitution, we can instead use double quotes, **list,** or **concat.**

```
set days 29
set yearMonths \
     "31 $days 31 30 31 30 31 31 30 31 30 31"
```

or

```
set yearMonths \
        [list 31 $days 31 30 31 30 31 31 30 31 30 31]
```

or

```
set yearMonths
            [concat 31 $days 31 30 31 30 31 31 30 31 30 31]
```

Of these three approaches, it is most likely you will use double quotes or the **list** command. Using the **list** command guarantees that the created list is anatomically correct, adhering to the rules defining a well-constructed Tcl list. **list** automatically places braces around items that may otherwise be interpreted based on their special meaning to Tcl. Note how the **list** command handles the $ substitution character in the list below.

```
set characterList [list @ % $ * ! % ( )]
echo characterList: $characterList
echo Length of characterList is [llength $characterList]
```

➡ characterList @ % {$} * ! % ( )
    Length of characterList is 8

concat and double quotes, on the other hand, will propagate unintentional errors. Although **concat** produces the same results, it is primarily used for converting multiple lists into a single list, such as

```
set people [concat {Joan Jean Jackie} {David Donald Dean}]
echo $people
```

➡ Joan Jean Jackie David Donald Dean

Building commands with `list`

The problem with deferred execution of commands containing variables is that sometimes errors result from an unexpected number of arguments. Perhaps you assumed that the variable substitution would result in a single word when, instead, the result contained two or more words. For example, suppose in the following example, the fictitious Tcl procedure GetUsersName returned Cowardly Lion instead of Lion.

```
set first [GetUsersName]
set cmd "set name $first"
...
eval $cmd
```

➡ Error: wrong # args: should be "set varName ?newValue?"

The error is stating that the **set** command was expecting no more than two arguments, the name of the variable and the word to be stored in the variable. Because the user typed in Cowardly Lion, the **set** command perceived a third word, Lion, generating an error.

Using the **list** command, you can anticipate this unexpected situation.

```
set first [GetUsersName]
set cmd [list set name $first]
...
eval $cmd
```

As described earlier, the **list** command makes the effort to generate a correct list. During Tcl evaluation, when Cowardly Lion is returned by the variable substitution of $first, **list** knows that Tcl substitution returns a value only *as a single word* and, therefore, represents that single word using braces:

```
set name {Cowardly Lion}
```

As a result, the during evaluation, the **set** command perceives the {Cowardly Lion} as a single argument and assigns it to the variable name.

Essential list-building complements: **split** and **join**

split and **join** are essential, complementary commands for decomposing and composing strings. **split** is ideal for processing output gathered from the user's environment, such as a directory location or the contents of a file. Recall from Chapter 2, *A Quick Start*, that **split** was used in the procedure GetUserList to break the long string representing the output of the UNIX who command into Tcl list items wherever the newline character occurred.

```
proc GetUserList {} {
        set whoList [exec /bin/who]
        set splitWhoList [split $whoList \n]
        return $splitWhoList
}
```

The following example decomposes the elements of a long pathname.

```
set pathItems [split "/usr/include/X11/bitmaps/xlogo16" /]
echo $pathItems
```

➡ {} usr include X11 bitmaps xlogo16

Although there are four directories and one file, a list of six items is returned. The item {} is the result of the **split** command looking at the first / and seeing nothing to the left of it; therefore, returning a null list.

```
set pathName [join $pathItems /]
echo $pathName
```

➡ /usr/include/X11/bitmaps/xlogo16

Convert a list into comma-delimited string.   **TASK**

```
set netList {routers bridges hubs sniffers}
# use join to insert a comma followed by a space
echo "Network concepts include [join $netList ", "]"
```

➡ Network concepts include routers, bridges, hubs,
sniffers

Tcl simple pattern-matching

Simple pattern-matching is supported by the use of a number of Tcl commands. Matching is performed in a fashion similar to that used by the C-shell's glob-style pattern-matching. For a pattern and a string to match, their contents must be identical, except that the following special sequences may appear in the pattern:

*	Matches any sequence of characters in string, including a null string.
?	Matches any single character in string.
[chars]	Matches any character in the set given by chars. If a sequence of the form x-y appears in chars, then any character between x and y, inclusive, will match.
\x	Matches the single character x. This provides a way of avoiding the special interpretation of the characters
*?[]\	in pattern.

Some of the Visual Tcl commands that use glob-style pattern-matching include:

- **string** match
- **lmatch**
- **switch**

Lists as stacks: lvarpop, lvarpush, lvarcat

Three commands, **lvarpop**, **lvarpush**, and **lvarcat** view Tcl lists as stacks of data. Like a pile of neatly stacked bricks, the most recently stored data can be retrieved easily by popping the stack with the **lvarpop** command. In contrast to most list-accessing commands that simply return list data, stack commands alter the stack as a result of their use. Rather than having to check how many items have been processed before ending a loop, with stack operations, processing is simply terminated when the stack is empty.

Echo the entire contents of a list one by one.   TASK

```
set itemList {one two three}
while {! [lempty $itemList]} {
      echo [lvarpop itemList]
}
```
➡ one
  two
  three

The same task can be accomplished with the looping **foreach** command (to be discussed in Chapter 7, *Flow and Development*, with the exception that the list's contents remain intact. In the example above, you will want to save the stack to a temporary variable if you need it for later use.

Example tasks

Use **lsearch** *to determine if a particular process is still executing.*   TASK

```
set pidList [split [exec ps -o pid -ef] "\n "]
if {[lsearch $pidList 9812] > -1} {
      echo "Process 9812 is still executing"
}
```
lsearch returns the index location of the first match it encounters. Keep in mind that a returned value of 0 means that the first item in the list was a match. Therefore, **lsearch** returns a −1 when no match is made.

Note that this example uses **split** to create a list of process IDs returned by **exec**. Why? Because *list commands process lists*. Using list commands on strings can produce unreliable results. Since **exec** returns a string, we use the **split** command to make sure that the string is parsed into list items wherever spaces or newlines occur. We specify spaces, since our match will fail if the process ID is prefixed with one or more spaces. Be sure to take a look at the contents of pidList to see how **split** has parsed the ps output string.

Sort the items in a list according to descending order.   TASK

```
set itemList {a e c d m j f}
echo [lsort -decreasing $itemList]
```
➡ m j f e d c a

lsort supports a number of options that affect how a list is sorted: -integer, -real, -floating, -increasing (the default behavior), and -command. -command can be used to provide your own sorting algorithm via a procedure.

Remove redundant items from a list.   TASK

```
set itemList {a b c c d l l e f g e}
echo [lrmdups $itemList]
```

➡ a b c d e f g l

TASK   *Replace all occurrences of John with "Mr. John Doe."*

```
set nameList {John Pete Dave}
set index [lsearch $nameList John]
set newNameList \
        [lreplace $nameList $index $index "Mr. John Doe"]
echo $newNameList
```

➡ {Mr. John Doe} Pete Dave

Note from Table 6–3 that **lreplace** requires *first* and *last* arguments. These arguments refer to a range of list items that are to be replaced. If there is a single item to be replaced, state the item's index twice, once representing *first*, the second representing *last*. This explains why $index is used twice in the example above.

When to pass a list or a variable name containing a list

Most Tcl commands that modify a list accept the list as an argument and return the modified list as a string value. For example, **linsert** inserts an item in a list and returns a new list as a command return value:

```
set list {a b c d}
set newList [linsert $list 4 e]
```

newList now contains {a b c d e}. The original list remains unmodified. Most Tcl commands operate in this manner. However, there are a few commands that manipulate data structures as pass-by-reference arguments. **lappend**, the Tcl command that appends items to a list, is an example of the latter case. Comparing it with **lindex**:

```
set listName {a b c d}
lappend varName e
echo $varName
```

➡ {a b c d e}

Other examples that accept lists as pass-by-reference arguments include: **append**, **array ctoken**, **global**, **lvarpush**, **lvarpop**, **incr** and the keyed list commands discussed below.

Keyed lists

Keyed lists are the Visual Tcl answer to structures in the C language. Contributed by the TclX library, keyed lists provide another choice for storing, organizing, and manipulating data. They are also key, so to speak, to the Visual Tcl callback mechanism, explained later in the book.

Table 6–4   Keyed List Commands

★	**keyldel** *listVar key*
★	**keylget** *listVar* [*key*] [*retVar* | {}]
★	**keylkeys** *listVar* [*key*]
★	**keylset** *listVar key value* [*key2 value2* ...]

A keyed list is a list of one or more lists that contain *keys* associated with a value. A keyed list can be used to contain database-like information. The example below suggests a keyed list that identifies location information about a company's employees.

```
{{name {John Doe}} {building {147 River St.} {office {A-123}}
```

A C structure that supported a similar view might look something like the following:

```
struct {
        char    *name;
        char    *building;
        char    *office;
} employeeLocale;
```

To build this keyed list, Visual Tcl provides the **keylset** command in the form:

```
keylset listVar key value [key2 value2 ...]

keylset employeeLocale name {John Doe}
keylset employeeLocale building {147 River St.}
keylset employeeLocale office A-123
```

If the key already exists in the variable employeeLocale, the current value associated with the key is replaced with the new value. If the key does not exist, it is appended to the keyed list, along with its associated value. **keylset** can also be used to determine whether a key exists in a list by replacing the value arguments with {}. A value of 0 is returned if the specified key cannot be located in the list.

Retrieve the keys in employeeLocale.

TASK

```
set listOfKeys [keylkeys employeeLocale]
echo "employeeLocale keys are: $listOfKeys"
```

➡ `employeeLocale keys are: name building office`

TASK   *Show the user's room number.*

```
set room [keylget employeeLocale office]
set name [keylget employeeLocale name]
echo "$name is located in office $room"
```

➡ `John Doe is located in office A-123`

Keyed lists for static structures, arrays for dynamic structures

It's a common situation to be faced with the decision of working either with an array or a keyed list. Keys in keyed lists can be treated in a way similar to the indexes of an array. One criterion to consider is the performance consequence. In general, for small amounts of data, keyed lists are most efficient. For large data situations, arrays are best.

A question to consider is "What is the nature of your data?" When you think about using a keyed list, think of it in terms of how you might make use of a C structure. A C structure is a static entity, where fields are not added and deleted over its lifetime. An array and its indexes, on the other hand, are designed to grow over time. If you are going to grow a data structure of labeled data, an array is probably the way to go.

An excellent strategy for aggregating data is to use an array to store keyed lists. For example, in our working `employeeLocale` example, an array could be used to represent an employee per array element.

```
set name "John Doe"
keylset employeeArray($name) building {147 River St.}
keylset employeeArray($name) office A-123
```

Nested keys

Keyed lists can also be nested in order to track data in enhanced detail. For example, instead of representing our employee in the previous format, {name {John Doe}}, we can organize each employee's name in the following manner:

```
keylset employeeLocale name.last Doe
keylset employeeLocale name.first John
```

Since the **keylset** command accepts one or more key-value pairs, the same two statements could be expressed as a single **keylset** command.

```
keylset employeeLocale name.last Doe name.first John
echo $employeeLocale
```

➡ {employee {{last Doe} {first John}}}

Strings

As one might expect from a string-based language, Visual Tcl supports a comprehensive set of string manipulation commands. Visual Tcl enhances an already extensive list of Tcl string commands with the addition of TclX library commands.

Table 6–5 String Commands

	append *varName* [*value value ...*]
★	**cequal** *string1 string2*
★	**cexpand** *string*
★	**cindex** *string indexExpr*
★	**clength** *string*
★	**crange** *string firstExpr lastExpr*
★	**csubstr** *string firstExpr lengthExpr*
★	**ctoken** *strName separators*
★	**ctype** [*-failindex var*] *class string*
	format *formatString* [*arg arg ...*]
	regexp [*switches*] *expr string* [*matchVar*] [*subMatchVar ...*]
	regsub [*switches*] *expr string subSpec varName*
★	**replicate** *string countExpr*
	scan *string formatString varName* [*varName ...*]
	string *option arg* [*arg ...*]
★	**translit** *inrange outrange string*

As you begin to explore the vast number of string commands and their options, you are likely to draw the conclusion that there appears to be a lot of overlap in the functionality offered by Tcl and TclX string commands. There are a number of factors you will want to consider when deciding which commands to select from, such as:

speed		For long string construction, **append** is superior to simple string concatenation.
script simplicity		**cequal** performs single string comparison. **regexp** is overkill for simple string compares.
power		**regexp**, on the other hand, is ideal for parsing complex strings.
portability		The Tk environment is not guaranteed to be extended with TclX. If your goal is to write code that can support both Visual Tcl and Tk scripts, you will want to avoid TclX string commands like **cequal**.
non-Tcl string handling		**regexp** and **regsub** support their own special characters, requiring you to "shift gears" when coding your Tcl script. Perhaps you may choose to minimize the use of string parsing that goes outside the Tcl view of strings.

string versus "c" commands

There is a great deal of functional overlap that occurs between the "c" commands of TclX and the Tcl **string** command. **string** is another example of a noun-verb command that supports a large number of string-handling options. The "c" commands, such as **cequal** and **cindex**, typically represent options within the **string** command that have been provided as individual commands and may or may not have simple additional features. Table 6–6 below presents a generalized comparison of possible overlap between the two categories of string commands.

Table 6–6   Tcl string options and TclX c command comparisons

TclX	*Tcl*	*Comments*
cequal	**string** compare	Both commands compare two strings. **string** compare is a superset of **cequal**. **cequal** reports 0 or 1, depending on equality. **string** compare reports -1, 0, or 1, depending on lexicographic relationships.
cindex	**string** index	Both return the index location of a character in a string. They are identical except that **cindex** supports len and end keywords, eliminating the need to calculate the length of the target strings and the index of its last character.

Table 6–6 Tcl `string` options and TclX c command comparisons (cont.)

TclX	Tcl	Comments
crange	**string** range	Both return a range of characters from a target string. **string** range supports the end keyword, while **crange** supports len and end keywords.
	string match	Supports simple pattern-matching.
	string first	Returns the position of the first match that occurs in a string.
	string last	Returns the position of the last match that occurs in a string.
clength	**string** length	Both return the length of a string.
	string tolower	Converts a string to lowercase.
	string toupper	Converts a string to uppercase.
	string trim	Removes indicated characters from the beginning and end of a string.
	string trimleft	Trims the left side of string only.
	string trimright	Trims the right side of string only.
cexpand		Expands backslash characters in a string to actual characters.
ctype		Tests whether characters in a string are of a given class, such as alphanumeric (see the extended discussion below). Performs a few numeric/ASCII conversions as well.
ctoken		Parses a token out of a character string.
csubstr		Returns a range of characters. Similar to **crange**, except that you can indicate how many characters after the first index to return.

The following tasks illustrate some of the features supported by Visual Tcl string handling.

Find Waldo in the string below.

```
echo [string trim "xxxxxwhere's waldo?xxxxxx" x]
```
➡ where's waldo?

TASK

Braces prevent backslash substitution that exists in our sentence below. Use the **cexpand** *command to remove the backslashes inside a curly-brace-quoted string.*

```
set line {This uses braces to \{highlight\} something.}
echo $line
```

➡ This uses braces to \{highlight\} something.

```
echo [cexpand $line]
```

➡ This uses braces to {highlight} something.

Note that the use of **cexpand** would not have been required, had we used double quotes instead of curly braces in the original string.

TASK

Compare the use of **cindex** *and* **string** *compare to find the last letter in a string.*

```
set aString "Scorpion"
echo "Last letter in $aString is \"[cindex $aString
end]\""
```

➡ Last letter in Scorpion is "n"

```
echo "Last letter in $aString is \"[string index
$aString \  [expr {[string length $aString] - 1}]]\""
```

➡ Last letter in Scorpion is "n"

Support for the end keyword clearly reduces the number of required calculations. The Tcl **expr** command is used to evaluate an arithmetic expression. Note that 1 must be subtracted before indexing the string to account for the fact that strings are indexed beginning with 0. Note that **clength** could have been used instead of **string** length.

TASK

Remove a line-labeling token from a string.

```
set aString "NAME: John Doe"
ctoken aString " "
echo $aString
# remove any leading spaces
set aString [string trimleft $aString]
echo $aString
```

➡   John Doe
   John Doe

ctoken is instructed to extract the first token that is terminated by a space character. The result is that NAME: is removed and aString is updated with the remaining portion of the string. The **string** command is used to trim any leading spaces that remain. When no trim characters are specified, **string** trimleft assumes that spaces are to be trimmed.

Write a procedure that checks a string to determine whether it is a commented line. The string may have been generated by the reading of a text file where comments are indicated with #.   **TASK**

```
proc CheckForComment {line} {
        # remove leading spaces and tabs
        set line [string trimleft $line " \t"]
        if {[cindex $line 0] == "#"} {
            # it's a comment!
            return 1
        } else {
            return 0
        }
}
```

Avoid == for string compares

Tcl supports the ability to compare two strings using the == operator in test expressions. Operators <, >, <=, >=, and != are also supported. (Operators are detailed in Chapter 7, *Flow and Development*.) However, in order to avoid errors or unexpected results, you should use **string** compare or **cequal** in expressions. If you fail to include a string operand as a variable or to quote it in double quotes an error will occur.

```
if {$name == Julie} {...            Not OK (generates a Tcl error)
if {$name == "Julie"} {...          OK
if {[cequal $name "Julie"]} {...    Better
```

Tcl uses string comparisons if the operands cannot be parsed as numbers.

Parsing strings with scan, format

format is ideal for organizing strings for output, as well as for converting values from one format to another. If you have a list of items to print out and you want them to appear in aligned columns, the use of conversion specifiers, (indicated with the % symbol), provides support controls for type specification, justification, and field width. **format** follows the same conventions as does ANSI C sprintf (see the **format** command in *Command Pages* for a list of supported conversion specifiers). **format** returns a string containing the conversions.

Format a set of values along with representative bar chart information.   **TASK**

```
foreach value {8 12 0 1 8 5} {
      echo [format "%2d %-s" $value [replicate X
$value]]
}
```

➡   8 XXXXXXXX
    12 XXXXXXXXXXXX
     0
     1 X
     8 XXXXXXXX
     5 XXXXX

The hyphen after the % conversion specifier indicates that the string should be left-justified. **replicate** is the TclX command that multiplies a string by a given value.

scan is also based on another ANSI C function, sscanf. **scan** is excellent for processing strings of information that follow a regular format. **scan** scans a string, looking for matches based on format specifiers, then updates variables, each with the value of the respective match. The following example extracts two values from the inputString, according to the format specifiers.

```
set info "Joe Jane 40 50"
set matchCount [scan $info "%s %*s %*d %d" name number]
echo $matchCount matches were made
echo Name:$name\tNumber:$number
```

➡ 2 matches were made
   Name:Joe   Number:50

The boundaries of the items that scan processes are delimited by whitespaces. Only two values are extracted in the example, since two of the specifiers contain *, indicating that **scan** should ignore their matching patterns.

regexp and regsub

If you have a lot of experience with using regular expression pattern-matching in UNIX shell scripting or with the UNIX **egrep** command, then you will be right at home with Tcl's support of the **regexp** and **regsub** commands. Their syntax as Tcl commands is shown below. Tcl's regular expressions are implemented using the public-domain Henry Spencer package.

regexp [switches] expr string [matchVar] [subMatchVar ...]

regsub [switches] expr string subSpec varName

The **regexp** command evaluates string, returning pattern-matched values in one or more variables (matchVar, subMatchVar), which can later be examined with Tcl $ substitution. For every pattern-matching expression, there is an associated variable that will be assigned to a variable. **regsub** uses the same pattern-matching rules as does **regexp**, however, it takes the further step of replacing matches with new values. A numeric switch is used to indicate how many string substitutions should be performed in the event of multiple pattern matches. Be sure to consult the *Command Pages* section for details.

regexp and **regsub** present windows into UNIX-style pattern-matching, where the meaning of Tcl special characters has no significance. To ensure their safe passage through the Tcl evaluation phase, pattern-matching expressions must be quoted with substitution-preventing braces.

lp is the System V UNIX command for printing files. In the process of setting up a print job, lp returns a request ID embedded in a sentence. The request ID takes the form of *printer name-number*, shown in the lp below.

```
request id is hp850c-12 (1 file)
```

The following example executes a print job using lp. The script uses **regexp** to extract the name of the printer from a request ID that is returned by lp. Since the actual request ID is the third item in the list string returned by lp, **lindex** is used to extract it.

```
set value [exec lp /etc/motd]
set reqId [lindex $value 3]
set match \
    [regexp {^([a-zA-Z0-9]*)-[0-9]*} $reqId {}
printerName]
if {$match == 1} {
    echo "Your print job has been submitted to:\
    $printerName"
}
```

➡ Your print job has been submitted to: hp850c

Of course, to make this script user-safe, you'll want to execute the lp command inside a **catch** script in the event that lp runs into an unanticipated problem.

Find other ways to parse the print job request ID string. Assume that the lp command has returned hplaser-99 *as the print job request ID.* **TASK**

```
echo printJob:$printJob
```

➡ printJob:hplaser-99

```
set tmpList [translit "-" " " $printJob]; # remove "-"
# use the scan command to extract the print string \
    and print job number
scan $tmpList "%s %d" name number
echo printer is $name, print job number is $number
```

➡ printer is hplaser, print job number is 99

```
set tmpList [split $printJob "-" ]
echo printer is [lindex $tmpList 0],\
        print job is [lindex $tmpList 1]
```

➡ `printer is hplaser, print job number is 99`

TASK *Convert all ! occurring in the first column of a file and replace with #.*

Here's the contents of our file, `/tmp/file`.

```
! this is a comment
        ! this is not a comment
this is ! not a comment
```

```
for_file line /tmp/file {
       if {[regsub {^!} $line {#} output] == 1} {
          echo $output
       }
}
```

➡ `# this is a comment`

Checking for character types in a string: `ctype`

The **ctype** command determines whether all characters in a string are of a specified class, returning 1 for true or 0 for false. Supported classes include alphanumeric (alpha), lower case (lower), hexadecimal digits (xdigit), and control characters (cntrl). Table 6–7 shows the complete list of classes.

```
set greeting "welcome"
if {[ctype lower $greeting] == 1} {
       echo "There are no uppercase letters in
\"$greeting\""
}
```

➡ `There are no uppercase letters in "welcome"`

Table 6–7 Supported **ctype** classes

```
alnum
alpha
ascii
char
cntrl
digit
graph
lower
ord
space
print
punct
upper
xdigit
```

In addition to performing checking, **ctype** also provides two conversion tasks:

1. Convert a character to its decimal numeric value
2. Convert a numeric value (0–255) to an ASCII character.

```
echo 86 is a \"[ctype char 86]\" in ASCII
echo "The ASCII letter V is the numeric value [ctype ord V]"
```

➡ 86 is a "V" in ASCII
    The ASCII letter V is the numeric value 86

Built-in variables

There are a number of standard Tcl variables built into the Tcl interpreter. Some, like env and args, provide environmental information. auto_path can be used to instruct the interpreter where to look for Tcl package libraries. Other variables, such as errorCode and errorInfo, supply your application with the error information that you can use to determine how and when to notify the user of your application. When assigned an integer, the variable tcl_precision establishes the number of significant digits to include when converting floating-point values to strings.

Table 6–8   Standard Built-in Visual Tcl Variables

```
argc
argv
argv0
auto_path
env
errorCode
errorInfo
tcl_precision
```

Accessing UNIX environment variables: env

UNIX environment variables such as LOGNAME, MAIL, SHELL, and HOME can be accessed easily from your script using the built-in env array. The Tcl interpreter builds the env array, using the name of each variable as an index name.

```
vtcl
vtcl> set env(HOME)
/u/fred
vtcl> set env(PATH)
/bin:/usr/bin:/usr/bin/X11:/u/fred/bin
```

When attempting to access environment variables from your script, be sure to check for their existence. Otherwise, a Tcl error will abort your script.

```
if {[info exists env(HOME)]} {
    set homeDirectory $env(HOME)
}
```

This example uses the **info** command to verify that the array element indexed by HOME actually exists before the subsequent code attempts to access its contents.

Accessing **argv** and **env** in procedures

As global variables, you must use the **global** command in order to make argc, argv0, argv, and env known to procedure scripts.

```
proc GetEnvInformation {} {
    global env
    if {[info exists env(DISPLAY)]} {
        return $env(DISPLAY)
    }
}
```

TCL_LIBRARY **for relocating the Visual Tcl startup library**

TCL_LIBRARY is a shell environment variable that can be used to redirect where the vtcl interpreter searches for essential startup libraries. The only time you might need to define the TCL_LIBRARY in your shell environment is in the event you need to locate the Tcl directory in another location.

Accessing the command line: **argc**, **argv0**, and **argv**

In keeping with its C namesake, argv is a Tcl list that will contain 0 or more list items representing the arguments passed to the application on the command line. argc is a simple variable that is assigned an integer, indicating the number of arguments present in argv. argv0 contains the name of the application. A fictitious Visual Tcl application named viewusers might be invoked as follows:

```
viewusers -machine machineName -sort
```

-machine *machineName* indicates that viewusers should list the users on *machineName*. -sort indicates that the list of user names should be displayed in alphabetical order. argc will contain the value 3, corresponding to the three arguments passed to viewusers, and argv0 will contain viewusers. The following code performs the task of processing command line options, taking advantage of two list processing commands discussed earlier.

```
while {! [lempty $argv]} {
    set arg [lvarpop argv]
```

```
    if {$arg == "-machine"} {
        set machineFlag 1
        set machineName [lvarpop argv]
    } elseif {$arg == "-sort" } {
        set sortFlag 1
    } else {
        puts stderr "$argv0:Invalid option: $arg"
        break ;# terminates the while loop
    }
}
```

Our example loops through the contents of argv until **lempty** determines that argv is empty. Treating argv as a stack, **lvarpop** pops the topmost value, reducing the list by one item with each pop. The **while** loop will continue until there are no more argv items to process. The **if** command is used to find an exact match between the argv arguments and the viewusers application's supported command line options.

Final Note

You can avoid a lot of potential errors by following the simple practice of using list commands to process lists and string commands to process strings. Since Tcl data structures are not self-defining, it is the command that projects structure and meaning onto the data structure. When you intermingle lists commands with strings, for instance, you may get unexpected results because the list command will project list structure onto the string.

Flow and Development

- ✔ Expressions
- ✔ Flow control commands
- ✔ Debugging and command tracing
- ✔ Reuse of package libraries
- ✔ Internationalization
- ✔ Performance issues and tips

*T*his chapter addresses a wide range of Visual Tcl features, ranging from base Tcl flow control commands to the TclX extensions for debugging, organizing, and internationalizing your code for localization in different languages. The first topic, Tcl expressions, applies to computational math as well as to test expressions that control the flow of your Tcl scripts.

Tcl expressions

The Tcl interpreter uses the **expr** command to evaluate expressions. New values are created by expressions that combine values and operators. The operators supported by Tcl, listed in order of precedence in Table 7–1, should be familiar to anyone with ANSI C experience.

The use of **expr** is not always obvious. For example, as we will see during our discussion of flow control, commands such as **if** and **while** require expression arguments for applying tests to conditions. In the code fragment below, the Tcl interpreter uses **expr** inside the **while** command to evaluate the test expression, $i < 10.

```
while {$i <10} {
    ...
}
```

Table 7–1   Bitwise and Logical Operators

Operator(s)	Description
– ~ !	Unary minus, bitwise NOT, logical NOT. Bitwise NOT may be applied only to integers.
* / %	Multiply, divide, remainder. The remainder will always have the same sign as the divisor and an absolute value smaller than the divisor.
+ –	Add and subtract.
<< >>	Left and right shift.
< > <= >=	Boolean less than, greater than, less than or equal to, greater than or equal to. Each operator produces 1 if the condition is true, 0 otherwise. These operators may be applied to strings as
== !=	Boolean equal, not equal. Valid for all operand types.
&	Bitwise AND.
^	Bitwise exclusive OR.
|	Bitwise OR.
&&	Logical AND. Produces 1 if both operands are nonzero, 0 otherwise.
||	Logical OR. Produces 1 if both operands are nonzero, 0 otherwise.
x?y:z	If-then-else (as in the C Language). If x evaluates to nonzero, then result is y, else z.

Arithmetic and Math operations

Tcl supports the full range of simple arithmetic operators, as well as a library of math functions. Precedence within expressions can be controlled with parentheses.

```
echo [expr {(15 + 5) * (8 / 4)}]
```
➡ 40

Tcl interprets strings that started with 0x to represent hexadecimal numbers. Octal numbers begin with 0, such as 0411. Numbers can also take on valid ANSI C formats, such as 10.03 and 3.1e+2. In the following list, all the numbers are equivalent.

```
88
8.800000e+01
0x58
0130
```

Table 7–2 Math Commands

expr *arg [arg ...]*
incr *varName [increment]*
★ **max** *num1 num2 [...numN]*
★ **min** *num1 num2 [...numN]*
★ **random** *limit* | seed *[seedval]*

The math functions, shown in Table 7–2 are built into the **expr** command as standard functional notation. Each of these functions is supported as an individual convenience procedure as part of the TclX library, listed in Table 7–3 below. The two Tcl scripts below produce the same result.

```
set result [expr floor(10.8)]    ;# the base Tcl way
set result [floor 10.8]          ;# the TclX way
```
➡ 10.0

In addition to the standard Tcl math functions, the TclX library adds **max**, **min**, and **random**.

Table 7–3 Math Convenience Procedures

★ abs	★ cos	★ hypot	★ sin
★ acos	★ cosh	★ int	★ sinh
★ asin	★ double	★ log	★ sqrt
★ atan2	★ exp	★ log10	★ tan
★ atan	★ floor	★ pow	★ tanh
★ ceil	★ fmod	★ round	

Although we refer to many of these procedures as *convenience procedures*, many of them are provided for historical reasons. Originally, base Tcl supported commands like **sin** and **cos**. Later, these were removed as commands and replaced as supported operations of the **expr** command. The TclX commands provide backward compatibility to the original math commands that are no longer supported in base Tcl.

TASK   *Use* **fmod** *to determine if this is a leap year.*

```
set year 1996
if {(([fmod $year 4] == 0.0) &&
    ([fmod $year 100] > 0 ||
     [fmod $year 400] > 0 ||
     $year > 1800 ) } {
        echo "$year is a leap year!"
}
```
➡ 1996 is a leap year!

Incrementing integers with `incr`

A common need in a script, such as a **while** loop, is to increment an integer by one. This could be done by the script

```
set count [expr {$count + 1}]
```

which adds 1 to the value stored in count, then updates count with the result. A more convenient approach uses the **incr** command.

```
incr count
```

Because **incr** accepts a pass-by-reference argument, the argument is updated in place (although **incr** also returns the value). An optional second argument overrides the default behavior of adding 1 to the value. The following adds 100 to the integer stored in count.

```
incr count 100
```

Supplying a negative number as the second argument instructs **incr** to decrement an integer by the amount specified.

```
incr count -100
```

String comparisons with `expr`

Normally used for numeric expressions, the **expr** command supports string-comparing operations with the operators <, >, <=, >=, ==, and !=. If **expr** determines that the operands are strings, it applies string-comparing logic. The trick is convincing **expr** that your operands are indeed strings. The example below will generate a Tcl syntax error because the literal string, Unix, is not enclosed in quotes.

```
if {$system == Unix} {...
```

In general, you should use string commands, such as **cequal** or **string** compare, in expressions. As you can see, there is no need to place quotes around a single word using a string-comparing command.

```
if {[cequal $system Unix]} {...
```

Recalling our final note in Chapter 6, *Data Structures*, you can avoid bugs by using commands that are intended for the data type you are working with. Although it's a nice convenience to use expressions for string comparison, the potential for creating bugs is much higher. Using native string commands eliminates the uncertainty of using a command like **expr** that must guess what behavior to use, based on the form of its operands.

Flow control

Visual Tcl supports the familiar set of control commands found in popular programming languages such as C and Pascal. Just like with C programming, a test expression that evaluates to nonzero is interpreted as a true condition. A zero result is interpreted as false.

Table 7–4   Flow Of Control Commands

break
error *message* [*info*] [*code*]
★   **commandloop** [*prompt1*] [*prompt2*]
continue
for *start expr next body*
foreach *varName list body*
if *expr1* [then] *body1* elseif *expr2* [then] *body2* elseif ...   [else] [*bodyN*]
★   **loop** *var first limit* [*increment*] *body*
switch [*options*] *string pattern body* [*pattern body* ...]
return [-code *code*] [-errorinfo *info*] [-errorcode *code*] [*string*]
source *fileName*
while *test body*

if

The **if** command executes a script if its associated test expression, shown as *expr* below, satisfies a test. In an **if** command containing multiple tests and scripts, no more than one can be chosen for execution. **if** supports a combination of formats.

```
if {expr} {              if {expr} {              if {expr} {
      . . .                    . . .                    . . .
}                        } else {                 } elseif {expr2}
{
                              . . .                    . . .
                        }                        } else {
                                                       . . .
                                                 }
```

TASK   *Assign the appropriate administrative permissions depending on the current user's role-based authorization.*

```
if {[cequal $userType "Administrator"]} {
      SetAdminPermissions
} elseif {[cequal $userType "BackupAdmin"]} {
      SetBackupAdminPermissions
} else {
      SetDefaultPermissions
}
```

switch

The **switch** command provides functionality similar to the **if** command with a "goto"-like approach. It provides a convenient format for handling multiple test conditions. For example, you can use the **switch** command to process the command line options supported by your application or to set options based on the buttons the user pushes on the user interface. We will show how **switch** can be used to set state, based on graphical user input, in our Rolodex example later in the book.

```
while {! [lempty $argv]} {
      set arg [lvarpop argv]
      switch -exact -- $arg
        -machine {
            set machineFlag 1
            set machineName [lvarpop argv]
        -sort {
            set sortFlag 1
        default {
            puts stderr "$argv0:Invalid option: $arg"
            break              ;# terminates the while loop
        }
      }
}
```

This script is a rewrite of the example in the previous chapter that used **if** to illustrate how to process the built-in `argv` variable. **switch** also supports simple pattern-matching when invoked with the `-glob` option, illustrated in the following example.

```
foreach arg $argv {
      switch -glob -- $arg {
          -? {
              echo $arg is a recognized option
              }
          default {echo $arg is not a recognized option }
      }
}
```

In this example, the pattern -? is used to identify traditional UNIX dashed single-character command line arguments such as -v and -f.

Be sure to terminate switch options with --

It is a common error to forget to turn off the processing of switch's supported options with --. Suppose that, in the previous example, we had neglected to included the double-dash string following -glob.

```
switch -glob $arg {
. . .
```

If we had specified a command line option such as -v to the file containing this script, we would have seen the Tcl error message:

➡ Error: bad option "-v": should be -exact, -glob, -regexp, or --

---

while

A tested loop is best suited for situations when it is unknown how many times a script will be executed. The **while** command executes a script until a condition fails its test. Building on the previous use of the argv variable, we can use **while** to process any number of command line arguments.

```
while {! [lempty $argv]} {
      set flag [lvarpop argv]
      ProcessCommandOption $flag
}
```

lvarpop actually removes the first item in a list each time it is executed. Eventually, the list will be zero in length. When needed, the **continue** command can be used to cause the **while** command to skip the rest of its script and immediately exercise its test expression argument. This effect is supported in all Visual Tcl looping control commands.

for

A counted loop is useful for methodically marching through data, one operation at a time. The number of maximum iterations is typically known in advance. The **for** command provides a **for** loop similar in format to the C language `for` loop. Its syntax supports four arguments:

for start test next body

The following example loops through a list of names, looking for a match. Of course, the same functionality is supported by the **lmatch** command.

```
set nameList {Apple IBM Microsoft HP SCO Sun Digital}
...
set maxIndex [llength $nameList]
for {set i 0} {$i < $maxIndex} {incr i} {
        if {[cequal [lindex $nameList $i] SCO]} {
            echo "SCO found"
            break
        }
}
```

Initialized to 0, i is incremented by the third argument containing the **incr** command, that we've chosen for this example. The **break** command is a Tcl exception that aborts looping commands such as **for**. The code fragment below illustrates a **for** command that decrements its counter with each loop. The loop terminates as soon as the test expression, $i > 0$, fails.

```
for {set i 100} {$i > 0} {incr i -1} {
        ...
}
```

foreach

The **foreach** command is a **for** loop designed for handling Tcl lists with performance advantages over using a conventional **for** or **while** loop. It is ideal for stepping through the items in a list one by one.

```
set count 0
set planetList {neptune mercury jupiter saturn}

foreach item $planetList {
        incr count
        echo "Planet \#${count} is $item"
}
```
➡ Planet #1 is neptune
   Planet #2 is mercury
   Planet #3 is jupiter
   Planet #4 is saturn

In the example below, the **array** command returns a list of array indexes that is then used to access individual array elements, one at a time.

```
set machine(Romulan) {Jay John Jil}
set machine(Scorpion) {Andy Louie Susan)

foreach machine [array index machines] {
      echo "Users on $machine are $machines($machine)"
}
```

➡ Users on Romulan are Jay John Jil
   Users on Scorpion are Andy Louie Susan

`loop` for speed

The TclX **loop** command was designed to execute a counting loop at high speed. Use the **loop** command if you know the end point of a loop, and increment it at a regular interval. The format of the **loop** command is

```
loop var start end [increment] body

loop i 1 128 1 {
      append asciiString [ctype char $i]
}
```

This example builds a string of the first 128 ASCII characters. **loop** can be used to count down by using a negative *increment* value. When not explicitly stated, the increment value defaults to 1.

Tcl exceptions: `break` and `continue`

Like Tcl errors, **break** and **continue** are also Tcl exceptions. Both commands terminate script execution within the looping commands of **for**, **foreach**, **loop**, and **while**. **break** and **continue** differ in the impact of their effect on a looping command. **break** terminates the looping command altogether; **continue** simply aborts or skips over the remainder of the executing body within the loop, sending execution back to the top of the loop.

```
foreach item {a b C d e F G h i J K l m} {
      if {[ctype lower $item]} {
          continue
      }
      lappend listOfUpperCaseLetters $item
}
echo $listOfUpperCaseLetters
}
```

➡ C F G J K

Including other scripts with `source`

When you spread your code across several files, the **source** command can be used to bring all of your source code together at run time. An alternative to **source**, called *package libraries*, is discussed later in the chapter.

TASK *Include scripts from another file in your current script without explicitly copying the source directly into your file.*

```
source /u/tcl/test/tools.tcl
```

Debugging and development

Visual Tcl provides the ability to trace completely the execution of your code as well as to monitor and track down performance issues.

Table 7–5   Debugging and Command Tracing Commands

★   **cmdtrace** *level* | on [noeval] [notruncate] [procs] [*fileid*] | off | *depth*
★   **profile** [-commands] on ; **profile** off *arrayVar*
★   **profrep** *profDataVar sortKey stackDepth* [*outFile*] [*userTitle*]
time *script count*
★   **times**

Tracing execution flow with `cmdtrace`

Littering your script with debugging **echo** or **puts** commands is made unnecessary by the **cmdtrace** command. **cmdtrace** prints a trace statement of all commands executed in the portion of the script that you are interested in. This gives you the ability to follow the flow of your code as it is executed and to view how the interpreter is performing parsing and substitution. This makes **cmdtrace** a great learning tool, as well as a debugging mechanism.

The following code illustrates how you can turn tracing on and off using a randomly chosen UNIX environment variable.

```
if {info exits env(TCLDEBUG)} {
        cmdtrace on [open cmd.log w]
}
```

In this example, if the environment variable TCLDEBUG exists at all, command tracing is turned on. This example illustrates the use of an optional second argument that accepts a file descriptor, returned by the call to **open**. The result is that all command tracing information is written to the file cmd.log. You can turn command tracing on and off anywhere within your script. The example below shows how you might bracket **cmdtrace** around a script that is giving you grief.

```
cmdtrace on
        ... little bit of troublesome code
cmdtrace off
```

Profiling your script with `profile`

You can gather statistical information about all of your procedures using the **profile** command. Specifying the -commands option, you can retrieve three categories of performance information about commands implemented as C functions in the interpreter. The information returned by **profile** includes

count   the number of times a procedure is executed

real   real-time information about how long a procedure executes

cpu   CPU utilization per procedure

The off option terminates profiling and stores the collected data into an array specified by the programmer. The complementary **profrep** command can then be used to print out a conveniently formatted statistical report.

```
proc ProcB {} {sleep 1}
proc ProcA {} {sleep 1; ProcB}
profile -commands on
ProcA
profile off stats
profrep stats calls
```

In this code fragment, profiling is turned on in order to profile the invocation of ProcA and the procedures and commands that occur during its execution. As profiling is turned off, the profile results are stored in the user-named array stats. **profrep** processes stats according to the order of calls and generates the following report. Units are in milliseconds.

Procedure Call Stack	Calls	Real Time	CPU Time
ProcA	1	2163	10
<global>	1	2163	10
sleep	1	1092	10
ProcA			
sleep	1	1071	0
ProcB			
ProcA			
ProcB	1	1071	0
ProcA			

Package libraries for code reuse

Once you start writing a few Visual Tcl scripts, you'll find that you tend to copy useful code from other files and include them in a new script. One of the first "reusable" procedures that you may commonly require is something like ExitCB, the callback procedure from the Goodbye button demo in Chapter 3, *Run-Time Environment*.

```
proc ExitCB {cbs} {
    VtClose
    exit 0
}
```

ExitCB invokes **VtClose** to disconnect the interpreter from the display server. **exit** then instructs the interpreter to terminate. As you might guess, this code will be useful for many of your Visual Tcl applications. So, rather than constantly rewrite it or cut and paste from older scripts, Visual Tcl makes it possible to create *package libraries* of dynamically loadable Tcl procedures. Package library files are referred to as *tlibs* (pronounced "tee-libs").

Table 7–6   Package Library Commands

★   **auto_commands** [-loaders]

★   **auto_load** [*command*]

★   **auto_load_file** *file*

★   **auto_packages** [-files]

★   **buildpackageindex** *libfilelist*

★   **convert_lib** *tclIndex packagelib* [ignore]

★   **loadlibindex** *libfile.tlib*

★   **searchpath** *path file*

    unknown *cmdName* [*arg arg* ...]

A package library is a file containing one or more packages of logically grouped Tcl procedures. For example, the Visual Tcl Vx commands are implemented as a package library in a file called vtcl.tlib. Look at the contents of the Tcl built-in variable auto_path to find vtcl.lib in the version of Visual Tcl that you are working with. Rather than loading all Tcl procedures stored in all package libraries, Visual Tcl loads only those packages of Tcl procedures that your script invokes. To thoroughly understand how you might take advantage of package libraries, let's take a look at how the interpreter processes commands that it cannot locate.

Where standard Tcl procedures reside

There are a number of built-in variables that describe the Visual Tcl environment. `auto_path` contains the list of directory locations that are searched by the Visual Tcl interpreter when it encounters a command that is neither a C function nor a procedure defined inside the application script. The procedures in these directories are contained and organized in files called *package libraries*. The location of Visual Tcl package libraries varies from platform to platform. For the SCO OpenServer environment, they are:

```
/opt/K/SCO/TclX/7.3.2a     location of Tcl, TclX procedures
/lib/vtcl                  location of Vx procedures
```

The search for a command

When the `vtcl` interpreter encounters a command for which it cannot locate a supporting command procedure or local Tcl procedure, it hands the command over to the **unknown** command. Originally a member of the TclX library, this base Tcl command simply extends the search taken to find a procedure definition for an unresolved command name. The **unknown** command searches:

1. known package library directories;
2. the UNIX environment for matching commands;
3. the Tcl history mechanism for a matching command, and, as a last resort,
4. attempts to expand the command to match an existing command.

Steps 2, 3, and 4 apply to the interactive vtcl shell session only. In other words, these steps are not followed if your script is executed as a file. The **unknown** service can be turned off by setting the built-in variable `auto_noload` to 1.

Package library conventions

The **unknown** command takes the first step of invoking the **auto_load** command to search all known directory locations (listed in the built-in `auto_path` variable) of package library files. A package file name is of the form

```
foo.tlib
```

where `foo` represents the name that you provide. A complementary named index file contains the `seek` addresses of each package of Tcl procedures contained within the package file. Its naming convention is

```
foo.tndx
```

The index file can be created explicitly with the **buildindexfile** command. This is usually unnecessary, because **auto_load** automatically reconstructs the index file if there have been any changes to the package file since the index file was last generated.

The package format

Package libraries are files containing a specified format of one or more packages containing Tcl procedures that you like to use over and over. A package identifies a group of related Tcl procedures, such as all of your home-grown procedures for dressing up a list widget.

```
#@package: package_name proc1 [... procN]
proc proc1 {} {
}
proc proc2 {} {
    ...
}
#@packend
```

The #@package delimiter describes the "public interface" of procedures that are supported by the package. There may also be other "helper" Tcl procedures that are located in the package for building the advertised package procedures, but they are private procedures that are not intended for external use.

```
#@package: directory_stack pushd popd dirs
```

@packend is entirely optional, since the current package definition ends at the next occurrence of #@package: anyway.

TASK

Earlier, in the discussion of the array command, we performed a search for a user listed in one of the list elements stored in the array. This could be useful elsewhere. Create a reusable package library for array-related Tcl procedures and initialize it with a procedure called SearchListArrayForItem.

```
#@package: arrayProcedures SearchListArrayForItem

proc SearchListArrayForItem {anArray} {
    ...
}

#@packend
```

TASK

As a temporary situation, you are constructing a package library in your home directory. Use **loadlibindex** *to load in a test package.*

```
loadlibindex /u/andrew/tcl/mytoys.tlib
```

If a matching index file is not present, **loadlibindex** automatically builds mytoys.tndx in /u/andrew/tcl.

Avoiding name collision

Within the package of related commands that you create, you'll probably have a number of helper procedures that are not intended for use outside of the package. Over time, as you build extensive libraries, you may encounter a problem with like-named procedures that results in errors. In the event that there are two procedures named sort, the interpreter simply uses the first procedure of that name that it finds. In order to minimize the potential for this kind of name collision, a good naming convention to practice is to name package library helper Tcl procedures using the package name as a prefix. For example,

```
#@package: arrayTools sortArray [... procN]
...
proc proc2 {arrayName} {
   ...
   arrayTools_sort $arrayName
   ...
}
proc arrayTools_sort {}
}
#@packend
```

By prepending the package name, followed by an underscore character in front of the helper procedure, there is much less likelihood of a potential conflict with another Tcl procedure having the same name (in this case, *sort*) located elsewhere in your code or another package library.

When to use source or package libraries

For modest-sized application development, there may not appear to be much difference between using the **source** command to include procedures from another file and using a package library. However, there are some factors you may want to consider:

1. Package-based Tcl commands are loaded on demand. Using the **source** command requires that your application must explicitly reference the file containing the needed Tcl procedures.

2. With the **source** command, you inherit all commands included in a file. With a package library, only those commands included in an individual package are loaded into your interpreter.

3. The interpreter looks in standard directories for package libraries. The **source** command requires that you must know the pathname of the file's location.

Bringing scripts together with `make`

Using commands like **source** and features like package libraries integrates your code during run-time execution. Another approach to consider is to build your scripts with a `makefile`. Inside your `makefile`, you can use the `cat` command to concatenate multiple scripts into a single executable script. This might also be a good time to remove those comments inside of looping commands to get the performance improvement you need. If your resulting script is excessively large, this may not be the best solution. This approach does, however, reduce the need to coordinate the location and use of multiple files when your application is installed.

Building internationalized scripts

Internationalizing your scripts makes them easy to localize in different foreign languages. Visual Tcl is 8-bit clean and built with ANSI functions supporting internationalized computing, such as the sorting of localized code sets. Extended with TclX internationalization commands, Visual Tcl scripts can be written to be language-independent, adapting to French, German, or any other language that can be supported in 8-bit ASCII. Using X/Open Portability Guide, Version 3 (XPG/3) message catalogs, Tcl strings translated into the user's language can be utilized in messages, widget labels, and wherever strings are displayed. If your script is truly internationalized using message catalogs, the only changes necessary to add new language translations are to the message catalog files. No change to the Visual Tcl script is required.

Table 7–7   XPG/3 Internationalization Commands

★	**catclose** `[-fail|-nofail]` *cathandle*
★	**catgets** *catHandle setnum msgnum defaultstr*
★	**catopen** `[-fail|-nofail]` *catname*

The three XPG/3 commands supported by Visual Tcl are listed in Table 7–7. Before we explain their use, let's address how message catalogs are created.

Building message catalogs

XPG/3-compliant operating systems provide the message catalog-building utility gencat. gencat is used to build formatted message catalogs that can be read by the Visual Tcl internationalization commands. To create a message catalog, you must first start with a message file that follows the formatting conventions legible by gencat.

```
$ This is a general comment in the input message file
$set 1 This is the header identifying a set of labels.
1 "Welcome to Visual Tcl"
2 "Do you want to save your editing?"
3 "This is a particularly long message that \
can be continued onto the next line."
...
$set 2 This is a set of menu strings
1 "File"
2 "Edit"
...
```

The text above illustrates the general format of a message input file that can be converted by gencat to an XPG/3 message catalog. Be sure to check the man page for gencat on your system. A set is a block of related messages. Its organization and definition are dependent on how you want to organize your messages. You can use this to make it easier for translators to create new catalogs by organizing related messages in groups of sets.

```
gencat msg.cat msg.src
```

gencat is used above to convert your source message file, represented by msg.src, to an XPG/3 message catalog. You can now use the commands listed in Table 7–7 to access the message catalog, msg.cat, from your script.

Accessing message catalogs

catopen opens the message catalog containing the localized messages that correspond to the language specified in the user environment's LANG variable. Be sure to check your system's implementation of environment variables and locale specifications. For this example, we'll reference our message catalog in a test location.

```
set fdMsg [catopen -nofail /tmp/msg.cat]
echo [catgets $fdMsg 1 1 "Visual Tcl"]
echo [catgets $fdMsg 1 2 "Save editing?"]
echo [catgets $fdMsg 1 8 "So long"]
catclose -nofail $fdMsg
```

➡ Welcome to Visual Tcl
Do you want to save your editing?
So long

catopen returns a file descriptor referencing the message catalog. The -nofail option is specified in order to allow processing to carry on even when no message catalog is located by **catopen**. -nofail is not actually required, since it is the default behavior of **catopen**. The result of a failed open is that the default strings, specified as the last argument in each **catgets** command, are returned as default strings in lieu of the message that might have existed in the missing message catalog.

The first **catgets** statement fetches set identifier 1, message number 1. The last call to **catgets** demonstrates the use of a default string. In this command, message number 8 is specified. Since there is no message 8 in our example message source file, the specified default message, So long, is returned by **catgets**. In the event that this is unintended by the developer, an updated message catalog containing set 1, message 8 can be generated, ending the use of the default string.

Updating localized strings with new information

You can use the **format** command to address strings where format specifiers are expected. For instance, a translated string may require a person's name.

```
6 "Welcome to Visual Tcl, %s"
```

The **format** command can plug in the value as read in by **catgets**.

```
set userName Janet
set formatMessage \
     [catgets $fdMsg 1 6 "Welcome to Visual Tcl, %s"]
echo "[format  $formatMessage $userName]"
```

➡ Welcome to Visual Tcl, Janet

Occasionally, a translation of a sentence changes the order that one might expect. For example,

```
"Saving file %s to directory %s"
```

might be reworked during a translation to

```
"The directory is %s that your file %s has been saved
to"
```

Using sequence numbering in format specifiers addresses this issue. This requires that each specifier contains an indexing number, followed by a $ character. The number represents the order that **format** should use to perform replacement. To deal with the message string above, we would rework it to incorporate index numbers that **format** can use to identify which variable to use in replacing each format specifier.

```
9 "Directory %2$s now contains your file %1$s"
```

The **format** command is instructed by the numbers in the format specifiers to use the corresponding variables in the **format** statement.

```
format "Directory %2$s now contains your file %1$s" \
      $fileName $dirName
```

This instructs **format** to use the value contained in the first variable, `fileName`, to replace the first specifier, `%1$s`. `%2$s` is then replaced by the contents of the second variable, `dirName`.

Performance considerations

As powerful as Tcl is, the reality is that is an interpreted language and will present occasional performance issues as you expand its use in your application development. The good news is that there are a number of things you can do before you throw your hands up and switch to C.

`lappend` is faster than `concat`

Using the **time** command, let's compare the following two uses of **concat** and **lappend**. The **time** command instructs the Tcl interpreter to execute a script for an indicated number of iterations. The default value of one iteration was used for the following tests.

```
set itemList {}
echo [time {
    loop i 0 2000 1 {
        set itemList [concat $itemList $i]
    }
}]
```

➡ 3220000 microseconds per iteration

```
set itemList {}
echo [time {
    loop i 0 2000 1 {
        lappend itemList $i
    }
}]
```

➡ 90000 microseconds per iteration

The loop using **lappend** is 97% faster than the **concat** loop.

append is faster than string concatenation

Compare the following:

```
echo [time {
    set string ""
    loop i 0 5000 1 {
```

```
        set string $string$i
    }
}]
```

➡ 8420000 microseconds per iteration

and

```
echo [time {
    set string ""
    loop i 0 5000 1 {
        append string $i
    }
}]
```

➡ 210000 microseconds per iteration

loop is faster than for

For instance, compare the following:

```
set fd [open /dev/null w]
echo [time {
    set limit 50000
    for {set i 0} {$i < $limit} {incr i} {
        puts $fd $i
    }
}]
close $fd
```

➡ 6790000 microseconds per iteration

and

```
set fd [open /dev/null w]
echo [time {
    set limit 50000
    loop i 0 $limit 1 {
        puts $fd $i
    }
}]
close $fd
```

➡ 2660000 microseconds per iteration

Other performance tips

The following tips can provide a base on which to expand from your own experiences, as well as from tips you see on the Net, where many of these originated.

Minimize Tcl code in memory

All Tcl code is stored in memory as a long string. It is then scanned and parsed on each execution. To minimize excessive scanning, remove all comments and whitespace from the inside of command loops.

Leverage built-in Tcl commands

When deciding to use **exec** to access external data or functionality, be sure to scrutinize the Tcl and TclX command set for the functionality you require. Familiarize yourself with noun-verb commands like **id**, **string**, **file**, and **info**, all of which have lots of hidden functionality.

Avoid large strings

Large strings cause swapping, particularly if they are to be parsed with list-processing routines. Read files one line at a time, particularly if they are large files.

Keyed lists versus arrays

Keyed lists become inefficient, due to a large number of keys or large blocks of key values. For large amounts of data, arrays are more efficient. Small keyed lists are more efficient than are small arrays.

Organize your code with package libraries

Take advantage of package libraries to deal with large applications that are slow to load. Procedures located in package libraries are loaded only on demand, thus reducing startup time. If your application contains lots of code that is rarely exercised, you may want to consider moving that code to a package library.

Data Access Commands

✔ File I/O commands
✔ File scanning
✔ Math commands
✔ UNIX process and signal commands

At this point, we have reviewed the command and data structures for manipulating information. This chapter explores the nongraphical Visual Tcl commands for retrieving information from the UNIX system, from data files or from other processes, through the richness of the TclX command set. TclX extends existing Tcl commands, provides comprehensive access to the UNIX environment and supports the kind of tools that turn Visual Tcl into an industry-strength development language. TclX makes it possible to stay within the language, reducing the need to rely on "outside" UNIX tools and utilities such as awk, wc, grep, or system tools that probe the UNIX system for user and file system information. It takes a while to learn all of the capabilities of Visual Tcl. It is common to see scripts written that execute UNIX commands unnecessarily. This chapter attempts to introduce just enough Visual Tcl to give you a sense of its completeness as a server-based development environment.

File I/O

Simple file access is greatly expanded by commands and procedures in the TclX library. A quick review of Table 8–1 reveals that there is very little file access functionality that cannot be performed by a Visual Tcl application.

Table 8–1 File I/O Commands

★   **bsearch** *fileId key* [*retvar*] [*compare_proc*]

     cd [*dirName*]

★   **chgrp** *group filelist*

★   **chmod** *mode filelist*

★   **chown** *owner*|{*owner group*} *filelist*

★   **chroot** *dirname*

     close *fileID*

★   **copyfile** [-bytes *num* |-maxbytes *num*] *fromFieldId
          toFieldId*

★   **dup** *fileId* [*targetFileId*]

★   **echo** [*str* ...]

     eof *fileId*

★   **fcntl** *fileId attribute* [*value*]

     file *option fileName* [*arg arg* ...]

★   **flock** *options fileId* [*start*] [*length*] [*origin*]

     flush *fileId*

★   **for_file** *var fileName body*

★   **for_recursive_glob** *var dirlist globlist body*

★   **frename** *oldPath newPath*

★   **fstat** *fileId* [*item*]|[stat *arrayvar*]

★   **funlock** *fileId* [*start*] [*length*] [*origin*]

     gets *fileId* [*varName*]

     glob [*switches*] *pattern* [*pattern* ...]

     lgets *fileId* [*varName*]

★   **link** [-sym] *srcpath destpath*

★   **mkdir** [-path] *dirList*

     open *fileName* [*access*] [*permissions*]

     pipe [*fileId_var_r fileId_var_w*]

     puts [-nonewline] [*fileId*] *string*

     read [-nonewline] *fileId* ; **read** *fileId numBytes*

★   **read_file** [-nonewline] *fileName* ; **read_file**
          fileName numBytes

Table 8–1   File I/O Commands (cont.)

★   **readdir** *dirpath*

★   **recursive_glob** *dirlist globlist*

★   **rmdir** [-nocomplain] *dirList*

     seek *fileId offset* [*origin*]

★   **select** *readfileIds* [*writefileIds*] [*exceptfileIds*]
              [*timeout*]

★   **server_info** *option hostname*

★   **server_open** [*option*] *host service*

★   **sync** [*fileId*]

     tell *fileId*

★   **unlink** [-nocomplain] *filelist*

★   **write_file** *fileName string* [*string* ...]

★   **umask** [*octalmask*]

Simple file access: open, close, eof, gets, puts

TclX provides the **copyfile** command for copying the remainder of the contents of one file to another file. The task below illustrates the use of common Tcl commands that achieve a simpler goal.

Copy the contents of file /tmp/data *to a new file. Append the contents if the file already exists.*   **TASK**

```
# open a file for reading
set fdIn [open /tmp/data.in r]

if {[file exists /tmp/data.out]} {
      # Open file for appending data
      set fdOut [open /tmp/data.out a]
} else {
      # Create the output file
      set fdOut [open /tmp/data.out w]
}

# begin the copy
while {![eof $fdIn]} {
      set record [gets $fdIn]
      puts $fdOut $record
}
close $fdIn; close $fdOut
```

Creating pipes with `open`

UNIX utilities can be opened for input in a manner that eliminates the need for storing information in intermediate Tcl variables. By prepending the pipe symbol, |, in front of the executable binary's name, input or output can be negotiated through the file descriptor.

```
open "|<binary>" r
```

The following example builds a Tcl list of available font names by retrieving the piped output provided by the X11 `xlsfonts` utility.

```
proc RetrieveFontList {} {
    set fd [open "|xlsfonts" r]
    while {![eof $fd]} {
        lappend fontList [gets $fd]
    }
    return $fontList
}
```

TASK   *Save the output of a script in compressed format.*

```
set fd [open "|gzip > tmp/output.gz" w]
foreach listItem $longListOfData {
    puts $fd $listItem
}
close $fd
```

This example sets off a write-only pipe to the GNU `gzip` compress utility. The same Tcl application can later use the `-d` option of `gzip` to uncompress the file and read in the previously compressed list information.

Visual Tcl file I/O is implemented on top of the `stdio` library. Files are buffered by default. You can use the **flush** command to force data through a pipe established with another process. Instead of **flush**, you can use the **fcntl** command to set the buffering mode to unbuffered.

Retrieving preformatted lists from a file: `lgets`

Like placing a bookmark in the book you're in the middle of reading, the state of your application can be saved by writing information out to a file State information can represent a script's internal mental note, such as "this user has indicated that the main list should always be displayed 8 rows high." This information can then be reloaded the next time your application is launched. Other state information might be information that the user wants the application to track between invocations.

Often, the data you save are in the form of a list or keyed list. **lgets** is the ideal read command for retrieving lists from a file.

Suppose we want to save a message that the user has typed into a text window provided by a Motif text widget. It's highly probable that the message contains a number of newlines. Using a keyed list, we will associate a time stamp with the user's message.

```
keylset userNote timeStamp [fmtclock [getclock] %r]
keylset userNote note [RetrieveMessageFromUser]
```

RetrieveMessageFromUser is our fictitious procedure that retrieves the message from the text widget. To save the keyed list, userNote, to disk, we can use **write_file** to blast the raw list into a file in the user's home directory, contained in homeDir.

```
write_file $homeDir/.msgrc $userNote
```

At a later point, the user reinvokes the application. One of the first chores it performs is to re-load the state information that was saved to .msgrc.

```
set fd [open $homeDir/.msgrc r]
set charsRead [lgets $fd keyList]
if {$charsRead > 0} {
        echo "Your last message, entered at\
            [keylget keyList timeStamp], said:"
        echo [keylget keyList note]
}
close $fd
```

➡ Your last message, entered at 09:21:45 AM, said:
There is a problem with John's computer.
Be sure to stop by and help him out.

lgets reads whole lists, not just lines like, **gets**. Newlines that may be quoted inside the list are read in just like any other character. In the process of reading a list, it discards file newlines, continuing to load the list until it reaches the end of the list. In the example above, **lgets** returns the number of characters it encounters, not including newlines. When used inside a loop, **lgets** should check for -1, meaning that an end-of-file (EOF) condition has been encountered.

For quick file access: `for_file, write_file`

When you want to quickly retrieve individual lines from a file, one by one in **while**-loop fashion, use **for_file**. There's no need for dealing with opening and closing file housekeeping.

```
echo The groups on this machine are:
for_file line /etc/group {
        echo [ctoken line :]
}
```

Complementing **for_file**, **write_file** is ideal for blasting data into a file with no looping required. For each string passed to **write_file**, a separate line is created in the output file.

```
write_file /tmp/hotdata \
    "Name: David" \
    "Occupation: struggling author"
```

Everything you ever wanted to know about a file: file and fstat

The **file** command is another noun-verb Tcl that supports extensive capability. The options supported by **file**, as shown in Table 8–2 illustrate the breadth of Tcl's access to file information.

Table 8–2   File command options

atime	extension	mtime	rootname	type
dirname	isdirectory	owned	size	writable
executable	isname	readable	stat	
exists	lstat	readlink	tail	

The TclX **fstat** command offers functionality similar to **file** stat, except that it works directly on open file descriptors.

```
file stat /etc/motd statArray
echo "File permissions for /etc/motd are: \
    [format "%o" [expr {$statArray(mode) & 07777}]]"
```
➡ File permissions for /etc/motd are: 644

Table 8–3   File stat array indexes

atime	gid	mtime	type
ctime	ino	nlink	uid
dev	mode	size	

Building network-enabled scripts: server_open

Through the TclX library, Visual Tcl can support TCP/IP sockets-based programming. Using the **server_open** command, it's possible to build your own Internet news browser.

Determine whether the system has sockets support using the **infox** *command. If sockets are supported, get the date and time from another server providing the Internet daytime network service.*

TASK

```
if {[[infox have_sockets] == 1]} {
    # open a socket to the inetd "daytime" service
    set fd [server_open -nobuf scorpion daytime]
    echo "The network time is [gets $fd]
}
```

➡ The network time is Fri Feb 16 22:31:05 PST 1996

When no buffering is specified with the −nobuf option, a single read-only file descriptor is returned by **server_open**. In this example, we want simply to fetch the daytime information in a read-only operation. When buffering is used, two file descriptors are returned by **server_open**, supporting read-write operations across a socket connection.

Example tasks

Determine whether a file name is a directory. If so, retrieve the files contained inside.

TASK

```
if {[file isdirectory $fileName] == 1} {
    set fileList [readdir $fileName]
}
```

Determine whether a file can be accessed by the script

TASK

```
if { [file exists /etc/motd] &&
    [file readable /etc/motd] } {
    set fd [open /etc/motd r]
}
```

In interactive shell mode, determine how many lines there are in a script file

TASK

```
vtcl
vtcl> set lines [read_file /tmp/script.tcl]
vtcl> llength $lines
207
```

This will actually count the number of newlines in the file because **read_file** uses **split** to return lines of file text as individual Tcl lists. You can add some code that ignores empty lists in lines.

Read the file again, this time ignoring empty lines.

TASK

```
vtcl
vtcl> set count 0
```

```
vtcl> for_file line /tmp/script.tcl {
=> if {[lempty $line]{
=> incr count
=> }
=> }
vtcl> echo Number of lines with code is $count
```
➡ Number of lines with code is 185

File scanning for Awk-like functionality

Visual Tcl supports the ability to perform Awk-like programming without having to leave the Tcl environment. With the TclX file scanning commands listed in Table 8–4, your script can scan a file, searching for matches based on regular expressions. With each match, a Tcl procedure that you provide is called to process data about the match, including the matching line itself.

Table 8–4   File Scanning Commands

★   **scancontext** [*option*]

★   **scanfile** [-copyfile *copyFileId*] *contexthandle fileId*

★   **scanmatch** [-nocase] *contexthandle* [*regexp*] *commands*

After opening a file for reading, using the base Tcl command **open**, the file descriptor is handed to the **scancontext** command, establishing a context for the scan to occur. **scanmatch** sets up the regular expression that will detect matches and the Tcl procedure that will process them. The file is scanned for matches on a per-line basis. With the context and matching criteria in place, the **scanfile** command is called to begin the actual scanning process. The context of the scan is ended when the EOF is reached.

The built-in variable matchInfo is an array that is updated with assorted information about each match. matchInfo is refreshed with new information at each pattern match.

Table 8–5   **matchInfo** indexes for pattern-matching information

line	The text of the line of the file that was matched.
offset	The byte offset into the file of the first character of the line that was matched.
linenum	The line number of the line that was matched. This is relative to the first line scanned, which is usually, but not necessarily, the first line of the file. The first line is line number 1.
handle	The file ID (handle) of the file currently being scanned.

Table 8–5 `matchInfo` indexes for pattern-matching information (cont.)

`copyHandle`	The file ID (handle) of the file specified by the `-copyfile` option. The element does not exist if `-copyfile` was not specified.
`submatch0`	The characters matching the first parenthesized subexpression. The second will be contained in `submatch1`, and so on.

The example below scans the Visual Tcl tlib package file for procedure names. The variable `auto_path` contains a list of known tlib package directories. It displays a list of procedure names and the line number on which they occur.

```
# Open the vtcl tlib and set the scan context
set fileName [lindex $auto_path 1]/vtcl.tlib
set fd [open $fileName r]
set scanId [scancontext create]

# Establish the pattern to look for (note that there's a
# space and a tab inside the square brackets.
set pattern {^proc[ 	]+([^ 	]*}
scanmatch $scanId $pattern {
        # extract the procedure name
        echo $matchInfo(submatch0)($matchInfo(linenum))
}

# begin the scan
scanfile $scanId $fd
close $fd
```

➡ VxMenu(36)
VxMenuGetButton(137)
_SetOptions(193)
VxOptionMenu(220)
VxOptionMenuGetSelected(230)
. . .

In the event that you want to build a file that includes all the lines where no match occurred, **scanfile** provides the `-copyfile` option for specifying the file descriptor of a file that has been opened for writing. All lines failing the test of the regular expression are then written to that file.

Tcl internal commands

Leveraging a large number of TclX commands, Visual Tcl supports a variety of general purpose commands for navigating the UNIX environment, manipulating user and process information as well as making inquiries of the run-time Tcl environment.

The **id** command supports options for

1. Set or retrieve the real and effective user ID
   id user
   id userid
2. Retrieve the process ID of the current process
   id process
3. Retrieve the process group ID of the current process.
4. Retrieve the effective user name, or effective user ID number.
   id effective user
   id effective userid

Perhaps the most useful general purpose command, **info** provides your application with the ability to query its own state, as well as the Visual Tcl interpreter. Some of the things you can do with **info** include:

1. Query the number of arguments passed to a procedure.
   info args *procName*
2. Retrieve a list of all procedure names that match a string pattern.
   info procs
3. Check for the existence of a variable.
   info exists *varName*
4. Retrieve a list of all current global variables.
   info globals
5. Retrieve the name of the current Tcl library.
   info library
6. Retrieve the current version of the Tcl interpreter.
   info tclversion

Be sure to examine the options to **info** listed in the *Commands* pages.

Table 8–6 Status Commands

★	**dirs**
★	**edprocs** [*proc* ...]
	history [*option*] [*arg arg* ...]
★	**id** *options*
	info *option*
★	**infox** *option*
★	**popd**
★	**pushd**
	pwd
★	**saveprocs** *fileName* [*proc* ...]
★	**showproc** [*procname* ...]

Using `info` to find variables

How can you be sure that these variables were actually created? The command

echo "The flower variables are: [**info** vars "flower?"]"

➡ The flower variables are flower1 flower2 flower3

uses the **info** command to list all of currently visible variables in the local and global namespace that match the pattern `flower?` (using the ? regular expression symbol).

Navigating the file system: `pushd`, `popd`, `cd`, `pwd`

pushd and **popd** are commands for going to and returning from directory locations.

Using the vtcl interactive shell, put the current directory on the stack and change directory to /tmp.   `TASK`

```
vtcl
vtcl> cd /tmp
vtcl> pushd /usr/lib/X11
vtcl> pwd
/usr/lib/X11
vtcl> popd
/tmp
vtcl> pwd
/tmp
```

Interactive session `history`

The **history** command is intended solely for creating a csh-like environment for the vtcl interactive shell. There are many options documented in the *Command Pages* section. Some **history** options include:

```
vtcl
...
vtcl>history           returns the last 20 commands
vtcl>!23               repeats the command that was entered on line 23
vtcl>!!                repeats the previous command
```

Viewing library procedures with `showproc`

Any procedure that is kept in a package library can be viewed from your interactive vtcl session with the **showproc** command. **showproc** displays all package procedures currently loaded into the vtcl session. To view individual commands, simply invoke **showproc** with the optional command name that you are interested in, such as the **pow** math command name.

When you use **showproc** in an interactive vtcl session, you may notice that there are a lot of TclX procedures not listed that you might have expected to see. For example, when you first enter a vtcl session, then type **showproc**, you won't see the **sin** Tcl procedure. However, if you execute one of the TclX math commands, such as **cos**, then type **showproc** again, all of the procedure scripts for TclX math commands appear, including **sin**. As you may have guessed, this behavior is due to the fact that the TclX commands implemented as Tcl procedures are maintained as packages in tlib libraries. Because procedures, and the package to which they belong, are loaded on demand, it isn't until a procedure in a TclX package is invoked that its entire package of procedures appears via **showproc**.

showproc, **edprocs**, and **saveprocs** are provided for the vtcl interactive shell environment and are not generally useful when executed from a script file.

Example tasks

TASK *Display the user's name using the **id** command.*

```
echo "Welcome to this application, [id user]"
```
➡ Welcome to this application, davidy

TASK *Use **showproc** to save all currently loaded procedures to a file for examination.*

```
write_file mystuff.tcl [showproc]
```

Process control, time and signals

Processes, such as Visual Tcl applications, have the ability to create, communicate with, and destroy processes.

Table 8–7   Process Control and Signal Commands

	exec [*switches*] *arg* [*arg* ...]
★	**execl** [-argv0 *argv0*] *prog* [*arglist*]
	exit [*returnCode*]
★	**fork**
★	**kill** [-pgroup] [*signal*] *idlist*
★	**nice** [*priorityincr*]
★	**pid** [*fileId*]
★	**signal** *action siglist* [*command*]
★	**VtAddInput** *fileID callback*
★	**VtRemoveInput** *fileID*
★	**wait** [-nohang] [-untraced] [-pgroup] [*pid*]

fork and exec with TclX

Through the TclX command library, Visual Tcl gives you the ability to fork and exec child processes. The **fork** command returns a child and parent process ID. **execl** replaces the current program, as you would expect from an **exec** command, thus never reaching the **echo** statement (assuming the call to vtcl doesn't fail). The vtcl command is passed to line script that causes it to sleep for 1 second, then to exit with a value of 12.

```
set processID [fork]
echo PID:$processID
if {$processID == 0} {
        # exec another vtcl process with a\
          little sleep script
        catch {execl vtcl {-qc {sleep 1;exit 12}}} msg
        puts stderr "execl failed: $msg"
        exit 1
}
set result [wait $processID]
echo Parent id of the child was [lindex $result 0]
echo Exit status was [lindex $result 1]
echo exit return code was [lindex $result 2]
```

➡ PID:0
   PID:699
   Parent id of the child was 699
   Exit status was EXIT
   exit return code was 12

wait waits on the child process ID until the child exits. The value returned to the script by **wait** is a list of three bits of information: the parent ID, a keyword EXIT, meaning that the child exited normally, and the number returned by the child's **exit** command.

Are you sure you need **exec**?

It's common to see scripts that use **exec** to launch UNIX utilities unnecessarily. By virtue of its TclX extensions, so much UNIX functionality has been folded into the Visual Tcl language that the need to create the overhead by the excessive use of **exec** is minimal. The functionality of many UNIX utilities is available as TclX built-in commands. For example, there's no need to perform the following command:

```
set currentDirectory [exec pwd]
```

since the pwd functionality is provided by the TclX command, **pwd**. Unless you are crafting a script that must be portable to other Tcl interpreters that may not be extended with TclX, be sure to check the tables in this book for the UNIX access functionality you need.

Monitoring an I/O stream: VtAddInput/VtRemoveInput

These two nongraphical Vt commands are provided to allow the processing of data returned by an external process, without interfering with the Visual Tcl event loop. See Chapter 21, *Non-GUI Vt Commands*, for an expanded explanation and example.

Time

Table 8–8   Time Commands

★   **alarm** *seconds*
★   **convertclock** *dateString* [GMT|{}] [*baseClock*]
★   **fmtclock** *clockval* [*format*] [GMT|{}]
★   **getclock**
★   **sleep** *seconds*

Retrieving the current time: `getclock` and `fmtclock`

Using the combination of TclX commands, **getclock** and **fmtclock**, we can retrieve the time from the system clock. Choosing from the list of field descriptors in Table 8–9, we can use **fmtclock** to define the format of the given time.

Table 8–9   `fmtclock` field descriptors for format argument

%%	Insert a %	%p	AM or PM
%a	Abbreviated weekday name	%r	Time as %I:%M:%S %p
%A	Full weekday name	%R	Time as %H:%M
%b	Abbreviated month name	%S	Seconds (00 – 59)
%B	Full month name	%t	Insert a tab
%d	Day of month (01 – 31)	%T	Time as %H:%M:%S
%D	Date as %m/%d/%y	%U	Week number of year (01 – 52), Sunday is the first day of the week
%e	Day of month (1 – 31), no leading zeros	%w	Weekday number (Sunday = 0)
%h	Abbreviated month name	%W	Week number of year (01 – 52), Monday is the first day of the week
%H	Hour (00 – 23)	%x	Local specific date format
%I	Hour (00 – 12)	%X	Local specific time format
%j	Day number of year (001 – 366)	%y	Year within century (00 – 99)
%m	Month number (01–- 12)	%Y	Year as ccyy (for example, 1990)
%M	Minute (00 – 59)	%Z	Time zone name
%n	Insert a new line		

```
set rawTime [getclock]
echo "Today is day number [fmtclock $rawTime %j%] of\
    [fmtclock $rawTime %Y%]"
```
➡ Today is day number 364 of 1995

getclock returns the system time as a UNIX integer value (of seconds). **fmtclock** then converts it into the format that has been specified. You can also use **fmtclock** to format the output of a file access, modified, or created time (atime, mtime, ctime) returned by the Tcl **file** command.

```
echo "/etc/motd was accessed\
      at [fmtclock [file atime /tmp/out] %r]"
```

➡ /etc/motd was accessed on 04:24:43 PM

TASK *Calculate how much time remains before Christmas.*

```
set christmasDay [convertclock "25 Dec 96"]
set today [getclock]
set days [fmtclock [expr {$christmasDay - $today}] %j]
echo "$days days till Christmas"
```

Signals

A *signal* is a notification that an event has occurred. An event can represent any number of things, such as the detection of activity on an open file descriptor or the death of a child process. There are also timed events that can be set to "go off" at some point. The **alarm** command can be used to set a timer. For example, suppose your graphical Visual Tcl script displays a clock that is updated every 5 seconds. You can use the **alarm** command to wake up a procedure that is responsible for updating the clock. The script below illustrates the general script mechanism that would handle a timed event.

```
signal trap SIGALRM {
      echo "An alarm has been caught"
      # update the visual clock here...
      # reset the timer
      alarm 5
}
alarm 5    # units in seconds
while {1} {sleep 1; echo "processing..."}
```

Keep in mind that Tcl signals receive attention *after* the interpreter has completed the command it is currently executing. When the interpreter completes execution of a command, it checks to see if there are any signals waiting for processing. If not, it moves on to the next command.

The TclX **sleep** command is used in the **while** loop simply to slow down the rate at which **echo** is executed. **sleep** has the profound effect of stopping the processing of all commands for the indicated number of seconds.

PART III

Visual Tcl

Motif and Visual Tcl

✔ Motif and Visual Tcl
✔ Event-driven programming
✔ Widgets, callbacks and the event loop

*D*eveloping applications that are more useful and friendly to users requires putting the keys in the hands of the user. Applications that are user-driven require an event-driven programming model in order to support to the seemingly unordered movements and clicks of a mouse. The OSF/Motif specification supports the combination of graphical controls, called *widgets*, and the event-driven model that provides the foundation for Visual Tcl GUI development.

This chapter provides a casual introduction to the basic concepts of the OSF/Motif toolkit, setting the stage for introducing GUI development with the Visual Tcl language. If you are already well versed in Motif concepts, you might want to jump to the next chapter. Also included is a short discussion on design strategies as you develop Visual Tcl applications.

The Motif look & feel

The improved usability of graphical applications is due in large part to the use of real-word concepts, such as *push buttons*, *lists* and *menus*. Usability has improved even further as developers begin to reuse common notions such as how a file pulldown menu looks. Overall, applications are looking more consistent now that there are fewer windowing standards, such as those found on UNIX, Windows, and the Macintosh; even these standards share levels of common heritage that help to present a reasonable consistency (as suggested in Figure 9–1, comparing two push buttons from different windowing systems).

Figure 9–1   Windows and Motif, side-by-side

Described in the *Motif Style Guide*, the OSF/Motif specification was largely modeled on top of the CUA specification that describes the Microsoft Windows look and feel. The OSF/Motif specification describes how a user interface should look and feel. The *look* is the appearance of a widget. A push button is rectangular in shape and chiseled for a three-dimensional appearance. The *feel* is how the widget interacts with the user. A push button simply appears to be depressed by the single click of the mouse button, creating the illusion of a real push button.

The OSF/Motif toolkit implements the Motif specification on top of the X windowing system. The X windows toolkit, Xt, provides the object-oriented foundation of widgets and widget resources, as well as the event-based engine that links user actions to functional code. Motif developers who work in the C language often move up and down the layers of Motif (Xm), Xt, and the X library in order to achieve the level of control that they need. Visual Tcl, on the other hand, was designed to present the developer with a single, high-level programming layer. With the trade-off of a certain amount of low-level control, the Visual Tcl developer benefits from reduced coding complexity, as well as from easier-to-maintain applications. The tools you decide to use depend on the challenges of your project's goals and constraints.

Since all user interface development in Visual Tcl is supported by Vt commands, the description of how to build Motif-based applications using Visual Tcl will require little discussion of X and Xt. Suffice it to say that X and Xt are sitting there, under the covers of the Vt command set, doing the right thing.

Event-driven programming

If you have performed a lot of shell scripting, you are probably used to writing applications that "fall through the code," executing each statement, stopping to wait for user input, and deciding what direction to take the user based on his or her response. Graphical user interface development, on the other hand, supports the developer's ability to present the user with a rich set of visual controls that support familiar navigation tools. The functional components of this interface are accompanied by features such as context-sensitive help or illustrative graphical images, designed to provide users with the additional information they might need to carry out a complex task. With all of these options, users are provided with the information needed to achieve their goals.

A user-driven environment is characterized by the generation of asynchronous events. User actions, such as

- the push of a button,
- the pressing of a keyboard key,
- the selection of an item in a list, or
- the movement of the mouse

require a model that can associate each event with the functional part of the application that performs the appropriate task.

Linking events to functionality

Event-driven programming links user actions with code that performs tasks. For example, when a user selects a name in a list of printers, the application directs itself to find the procedure that processes that action. The response may be to display a dialog containing extended information about the selected printer or to designate it as the default printer. Let's take a look at widgets and their callback resource.

Widgets and callbacks

A widget is an intelligent object that contains all the knowledge necessary to display its advertised behavior. Widgets provide a public interface to the programmer, as well as to the user's configuration environment, through attributes called *resources*. Widget resources affect different aspects of the widget, depending on the type of widget. A label widget, for instance, supports resources affecting the font that displays characters, as well as resources that control its background color and its dimensions. A list widget has similar resources as well as resources that control the number of rows it should display.

Widgets are connected to functional code by the *callback resource*. The callback resource identifies the name of a procedure to invoke when a user action is detected. There are different types of callbacks that are invoked, depending on the nature of the event and the widget involved in the event. Is the event a single click or a double click? Is the event simply the crossing of the mouse across the boundaries of the widget?

During the development of an application, the developer must register the callbacks that are to be associated with the types of events that are to be supported. In Visual Tcl, a callback is a Tcl procedure is associated with (1) a particular widget and (2) a particular event type supported by the widget. The Tcl procedure provides the functional computing that actually makes the printer the default printer or invokes other Vt building commands to display extended information about the printer. So, a single widget may generate different callbacks (procedures), depending on what kind of user event it detected.

The event loop

The process of responding to user-generated events does not begin until the application enters an *event loop*. The event loop acts as traffic cop, taking incoming callback requests from widgets and vectoring them to the named Tcl procedure. Once the procedure has completed its function, control is handed back to the event loop for further user events. In Visual Tcl, the event environment is entered once the **VtMainLoop** command is invoked. Recall that the Visual Tcl environment is provided by a client/server relationship of the vtcl interpreter and Motif display engine.

Visual Tcl Concepts

✔ Widget naming
✔ Vt command anatomy
✔ Visual Tcl resources
✔ Visual Tcl program anatomy
✔ Vx convenience routines

Visual Tcl supports a major portion of the OSF/Motif version 1.2 toolkit. Many Motif principles show through the Visual Tcl programming interface, however, there are a number of concepts unique to Visual Tcl. This chapter introduces common concepts that apply to Visual Tcl programming in general.

Some concepts, useful hints and practices, and interesting functionality and commands are introduced, expanded on later.

Anatomy of a Vt command

Motif widgets and widget resources are created, destroyed, modified, queried, displayed, hidden, and organized with Vt commands. Vt commands are C function extensions of the Tcl interpreter. Like any other Tcl command, they return an internal return code to the interpreter. They process their own arguments, apply their own meaning, and alert the interpreter when there is an error, providing the interpreter with a meaningful error message to pass along to the user.

Vt commands follow the general format of

```
Command [handle] [-option [optionArgs]]
```

Command	a supported Vt command.
handle	the name assigned by the programmer to an object, building on the name of a parent widget.
option	a valid option, typically representing a widget resource.
optionArgs	a valid option argument.

Vt commands, such as widget-creation commands, return a string value. Other Vt commands return no value. Before we go into detail about Vt commands, let's talk about how widgets are named.

Widget naming

A Visual Tcl graphical interface is composed of parent and children widgets organized as a hierarchical tree of names, much like a family tree. A Main dialog parent contains a child check box. The child check box becomes the parent that contains child toggle buttons. The top level parent is the *application widget*, which is retrieved from the display server by the **VtOpen** command. The naming format used for widget names supports a dot-delimited notation:

    .<application widget>.<ancestor>.<parent>.<child>

The application widget is always prefixed with a period, as a result of its creation. As you can see in the following example, the name of the handle influences the name of the application widget that results from its creation. demoApp is an example of a Vt handle. The handle is a string that is to be included in the widget naming process. .demoApp is the official application widget name retrieved by **VtOpen**.

echo [**VtOpen** demoApp]

➡ .demoApp

Every Visual Tcl widget receives a name as a result of its creation. Vt widget-creating commands, such as **VtLabel**, return the entire name of the new widget, prefixed with the application widget name and the names of all of its ancestors in between.

Figure 10–1 Label widget name

.demoApp.mainDialog_popup.mainDialog.mainDialog.welcomeLabel

Figure 10–1 shows a Visual Tcl applet that simply displays the label "Welcome to Visual Tcl" in the center of its main dialog. Let's examine the meaning of each component of the label widget name.

`.demoApp`	The application widget name, specified by the developer, with the dot prefix added by **VtOpen**.
`.mainDialog_popup` `.mainDialog`	Two intermediate internal parent widgets, invisible to the script, constructed by the display server incorporating a portion of the handle name.
`.mainDialog`	The handle of the Main dialog, assigned by the developer.
`.welcomeLabel`	The handle of the label, assigned by the developer. This component of a handle is referred to as the *short name*.

The demoApp applet was created by the following script.

```
set appName [VtOpen demoApp]
set mainDialog [VtFormDialog $appName.mainDialog
        -title "Label Demo"
        ]
set welcomeLabel [VtLabel $mainDialog.welcomeLabel \
        -label "Welcome to Visual Tcl"
        ]
VtShow $mainDialog
VtMainLoop
```

Let's review the script, tracking the construction of the widget name that eventually gives us the label name.

1. **VtOpen** establishes a connection with the display server, passing it the demoApp handle and receiving the official application shell name, .demoApp, in return. This value is stored in the variable appName, for reasons that we will discuss soon.

2. **VtFormDialog** creates the main window for demoApp. Building on the parent name stored in appName, we provided a new handle, $appName.mainDialog. A handle consists of two components

parent name	The long portion, containing the parent name ($appName)
short name	The programmer-specified component (.mainDialog)

   The main window's widget name returned by the display server is stored in the variable mainDialog. The display server has inserted two intermediate parent widget names, .mainDialog_popup and .mainDialog.

3. **VtLabel** creates a label containing the "Welcome to Visual Tcl" string that is placed inside the main window dialog. This time the display server simply returns the long handle name—unaltered—as the widget name giving us the name shown in Figure 10–1.

4. **VtShow** instructs the display server that it's time to tell the X server to display the completed interface, represented by the main window's dialog widget.

5. **VtMainLoop** puts the script into an event loop, waiting for input from the user.

Components of a widget name

Clearly, there is some extra work performed by the display server as it services the widget-building requests of the demoApp script. A widget name is constructed from a number of sources:

- the short name portion of the handle assigned by the programmer,
- the long parent widget name portion of the handle, and,
- one or more internally generated display server widget names.

The "surprise" internal widget names that are inserted in the final widget name are a by-product of the "layer of policy" supported by the Visual Tcl display server. Commonly needed widgets like the Form dialog are provided by Visual Tcl with a single Vt command. In order to achieve this, the display server supports the **VtFormDialog** by constructing the dialog from a collection of widgets. It is the added widgets that result in the additional widget names returned by **VtFormDialog**.

This is an example of how Visual Tcl supports easy, rapid development of Motif applications. In a conventional Motif development environment, you would have had to build the Main dialog widget by bringing together different contributing widgets. Although the example doesn't make it obvious, the composite widget provided by the **VtFormDialog** command supports many additional features, including OK, Cancel, Apply, and Help buttons. Depending on which additional options you choose, the **VtFormDialog** will return a different widget name, reflecting the additional widgets that went into the construction of the resulting dialog.

Visual Tcl widget naming and the Tk programmer

If you are Tk programmer, you are used to controlling the entire naming of a widget. As we have seen, although Visual Tcl widget naming uses a form similar to Tk naming, there is a different strategy for generating widget names.

Using widget names after creation

Having seen how long a widget name can get for a very small applet, it becomes clear why we are using the practice of storing widget names in variables as they are returned by Vt commands. Widget names are long, and they get longer as your application design grows with the addition of child dialogs. Imagine having to type in every widget name built inside a complex application. Another reason to store widget names in variables is that you are not going to know the widget's name until it's generated at run time by the display server, so you need a variable to store the run-time-generated widget name.

Once you have amassed a bunch of widget names stored in variables, what are the kinds of things you can do with them?

- Modify a widget resource such as its color resource or font resource
- Retrieve the current value of a widget resource
- Refer to a neighbor widget during the layout of a dialog
- Build child widgets contained by the parent (as illustrated by the script above)

For example, widget resources can be changed with the **VtSetValues** command. **VtSetValues** uses the widget name in order to identify which widget to modify. To change the label resource for our demoApp applet after the label has been created, we might add the command:

```
VtSetValues $welcomeLabel\
      -label "Welcome to Widget Naming"
```

Conversely, current widget resource values can be retrieved with the **VtGetValues** command.

Unique names and handles

You can see the benefit of storing the widget's name in the variable. We will soon see many examples of referencing other widgets. Unique widget names are required in order to reference widgets after their creation. Since there are so many situations that demand unique names, the default behavior of the Visual Tcl display server requires their use. If the demoApp script had been built with two label widgets, we could not have updated either of the labels without a unique widget name distinguishing one widget from the other. This is where the value of carefully considered handle short names becomes apparent.

Assigning *meaningful* handle names is not a requirement, however, it is extremely useful. Names like printerList or userName or cardID will make it easier to track widgets in large applications. Additionally, with the **VxGetShortName** convenience command, callback procedures can actually use the handle short names to extract useful information, which we'll explore later in this section.

> ### Handles as variable names
>
> This book uses the convention of using the handle name (minus the parent prefix) for the variable name that is assigned the widget name value returned from the Vt widget creation command.
>
> **set** nameLabel [**VtLabel** $parent.nameLabel ....

Using nonunique names

There are cases where it is not always necessary to uniquely name a widget. Visual Tcl supports the ability to override the default unique name requirement by providing the

```
-allowDuplicateName
```

option as part of the *object class*, described later.

Hierarchical naming

You may be wondering how you can guarantee unique names if your application makes use of dozens of widgets located here and there. Hierarchical naming takes care of most of this problem. The demoApp script illustrated a simple, linear widget naming tree. Most of your scripts won't be so simple. Let's examine a slightly more complex main dialog and how its naming tree might appear .

Figure 10–2   Two toggle widgets in a dialog

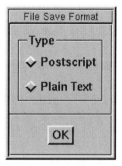

File Save Format (Figure 10–2) is a dialog that presents the user with the ability to select a format for an output file. The choices are postscript format or plain text. Toggle buttons that are inside a radio box behave as radio buttons, enforcing one-choice-only behavior. This applet contains seven primary widgets. The table below lists the short name portion of the widget name and a description of its function.

Short name	Description
`saveFormatDemo`	The application widget
`mainDialog`	The Main Form dialog
`typeFrame`	A widget that provides the "etched-in" box and "type" title around the radio box
`radioBox`	The manager widget that causes its toggle-button children to behave like radio buttons
`postTog`	A toggle button for selecting Postscript type
`textTog`	A toggle button for selecting Plain text type
`OK`	A push button for exiting the applet

The names we have chosen for each widget handle short name are intended to imply the functionality of each widget, as well as to be unique. Insuring a unique name is made easy by the nature of a tree naming structure. The points to focus on are the leaf node names `.postTog` and `.textTog`. As long as they are unique, the entire widget name for each of them is unique. Figure 10–3 illustrates the naming structure of File Save Format.

Figure 10–3   File Save Format applet widget name tree

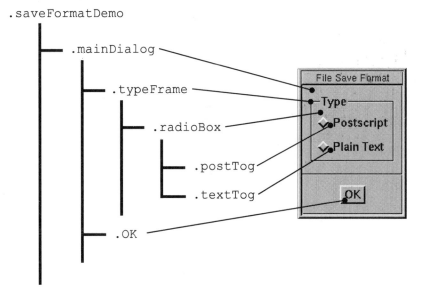

Anatomy of a Visual Tcl program

There are few absolute rules about how to organize your Visual Tcl script. However, there are advantages to organizing it in a consistent manner to go along with using a consistent approach to variable, widget, and procedure naming.

Although there will always be variations, the typical steps followed by a Visual Tcl application can be summarized as:

1.   Define procedures and callbacks
2.   Establish a connection with the Visual Tcl display server
3.   Create the main window
4.   Display (or realize) the main window
5.   Enter the main event loop

There are a few factors that influence this ordering. First of all, the connection with the display server must be established before Vt widget-creation commands can be used. Next, the main window should be displayed before entering the event loop. If the event loop took over flow control before the display server was instructed to render the Main dialog (using **VtShow**), there would be no way for the user to see that the application is waiting for input. Finally, once the flow of control enters the main loop represented by the **VtMainLoop** command, no parsing of the script may occur past that point, until the loop is terminated with **VtClose**. Figure 10–4 illustrates a very simple bit of code, using the flow of Visual Tcl commands.

Figure 10–4   Typical Visual Tcl script skeleton

```
#!/bin/vtcl

# define a callback that shuts down our application
proc QuitCB {} {
    VtClose
    exit 0
}

# Establish a connection with the Visual Tcl display
server
set app [VtOpen simpleDemo]

# Create our main window
set mainWindow [VtFormDialog $app.mainW \
    -okCallback QuitCB \
    -title "Simple Demo" \
    ]

VtLabel $mainWindow.labelW \
    -label "Hello World"
```

```
# Display the main window dialog
VtShow $mainWindow

# Enter the event-driven environment
VtMainLoop
```

Callbacks

Callbacks are widget resources represented by Tcl procedures that are invoked when a user triggers an event related to a specific widget. Callback procedures are registered with a widget, when the widget is created or after the widget is created, using **VtSetValues**.

The Visual Tcl callback mechanism is quite simple. With the exception of the separator widget, every widget supports at least two types of callback options.

-callback   A generic callback that returns a value relevant to the type of widget.

-shortHelpCallback   A focus event callback that is triggered when the mouse cursor crosses the boundary of a widget.

When a callback procedure is registered, the name of the procedure is stored with the display engine, where it is associated with the indicated widget. When a user event occurs, the display server checks the widget involved to determine whether any callbacks are registered. If so, the name of the callback procedure is sent back to the vtcl interpreter and the executing main loop, which directs the interpreter to evaluate the procedure.

Vt programming in the vtcl interactive shell

You can use the vtcl interactive shell to program with Vt commands. Though this is extremely useful for non-Vt commands or for trying out simple Vt command examples, you'll soon see the limitations of graphical development through a shell interface.

```
vtcl
>VtOpen a

.a
>VtLabel .a.b -label "hello world"
.a.b
>VtShow .a.b
```

VtLabel is a simple command that doesn't cause additional intermediate widget generation by the display server. As a result, the handle will be the same name as the returned widget name, making it easy to avoid the need to store widget names in variables.

Visual Tcl directories and files

The Visual Tcl environment consists of its executable interpreter and display server binaries, the Visual Tcl package library, and the default resource file that affects Visual Tcl's default resource values. The location of these files and directories varies from port to port. Check the appendix to find the exact location.

`../bin/vtcl`	the binary for the Visual Tcl interactive shell and interpreter.
`../lib/vtcl/vtcl.tlib`	the package library of Vx convenience commands.
`../lib/vtcl`	the directory containing `main.c`, `libvtcl.a`, and `vtcl.h` for extending the Visual Tcl interpreter with C function-based commands.
`../app-defaults/Vtcl`	X resource file for SCO Visual Tcl

If the files contained in `../lib/vtcl` are moved to a directory other than `/lib/vtcl`, their new location should be set in the environment variable VTCL_HOME. The vtcl interpreter can be pointed to the supporting Tcl library location, when moved from its default location, with the TCL_LIBRARY environment variable.

Visual Tcl option classes

Motif widgets of are built on top of an object-oriented infrastructure. High-level widgets inherit their features from lower-level widgets. For example, push buttons and toggle buttons inherit resources supported by the label class. As a result, the resource for label alignment (left, center, right) is supported by both of these widgets.

Since Visual Tcl represents widget resources as command options, it's not surprising that many Vt commands support similar options. Reflecting the Motif widget hierarchy, Visual Tcl options are grouped into different classes. Different Vt commands support different combinations of option classes, depending on the nature of the widget supported by the command. The Visual Tcl option classes are

- Label class
- Dialog class
- Form class
- Object class
- Geometry class

Most options can be used to set resources at widget creation time. Many resources can be set, as well as retrieved, after the widget has been created. For instance,

```
# Create a label widget with a Welcome string.
VtLabel $mainDlg.label -label "Welcome to Visual Tcl"
```

```
# Retrieve the label of a label widget
set label [VtGetValues $mainDlg.label -label]
echo $label
```

➡ "Welcome to Visual Tcl"

```
# Change the label to say goodbye.
VtSetValues $mainDlg.label -label "Goodbye for now"
```

The display server and Motif resources

The real Motif application is the daemon process Visual Tcl display server, xm_vtcld. The interpreter has no Motif code. The side effect of this architecture is that the display server daemon must be stopped and restarted in order for changes to X resource files to be loaded into the display server's resource database. A quick way to achieve this is to type the following at your UNIX command line.

```
vtcl
>VtOpen x
.x
>VtQuitServer
>exit
```

The **VtQuitServer** command kills the xm_vtcld display server daemon. The next time you run a Visual Tcl script, the display server will load any X resource file changes, such as those in /usr/lib/X11/app-defaults/Vtcl and in your home directory .Xdefaults file.

Inside your .Xdefaults file, you can refer to certain resources in a specific Visual Tcl application by prefixing the resource with the handle name passed to **VtOpen**.

If the name of the application handle is userAdm, as specified in

```
set appName [VtOpen userAdm]
```

you could specify the background color used by that application only with the following entry in .Xdefaults.

```
userAdm*background:   blue
```

Vx convenience routines

Throughout the example code that follows, we'll be taking advantage of some Visual Tcl convenience procedures called *Vx commands*. These commands are provided for the following reasons.

Convenience The majority of Vx commands were created to address commonly needed widget configurations, such as **VxText** and **VxList**, which put a title on top of a text or list widget.

Other, more complex tasks are encapsulated in commands like **VxAlignedForm**, which makes it easy to create attractive data-entry forms with columns of labels and associated widgets neatly aligned. Other commands, such as **VxGetVar** and **VxSetVar**, provide the ability to preserve and retrieve data that is accessed from within callback procedures.

Widget Emulation   Visual Tcl does not support a native spin button widget. However, the Vx command **VxSpinButton** and its support Vx routines provide a good emulation.

Viewing the scripts over time, you will probably want to create your own widget convenience routines that support the Vx routines and can provide you with implementation strategies. The Vx commands are documented in Part IV, *Command Pages*.

Charm (SCO OpenServer)

Charm-specific resource options

    VtInfo -charm

will return a value of 1 if the display server is linked with the Charm library. A design goal of Visual Tcl was to reduce the need to write significant environment-specific scripts, making it so that one script would work in both character and graphical environments.

Visual Tcl supports the special-casing of Vt command options to refer to character-only environments. For instance, interpreting 10 pixels as 10 characters would produce undesirable effects, prefixing

```
-CHARM_rows 8
-MOTIF_rows 16
-CHARM_rightOffset 1
-rightOffset 10
```

Navigation and selection in character mode

The following keys are used in the Charm user interface for navigation and selection:

Arrow keys   Open hidden lists (for example, <down arrow> opens drop lists in combo boxes and in options menus), moves up, down, and between menus, moves between toggle buttons.

<Ctrl>R   Refreshes screen.

<Ctrl>A	Provides lead-in characters to mnemonic shortcut. This is provided because <Alt> is not normally detected on a character terminal.
<Esc>	Cancels dialogs and closes menus, canceling any selection.
<Enter>	Moves between input areas, accepts selection, activates buttons.
<F1>	Provides context-sensitive help.
<F2>	Generates a one-page help screen, listing the most commonly used keys in the Charm environment.
<F10>	Moves to the menu bar from the main body of the screen.
<Space>	Selects a check box or toggle button item, selects an item from multiple-select lists, and activates buttons.
<Tab>	Moves between input areas on the screen.

A development strategy

If you are developing an application to work in both worlds—character and graphical—experience has demonstrated that the best approach might be to perform your initial development using the character display server. Going from character to graphical environment presents fewer issues of adjusting offset values and so on, as compared to going from graphical to character environment.

Callbacks

✔ The `-callback` option

✔ The callback keyed list

✔ Maintaining dialog-specific persistent data across callbacks—**VxSetVar**, **VxGetVar**

✔ Preventing accidental callback execution—**VtLock**, **VtUnLock**

✔ Passing additional arguments to callback procedures

Callbacks tie functional code to user events. When a user clicks on a button widget, a procedure that has been registered as the button's callback is executed. A callback is typically registered during the creation of a widget.

```
VtPushButton $mainDialog.pushB \
        -label "Push Me!" \
        -callback SaySomethingCB
```

This example assigns the Tcl procedure SaySomethingCB as the callback for the .pushB push button widget. The procedure has been defined as follows:

```
proc SaySomethingCB {cbs} {
        echo I've been pushed!
}
```

All callback procedures receive at least one argument. Since SaySomethingCB was listed in the **VtPushButton** command as having no arguments, it will receive one argument. The minimum argument that it receives is a keyed list containing details returned by the display server about the event and the widget that was associated with the event. Borrowing from the Motif convention, this book will name the keyed list cbs.

The keys in the keyed list identify each piece of callback information. Their meanings are listed in Table 11–1.

Table 11–1   Callback argument keys

widget	The name of the widget in which the event occurred.
dialog	The name of the form dialog in which the widget resides.
value	A value corresponding to the contents or the state of the widget. The exact content and meaning of the data for this key depend on the widget, usually corresponding to the data in the field specified for the widget. For example, the value associated with a check box will contain a list of each toggle button that is currently selected. A list widget value will contain one or more currently selected list items.
mode	Contains a value indicating what caused the callback to activate. The potential values are listed in Table 11–2.

Only the keys widget and dialog are guaranteed to appear in all forms of the callback keyed list. For callbacks registered with the -callback option, mode and value are also provided.

Using the keyed list command **keylget**, we can extract information from each key in the cbs keyed list that was passed to SaySomethingCB.

```
proc SaySomethingCB {cbs} {
        echo I've been pushed!
        echo "dialog: [keylget cbs dialog]"
        echo "widget: [keylget cbs widget]"
        echo " value: [keylget cbs value]"
        echo "  mode: [keylget cbs mode]"
}
```

➡ dialog: .demo.mainForm_popup.mainForm.mainForm
    widget: .demo.mainForm_popup.mainForm.mainForm.pushB
     value: Push Me!
      mode: select

From these data, we can determine the name of the dialog in which the widget resides (i.e., its parent), the widget's name, the value of the label on the push button, and the mode describing how the event was detected by the widget (i.e., it was selected, or pushed).

Table 11–2   Possible mode key values

changed	The user interacted with the widget and moved focus away from it. This implicitly indicates that the user has finished interaction with the widget. This usually corresponds to a value change and loss of focus (for example, by tabbing or selecting another widget).

Table 11–2 Possible mode key values (cont.)

`done`	The user interacted with the widget and implicitly indicated that he or she had finished interaction. This usually corresponds to an <Enter> keypress.
`internalTraverse`	This applies only to **VtList** and **VtDrawnList**. It occurs when the user is traversing the list, using up or down arrow keys.
`select`	The user selected something from the widget. This usually corresponds to a <Space> keypress or a mouse button click.
`selectSame`	The user selected a value that is already selected. This usually corresponds to the user selecting a button that is already selected.

Learning callback information

Be sure to take advantage of the fact that it's so easy to dump the values of variables in a scripting language. The callback's keyed list is highly variable in its contents, depending on the widget. Putting in a simple statement like

echo value:[**keylget** cbs value]

will help you ramp up quickly on the characteristics of each widget callback.

Passing additional callback arguments

The -callback option accepts only one argument. In order to pass arguments to the procedure and still satisfy the -callback argument restriction, the procedure name and its arguments must be quoted.

```
...
-callback {SaySomethingCB Mark}
```

Let's redefine the callback procedure to accept an additional argument.

```
proc SaySomethingCB {name cbs}
     echo "Thanks for pushing me, $name"
}
```
➡ Thanks for pushing me, Mark

Sometimes you may want to pass the contents of a variable to a callback procedure. This would require using double quotes for quoting.

```
set name Mark
...
-callback "SaySomethingCB $name"
```

A variable that is passed to a callback procedure using variable substitution must exist at the time the widget creation command is evaluated. If the variable is not created, you'll receive a Tcl error. If you need access to a variable, it is best to access the variable using the **global** command from inside the callback procedure.

Using the dialog name

Using the callback keyed list widget key and its associated widget name value, you can find out more details about the affected widget using **VtGetValues**; you can make changes to its resources using **VtSetValues**.

It may not seem obvious at first, but there is also a number of things you can do with the dialog name associated with the dialog key.

Launching a new dialog

Probably the most common use of the keyed list dialog key is to use the dialog's name as a parent to children dialogs. For example, suppose your application's main window has a Close button for exiting the application. If you decide to put up a Question dialog that asks the omnipresent "Are you sure?" question, you must provide a parent widget to the dialog. The following example shows the callback procedure that is associated with the application's Close button.

```
proc CloseCallbackCB {cbs} {
    # retrieve that parent dialog's widget name
    set Dialog [keylget cbs dialog]
    set qDlog [VtQuestionDialog $Dialog.questionDlg\
        -message "Are you sure you want to exit?"
        -okCallback CloseApplicationCB \
        ]
    VtShow $qDlog
}
```

Notice that there's no call to **VtMainLoop** after the **VtShow** command. That's because *there's no need for more than one call to* **VtMainLoop** *in a Visual Tcl application.* When the callback procedure has completed, control falls back into the main loop, waiting for another event.

Removing the dialog

The OK button normally removes its parent dialog from the screen after it has completed the dialog's task. The Cancel button simply removes the dialog with no action taken. To do this for dialogs created with **VtFormDialog**, discussed later, the OK or Cancel callback procedure must destroy or hide the parent (for later reuse with **VtShowDialog**). The commands **VtDestroy** and **VtHide** accomplish this. Both require the name of the dialog which can be fetched from the callback's keyed list.

VtDestroy [**keylget** cbs dialog]

or

VtHide [**keylget** cbs dialog]

This same task may also be achieved with the **VtDestroyDialog** and **VtHideDialog** commands. Both commands require only the name of any child widget contained within the dialog. Each command uses the child widget to walk itself up the widget tree until it finds the parent dialog.

VtDestroyDialog [**keylget** cbs widget]

or

VtHideDialog [**keylget** cbs widget]

The Motif message dialogs and selection dialogs provide automatic destruction of the dialog when the OK or Cancel buttons are used.

Preventing multiple callbacks

When a user clicks on a push button that results in a new dialog, there is the chance that the user, out of habit, will double-click, resulting in two distinct callbacks and causing a dialog to try to build itself twice. There are two approaches to preventing the likelihood of situations like this.

-autoLock *listOfProcedureNames*

When you create a widget with a callback, you can pass it the -autoLock option, specifying the name of the callback procedure. This instructs the display server to stop user input until the lock is removed by an explicit call to the **VtUnLock** command.

VtLock

VtLock is a command that has the same effect as -autoLock. Both approaches cause the cursor to change to a watch cursor, denying user input. **VtUnLock** also unlocks this state.

Saving persistent data

Callback procedures often require the ability to access widgets located elsewhere in the current dialog. For instance, if a user selects the OK button in the dialog's action area, the callback for the OK button may be responsible for carrying out the dialog's functionality, such as adding a user. The command that performs the UNIX-level task of adding a user may have already been constructed during the series of callback actions as the user modified the values displayed by individual widgets in the control area of the dialog. How does the OK callback procedure locate the command (or build it, if it hasn't yet been constructed)?

The Vx commands **VxSetVar** and **VxGetVar** store persistent data by associating them with a specific dialog. The command format for creating a persistent variable is:

VxSetVar *dialogName variableName value*

This command takes a variable and its contents and stores them with the name of the dialog. Arrays are supported, as are scalar variables. To retrieve the data, you provide the dialog's name and the name of the variable. The dialog's name, of course, is available from the `dialog` key in the callback's keyed list.

VxGetVar *dialogName variableName*

These Vx commands provide an attractive alternative to using global variables, since the potential for naming conflicts is limited to the scope of the dialog and not to the entire application name space.

In the following example, let's assume that the user is in a dialog that loads a file into an editor. The user selects the toggle button for "read only" mode, choosing to browse the file when the editor starts. The toggle button's callback procedure executes the following script fragment.

```
set dialog [keylget cbs dialog]
set readOnlyMode [keylget cbs value]
VxSetVar $dialog readOnlyMode $readOnlyMode
```

Now the data associated with the variable name `readOnlyMode` are stored with the parent (i.e., the dialog) of the toggle button. Since a toggle button is Boolean, the value it sends to the callback is either 1 or 0.

The user selects the OK button in order to begin the loading of the file and the start of the editor. The OK button's callback procedure uses **VxGetVar** to locate the variable, set earlier by the toggle button callback.

```
proc LoadFileOKButtonCB {cbs} {
    set dialog [keylget cbs dialog]
    set readMode [VxGetVar $dialog readOnlyMode]
    if {$readMode == 1} {
        # load file as read-only
        ...
}
```

VxSetVar and **VxGetVar** are particularly useful for storing the names of widgets in other dialogs, such as a label widget used for a status bar, giving child dialogs the ability to update widgets elsewhere in the application.

Accessing Resources

✔ Updating resources with **VtSetValues**
✔ Retrieving resource values with **VtGetValues**
✔ The Object class

*R*esources are the public interface provided by widgets for reading or modifying look and feel. **VtSetValues** and **VtGetValues** give your application the level of control you need to build a dynamic, highly integrated graphical application.

The Object class is inherited by all Visual Tcl widgets. Its resources range from font and color management to context-sensitive help support.

Setting resources

There are three ways to specify a widget resource. Most often resources are set according to default resource values that are used when a widget is created. For example, the foreground color for a label widget is set according to the default foreground color specified in the app-defaults X resource file, Vtcl. The advantage of allowing resources to be set this way is that your application will look and feel more like other Motif applications that are sharing the same resource files. For example, the same font will be used for different labels in push buttons.

Individual widget resources can also be explicitly set during creation with Vt command options.

```
VtToggleButton $mainDialog.togB -label "Symbolic"
```

In this script, the toggle button creation command sets the label resource in a toggle button to display the string "Symbolic".

The third way to set a widget's resource is with the **VtSetValues** command. **VtSetValues** provides the ability to perform dynamic changes to resources of existing widgets, often in response to changing conditions or user actions.

```
VtSetValues $mainDialog.togB -label "Numeric"
```

Here we have changed the toggle button's label.

Getting resources

Widgets can be examined for the values of their resources. Although values are often provided as part of a callback event, often you may need to retrieve a value from another widget, unrelated to the event, in order to collect all the information you need to carry out a task.

Figure 12–1   Simple file creation dialog

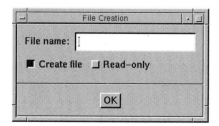

The following example is a callback procedure for an OK button. Viewing Figure 12–1, the user will probably select the OK button, thinking the task complete. Making sure that all the data required for the task have been provided by the user, ProcessUserInfoCB uses **VtGetValues** to retrieve the current value in a text field widget. In this example, the program requires that the user enter a file name into the text field.

```
proc ProcessOKCB {cbs} {
        set name [VtGetValues $mainDialog.nameText -value]

        # remove any inadvertent spaces
        set name [string trim $name]

        if {[clength $name] == 0} {
           ShowError "You forgot to enter a file name!"
        }
        ...
}
```

Not all resources can be set or retrieved. The options listed with each option class and Vt command in *Command Pages* at the back of the book provide information regarding supported access to Visual Tcl widget resources.

The Object class

The Object class is the most generic collection of resources, representing options that are supported by virtually all Visual Tcl widgets.

Overriding widget name uniqueness

```
-allowDuplicateName
```

By default, all widget names must be unique. Let's take the example of a situation where you may not want the display server to scrutinize for unique widget names. Suppose you want to print a list of names as labels in a form.

```
foreach name {Alan Betty Charlie Diane} {
        VtLabel $mainDialog.label \
            -allowDuplicateName \
            -label $name
}
```

The option -allowDuplicateName instructs the display server to refrain from requiring a unique widget name. Our goal with the example above was simply to display a list of names represented with label widgets. Had we needed to refer to these widget names from elsewhere in our code, then we would have had to generate unique names in order to prevent an error resulting from using an ambiguous name.

Managing color

```
-background string
-foreground string
```

In order to promote the portability of your scripts, Visual Tcl supports a predefined set of symbolic names that index the actual color resources listed in the app-defaults Vtcl resource file.

Table 12–1   Symbolic color names

```
urgentColor
highlightColor
foregroundColor
backgroundColor
altBackgroundColor
```

To override the colors in `./app-defaults/vtcl`, you can redefine these resources in your home directory's `.Xdefaults` file. You can also add your own symbolic color name to an X resource file, then refer to it using one of these two color resource options.

In your `.Xdefaults` file:

```
*dramaticColor:        red
```

Then, after restarting the display server in order to update its resource database, you can access `dramaticColor` from your script.

```
VtLabel $mainDialog.warningLabel \
        -label "You've entered an illegal value" \
        -foreground dramaticColor
```

Managing fonts

```
-font string
```

As with colors, Visual Tcl supports a predefined set of symbolic font names that index the real font name listed in the `app-defaults/vtcl` resource file. If your script contained direct references to the actual font names, the script would terminate on any system that might not support that font.

Table 12–2   Symbolic font names

smallPlainFont	medPlainFont	largePlainFont	monoNormalFont
smallBoldFont	medBoldFont	largeBoldFont	monoBoldFont
smallItalicFont	medItalicFont	largeItalicFont	monoItalicFont

To create your own symbol name, you can simply add the name and its associated font name to your X resource file. For instance,

```
*myFont   -misc-fixed-bold-r-normal--0-0-75-75-c-0-iso8859-1
```

Remember to kill and restart the display engine in order for `myFont` to become an available resource.

Widget dimensions

```
-height integer
-width integer
```

A widget's dimensions can be "hard-coded" with the options -height and -width. For fine tuning the placement of your dialog layout, you can also retrieve these resources with **VtGetValues** in order to determine the current dimensions of a widget, in pixels. For each widget that you are interested in sizing, be sure to verify whether there is another option already provided for dictating dimension, such as the number of rows in a list widget in order to state the required height.

Widget availability and sensitivity

```
-hidden boolean
```

The -hidden option gives you the ability to delay the rendering of a widget until you instruct the display server to render it. Perhaps you want to create a label widget that doesn't appear on the interface of a dialog until a task is completed or the user performs some action.

When you are ready to make the widget visible, you can use **VtShow**.

```
-sensitive boolean
```

Depending on an existing condition, such as user access permissions, you may want to make a widget insensitive. In this state, a widget does not accept user events, although it can be seen by the user.

Figure 12–2   Using insensitivity to prevent widget access

Figure 12–2 illustrates the use of -sensitive to indicate the authorizations available to a user. In this case, the user can choose the privilege to backup files, but not to restore them.

The sensitivity resource has a distinct advantage over hiding widgets altogether. First, screenshots in help manuals are consistent with what the user sees on the screen (i.e., now "missing" widgets). Secondly, it's a good thing to show all the available options so that a user can see that they may log into the system with another userID.

Short help

```
-shortHelpCallback cmd
-shortHelpString string
```

The use of short help has been popularized by applications like Microsoft Word, which display a short explanation of the object on which the mouse cursor currently rests. These kinds of messages are particularly useful in an interface that is cluttered with numerous buttons and pulldown menus.

```
VtPushButton $mainDialog.pushB \
        -pixmap /lib/pixmaps/sort.px \
        -shortHelpCallback PostShortHelp \
        -shortHelpString "Sort user list alphabetically"
```

The effect of -shortHelpString is to associate its string argument with a key, helpString, that will be included in the callback procedure's keyed list argument.

```
proc PostShortHelp {cbs} {
        global shortHelpLabel
        set message [keylget cbs helpString]
        VtSetValues $shortHelpLabel -label $message
}
```

Storing data inside widgets

```
-userData string
```

A large application can get cluttered with global variables containing state information about each widget. Visual Tcl widgets provide the ability to store information "inside" each widget. For example, suppose you want to know whether the user has selected a push button at least once before. The following example assumes that the push button's widget name is stored in the variable taskPushB:

```
VtSetValues $mainDialog.taskPushB \
        -userData "PreviouslyPushed:True"
```

This information remains through the lifetime of the widget, accessible any time throughout your application. The information you store can be in any string format that you choose. In the example above, **VtGetValues** can be used at a later date to retrieve the information, parse it, and make a determination.

Access to Motif resources

```
-xmArgs list_of_string_pairs
```

Visual Tcl provides a way to get access to Motif resources when there is no support provided by a Visual Tcl option. This option, however, should be used sparingly, especially if you anticipate the porting of your application to the Windows environment.

Future versions of Visual Tcl will support non-Motif environments, such as MS Windows, where the -xmArgs option will have no effect. But, if you're in a pinch, -xmArgs may meet your needs.

Motif resources start with the characters XmN, as in XmNbackground. -xmArgs will assume XmN if you specify the resource without these leading characters in your argument. Either of the two versions below will work.

```
. . .
-xmArgs "background red foreground green"
. . .
-xmArgs "XmNbackground red XmNforeground green"
```

Use of -xmArgs is shown in the chapter *Geometry Management*.

Miscellaneous object class resources

F1 key for context-sensitive help (SCO only)

`-helpCallback cmd`

Your script can define a callback procedure, cmd, that is invoked when the user presses the keyboard <F1> function key. Among the callback information that is returned is the name of the widget that the mouse cursor was currently overlapping. This provides a powerful mechanism for building your own context-sensitive house.

You have the options of specifying a callback procedure that is specific to the particular widget or specifying a generic callback, shared by all your widgets, that simply checks the keyed list to determine which widget was involved at the time the <F1> key was pressed.

This feature is supported on SCO OpenServer systems only.

Accessing relative widget and font size information

`-baseLineList`

This resource is used to retrieve the distance, in pixels, from the top of a widget to the bottom of the font that it may use. This may be useful in calculating changes you might want to make to the height of a widget.

Figure 12–3   Toggle button with border width of 2 pixels

Setting border size

```
-borderWidth integer
```

This option sets the border width, in pixels, around a widget. By default, a widget's border has a width of 0, making it invisible. A border width of two pixels was placed around the toggle button in Figure 12–3.

Global error callback

```
-errorCallback cmd
```

This resource can be set to invoke a command or procedure in the event of an error that occurs inside a widget's callback. This takes effect on any errors that occur inside the callbacks of widgets that haven't set this resource. Typically, an -errorCallback is defined for an entire script using the **VtSetAppValues** command.

```
set appName [VtOpen demo]
VtSetAppValues $appName \
    -errorCallback HandleErrorsCB
```

The procedure HandleErrorsCB can access a key called results in its callback keyed list argument.

Preventing user input

```
-autoLock list_of_callback_procedure_names
```

It is possible for a user to accidentally double-click on a button that brings up another form and get two resulting forms. There are also times when a form needs time to perform calculations before it decides to make certain widgets insensitive. To control these situations, Visual Tcl supports the ability to lock the display server from accepting any more input until it is explicitly unlocked.

```
VtPushButton $displayTaskFormPushB \
    -label "Admin chores..." \
    -callback DisplayTaskDialogCB \
    -auto_lock DisplayTaskDialogCB
```

The example above instructs the display server to stop processing user input until instructed to resume. Inside the callback DisplayTaskDialog, a call to **VtUnLock** unlocks the display server. Any user input during the locked period is thrown away.

```
proc DisplayTaskDialogCB {cbs} {
    ...
    VtUnLock
}
```

Geometry Management

✔ The row-column widget—**VtRowColumn**

✔ The form widget—**VtForm**

✔ The frame widget—**VtFrame**

✔ The Geometry class

✔ The Form class

Geometry management addresses the widgets that are arranged in a dialog window and the behavior they exhibit in the event that the user chooses to resize the window. Inherited from its Motif roots, Visual Tcl supports two widgets, called *geometry managers*, for managing widget layout.

A geometry manager is just like any other widget, except that it performs a role "behind the scenes" in support of children widgets. A manager widget manages its children by controlling their size and position. Different geometry managers use different techniques and strategies for controlling widgets. Once you understand the geometry requirements for your design, choose the manager that best achieves your design needs.

Using color to "see" manager widgets

Working with Motif geometry management can be quite tricky at times, depending on the complexity of your widget layout needs. By setting the background color of the manager that you use, you will be able to visually see a portion of its behavior. This becomes particularly useful when you are using geometry managers in a nested fashion, such as a form in a form.

Using color to "see" manager widgets (cont.)

```
VtForm $mainDialog.form \
   -background highlightColor
```

or

```
VtForm $mainDialog form \
   -xmArgs "background green"
```

Since this is used for debugging purposes, you'll want to be sure to remove this code when you are finished.

How widgets plug into managers

A widget can be arranged in a geometry manager by creating the widget as a child of the manager widget.

```
set rowColumn [VtRowColumn $mainDialog.rowColumn \
      . . .
]
. . .
VtLabel $rowColumn.label \
      . . . .
```

This code fragment demonstrates how to use widget naming to cause the label widget to be inherited by the row-column widget. The label widget is now under the control of the row-column geometry manager widget.

Row column for convenience

Created with the **VtRowColumn** command, the row-column widget is usually used to organize child widgets along rows and columns. It is already used, transparent to the programmer, by many other widgets, such as menu bars, pulldown menus, radio boxes, and option menus. Within the row-column widget, there are three types of *packing* behaviors from which to choose.

- NONE
- TIGHT
- COLUMN

    Compared with form-based geometry management, it is probably easier to use row-column management. A trade-off is made by the effects that row-column widgets have on their managed widgets. If you are dealing with simple design that requires a regular pattern of widget arrangement, row-column management is the way to go.

Column packing for spreadsheet-style placement

Setting the -packing option to COLUMN will turn the row-column widget into a spreadsheetlike manager, providing simple widget placement at the expense of a lack of per-widget control.

Figure 13–1   Effects of different single-column row-column orientations

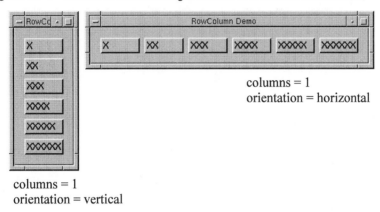

columns = 1
orientation = horizontal

columns = 1
orientation = vertical

Within the COLUMN behavior, there are resources that instruct the row-column widget with respect to orientation and the number of columns to use. The default – vertical orientation results in column-major behavior where managed widgets, such as the push buttons in the two example figures (Figure 13–1 and Figure 13–2) are laid out, starting at the top of the column.

Figure 13–2   Orientation effect on multi-column row-column managers

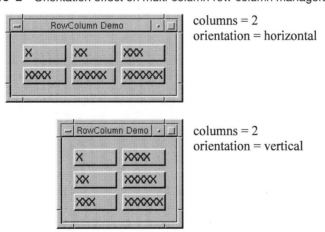

columns = 2
orientation = horizontal

columns = 2
orientation = vertical

In the case of multiple columns, specified with the −numColumns option, the
row-column manager calculates the number of rows it needs to fill out the number of
requested columns. If there are eight widgets to manage in a vertical orientation and four
columns are requested, the row-column manager will create two rows by four columns. In
a horizontal orientation, the configuration will be four rows by two columns.

Figure 13–3   Row-column widget with heterogeneous managed widgets

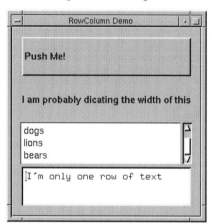

A major side effect of COLUMN behavior is that all managed widgets must conform
to the size of the largest widget. Figure 13–3 illustrates the effect on widgets of different
types.

Data entry dialogs are commonly used by an application to gather text-based
information from its user. A simple data entry dialog pairs off two types of widgets: a
label and an associated text field. Let's build one with **VtRowColumn**.

In order to produce the effect we want of labels preceding text fields, the easiest
approach is to set the row-column orientation to horizontal. Then, in our script, we can
alternate label, column, label, column, and so on.

The following script builds four rows for labeled text fields, using the names in
labelList to build them. The number of columns (from a horizontal perspective) is
calculated, based on the number of labels to be used.

```
set labelList {Name: Address: Phone: E-mail:}
...
set rowColW [VtRowColumn $mainForm.rowColW \
        -horizontal \
        -rightSide FORM \
        -bottomSide FORM \
        -numColumns [llength $labelList] \
        -packing COLUMN \
        ]
```

Now that our row column widget is created and configured, we use a loop command to process each label.

```
foreach label $labelList {
    VtLabel $rowColW.$label \
        -label $label \
        -labelRight
    VtText $rowColW.text${label} \
        -rows 1
}
```

The result of this code fragment is shown in Figure 13–4. Using a label alignment resource, -labelRight, we've made each label right-justified in order to associate each one next to its respective text field. Note that we're constructing the text field handle by concatenating text with the current label's name. Therefore, the first widget's name would be

```
$rowColW.textName:
```

Figure 13–4   Data entry dialog built with **VtRowColumn**

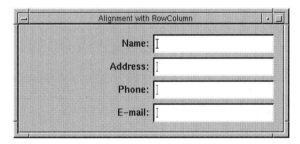

Once again, the side effect of keeping widgets to a uniform size is reflected in the resulting dialog. Using form-based management, described below, we'll revisit this example and see how we can eliminate all of the wasted space to the left of the labels.

NONE packing for *x-y* placement

Although Visual Tcl does not support the bulletin board manager widget, it can be emulated using packing set to NONE. When packing is set to NONE, the row-column widget turns packing off, requiring that the widget location be specified using x-y coordinates.

Figure 13–5 below uses NONE packing to simulate an x-y coordinate graph. This script fragment is used to build an example

```
set rowColW [VtRowColumn $form.rowcol \
    -packing NONE \
    ]
```

```
set lociList \
    {0,0 10,20 10,80 20,40 80,80 0,120 120,0 120,120}

foreach locus $lociList {
        # extract the individual x and y values
        scan $locus "%d,%d" x y

        VtLabel $rowColW.$locus \
            -font smallPlainFont \
            -label "($locus)" \
            -xmArgs "x $x y $y"
}
```

Figure 13–5   Row-column widget with NONE packing

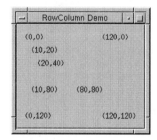

This script makes use of -xmArgs in order to set the XmNx and XmNy resources for placing the labels. The next release of Visual Tcl will support additional options for x-y placement, eliminating the need for using -xmArgs.

TIGHT packing for retaining widget size

In an earlier example, we demonstrated the awkward combination of managing heterogeneous widgets inside a row-column widget supporting COLUMN behavior. Taking that same example and specifying TIGHT packing generates a more reasonable effect, shown in Figure 13–6.

Forms for relative placement

The form manager widget supports the placement strategy of placing widgets relative to each other and to the form itself. Relative to the row-column manager widget, this approach provides the programmer with a greater deal of control over the behavior and placement of individual widgets. Widget A can be aligned so that its top is aligned with the bottom of Widget B. Widget C can be "attached" to the bottom of the form so that when the window is stretched, the widget stretches, too.

Relative placement is achieved via *attachments*, describing how one widget relates to another widget or the form. The options that support attachment resources are members of the *geometry class*, listed later in this chapter.

Figure 13–6   Improved effect of TIGHT packing

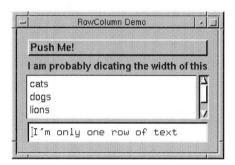

VtForm and VtFormDialog

There are two widgets that provide form manager functions. **VtForm** is a form widget that can be placed inside other forms or dialogs. **VtFormDialog** is actually a composite widget that supports additional features, such as built-in OK, Cancel, Apply, and Help buttons, in addition to providing form manager services. **VtFormDialog** will be discussed at length in Chapter 14, *Dialogs*.

Types of attachments

There are four kinds of attachments, represented by the following four resource values.

NONE	No attachment at all.
FORM	An attachment to the edge of the immediate parent form.
widget	An attachment to another widget, specified by its name.
integer	An imaginary line, some percentage of the distance across a form. Keep this in mind when we discuss -fractionBase, below.

In the script fragment below, the form options translate as "attach my right side to the form" and "attach my top side to the widget" (named in $anotherLabel).

```
VtLabel $mainDialog.label \
        -rightSide FORM \
        -topSide $anotherLabel
```

Attachments to FORM

When you place the first widget in a form, it is attached by default to the top and left side of the parent form, reflecting the options

```
-topSide FORM
-leftSide FORM
```

The other sides of the widget are set to NONE. Each subsequent widget that is added to the form receives the default options of

```
-topSide <name of previous widget>
-leftSide FORM
```

The result is that you have a vertical column of vertically attached widgets, anchored to the left side of the form. Expanding the size of the window will show no change in widget size or placement.

A push button with a pixmap label (dialog A, Figure 13–7) has been added to the form by simply using the default values for attachment. The form has been created with a height and width of 150 pixels. The default attachment values are shown in parentheses. Since they are defaults, you don't need to specify them in your script. When you expand the window containing the form, the managed widget shows no change.

In the same figure, dialog B shows the result of attaching the right side of the same push-button widget to FORM. The attachments may have been made during the creation of the push button or later, using **VtSetValues**.

VtSetValues $form.pushB -rightSide FORM.

No matter how it was achieved, the net effect of the new attachment is that the button is stretched across the form. Enlarging the window with the mouse would only cause the button to stretch even further.

Figure 13–7   Positioning a push button relative to a form

Dialog A

(-topSide FORM)
(-leftSide FORM)

Dialog B

(-topSide FORM)
(-leftSide FORM)
-rightSide FORM

In Figure 13–8, we have removed some of the attachments with the NONE resource value. The button in dialog C, having been detached from the left side, assumes its natural dimensions at the right side of the form. Expanding the size of the window causes the push button to move along with the right side.

In dialog D, the default attachments are completely removed. The addition of an attachment to the bottom of the form causes it to move the bottom right portion of the form.

Figure 13–8   Effects of removing attachments

Dialog C

(-topSide FORM)
-leftSide NONE
-rightSide FORM

Dialog D

-topSide NONE
-leftSide NONE
-rightSide FORM
-bottomSide FORM

When attachments aren't working right

Motif attachment is not the easiest concept to work with, an opportunity not unrecognized by the large community of interactive design tool makers. As suggested earlier, temporarily changing the color of the geometry manager may assist your efforts. Usually, however, the problem is that you have forgotten about the default attachments provided by Visual Tcl. If you're not sure about the default behavior, you can also do the following before adding attachments.

```
VtSetValues $form.widget \
   -leftSide NONE \
   -rightSide NONE \
   -topSide NONE \
   -bottomSide NONE
```

Widget-to-widget attachment and alignment

To put two widgets side by side, you usually specify the relative attachment in the second widget created.

```
VtPushButton $form.surfPushB \
    . . .

VtPushButton $form.wizardPushB \
    -leftSide $form.surfPushB \
    . . .
```

The problem here is that the attachment specification isn't complete. All we have done is to place the second widget, .wizardPushB, so that surfPushB is to the left side. In order to get the desired effect, we need to indicate that it also should align with the top of the other widget.

```
VtPushButton $form.surfPushB \
    . . .

VtPushButton $form.wizardPushB \
    -leftSide $form.surfPushB \
    -alignTop $form.surfPushB
```

You can also work with the combination of setting attachments at widget-creation time and modifying them with **VtSetValues** later. For example, suppose that in our working example we want the buttons next to each other, but if the window is enlarged, we want the right button to move with the right side of the form, leaving the left button in its current position.

```
VtSetValues $form.wizardPushB \
    -leftSide NONE \
    -rightSide FORM
```

This command separated the two sides of the widgets, freeing wizardPushB to move with the movement of the right side of the form, without getting stretched between the left push button and the form in the process.

Forms in forms

Figure 13–9   Data entry form created with **VxAlignedForm**

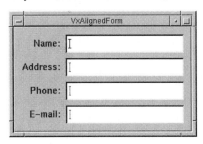

Sometimes, in order to get the layout effect that you need, you will want to put forms inside other forms. There is really no limit to this flexible strategy. If you recall, we built a data-entry dialog with a row column widget in Figure 13–4. The problem was that because row column packing, when set to COLUMN, makes all the widgets the same width, there was a lot of clear area to the left of the right-aligned labels.

VxAlignedForm is an example of a command that applies nested forms to solve a problem. Applying this command to the same data-entry dialog generates the dialog in Figure 13–9, with the leading clear area removed. The sketch of forms and their attachments in Figure 13–10 shows the relationship of widgets and form widgets used to construct the improved data-entry dialog.

Figure 13–10   Outline of forms, widgets, and attachments

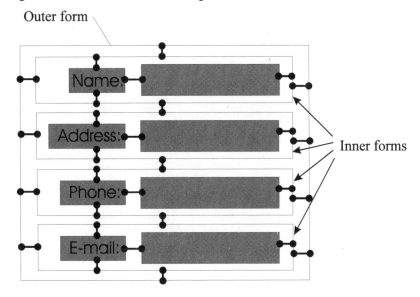

Each label-text widget pairing (both shown in gray) is placed in its own form, where attachments are made relative to that form. Attempts to define attachments that refer to objects outside of the immediate parent form will generate errors.

Frame widget for appearances

Although it is also a manager widget, the frame widget is a purely cosmetic member of the manager family, providing the familiar Motif chiseled look around other widgets. The frame can also provide a title for the framed object. The frame widget is classified as a manager because it manages the child widget that it contains by wrapping itself around the child. The frame can host only a single managed widget. Therefore, in order to frame multiple widgets, it is usually another manager widget that is placed inside a frame.

```
set frameW [VtFrame $mainDialog.frameW \
        -shadowType ETCHED_OUT \
        -title "Choices" ]
set rbox [VtCheckBox $frameW.rbox ]
VtToggleButton $rbox.tog1 -label "Shutdown Computer"
VtToggleButton $rbox.tog2 -label "Restart Computer"
```

Figure 13–11   A framed radio box using ETCHED_OUT

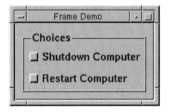

The supported resource values for etch types are:

IN	presents the managed widget on a sunken surface
OUT	presents the managed widget on a raised surface
ETCHED_OUT	puts a raised border around the managed widget
ETCHED_IN	puts a sunken border around the managed widget

An attachment rule: *never attach outside a parent*

In a complex dialog, it may be tempting to attach a widget to another widget that is contained by another parent. This will always result in an error. For example, suppose you have two frames, each containing complex form managers. In order to position objects relative to one another between the two frames, you can perform only frame-to-frame attachment.

> ## An attachment rule: *never attach outside a parent* (cont.)
>
> When you specify an attachment option such as
>
> ```
> -rightSide FORM
> ```
>
> Visual Tcl expects that the form you are referring to is the immediate parent form. A widget cannot specify another form unless the form is simply another widget that shares the same parent.

Geometry class

The Geometry class supports all widgets that are children of form widgets created by **VtForm** and **VtFormDialog**. Many of the options in this class have been discussed in detail earlier in this chapter.

```
-above widgetName
-below widgetName
```

These two options read "put me above" and "put me below" the referenced widget.

```
-alignBottom widgetName
-alignLeft widgetName
-alignRight widgetName
-alignTop widgetName
```

Widgets that place themselves relative to the top, bottom, left, and right of other widgets are using the target widget's edges for reference.

```
-bottomSide widgetName |FORM | distance | NONE
-leftSide widgetName | FORM | distance | NONE
-rightSide widgetName | FORM | distance | NONE
-topSide widgetName | FORM | distance | NONE
```

These resource options have been previously addressed. distance represents a percentage of the form width and height. For example, -leftSide 10 would indicate that the left side of a widget is to be 10% away from the left side of the form. Illustrated in Figure 13–12, the following three labels were placed using percentage values.

```
VtLabel $mainDialog.label25 -label 25% -leftSide 25
VtLabel $mainDialog.label50 -label 50% -leftSide 50
VtLabel $mainDialog.label75 -label 75% -leftSide 75
```

Figure 13–12   Effect of percentage-based placement

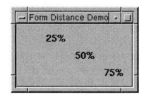

```
-bottomOffset integer
-leftOffset integer
-rightOffset integer
-topOffset integer
```

Offsets indicate in pixels how much distance is to be placed between a widget and its relative widget or form edge. To place widgets closely together, specify an integer value of 0. This is a common practice when placing a label widget acting as a title above another widget.

Form class

The form class addresses resources that affect how forms treat all of its children widgets.

```
-horizontalSpacing integer
-verticalSpacing integer
```

Spacing resources set the pixel distance between objects in a form. The default for horizontal is 5 pixels; vertical is 10 pixels.

```
-marginHeight integer
-marginWidth integer
```

-marginHeight refers to the distance between managed children and the edge of the form—10 pixels is the default distance in both height and width. If you want managed widgets to butt up against the edge of the form by default, set these option resources to 0.

```
-resizable boolean
```

By default, if you add a large widget to a form, the form will resize to accommodate the dimensions of the widget, if necessary. This behavior can be rather irritating if you are, for instance, constantly updating a label widget with variable-length strings. Setting the form's resizable resource to 0 will direct it to avoid resizing when its children change dimensions.

Dialogs

✔ The main window—**VtFormDialog**

✔ Motif dialogs—**VtInformationDialog**, **VtErrorDialog**,
   VtMessageDialog, **VtQuestionDialog**, **VtWarningDialog**,
   VtWorkingDialog

✔ Controlling the Motif window manager

✔ The Dialog class

A main window is a dialog that acts as an instrument panel—coordinating, organizing, informing, and presenting to the user the tasks supported by your application. Dialog formats range from simple Message dialogs with OK, Cancel, and Help buttons at the bottom of the window to full-blown main windows with a menu bar of pulldown menus. The dialog you choose is reflective of the nature of your application. If you are writing a simple configuration front-end, it *may* be that you choose to build a simple, custom dialog with a few buttons and text fields, and action buttons (OK, Cancel, and Help) at the bottom. If, on the other hand, you are building a full system administration application, such as a printer account manager, then you are probably going to want to incorporate a complete Main dialog with pulldown menus for organizing lots of functionality.

Visual Tcl supports the ability to create custom dialogs from scratch, as well as to choose from precanned Message dialogs that are designed to perform singular tasks, such as requesting confirmation or warning about an error situation.

Building dialogs with `VtFormDialog`

You have probably noticed by now that most of the GUI examples in this book make use of the command **VtFormDialog** to create the main window. The main window is the dialog that serves as the home base from which the user navigates through the rest of your application. **VtFormDialog** was designed to support two of the most common dialog configurations: main windows and custom dialogs containing familiar OK, Cancel, and Help buttons at their base. For full-function applications, menu bars are added to a main window using the **VtMenuBar** command. Secondary dialogs are launched from the main window, presenting discrete, well-defined tasks.

Figure 14–1   Visual Tcl dialogs

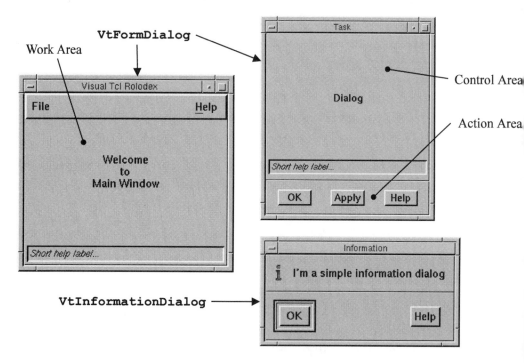

A main window is dominated by the large work area where a master list widget might be used to display all of the available printers in a printer management application. The work area is actually a form widget. In essence, **VtFormDialog** is very much like **VtForm**, with the exception that it throws in lots of added features, such as standard action buttons and window manager controls, discussed below.

A standard dialog, on the other hand, has two areas. The *control area* is populated with buttons, toggles, lists, and other widgets that present the user with choices and state information supporting the task at hand. The user reviews the control area, making modifications where necessary, in order to set up the criteria for carrying out the dialog's stated task. One of the control area's widgets might provide a selection list of devices to which to attach a new printer. Selecting the OK button in the action area instructs the application that the user has completed setting and reviewing the conditions, and it's time to carry out the task.

Displaying an action area

By default, **VtFormDialog** creates a form-based window with no action area where OK, Cancel, Apply, Reset, and Help buttons might be located. They are automatically added when you specify options such as -ok or -help. These and other related options are members of the Dialog class, discussed below. The following script fragment illustrates how to instruct **VtFormDialog** to create a custom dialog with an action area, like the one in Figure 14–1.

```
set mainDialog [VtFormDialog.mainForm \
      -title "Task" \
      -ok \
      -okCallback MakeTaskHappenCB \
      -help \
      -helpCallback DisplayHelp \
      ]
```

-ok and -help indicate that only the OK and Help buttons should be displayed. Their labels can be changed using -okLabel.

```
-okLabel "Close"
```

The form work area

VtFormDialog supports a form-based work area for widget placement that can be treated as though you are dealing with the **VtForm** command. When attaching widgets to the bottom of the form, you simply use

```
-bottomSide FORM
```

just like you would inside any form. There's no need to worry about the buttons in the action area, if you specified that they be added. All of the inner geometry of the action area is hidden from your application.

Retrieving button names

There may be occasions when you need access to the built-in buttons of the **VtFormDialog** action area. For instance, you may wish to remove sensitivity from the OK button. To do this, you need the widget name of the OK button, which is known only by the dialog. Using the same options that instruct **VtFormDialog** to build the buttons, you can retrieve their widget names.

```
set Okbutton [VtGetValues $formDialog -ok]
VtSetSensitive $Okbutton FALSE
```

Linking the <Esc> key to dialog buttons

Using -cancelButton in **VtFormDialog** only, you can link the callback of a dialog push button to the <Esc> key. Typically, the <Esc> key is linked to the Cancel button where it's assumed that the user doesn't want to perform the task and wants the dialog simply to go away. To specify which button to link the <Esc> key to, you pass the button's token. If you link it to your own widget, specify the widget name.

-cancelButton OK | APPLY | RESET | CANCEL | HELP | *widgetName*

Motif message dialogs

Message dialogs are pop-up dialogs that typically serve a very specific task (Are you sure? Is this OK? Danger, you're about to lose everything!). The task is very simple and often very important. The pop-up has its own window and, therefore, appears on top of or outside the main window, making it clear to the user that this is something that requires attention, even if it's only an informative "I just performed an automatic save of your work."

Visual Tcl supports six commands for creating Motif dialog boxes.

- **VtInformationDialog**
- **VtErrorDialog**
- **VtMessageDialog**
- **VtQuestionDialog**
- **VtWarningDialog**
- **VtWorkingDialog**

Because you don't design these from scratch, your application is guaranteed to appear consistent with the message dialogs of other Motif applications that also take advantage of dialog boxes. Instead of providing a form-based work area, each message dialog combines a label widget message following its own built-in distinctive pixmap that indicates the nature of the dialog. The only exception to this is the generic Message dialog that displays no pixmap. All six Message dialog boxes support the same

-message *messageString*

option to indicate the message that is to be displayed. Left-justified alignment is supported, making it convenient to use embedded newlines in your message string (see Figure 14–2 for an example using an embedded newline).

By default, Motif dialogs display the OK, Cancel, and Help buttons unless the command is called with at least one button-specific option. Then you must specify each button that you want. Pressing OK and Cancel automatically makes the dialog go away.

```
-autoDestroy boolean
-autoHide boolean
```

These two options, members of the dialog class, control this behavior and are described below.

Intercepting the window manager Close button

It's a rude thing when an application is closed by using the window manager Close button from the window Menu Button (see Figure 14–3, page 205), rather than by using the Exit or OK buttons you've assigned for such occasions. Because your application wasn't prepared, data may have been left in an inconsistent state or simply lost. You can prevent this situation by using -wmCloseCallback to attach a callback that keeps control of the exiting process.

In a simple main dialog, you may simply choose to specify the same callback for handling the user's intent to close the application.

```
VtFormDialog $app.mainDialog \
    ...
    -okCallback CloseCB \
    -wmCloseCallback CloseCB
```

From your CloseCB callback, you can use one of the standard Motif dialogs to post remaining outstanding issues that the user should know about.

Figure 14–2   **VtQuestionDialog** with Cancel button relabeled to "Discard"

The question in Figure 14–2 was posted with the following script fragment.

```
VtShow [VtQuestionDialog $mainForm.closeQuestion \
    -ok \
    -okCallback SaveDataCB \
    -cancelLabel Discard \
```

```
-cancelCallback ShutdownCB \
-help \
-message \
  "Would you like to save your data\nbefore \
      exiting?"]
```

Recycle dialogs with VtHide and VtShow

In the event that you are building a time-intensive custom dialog that may be posted more than once during the lifetime of your application, you can recycle your dialog with the combination of **VtShow** and **VtHide** (also known as **VtShowDialog** and **VtHideDialog**).

VtShow tells the display server to render a dialog or other graphical object. **VtHide** does the opposite. Rather than destroy the dialog with **VtDestroyDialog**, use **VtHide** to simply remove the dialog from view; before it is required again, use **VtSetValues** to clear old values and reset the dialog's control area to the proper values.

The dialog class

The dialog class provides options for **VtFormDialog**, **VtSelectionDialog**, and **VtFileSelectionDialog**. Keep in mind that the descriptions of the behavior of all of the options supporting the standard action area buttons of the dialog commands are described by the *Motif Style Guide*. You have the ability to make them do just about anything, but that might lead to some very unpleasant surprises for your application's users.

Dialog buttons

```
-apply
-applyCallback cmd
-applyLabel string
```

These options support the Apply button (selected by the user to make an action take place), but leave the current dialog in focus. Used with **VtGetValues**, -apply can be used to retrieve the widget name of the **VtFormDialog**'s Apply button.

```
-cancel
-cancelCallback cmd
-cancelLabel string
```

These are the form options that suggest that no action take place. Any changes made to the control area of the form are to be thrown away. The dialog is closed. Used with **VtGetValues**, -cancel can be used to retrieve the widget name of the **VtFormDialog**'s Cancel button.

```
-defaultButton OK | APPLY | RESET | CANCEL | HELP | widgetName
```

The Default button specifies a button that is to be selected when/if the user selects the <Enter> key. This is most commonly used for simple dialogs where the user is confirming what appears on the screen, pressing <Enter> to make the action occur. If you build your own dialog from scratch, you can specify the widget name of a push button. This option is not supported by **VtSelectionDialog** or **VtFileSelectionDialog**.

```
-ok
-okCallback cmd
-okLabel string
```

These options support the OK button. Selecting the OK button means "carry out the action and close the dialog." Used with **VtGetValues**, -ok can be used to retrieve the widget name of the **VtFormDialog**'s OK button.

```
-reset
-resetCallback cmd
-resetLabel string
```

These options support the Reset button. Reset supports the same effect as does Cancel, except that the dialog remains displayed. Used with **VtGetValues**, -reset can be used to retrieve the widget name of the **VtFormDialog**'s Reset button.

```
-help
-helpLabel string
-helpCallback cmd          (not supported in SCO OpenServer Release 5)
```

These options support the Help button. Used with **VtGetValues**, -help can be used to retrieve the widget name of the **VtFormDialog**'s Help button.

Help and SCO OpenServer Release 5 users

SCO Visual Tcl's on-line help mechanism is hard-wired to the SCO OpenServer Release 5 Mosaic browser. There is no public API, so there is no support for providing your own help mechanism. As a result, the only way to provide a functioning Help button at the bottom of your dialog is to (1) provide your own dialog action area, building buttons from scratch and including a Help button or (2) use the ability to relabel one of the dialog buttons, pointing its associated callback to your own on-line help dialog.

For all non-SCO versions of Visual Tcl, the -helpCallback option is supported for providing your own help callback for the standard Help button.

Closing Motif dialogs

```
-autoDestroy boolean
-autoHide boolean
```

When set to true (the default behavior), these options can make it so that the dialog simply disappears when the user selects OK or Cancel. The difference between the two options is that -autoDestroy permanently destroys the dialog, whereas -autoHide simply requires that the application use **VtShow** to redisplay the dialog. This option supports only the precanned Motif dialog boxes and the selection dialogs.

Modeless for simultaneous dialog interaction

```
-modeless
```

By default, Visual Tcl dialogs are modal, meaning that the focus for user events is always on the topmost dialog. To override this behavior, -modeless is provided, giving the user the ability to move back and forth through posted dialogs.

Take care with modeless behavior

Although the spirit of graphical application behavior supports building modeless dialogs that contribute to the user's sense of control, there is an overhead cost that you should take into account. Modal dialogs relieve you of having to deal with issues of data and state consistency between dialogs. A modeless environment means that you must provide mechanisms that check for consistency, since the flow of control and the places where variables and other data structures (and files) can be updated require tracking.

Visual Tcl is designed to leverage the advantage of script-based GUI development. It's targeted at small- to medium-sized applications and configuration tools. Staying modal is probably the best way of maximizing Visual Tcl as a rapid application development environment.

Figure 14–3   Motif window manager controls

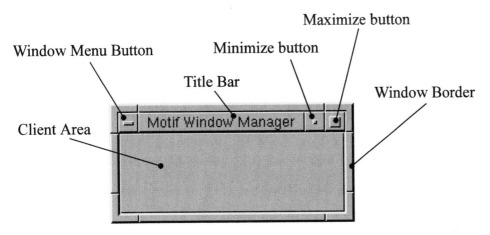

Controlling the Motif window manager

```
-wmDecoration ALL │ RESIZE │ TITLE │ BORDER │ MENU │
        MINIMIZE │ MAXIMIZE
-wmShadowThickness integer          (SCO Charm only)
```

Your dialog can control certain features of the window manager. For example, with the following script fragment, you can indicate that only the title bar and border are to be displayed.

```
VtFormDialog $appName.dlog \
        -wmDecoration {TITLE BORDER}
```

You must carefully consider the situation that you leave your user in by turning off certain window manager controls. Remember that the idea behind graphical applications is to give your user a sense of control and flexibility.

MINIMIZE and MAXIMIZE affect only the very first dialog of your application. -wmShadowThickness specifies a "shadow" to put around a dialog. This is very useful for making one character dialog appear to be above another dialog.

Labels and Buttons

✔ Using labels to inform—**VtLabel**

✔ Buttons—**VtPushButton**

✔ Setting state with buttons—**VtToggleButton**

✔ Presenting choices—**VtRadioBox, VtCheckBox**

✔ The Label class

*L*abels provide your interface with text and graphical pixmaps, giving your user the information necessary to navigate through your application. Labels are read-only widgets, not supported by a callback option other than the short help callback resource. Updated via **VtSetValues**, labels can take on a dynamic role, providing ongoing status information. Modest animation can be created when the label is updated with a series of in-place pixmaps.

The Motif Label class is the foundation for many other widgets, including push buttons and toggle buttons. Push buttons are labels that feature callback capability. They play a role in pulldown menus, as well as in dialogs, where they may be used to present a user with a choice of actions.

Toggle buttons are a simple version of buttons, representing the Boolean condition of on or off. When used inside radio boxes or check boxes, toggle buttons become even more useful when providing users with a range of choices from which to select.

Labels

Label widgets are created with **VtLabel**. Using the -label option, they can be updated with **VtSetValues** and retrieved with **VtGetValues**.

Labels support an alignment resource. They can be left-justified, centered, or right-justified. In the following example, the label "Name:" is right-justified in order to make sure that it butts up against its companion text widget, both contained in a row column widget. The result is displayed in Figure 15–1.

```
set rowcol [VtRowColumn $mainDialog.rowcol \
        -vertical \
        -numColumns 2 ]
VtLabel $rowcol.label \
        -label "Name:" \
        -labelRight
VtText $rowcol.text \
        . . .
```

Figure 15–1   Right-justified label

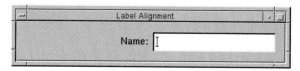

Using the TclX **alarm** command, we can use a label widget to create a digital clock that is updated every second. This example is a complete script. The **signal** command interprets % symbols in its own way (see the **signal** command description in *Command Pages*). Therefore, we put the **fmtclock** command in its own procedure.

```
proc GetClock {} {
        return [fmtclock [getclock] %T]
}

set app [VtOpen app]
set mainDialog [VtFormDialog $app.mainD \
        -title "Label Demo" \
]
signal trap SIGALRM {
        VtSetValues $mainDialog.clockLabel \
            -label [GetClock]
        alarm 1          ;# reset the timer
}

VtLabel $mainDialog.clockLabel \
        -label [GetClock]
alarm 1          ;# units in seconds
```

```
VtShow $mainDialog
VtMainLoop
```

Figure 15–2   A simple label widget clock

The label widget also supports pixmaps using the -pixmap option. Visual Tcl supports pixmaps that are in the XPM3 format. If you have pixmaps that are in the XPM1 format, public domain conversion utilities are widely available. SCO users can use SCOpaint to generate XPM3 pixmaps. SCOpaint also can load in XPM1 pixmaps and save them to disk in XPM3 format.

Labels can display strings on multiple lines by using the \n backslash sequence. Its behavior, however, is to center-justify each string per line.

Push buttons

Push buttons are used in pulldown menus, as well as in stand-alone buttons on a form. In both situations, they most commonly invoke the creation of a child form. Anybody who has ever selected the Open button inside the file pulldown menu in just about any common application has used a push button to launch a dialog (a File Selection dialog, in this example). By convention, push buttons that lead to another dialog contain a label string that ends with three dots "...".

Because they inherit the label class, push buttons can display both strings and pixmaps. Pixmaps can be changed dynamically. The default alignment for buttons is left. To center the label on your push button, using the -labelCenter option.

An armed push button

In addition to standard pixmap support, you can specify an additional pixmap that is displayed when the user pushes the button with the left mouse button. The option for this is -armedPixmap.

Push button callbacks

A push button callback procedure receives a keyed list argument with the additional keys of value and clickCount. The value key will contain the label assigned to the push button. The clickCount key represents the number of times the user clicked the button. Though not recommended, you could use this value to cause the callback to react differently to a double click, for instance.

Toggle buttons

Toggle buttons are simple little widgets used to present a Boolean choice. The example in Figure 15–3 shows a toggle button used to represent a read-only mode that may, for instance, apply to a task that views the contents of a file.

Figure 15–3   A selected toggle button

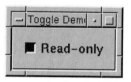

In this example, the default setting of "on" was set by the option -set, which accesses 1 or 0 (on or off). -set can also be used with **VtSetValues** to change the toggle button's state and with **VtGetValues** to retrieve its state.

Radio boxes and check boxes

The use of a toggle button is greatly enhanced when it becomes a child of a radio box or a check box. These parent widgets are actually row column widgets that contribute unique behavior to the toggle buttons they inherit.

RadioBox   Created with **VtRadioBox**, toggle button children display a "one-of-many" behavior, allowing the user to select only one item from a list of toggle buttons. The shape of the toggle button takes on a diamond appearance. A default selection can be created by specifying the name of the toggle button to the -value option.

CheckBox   Created with **VtCheckBox**, toggle button children display "one-or-more" behavior, allowing users to select as many items as they choose. Toggle button shape is unaffected, retaining its rectangular shape.

Figure 15–4 shows a check box and a radio box side by side, each wrapped with a frame widget (including title). The radio box was created with the following script fragment. cframe contains the widget name of the check box. Note how the widget naming is performed in order to indicate that the toggle buttons are to be inherited by the radio box (and that the radio box is to be inherited by the frame).

```
set rframe [VtFrame $mainDialog.rframe \
        -shadowType ETCHED_OUT \
        -title "Memory size" \
        -leftSide $cframe \
        -alignTop $cframe ]
set rBox [VtRadioBox $rframe.rBox \
        -callback ProcessSelectionCB ]
VtToggleButton $rBox.8 -label "8 Meg"
VtToggleButton $rBox.16 -label "16 Meg"
VtToggleButton $rBox.32 -label "32 Meg"
VtSetValues $rBox.16 -value 1    ;# set as default on
```

Figure 15–4   Check box and radio box, both with frames

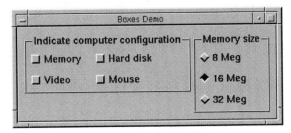

Callbacks can be handled in two ways. You can assign a callback either to each toggle button or to the radio box, as we have in this script fragment. The radio box callback, ProcessSelectionCB, will receive a keyed list containing a key called value. It will contain the name of the toggle button that was selected. For check boxes, value will contain a list of zero or more selected toggle buttons.

The callback keyed lists of radio boxes and check boxes display interesting results. The callback keyed list associated with **VtRadioBox** will grow and shrink, depending on the number of toggle buttons that have been selected. If buttons A, B, and D have been selected from a box containing four buttons, the widget names for the selected buttons will be contained in the value key.

The callback associated with the radio box widget will simply return the name of the selected child toggle button. If, however, you decide to assign a callback per toggle button in a radio box, you may receive two callbacks when a selection is made. Since only one toggle button can be "on" at a time, the first callback will be the result of a previously selected toggle button being turned off. The second callback will be the result of the selection of the other toggle button. If you are not concerned about which button is being unselected, you may want to simply assign a callback to the parent radio box.

Extracting information from widget names

Let's assume the user selected "32 Meg" in the Figure 15–4 radio box. Our callback will extract the name of the widget from the keyed list using the `value` key.

```
proc ProcessSelectionCB {cbs} {
  set selectedWidget [keylget cbs value]
  echo $selectedWidget
}
```

➡ `.app.mainD_popup.mainD.mainD.rframe.rBox.32`

This is nice, but what do we do with it? Note that the handle that we assigned to the toggle button included the short name *32*. This pragmatic name was chosen so that we could use the Vx command **VxGetShortName** to extract the 32 and use it as meaningful information.

```
echo "You are lucky to have \
    [VxGetShortName $selectedWidget] Meg of
memory."
```

➡ You are lucky to have 32 Meg of memory.

Of course, instead of echoing this reply, we could have used the information to store in a configuration file.

Because radio boxes and check boxes incorporate row-column widgets, they support the same row-column options:

> `-horizontal` and `-vertical` for column orientation
> `-numColumns` for specifying one or more columns of toggle buttons
> `-spacing` for indicating the pixel separation between toggle buttons

The Label class

The Label class represents the resource options that are inherited by label, push button, and toggle button widgets.

> `-accelerator` *string*
> `-acceleratorString` *string*
> `-mnemonic` *char*

Discussed later during the construction of the Rolodex program, any button can be selected with a combination of key strokes, using accelerators or mnemonics. A mnemonic allows you to select, for instance, a button in a visible menu item by pressing the character, highlighted by an underscore. An accelerator allows you to select a menu button without even seeing the item. For instance, you can add an accelerator to the button that saves a file to disk. For an accelerator, the convention is to require the <Ctrl> key, in addition to the underscored letter.

```
-label string
```

This option is used to create or update a label string.

```
-labelCenter
-labelLeft
-labelRight
```

The default behavior of a label is to be aligned to the left. These options control label alignment.

```
-pixmap filename
-insensitivePixmap filename
```

Pixmaps can be supported by all members of the label class. An insensitive pixmap can be indicated, causing it to be used when the widget has been set to be insensitive (i.e., not allowing user input). Use of the **VtSetSensitive** command or the -sensitive option on the label or button widget will cause the insensitive pixmap to be displayed.

```
-recomputeSize boolean
```

This option, when set to false, or 0, prevents the label or button from resizing itself if the label or pixmap assigned to it grows larger than its original dimensions. In order to keep the rest of your dialog from resizing around it, setting the widget's recomputeSize option to false is a good idea. If you are going to change the contents of the widget, make sure you've allocated enough space to accommodate the changes in size of the label string or pixmap.

Selection Dialogs

✔ **VtSelectionDialog** for potentially large list selections

✔ **VtFileSelectionDialog** for accessing files

*T*he **VtFormDialog** was provided by Visual Tcl to enhance the ability to build commonly needed main window and custom dialogs with as few commands as possible. Motif takes this one step further by providing two dialogs that build on two specific tasks common to most application needs. **VtSelectionDialog** provides a dialog solely for the purpose of allowing the user to select an item, either by typing in the selection or by choosing from a list. **VtFileSelectionDialog** provides the even more focused task of furnishing the user with a selection of directories and files, providing the ability to filter the view so that only certain matching files are presented.

VtFileSelectionDialog

In addition to standard Dialog class options, the **VtFileSelectionDialog** command supports options for reworking its appearance as required by your application. For example, you can redefine the labels identifying the file and directory list widgets and the filter text field with the following options.

```
-dirListLabel string
-fileListLabel string
-filterLabel string
-selectionLabel string
```

These options all support the ability to rework the predefined labels in the File Selection dialog.

```
-filter string
```

The filter string specifies the matching pathname from which to generate a list of directories and files. To list all the files in the /tmp directory, the filter would be /tmp/*.

```
-hideDirList
-hideFilter
```

These options indicate that the filter text field and the directory list widget should not be realized (displayed). The option

```
-selection string
```

sets the name of the file to occur in the selection text box at the bottom of the dialog.

Figure 16–1   Reconfigured File Selection dialog

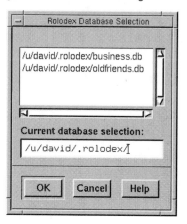

Loading a Rolodex database

For the Rolodex application, we want to use the File Selection dialog to present the user with a selection of Rolodex databases for loading or saving. We have the following design requirements for the database Selection dialog.

1. We want to reduce the chances of the user accidentally selecting a non-Rolodex database file.

2. We want to take the user straight to the Rolodex databases.

```
proc OpenRoloDatabaseCB {cbs} {
        global userDirectory
        set parent [keylget cbs dialog]
        VtShow [VtFileSelectionDialog $parent.dbaseLoadDlg \
            -title "Rolodex Database Selection" \
            -hideFilter \
            -hideDirList \
            -selectionLabel "Current database selection:" \
```

```
        -okCallback ProcessDataBaseSelectionCB \
        -filter $userDirectory/.rolodex/*.db \
    ]
}
```

The filter option is used to show only those files that end with .db, since there are other files, such as the user's configuration file, in the Rolodex directory. We have indicated that the filter text field need not be displayed. Also, we have hidden the directory list to discourage the user from getting lost elsewhere in the directory hierarchy.

The OK and Cancel buttons automatically destroy the dialog. You can change this behavior with the option -autoHide (if you prefer to simply hide the dialog). All of the dialog's action area buttons—OK, Cancel, Filter, and Help—are displayed by default. Using the button options, such as -ok, will imply that only the buttons represented by specified options are to appear. The Filter button is always displayed.

VtSelectionDialog

The Selection dialog is very similar in its behavior to the File Selection dialog, particularly its action area buttons and their default behavior. However, there is significantly less flexibility, particularly if you want to rename the labels for the list and text widgets. In addition to standard Dialog class options, **VtSelectionDialog** supports the following options.

-filename *string*	A (full path) file containing a list of items to be displayed.
-itemList *list*	A list of items to be displayed.
-selection *string*	An item to be highlighted by default.

Specifying a Rolodex entry type

When a user adds a new Rolodex entry, he or she must indicate how the entry is to be classified. Is it a colleague, a friend, or a WEB site? Because we want the user to be able to add new classifications that can then be used for filtering, we have chosen the Selection dialog that combines list selection with the creating of new list items. The following callback, invoked from the data entry dialog, presents the user with the request for classification.

```
proc SelectDataTypeCB {cbs} {
    set parent [keylget cbs dialog]
    VtShow [VtSelectionDialog $parent.dbaseLoadDlg \
        -title "Rolodex Entry Classification" \
        -itemList [GetClassificationList] \
        -okCallback InsertItemType \
    ]
}
```

Figure 16–2   Presenting a list of classifications with `VtSelectionDialog`

Scales

✔ The scale widget—**VtScale**

A scale widget is one of the more intuitive Motif widgets. Sliding a scale back and forth presents the user with a dynamic sense of how a current value fits in with a range of possible values. When used as a gauge, a slider serves as a progress indicator, such as the anticipated amount of time it takes to install a software product.

Using scale as a gauge

The UNIX df command reports the amount of unused disk space in a UNIX file system. On an SCO OpenServer system, the command

```
df -v
```

reports how file system space is currently utilized in the following formatted output.

```
Mount Dir   Filesystem   blocks    used      free      %used
/           /dev/root    1076364   1004654   71710     94%
/stand      /dev/boot    90000     16084     73916     18%
/u          /dev/u       800000    449196    350804    57%
```

Let's create a gauge of file system space usage, based on the scale widget. Our application will be dynamic, adapting to the number of file systems by providing a scale widget for each file system. It will graphically reflect the percentage of file system space currently used.

First, we need to parse the output of df -v. The data we are interested in are contained in the last column, %used.

```
proc FetchDiskFreeValues {arrayName} {
    upvar $arrayName ar
    # convert output into a list of lists.
    set dfList [split [exec df -v] \n]
    lvarpop dfList        ;# get rid of column headings
    foreach row $dfList {
        set used [lindex $row 5]
        set ar([lindex $row 0]) [ctoken used %]
    }
}
```

The procedure FetchDiskFreeValues parses and returns the output from df that interests us. An array is updated via call-by-reference, using the name of each file system as the element index name. **ctoken** has the nice property of returning the string preceding the specified token, % in this case. We use it to extract the percent integer.

With data in hand, let's construct the GUI-building portion of our application.

```
set app [VtOpen dfscale]
set mainDialog [VtFormDialog $app.mainDialog \
        -title "% Disk Usage" \
        ]
FetchDiskFreeValues dfDataArray
foreach filesys [array name dfDataArray] {
    VtScale $mainDialog.$filesys \
        -title "File system: $filesys" \
        -value $dfDataArray($filesys) \
        -rightSide FORM
}
VtShow $mainDialog
VtMainLoop
```

Figure 17–1   Using three scale widgets to show disk usage

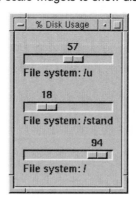

The output of our complete application is shown below (Figure 17–1). There are a number of enhancements that can be added, such as labels at either end of the scale, indicating 0% and 100%. Also, using a command like

VtSetValues $labelWidget -value $updatedValue

this application can be enhanced to update each slider with changes in the file system disk usage.

Scale options

```
-horizontal
-vertical
```

The **VtScale** command creates a scale oriented horizontally by default.

```
-length integer
```

The length of the scale can be set with -length where the integer is multiplied by the maximum font width used to display the value.

```
-max integer
-min integer
```

These two options establish the upper and lower boundaries for the displayed legal scale value.

```
-readOnly
```

When rendered in read-only mode, the slider turns to a stippled color. User input is ignored. The problem with this behavior is that it does not make for an attractive display when used as a progress indicator.

```
-showValue boolean
```

This option is used to turn off the display of the current value. By default, the value is displayed.

```
-title string
```

A string is placed below the scale widget.

```
-value integer
```

sets the current value within the limits allowed by -min and -max.

Text Widget

✔ Text and text fields —**VtText**
✔ Controlling the current focus with **VtSetFocus**

*T*he **VtText** command is commonly used to create simple editors or file browsers. **VtText** supports the ability to perform basic text widget operations, representing a subset of the features available in a full Motif text widget.

By indicating the number of desired rows, you can create a single line text field or a multiline text window with vertical and/or horizontal scrollbars. The following example is a fully functioning file browser, browsing a cron file as an example.

```
set app [VtOpen app]
set mainDialog [VtFormDialog $app.mainD \
    -title "Text Widget Browser" \
]
VtText $mainDialog.text \
    -filename /usr/spool/crontab/root \
    -columns 80 \
    -rows 10 \
    -verticalScrollBar 1\
    -rightSide FORM \
    -bottomSide FORM
VtShow $mainDialog
VtMainLoop
```

Figure 18–1   A simple, but complete cron browser

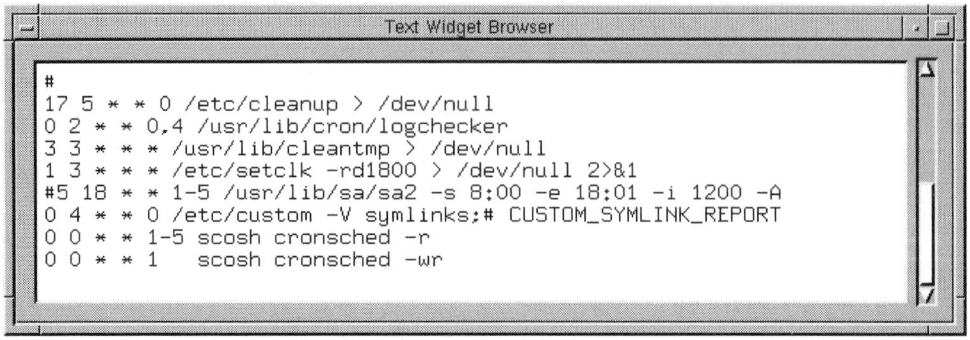

```
#
17 5 * * 0 /etc/cleanup > /dev/null
0 2 * * 0,4 /usr/lib/cron/logchecker
3 3 * * * /usr/lib/cleantmp > /dev/null
1 3 * * * /etc/setclk -rd1800 > /dev/null 2>&1
#5 18 * * 1-5 /usr/lib/sa/sa2 -s 8:00 -e 18:01 -i 1200 -A
0 4 * * 0 /etc/custom -V symlinks;# CUSTOM_SYMLINK_REPORT
0 0 * * 1-5 scosh cronsched -r
0 0 * * 1   scosh cronsched -wr
```

This script is very similar to the one used to provide a simple help system in the Rolodex program discussed in subsequent chapters.

Text widget callbacks

Unlike most other widgets, the information a user enters into a text widget is largely unrestricted. This makes the text widget an extremely versatile widget when dealing with a situation where it's impossible for the application to know the expected values. However, this degree of flexibility creates the potential for lots of errors from typos, invalid data types and other error situations the user can create during free-format data entry.

In order to provide the developer with enough tools to give the user as much immediate feedback as possible, **VtText** supports a number of callbacks not available with other widgets.

Single line text callback

A text field is a single line text widget, commonly used to receive discrete values, such as an IP address or a machine name, as opposed to a multiline file editor which may be less discriminating. A distinguishing behavior of a text field is the effect of selecting the <RETURN> key. The text cursor has no where to go since it's restricted to a single line of text. Therefore, the implication of a text widget that detects the pressing of a <RETURN> key is that the user has completed entering the string value.

The option that supports a <RETURN> key event is:

```
-callback procedure
```

This callback is not supported when a text widget is created to support more than one line of text since the nature of a <RETURN> key press changes from "done" to "put me on the next text line."

Examining text character-by-character

A good user interface design ensures that the user cannot create an error situation by entering bad data. At the very least, the quality of data the user enters should be checked on a per-key basis. The user is then prevented from typing in a large amount of data only to find out that there's an error when he finally selects the OK button.

In the example of a text field widget that is used for accepting an IP address from the user, the callback

```
-valueChangedCallback procedure
```

can be used to verify each character as it is typed in. -valueChangedCallback supports character-by-character scrutiny, invoking a callback every time the user performs a keystroke.

```
VtText $mainDialog.ipAddress
...
    -valueChangedCallback CheckForValidAddressCB
```

This callback script fragment might be supported by the procedure in the following example.

```
proc CheckForValidAddressCB {cbs} {
        set value [keylget cbs value]
        set lastCharEntered [cindex $value end]
        if {[regexp {[0123456789.]} $lastCharEntered] == 0} {
                # keep focus on the current text field
                VtSetFocus [keylget cbs widget]
                PostErrorDialog [keylget cbs dialog] \
                        "\"$value\" not a valid IP address character"
        }
}
```

In a dialog that contains text editing functions, some of the buttons, such as a delete button may be insensitive to user input since there is no text to edit. Illustrated in Figure 1-2, as soon as text is detected via the -valueChangedCallback, then the associated callback can be used to make the related editing buttons sensitive to user input.

Figure 18–2   Using valueChangedCallback to sensitize buttons

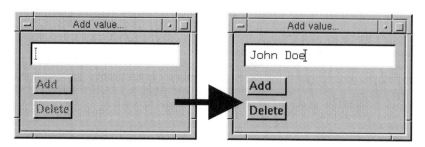

Detecting when the user moves on

The callback option

```
-losingFocusCallback procedure
```

sets up a callback for examining the text or text field's current value when the user decides to move onto another widget. The procedure in this case may apply full examination of the value that was just entered. Building on our previous example, the application may now examine the entire IP address entered for validity.

Controlling user input focus

In a data-entry style dialog, containing multiple text fields, it's often desirable to dictate where the user input focus should go when the user completes filling in the previous text field.

VtSetFocus *widgetName*|-dir *direction*

Table 18–1   Directions for setting focus

DOWN	HOME	LEFT	NEXT_TAB_GROUP
NEXT	RIGHT	UP	PREVIOUS_TAB_GROUP

Used inside the procedure associated with a text field <RETURN> user event, **VtSetFocus** can be used to progress a user step-by-step, moving to the next widget, field or otherwise, where the next bit of information is required.

As an alternative to keeping track of widget names in a form, the -dir option gives your application to set focus in a relative sense. A *Tab group* is a keyboard traversal concept that occurs within objects that contain related objects, such as all of the buttons in a dialog's action area (OK, Cancel, Help), the toggle buttons in a check box or the push buttons in a pulldown menu. Once focus is set inside a tab group, keyboard control shifts from the TAB key to the arrow keys, in order to cycle focus across the related widget objects.

VtSetFocus is particularly useful for returning the user's input focus to any widget where an error condition has been detected. Explained with a short help message, the user can then make the necessary correction.

Other Text widget options

```
-columns integer
-rows integer
```

-columns dictates the width of a Text widget by multiplying the integer value by the width of the maximum width of the current font.

```
-value string
-filename string
```

Initial text can be loaded by string or simply passing a file name to be read in. -filename is inherently read-only. To save editing, you must build file-writing logical that writes changes back out to the file.

```
-verticalScrollBar boolean
-horizontalScrollBar boolean
```

Scrollbars do not appear unless specified.

```
-noEcho
-readOnly
```

-noEcho can be used to create text fields for passwords. -readOnly prevents user input from altering the displayed text.

```
-wordWrap
```

Turns word wrap behavior on.

Option Menu and Combo Box

✔ Menus in dialogs—**VtOptionMenu**

✔ Combining text and list widgets—**VtComboBox**

*T*he option menu and combo box are two powerful, choice-driven widgets that support convenience and flexibility. Using these widgets in your custom dialogs helps to prevent user errors, since they are selecting from a set of valid options.

The option menu provides a predefined list of legal choices from which to choose. This widget should be used for a limited set of values, since its displayed list can grow outside the boundaries of the user's screen! It's generally recommended that you do not exceed around ten items or so.

If the number of values is a potential concern, the combo box might be a better choice. As the name implies, the combo box widget provides a combination of the text field widget and a list widget. This combination is flexible in that the user can select from a list of values or may enter a new value. The list portion of the combo box gives it greater scalability to display a variable number of values, as compared with the option menu.

Option Menu

Just like a pulldown menu, an option menu is constructed by placing push buttons on the option menu. The option menu is created first with **VtOptionMenu**, then child push buttons are added.

Figure 19–1   Selecting from option menu

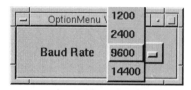

The option menu in Figure 19–1 provides the user with a selection of modem baud rates. This dialog was created with the script fragment illustrated below.

```
set rowCol [VtRowColumn $mainDialog.rowCol \
    -horizontal \
    -numColumns 1 \
    -rightSide FORM \
    -bottomSide FORM ]
set baudLbl [VtLabel $rowCol.baudLbl \
    -label "Baud Rate" \
    -labelRight ]
set optBaudRate [VtOptionMenu $rowCol.optBaudRate \
    -callback RetrieveBaudRate ]
foreach item {1200 2400 9600 14400} {
    set button${item} \
        [VtPushButton $optBaudRate.$item -label $item]
}
# indicate a default value
VtSetValues $optBaudRate -selectedWidget $button9600
```

A **foreach** loop is used to load each of the buttons. The name of the button was crafted to make sure that each button's handle short name contained its baud rate label. This makes it possible to use **VxGetShortName** in the option menu callback to extract the baud rate from the callback information, which returns a value containing the name of the selected push button.

```
proc RetrieveBaudRate {cbs} {
    set value [keylget cbs value]
    set baudRate [VxGetShortName $value]
    ...
}
```

Combo box

The combo box widget brings together the behaviors and benefits of two widgets, the text field widget and a list widget, providing functionality similar to a selection box, but with more flexibility for integrating into custom dialogs. The user has the ability to select from a list of values or to enter a new value.

Figure 19–2 Combo box for list and text features

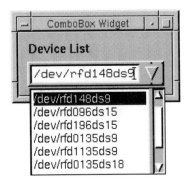

Combo box callbacks

`-callback` *cmd*

This callback is invoked when the value is changed and the widget loses focus, or when the user has pressed the <Enter> key.

`-dropListCallback` *cmd*

sets the callback `cmd`, called when the drop list on the combo box is opened. The value supplied to the callback represents the value indicated in the text field.

`-valueChangedCallback` *cmd*

Leveraging the `-valueChangedCallback` of a text field, the application can scrutinize text data as they are entered by the user.

Other Combo box options

Other options set the callback `cmd` called after text is deleted from or inserted into the widget.

`-columns` *integer*
`-rows` *integer*

`-columns` defines the width of the list portion of the combo box. If the values in the list are wider than the width value, a horizontal scrollbar is added. `-rows` specifies the number of rows displayed when the drop list is popped up. If the number of list rows specified exceeds six, a scrollbar is added.

`-itemList` *list*

sets a list of items for the combo box object. If the number of list rows specified exceeds six, a scrollbar is added.

`-value` *string*

You can use this option to set the initial value in the text field portion of the combo box.

CHAPTER 20

Lists and Drawn Lists

✔ Simple lists with **VtList**
✔ Hierarchical, graphical lists with **VtDrawnList**

*P*erhaps the biggest challenge to your application is its ability to scale to its user's environment. Just when you think you've constructed the most robust script possible, you hand it to somebody to try, and it blows up on the first attempt. A script that aborts is not the only problem. If you developed your script in a small, local-area network, and try it on the company wide-area network, you may discover that the widget you thought would be ideal for representing resources is no longer adequate to handle the expanded amount of data.

Lists are ideal for displaying large amounts of information within a small screen. Visual Tcl provides two list widgets. A list widget is a common site for most users of e-mail applications or user administration tools. Any application that revolves around manipulating resources, such as pieces of e-mail, newsgroup posts, users, or printers typically makes use of the flexibility of a single-column list widget. The tasks boil down to "add an item," "remove an item," "select an item," "sort an item," and so on.

VtList supports a conventional Motif list widget that is ideal for displaying a moderate amount of data. For extremely large data management, the **VtDrawnList** provides a graphical list widget that supports a number of advantages over the conventional list widget, including the ability to handle proportional fonts in columns and to display pixmaps anywhere within rows of list items. The most prominent feature of the drawn list is its ability to represent information hierarchically. With the right design, a hierarchical view using "drill-down" navigation can scale to almost any environment.

The list

The list widget is a natural choice for building a simple crontab file editor. The design we've chosen combines a list widget with a text widget inside a row column widget for easy geometry management. The result of the code shown below is displayed in Figure 20–1.

```
set app [VtOpen cronDemo]
set mainDialog [VtFormDialog $app.mainDialog \
    -title "Cron File Editor" \
    -okLabel "Add Record" \
    -okCallback AddRecordCB \
    ]

set cronFile /usr/spool/cron/crontabs/root

set rowC [VtRowColumn $mainDialog.rowC \
    -packing TIGHT \
    -rightSide FORM \
    -bottomSide FORM ]

# read_file returns a string, \
  so we need split to create a list

set listW [VtList $rowC.listW \
    -itemList [split [read_file -nonewline $cronFile]
\n] \
    -rows 8 \
    -columns 80 \
    -selection SINGLE \
    -topItemPosition 0 \
    -callback RecordToTextFieldCB \
    -defaultCallback DeleteRecordCB \
    ]

set textW [VtText $rowC.textW \
    -rows 1 \
    ]
# store widget names with the dialog for callback access
VxSetVar $mainDialog textW $textW
VxSetVar $mainDialog listW $listW

VtShow $mainDialog
VtSetFocus $textW      ;# must occur after VtShow
VtMainLoop
```

Notice that a scrollbar has been created automatically. This occurs whenever the number of list items exceeds the number of displayed rows.

```
-scrollBar boolean
```

forces **VtList** to display a scrollbar at all times. A horizontal scrollbar appears only when -width or -columns is specified. Otherwise, the list grows sideways to accommodate the widest item.

Figure 20–1   A cron editor dialog with list and text widgets

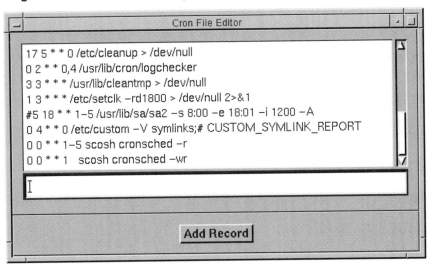

We've also relabeled the OK button to "Add Record." The AddRecordCB appears below. It's designed to copy the value typed into the text widget and add it to the list using **VtListAddItem**, one of the seven list widget manipulation routines. The first item in a list occupies position 1. Position 0 means "end of the list." AddRecordCB performs the addition of the text string to the end of the list widget.

To scroll the newly added item to the middle of the eight-row-high list, we've used **VtListGetItem** to return all of the list's items in order to calculate the total number of items. -topItemPosition indicates which item to scroll to the top of the visible list. By adding 4 to the new item's position, we're ensuring that it will appear in the middle of the list. The fact that we've shown the new item as selected with **VtListSelectItem** does not make it automatically appear in the viewable list widget if position 0 happens to occur out of view.

```
proc AddRecordCB {cbs} {
        set dialog [keylget cbs dialog]
        set textW [VxGetVar $dialog textW]
        set listW [VxGetVar $dialog listW]
        set string [VtGetValues $textW -value]
        VtListAddItem $listW \
            -item $string \
            -position 0
        # highlight the new item
        VtListSelectItem $listW -position 0
        set length [llength [VtListGetItem $listW -all]]
```

```
        VtSetValues $listW -topItemPosition [incr length -4]
    }
```

There are two other callbacks defined in the call to **VtList**.

```
    . . .
    -callback RecordToTextFieldCB \
    -defaultCallback DeleteRecordCB
```

RecordToTextFieldCB copies the selected item to the text widget. It is executed as a result of a single click of the left mouse button. A double click, on the other hand, invokes the callback associated with -defaultCallback. The effect is to delete the currently selected item.

```
    proc RecordToTextFieldCB {cbs} {
        set dialog [keylget cbs dialog]
        set widget [keylget cbs widget]
        set value [lindex [keylget cbs value] 0]
        set textW [VxGetVar $dialog textW]
        VtSetValues $textW -value $value
    }
```

Since the selected item is returned as a value key in RecordToTextFieldCB's keyed list, there's no need to use any **VtList**-related command. **VtSetValues** takes care of updating the text widget.

If you were to echo the contents of cbs in any of the **VtList** callbacks, you'd see that the value key's value is not a string, but is instead a list of lists. That's because the list widget is capable of returning more than one selected item when a user input event occurs. For example, if the -selection option specifies a MULTIPLE or EXTENDED selection mode, more than one item can be selected at a time using the <Ctrl> and <Shift> keys. Therefore, value's natural state is to represent values as a list of lists.

As a result, in order to extract even a single value from a list of lists, we've chosen to use **lindex**. The following describes the four supported **VtList** selection behaviors.

```
    -selection SINGLE | EXTENDED | MULTIPLE | BROWSE
```

BROWSE   An item is always selected with a solid line. The user cannot
                unselect the item.

SINGLE   Supports simple select and deselect, one item at a time.

EXTENDED   **VtList** only. An item is always selected. Dragging the mouse,
                with the left button pressed, extends the selection to additional
                items. You can select multiple items by pressing the <Ctrl> key
                while selecting with individual mouse clicks. Pressing the <Shift>
                key causes the selection of all items between the current item and
                the last selected item.

MULTIPLE   **VtList** only. Noncontiguous selection is supported, not
                requiring the <Ctrl> key. Drag selection is not supported. The
                callback specified by -callback is invoked with each selected
                item.

The remaining callback, invoked by a double click of the mouse, deletes the currently selected record using **VtListDeleteItem**.

```
proc DeleteRecordCB {cbs} {
        set widget [keylget cbs widget]
        set value [lindex [keylget cbs value] 0]
        VtListDeleteItem $widget -item $value
}
```

The three remaining **VtList** commands that have not been used in this example are:

VtListDeselectItem   Removes the highlighting of the currently selected item.

VtListGetSelectedItem   Returns the position numbers of currently selected items.

VtListSetItem   Sets an existing item to a new value.

Common features of most of the **VtList** commands are that they support the ability to modify the entire list by using -itemList, they can locate items by position using -position, and they can locate an item by matching its contents with -item.

The drawn list

The drawn list widget provides the primary data view in our Rolodex example application. The drawn list gives us the ability to build a significantly large Rolodex database without losing the ability to easily track and organize the data we collect over the years about people, businesses, restaurants, and WEB sites. Before we construct this list with the **VtDrawnList** command, let's review some key features of the drawn list.

Column list support

One of the shortcomings of a simple list widget is its handling of nonproportional fonts. No matter how much you try to format a row of data so that its columns line up with other rows, this is virtually impossible to achieve with a list widget. The only way to achieve alignment of columns of data in a list widget is to use fixed fonts. Compare the alignment with a fixed-length font, such as Courier:

```
1234567890
abcdefghij
ABCDEFGHIJ
```

to that with a proportional font such as Times New Roman:

1234567890

abcdefghij

ABCDEFGHIJ

The drawn list widget supports the ability to organize data by columns. Each column is constructed based on the format information provided, including column width and width of the gap between columns. Columns have data types as well, including the support for pixmaps, discussed below. Format information can be specified on a per-row basis.

In addition to in-list columns, a label field above the drawn list is provided and is controlled by column-based formatting, as well.

Hierarchical lists for high-volume data management

The migration of applications to the graphical environment got an earlier start in the area of network management. The need to display huge amounts of management information in a wide area network could be addressed only by pixmap-based representations. Overwhelming views of flattened data have been replaced by icons representing collections of management data. A network administrator can drill down these icon-based collections, viewing data and increasing details of information.

This hierarchical view of data can be applied to many types of relationships, some of which are represented in Figure 20–2.

Figure 20–2   Types of hierarchical relationships

Directory	*Object*
File	Attribute
File	Attribute
...	...

Person	*DCE Cell*
Data	Object
Data	Object
...	...

The drawn list is the focal point widget of the Visual Tcl language. Because of Visual Tcl's roots in systems management and the need to support the development management applications that must scale to deal with large, server-based management environments, the drawn list and its ability to support a hierarchical view was essential. Its hierarchical behavior is provided by the ability to support in-line pixmaps, in any column, as well as the ability to format columns on a per-row basis.

The Rolodex main window drawn list

Our Rolodex main window uses a drawn list widget to show a monoclinic hierarchical list—a list containing a single layer of expanded information underneath the top layer. For example,

Person
  Phone Number
  Address
  E-mail

represents a simple hierarchical relationship that we use every day. When we need to read information about people, the Rolodex program will support the ability to drill down to the level below *Person*.

Elements of a drawn list

Let's review some key components of a drawn list before we build some manipulation routines for the Rolodex program.

Pixmaps

During the creation of the drawn list widget, the option `-pixmaps` is used to pass the names of pixmaps that will be used during the lifetime of all drawn list operations. References to these pixmaps will be made in the format list, explained below, by indexing their position in the pixmap list.

```
VtDrawnList $mainDialog.roloDrawnL \
        -pixmaps {business.px restaurant.px face.px } \
        ...
```

To indicate that the `person.px` pixmap is to be used, it would be referenced with a 0.

Format

The format of each item in a drawn list can be specified as a default format in the **VtDrawnList** command or on a per-list-item basis, such as with **VtDrawnListAddItem**. A typical example of a format option might look like the following:

```
-formatList {{ICON 2 5} {STRING 25 5 5} {DATA}}
```

This example indicates that the first field is reserved for a space wide enough to accommodate two icon pixmaps. There should be a margin of 5 pixels to the left of the icon. The second field specifies that a column of 25 character width will be reserved for a string. This string will have margins of 5 pixels to the left and to the right. The third field is similar in function to the `-userData` option of the Object class, which gives you the ability to store information inside a widget that can be examined by interested code elsewhere in your application. The significance of DATA is that you can store hidden information on a per-row-item basis!

```
type width [leftMargin rightMargin]
```

The type field supports three possible format identifiers.

ICON

designates a pixmap or a built-in *connection icon*, which can be specified

CONNECT_L

CONNECT_I

CONNECT_T

CONNECT_H

NO_ICON

L, I, T, and H correspond to four built-in pixmaps (L shape, vertical line, a T-bar, and a horizontal line), providing symbols that can be used to represent hierarchical relationships between items in the drawn list. NO_ICON represents an empty pixmap when whitespace is needed.

STRING

A string. Be sure to use Tcl quoting so that the string is perceived as a single word.

DATA

For storing hidden application-specific data that can later be retrieved for interpretation.

Field elements

Icons and strings are inserted into the drawn list through the -fieldList option of the **VtDrawnListAddItem**. The following is an example of a **DrawnList** command that inserts a new row item. This item will look like

```
VtDrawnListAddItem $mainDialog.drawnL \
    -formatList {{ICON 2 5} {STRING 25 5} {DATA}} \
    -fieldList "{CONNECT_L 2} {I'm a second level object} EXPANDED"
```

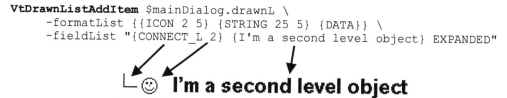

For the first field, the CONNECT_L corresponds to the L-shaped icon. The 2 is indexing the third icon listed earlier in the -pixmap option, corresponding with face.px. The second field is assigned the string, I'm a second-level object. The final field is assigned the string EXPANDED, which is an application-specific word that we can store with the item when it is added to the list. We'll show how we use this stored information later in the chapter.

Creating a drawn list

Let's begin building our drawn list. The code fragment below sets the foundation for the drawn list widget. It specifies the pixmaps we will index by numeric position. The -defaultCallback option specifies the callback procedure to invoke if the user double-clicks on an item. We choose not to use the single-click -callback option.

There are 60 columns requested, which is calculated according to the widest default font width. The top and left sides of the form are already attached by default; we've attached the right side to the form. Though not shown here, we've attached the bottom to the short help label at the bottom of the window, after creating the label. This geometry strategy is explained in detail in Chapter 20, *Menus and Pulldowns*.

Because we are creating a drawn list for hierarchical relationships, we want to define the formatting of list items on a per-item basis. Therefore, there is no use of format option information so far.

```
set drawnL [VtDrawnList $mainDialog.roloDrawnL \
        -iconList {person.px colleague.px \
            business.px restaurant.px web.px} \
        -defaultCallback ExpandOrCollapseCB \
        -font largeBoldFont \
        -columns 60 \
        -rows 16 \
        -rightSide FORM \
]
```

Figure 20–3   Main window with empty drawn list

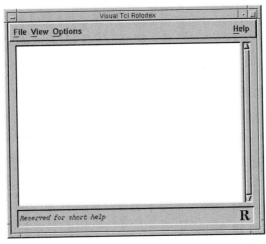

Adding and removing list items

It's time to retrieve information stored in the Rolodex database and convert it into rows of graphical information in a drawn list widget. The Rolodex application organizes each Rolodex entry into the format of a keyed list. Each keyed list is then stored in an array, using the name of the entity that represents the Rolodex entry as the array's index. This very abbreviated example shows how Rolodex information is organized.

```
set roloArray("Joe Doe") \
    [list {icon 0} {phone 408-555-1234}]
set roloArray("SC Coffee") \
    [list {icon 1} {phone 408-555-4321}]
```

We are going to use the -recordList option to load in all of the initial information with a single call to the **VtDrawnListAddItem** command. -recordList expects a list of lists, where each list is an individual item for the drawn list. The following script fragment builds a list of lists, using **lappend**. Each element from the array is processed using a **foreach** loop. **append** builds up the list item with increasing bits of information.

```
foreach item [lsort [array names roloArray]] {
    append tmpVar " [keylget roloArray($item) icon]"
    append tmpVar " [list $item]"
    append tmpVar " COLLAPSED"
    lappend recordList $tmpVar
    unset tmpVar
}
```

After the contents of tmpVar are inserted into recordList, tmpVar is destroyed so that it can be created again for constructing the next list item.

```
VtDrawnListAddItem $drawnL \
    -recordList $recordList \
    -formatList {{ICON 1 5} {STRING 35 5} {DATA}}
```

The result is that we now have a drawn list full of Rolodex entries.

Figure 20–4   A populated drawn list

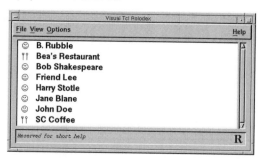

Expanding and collapsing

When we created the drawn list with **VtDrawnList**, we specified the -defaultCallback option to invoke ExpandOrCollapseCB when the user double-clicks on an item. The job of ExpandOrCollapseCB is to decide whether the selected item is to be expanded or collapsed ("rolled up"). It checks the selected item for the DATA field that we initialized with the string COLLAPSED during the creation of the list items.

ExpandRecord creates the illusion of drilling down the hierarchy of the selected item. A leaf node of the hierarchical tree appears to expand with additional nodes. The result is that an indented set of related information "contained" by the selected item is revealed in the list.

The illusion of expansion is created by inserting new drawn list items, taking advantage of the built-in connection icon pixmaps, as we have chosen to do for the Rolodex application.

```
proc ExpandOrCollapseCB {cbs} {
        set drawnL [keylget cbs widget]
        set position [keylget cbs value]
        set status [VtDrawnListGetItem $drawnL \
            -position $position]
        if {[lindex $status 2] == "COLLAPSED" } {
            set name [lindex $status 1]
            ExpandRecord $name $position


        }
}
```

ExpandOrCollapseCB acts on the position information supplied by the keyed list to retrieve information about the selected item using **VtDrawnListGetItem**. Noting that the selected item is COLLAPSED, the name of the Rolodex entry, such as "Bea's Restaurant," is extracted with **lindex** and passed to ExpandRecord, along with the position.

ExpandRecord uses the name to retrieve additional information about Bea's Restaurant. It then loops through the information, adding it as individual rows of data to the drawn list. In addition to the data, such as phone number and address, the row appears indented, due to the use of prefixed icon connection icons.

```
proc ExpandRecord {name position} {
        set info $roloArray($name)
        set newRowCount [llength $info]
        foreach item [keylkeys info]
            incr length -1
            if {[cequal $item "icon"]} {
                if {$length == 0} {
                    append fieldList " \"CONNECT_L "
                } else {
```

```
                      append fieldList " \"CONNECT_T "
                  }
                  append fieldList " [keylget info icon]\" "
              } else {
                  append fieldList " \"[keylget info $item]\"
       "
              }
              append fieldList " CHILD "

              VtDrawnListAddItem $drawnL \
                  -formatList {{ICON 2 5} {STRING 25 10} {DATA}} \
                  -fieldList $fieldList \
                  -position [incr position]
          }
      }
```

ExpandRecord generates the expanded list shown in Figure 20–5. The **foreach** loop processes every key representing bits of information about Bea's Restaurant. Inside the loop, a check is made for the last piece of information so that a terminating L-shaped connector icon is appended. When the item is constructed, the hidden data string "CHILD" is added. This information will be used by another callback to determine whether it is dealing with a first- or second-level of hierarchy. Finally, with the entire fieldList constructed, **VtDrawnListAddItem** inserts the item at the next calculated position.

Figure 20–5   Double click expands info on Bea's Restaurant

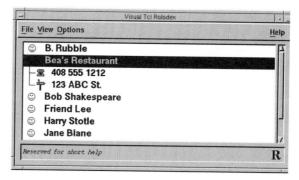

Adding drawn list labels

If you are using the drawn list widget for displaying columns of aligned proportional fonts, you may want to take advantage of the support for adding a label at the top of the drawn list. The same approach and format identifiers are used for the label as were used for creating drawn list items.

```
-labelFormatList list
-labelList list
```

The one exception is that icons are not currently supported for inclusion in labels.

Options common to lists and drawn lists

```
-defaultCallback cmd
```

This option indicates the callback procedure to invoke when the user double-clicks the mouse or presses <Enter>.

```
-topItemPosition integer
```

You can shift the view of the list, indicating that an in item, identified by its list number, is to be

```
-columns integer
```

This option indicates the number of columns to display, calculated by multiplying the integer by the current font character width. The option

```
-rows integer
```

sets the number of character rows displayed in a list or drawn list to `integer`.

Menus and Pulldowns

✔ Menu bars—**VtMenuBar**

✔ Pulldown menus—**VtPulldown**

✔ Accelerators and mnemonics

✔ Short help and the short help callback

Most functionally rich applications feature *main menus* located at the top of the main window. The main menu consists of a menu bar of labeled categories, such as *file*, *edit*, and *help*. The selection of a menu bar category generates the presentation of a column of push buttons on a pull down menu. A cascade button may lead to more menus of buttons.

```
MenuBar->PullDown->PushButton/PushButton/PushButton
MenuBar->PullDown->CascadeButton->PushButton/PushButton
MenuBar->PullDown->PushButton/ToggleButton/ToggleButton
```

The advantage of menu bars is the ability to move functionality off of the main window and into logically grouped pulldowns. An application that supports a task or two probably does not need to leverage the benefits of a menu bar.

The menu bar itself is a row column manager widget and does not support a public callback. Instead, it leads the user to the button-based callbacks organized in the pulldown it organizes.

VtMenuBar

The script below adds a new procedure called `BuildMenuBar`. Inside `BuildMenuBar`, the **VtMenuBar** command is invoked to create the menu bar widget, which will automatically appear at the top of the main window dialog.

The help menu item is created within the context of the **VtMenuBar** command, in response to the -helpMenuItemList option. This is the only menu bar pulldown that is built in and is done so because the help item is such a standard feature of any menu bar. Visual Tcl automatically places the help menu item to the far right end of the menu bar. The list passed to -helpMenuItemList indicates which push buttons should appear in the pulldown. Many of the support help menu items are supported on SCO platforms only; therefore, we are using only the ON_VERSION item. The version number of your application can be set with the **VtSetAppValues** command.

```
proc CloseCB {cbs} {
     VtClose; exit 0
}
proc BuildMenuBar {dialog} {
     set menuBarW [VtMenuBar $dialog.menuBarW \
         -helpMenuItemList {ON_VERSION} \
         ]

     set filePullD [VtPulldown $menuBarW.file \
         -label "File" \
         ]
     set openPushD [VtPushButton $filePullD.open \
         -label "Open..." \
         ]
     VtSeparator $filePullD.sep

     set quitPushB [VtPushButton $filePullD.quit \
         -label "Quit" \
         -callback CloseCB \
         ]
}
set app [VtOpen rolodex]
set mainForm [VtFormDialog $app.mainF \
     -title "Visual Tcl Rolodex" \
     -wmCloseCallback CloseCB \
     ]

VtSetAppValues $app \
     -versionString "Visual Tcl Rolodex\nVersion 1.0"
BuildMenuBar $mainForm

VtShow $mainForm
VtMainLoop
```

VtPulldown

In the script above, we have created an additional menu bar item, File. Typical menu items take the following widget creation path.

VtMenuBar->VtPulldown->VtPushButton

The `CloseCB` callback is plugged into the `Quit` push button. This procedure is now invoked from both the pulldown menu and the Motif window manager. The result of these few menu-building commands is shown in Figure 21–1.

Figure 21–1   File pulldown menu

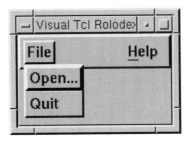

Cascading menus and radio behavior

Our Rolodex program has the ability to change the size of the font that it displays in the drawn list widget. The following code adds a view pulldown menu that inherits three children. Two are push buttons, Expand and Collapse. These are linked to the same Rolodex callback, `ExpandOrCollapseCB`, discussed earlier in *Lists and Drawn Lists*.

```
set viewPullD [VtPulldown $menuBarW.view \
        -label "View" \
]
set fontPullD [VtPulldown $viewPullD.filter \
        -label "Fonts"\
        -radioBehavior 1 \
]
VtToggleButton $fontPullD.12 -label "12 pt" \
        -callback SetFont
VtToggleButton $fontPullD.14 -label "14 pt"\
        -callback SetFont
VtToggleButton $fontPullD.16 -label "16 pt"
        -callback SetFont
```

The other child is another pulldown labeled *Fonts*. A child pulldown becomes a push button that generates a cascading menu when selected. The cascading menu presents three fonts from which to choose. Radio-box-like behavior is turned on with the `-radioBehavior` option.

Figure 21–2   Cascading menu with radio behavior

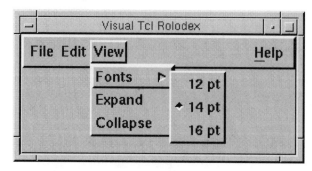

Accelerators and mnemonics

As a user of your application becomes more and more familiar with its function, he or she can take advantage of advanced navigation tools, such as mnemonics and accelerators. A *mnemonic* is a letter in a menu button label that can be pressed in order to activate the button. The first character in the label string that exactly matches the mnemonic is underlined when the button is displayed.

```
-mnemonic char
```

The display server automatically adds <Alt>mnemonic as an accelerator for the menu.

```
-accelerator string
```

This option establishes the widget's accelerator, represented by a keystroke sequence involving <Ctrl> or <Alt> keys. This is done in order to distinguish accelerators from ordinary keypresses. To specify the accelerator <Ctrl>E, the string Ctrl<Key>E is used.

```
-acceleratorString string
```

The accelerator string that your user sees on a menu push button is set with this option. To specify that <Ctrl>E is the accelerator, replace string with Ctrl+E. Accelerator text is displayed only on push buttons and toggle buttons in a pulldown.

```
set expandPushD [VtPushButton $viewPullD.expand \
        -label "Expand" \
        -shortHelpCallback SetShortHelp \
        -shortHelpString  \
           "Expand current selection for more information" \
        -acceleratorString "Ctrl+E" \
        -accelerator "Ctrl<key>E"
]
set collapsePushD [VtPushButton $viewPullD.collapse \
        -label "Collapse" \
        -shortHelpCallback SetShortHelp \
        -shortHelpString "Hide expanded information" \
```

```
      -acceleratorString "Ctrl+C" \
      -accelerator "Ctrl<key>C"
]
```

The code above shows how accelerators are specified, as well as short help information, discussed below. Figure 21–3 shows the results of both accelerators and short help.

Short help

With all of the functionality that can be represented with pulldown menus, the user is going to need as much help as possible navigating around your application. A simple but useful mechanism is provided by short help.

The main window of the Rolodex was constructed with a label at the bottom, provided solely to support the display of short help messages.

Figure 21–3   Accelerators and short help

PushButton with Accelerator

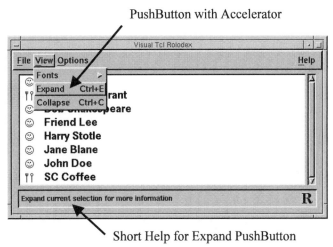

Short Help for Expand PushButton

```
      -shortHelpCallback cmd
      -shortHelpString string
```

The following provides an example of a short help callback. Note the keyed list callback key `helpString`. It contains the string that was defined with `-shortHelpString`.

```
proc SetShortHelp {cbs} {
      set dialog [keylget cbs dialog]
      set message [keylget cbs helpString]
      set helpLbl [VxGetVar $dialog ShortHelpLabel]
      VtSetValues $helpLbl -label $message
}
```

Non-GUI Vt Commands

✔ Monitoring I/O of other processes—**VtAddInput**
✔ Performing work during idle time—**VtAddWorkProc**

*T*here are a number of nongraphical functions that are commonly needed by graphical applications, particularly in the systems management application environment. One is to monitor other processes that have their own loops, performing work for a management application, such as the network `ping` command. At other times, there is also the need to perform lengthy tasks that should not bring the support of user input to a halt. Once handed the execution control by the event loop, some procedures may "run away," making your application appear to be frozen to the user. This is an all-too-common occurrence when applications are developed in a small engineering local-area network, displaying entirely different behavior when they are executed in a production, large-scale network environment.

Event loops and external processes

The challenge of writing an application that leverages another continually running process is that the event loop cannot take care of its own chores of processing user input. A common command used in systems administration is the UNIX `find` command. If you launched a `find` that searched for core files on a large disk, your application's event loop could be locked up a long time waiting for `find` to return matched files.

Visual Tcl provides the ability to set up a file stream I/O interaction with another process, using the **VtAddInput** and **VtRemoveInput** commands. **VtAddInput** registers a callback procedure that is invoked whenever activity is detected on the input

file descriptor. The file descriptor is passed as an argument to the procedure so that the
input can be read and processed.

```
set pipe [open "|ping ftp.prenhall.com" r]
VtAddInput $pipe ReadPingData
```

This complete script opens a read pipe to the network ping command, which is
launched in the process. With each reading of data from ping, the ReadPingData
callback procedure is invoked, with the file identifier passed as an argument.

```
proc SayHelloCB {cbs} {
    echo Yes, I'm here
}

proc ReadPingData {id} {
    global pipe lbl
    set response [gets $id]
    if {[eof $id]} {
        VtRemoveInput $id
        close $pipe
        VtSetValues $lbl -label "Ping session
completed"
    } else {
        VtSetValues $lbl -label $response
    }
}
set app [VtOpen demo]
set mainF [VtFormDialog $app.mainF]
set lbl [VtLabel $mainF.lbl]

# ping -c 10 creates 10 pings, then ping terminates
set pipe [open "|ping -c 10 ftp.prenhall.com"]
VtAddInput $pipe ReadPingData

VtPushButton $mainF.Test\ MainLoop -callback SayHelloCB
VtShow $mainF
VtMainLoop
```

The effectiveness of **VtAddInput** depends on the nature of the process from
which you are awaiting input. A command like ping returns data to read at regular,
relatively evenly spaced intervals, giving VtMainLoop enough time to handle most user
input events in the meantime. However, if you create a pipe to the UNIX find command
and it returns every file name on your hard disk, you are likely to overwhelm the main
loop's ability to process user input. A possible solution to this is to write your own script-
based process that acts as a proxy by executing the find command, bundling up the data,
then sending it back to the parent script in packages that can be handled without
overwhelming the event loop.

VtAddWorkProc

The primary function of the main loop is to redirect user input events to callback procedures. If a task results in keeping the loop inside of a procedure, the application will not respond to user input, since control has not yet returned to the main loop.

A *work proc* is a procedure that receives attention from the main loop when it is not busy processing a user input event. A work proc is created by the command

VtAddWorkProc *procedureName*

The procedure, named by *procedureName*, receives a minimum of one argument, which is a work proc ID. The work proc ID is used by the **VtRemoveWorkProc** command in order to halt the work proc procedure. The key to a good work proc is its ability to pick up from where it left off by tracking its own state between sessions when the event loop takes back control. Like **VtAddInput**, **VtAddWorkProc** can overwhelm the event loop as well, if asked to perform a compute-intensive operation.

Design Issues for Configuration Scripts

✔ Suggested steps to take when designing configuration tools

The life cycle of system administration is characterized by two phases: configuration and ongoing administration. Ongoing administration represents the long-haul aspect of systems management, making modest changes on a daily or weekly basis, such as adding users to the system. Configuration represents installation and initialization activities of system and application software, as well as hardware components. In the UNIX environment, the configuration phase of installation is typically characterized by nongraphical scripts issuing a series of questions. "Plug 'n play" devices are emerging, with the hope of reducing the number of details that an administrator must worry about during installation. With the ongoing evolution of graphical operating systems, users are raising their expectations of applications that present them easy-to-understand controls. For software and hardware developers, providing user-friendly configuration tools has become an integral part of the challenge for competitive features.

Building configuration applications presents some unique design issues. Ralf Holighaus of NetCS, an ISDN technology company in Berlin, Germany, provided *The Visual Tcl Handbook* with some guidelines for the design of graphical configuration utilities, based on his experience and the experience of his co-workers. Clearly, many of these steps apply to nonconfiguration management tool design, as well. The purpose of this discussion is to help you construct your own structured approach to graphical configuration tool design.

Figure 23–1   Typical configuration interface

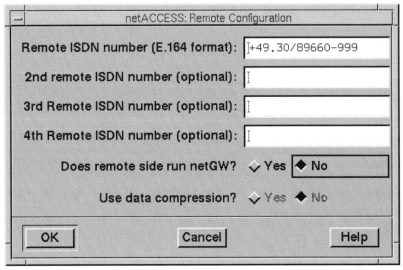

Development steps

Configuration tool design can be organized into categories of issues. The following list attempts to organize some of the thought process that is required.

Parameter definition

Identify the information that your product requires during the configuration phase. For example, if your application supports modem services, you may require baud rate, flow control, and modem manufacturer information. If your product is large and divided into distinct components, you may decide to present the user with the choice of installing individual packages now, installing later, or not installing at all. Of course, progress indicators during a lengthy installation are essential.

Forms layout definition

With parameters in hand, you can now begin to consider which widgets best present and gather choices to and from the administrator. There are widgets for providing feedback, widgets for presenting explanation, widgets for presenting simple choices, and widgets for presenting choices from long lists.

Instead of one large form, you may divide choices into logical groups of individual forms. This also gives your configuration tool the option of displaying or not displaying forms, depending on answers provided by the user in earlier forms.

Some forms may be applicable only during installation, while other forms are to be used for ongoing systems administration, as well.

Forms implementation

Carry out the implementation of the form. This can be done without supporting callback procedures. Temporary hard-coded values help to create the illusion of functionality that can be used during initial user testing.

Procedure definition

Identify the procedures behind the widgets, including callbacks and procedures that sort out data for display and possible execution. In the process of performing this exercise, you may identify extensions to the vtcl interpreter that are required for performance reasons. However, this should be considered only as a last resort, to minimize issues such as version control of the Visual Tcl interpreter.

Procedure implementation

When implementing procedures and callbacks, initially you may want to add only enough functionality to increase the testability of your configuration tool during user testing. Once you feel the design of your forms are solid, you can then enhance and bulletproof the implementation of these procedures.

Chaining everything together

This phase creates the illusion of a seamless series of configuration steps.

Final tests

There's nothing like watching a customer use your graphical interface for the first time. Assumptions about how you expected a user would progress through your screens fly out the window, requiring rework. Luckily, because you're taking advantage of a script-based tool like Visual Tcl, you can allocate more of your time on good user testing and less time on programming.

Parameter definition

The most difficult phase of configuration tool design focuses on how to present and retrieve parameter information to and from the user. The better the design, the greater the overall impression that your application makes to users and administrators. Let's take a closer look at the issue of mapping parameter requirements to graphical design.

What parameters do we need?

Identify the information that your product requires during the configuration phase.

How do they depend on each other?

What if a user cannot provide support for more than a 9600 baud rate? Perhaps features in your application are meaningless at a low baud rate, making it unreasonable to expect the user to provide answers to other questions. You can handle this by simply stippling out choices that are no longer applicable. Note in Figure 23–1 that the compression option is stippled out (i.e., made insensitive to user input), the result of an earlier answer that indicated to the configuration script that data compression would not be possible, due to missing software on the remote client.

You could also remove the choices altogether, but you probably want to avoid forms that are too dynamic, since this presents additional design issues that make it difficult to test all of the possibilities. Also, you may want users to be aware of the kinds of features they can take advantage of if they decide to purchase a more powerful modem.

What default values are appropriate?

Default values have a tremendous impact on who can use your product's configuration tools. The more intelligence you can put into the configuration phase, the more you provide for user-based self-administration, reducing the support burden of both administrators and your own support department.

Default values can affect the granularity of the forms you provide. Perhaps by presenting a simple, initial form that asks a few questions, you can follow up with subsequent forms that provide very accurate default values, based on the answers to a few simple questions.

How can we group parameters together?

By identifying and organizing parameters as related collections, half of your design is done. Parameters can be organized as one form per collection or as a larger form, using separators to distinguish one group from the other.

What are the allowed ranges of parameter values?

For each parameter, build a list of potential values. Identify which values depend on the user-selected values of other parameters.

Which widget fits best to enter/modify a parameter value?

Widgets with a fixed set of options are always better than a stack of text widgets that does little to improve the user's chance of entering correct values. Also, with fixed options there is less dependence on your code to process answers for accuracy. An option menu widget is ideal for providing up to 12 choices. If a particular parameter supports more than 12 choices, perhaps a selection box is required.

The bottom line is, if possible, to *avoid generating forms dynamically!* Dynamic generation usually means using lots of text fields that are susceptible to user pilot error. Also, documenting dynamic interfaces is virtually impossible, especially with screen shots. Provide choices whenever possible.

How do we store these parameters?

Many applications read startup configuration files when invoked by the user. The output generated for your application's configuration script is likely to generate or modify a user-specific configuration file.

The Rolodex program saves configuration information in the format of a Tcl command. The file can then be loaded in with the **source** command as though it were part of the application.

Whatever approach you decide to take to design configuration scripts, with graphical scripting languages like Visual Tcl, you now have the opportunity to build tools that enhance the utility of your product.

PART IV

Command Pages

Control

Table 24–1 Commands for control

Command	Tcl	TclX	Short Description
break	✔		Abort looping command
catch	✔		Evaluate script and trap exceptional returns
commandloop		✔	Create an interactive command loop
continue	✔		Skip to the next iteration of a loop
error	✔		Generate an error
eval	✔		Evaluate a Visual Tcl script
for	✔		Perform a "for" loop
foreach			Iterate over all elements in a list
if	✔		Execute scripts conditionally
loop		✔	Perform higher performance "for" loop
proc	✔		Create a Visual Tcl procedure
rename	✔		Rename or delete a command
return	✔		Return from a procedure
source	✔		Evaluate a file as a Visual Tcl script
switch	✔		Evaluate one of several scripts, depending on a given value
uplevel	✔		Execute a script in a different stack frame
while	✔		Execute a script repeatedly as long as a condition is met

break   Tcl

Syntax

```
break
```

Description

This command may be invoked only inside the body of a looping command, such as **for** or **foreach** or **while**. It returns a TCL_BREAK code to signal the innermost-containing loop command to return immediately.

catch   Tcl

Syntax

```
catch script [varName]
```

Description

The **catch** command may be used to prevent errors from aborting command interpretation. **catch** calls the Tcl interpreter recursively to execute *script* and always returns a TCL_OK code, regardless of any errors that might occur while executing *script*. The return value from **catch** is a decimal string, giving the code returned by the Tcl interpreter after executing *script*. This will be 0 (TCL_OK) if there were no errors in *script*; otherwise it will have a nonzero value corresponding to one of the exceptional return codes. If the *varName* argument is given, it gives the name of a variable; **catch** will set the variable to the string returned from *script* (either a result or an error message).

commandloop   TclX

Syntax

```
commandloop [prompt1] [prompt2]
```

Description

This command creates an interactive command loop for the current Tcl interpreter. It receives commands from *stdin* and executes them. It is useful for Tcl scripts that do not normally converse interactively with a user through a Tcl command interpreter but sometimes want to enter this mode.

prompt1 is a Tcl command string that is evaluated to determine the text of the prompt string. The old value of *tcl_prompt1* is saved and prompt is set to this value for the duration of the command loop. *prompt2* is a command string that is evaluated to determine the "down-level prompt," which is the prompt issued for continuation of input. The old value of *tcl_prompt2* is saved and the prompt is set to this value for the duration of the command loop.

When the command terminates, the variables for the prompt hooks will be set to their old values. If these arguments are not specified, the prompt hooks use their current values.

continue   Tcl

Syntax

`continue`

Description

This command may be invoked only inside the body of a looping command, such as **for**, **foreach**, or **while**. It returns a TCL_CONTINUE code to signal the innermost-containing loop command to skip the remainder of the loop's body but continue with the next iteration of the loop.

Example

The following code loops through a list of items, skipping the remainder of the processing inside the loop when a special list item is detected.

```
echo The following planets have no Chevrolets
foreach item {Mercury Venus Earth Mars Jupiter Saturn} {
    if {$item == "Earth"} {
        continue
    }
    echo $item
}
```

➡ The following planets have no Chevrolets
   Mercury
   Venus
   Mars
   Jupiter
   Saturn

error   **Tcl**

Syntax

error *message* [*info*] [*code*]

Description

This command returns a TCL_ERROR code, which causes command interpretation to be unwound. *message* is a string that is returned to the application to indicate what went wrong. If the *info* argument is provided and is not empty, it is used to initialize the global variable errorInfo. errorInfo is used to accumulate a stack trace of what was in progress when an error occurred; as nested commands unwind, the Tcl interpreter adds information to errorInfo. If the *info* argument is present, it is used to initialize errorInfo, and the first increment of unwind information will not be added by the Tcl interpreter. In other words, the command containing the **error** command will not appear in errorInfo; in its place will be *info*. This feature is most useful in conjunction with the **catch** command: If a caught error cannot be handled successfully, *info* can be used to return a stack trace reflecting the original point of occurrence of the error:

```
catch {...} errMsg
set savedInfo $errorInfo
...
error $errMsg $savedInfo
```

If the *code* argument is present, its value is stored in the errorCode global variable. This variable is intended to hold a machine-readable description of the error in cases where such information is available. If the code argument is not present, errorCode is automatically reset to NONE by the Tcl interpreter, as part of processing the error generated by the command.

eval   Tcl

Syntax

eval *arg* [*arg* ...]

Description

eval takes one or more arguments, which together comprise a Tcl script containing one or more commands. **eval** concatenates all of its arguments in the same fashion as does the **concat** command, passing the concatenated string to the Tcl interpreter recursively and returning the result of that evaluation (or any error generated by it).

for   Tcl

Syntax

for *start test next body*

Description

This is a looping command, similar in structure to the C for statement. The *start*, *next*, and *body* arguments must be Tcl command strings, and *test* is an expression string. The **for** command first invokes the Tcl interpreter to execute *start*. Then it repeatedly evaluates *test* as an expression; if the result is not zero, it invokes the Tcl interpreter on *body*, then invokes the Tcl interpreter on *next*, then repeats the loop. The command terminates when *test* evaluates to 0. If a **continue** command is invoked within *body*, any remaining commands in the current execution of *body* are skipped; processing continues by invoking the Tcl interpreter on *next*, then evaluating *test*, and so on. If a **break** command is invoked within *body* or *next*, the **for** command will return immediately. The operation of **break** and **continue** are similar to the corresponding statements in C. The command returns an empty string.

Example

```
echo "Begin incrementing i from 0 to 9"
for {set i 0} {$i < 10} {incr i} {
    echo "i = $i"
}
```

foreach   Tcl

Syntax

foreach *varName* *list* *body*

Description

In this command, *varName* is the name of a variable, *list* is a list of values to assign to *varName*, and *body* is a Tcl script. For each element of *list* (in order from left to right), **foreach** assigns the contents of the field to *varName* as if the **lindex** command had been used to extract the field, then calls the Tcl interpreter to execute *body*. The **break** and **continue** statements may be invoked inside *body*, with the same effect as in the **for** command. The command returns an empty string.

Example

```
set spectrumColors {blue green yellow orange red}
echo "The colors of the spectrum are: "
foreach color $spectrumColors {
        echo $color
}
```

➡ The colors of the spectrum are:
blue
green
yellow
orange
red

if   Tcl

Syntax

if *expr1* [then] *body1* elseif *expr2* [then] *body2* elseif ...
    [else] [*bodyN*]

Description

The **if** command evaluates *expr1* as an expression (in the same way that **expr** evaluates its argument). The value of the expression must be Boolean (a numeric value, where 0 is false and anything is true, or a string value such as true or yes for true and false or no for false); if it is true, then *body1* is executed by passing it to the Tcl interpreter. Otherwise, *expr2* is evaluated as an expression; if it is true, then *body2* is executed, and so on. If none of the expressions evaluates to true, then *bodyN* is executed. The then and else arguments are optional "noise words" to make the command easier to read. There may be 0 or more elseif clauses. *bodyN* may also be omitted, as long as else is omitted, too. The return value from the command is the result of the *body* script that was executed. An empty string will be returned if none of the expressions was nonzero and there was no *bodyN*.

Example

```
if {$nodeCount > 1024 } {
        echo "I don't scale to large networks very well!"
} elseif {$nodecount < 32} {
        echo "You spent way too much money for me!"
} else {
        echo "You are getting excellent cost/performance"
}
```

loop   TclX

Syntax

loop *var first limit* [*increment*] *body*

Description

loop is a looping command, similar in behavior to the Tcl for statement, except that the **loop** statement achieves substantially higher performance and is easier to code when the beginning and ending values of a loop are known and the loop variable is to be incremented by a known, fixed amount every time through the loop.

The *var* argument is the name of a Tcl variable that will contain the loop index. The loop index is set to the value specified by *first*. The Tcl interpreter is invoked upon *body* 0 or more times, where *var* is incremented by *increment* every time through the loop, or by 1 if *increment* is not specified. *increment* can be negative, in which case the loop will count downward.

When *var* reaches *limit*, the loop terminates without a subsequent execution of *body*. For instance, if the original loop parameters would cause **loop** to terminate, i.e., *first* is 1, *limit* is 0, and *increment* is not specified or is not negative, *body* is not executed at all, and **loop** returns.

first, *limit*, and *increment* are integer expressions. They are evaluated only once at the beginning of the loop.

If a **continue** command is invoked within *body*, any remaining commands in the current execution of *body* are skipped, as in the **for** command. If a **break** command is invoked within *body*, the **loop** command will return immediately. **loop** returns an empty string.

proc   Tcl

Syntax

proc *name args body*

Description

The **proc** command creates a new Tcl procedure named *name*, replacing any existing command or procedure of that name. Whenever the new command is invoked, the contents of *body* are executed by the Tcl interpreter. *args* specifies the formal arguments to the procedure. It consists of a list, possibly empty, each of whose elements specifies one argument. Each argument is also a list, with either one or two fields. If there is only a single field in the specifier, then it is the name of the argument; if there are two fields, then the first is the argument name and the second is its default value.

When *name* is invoked, a local variable is created for each of the formal arguments to the procedure; its value is the value of the corresponding argument in the invoking command or the argument's default value. Arguments with default values need not be specified in a procedure invocation. However, there must be enough actual arguments for all the formal arguments that do not have defaults, and there must not be any extra actual arguments. There is one special case to permit procedures with variable numbers of arguments. If the last formal argument has the name args, then a call to the procedure may contain more actual arguments than the procedure has formals. In this case, all of the actual arguments, starting at the one that would be assigned to *args*, are combined into a list (as if the **list** command had been used); this combined value is assigned to the local variable *args*.

When *body* is being executed, variable names normally refer to local variables, which are created automatically when referenced and deleted as the procedure returns. One local variable is automatically created for each of the procedure's arguments. Global variables can be accessed only by invoking the **global** command or the **upvar** command. The **proc** command returns an empty string. When a procedure is invoked, the procedure's return value is the value specified in a **return** command. If the procedure does not execute an explicit **return**, its return value is the value of the last command executed in the procedure's body. If an error occurs while executing the procedure *body*, the procedure as a whole will return that same error.

Example

This example shows how to use the keyword args to allow for C varargs-style behavior.

```
proc DoSomething {args} {
      foreach value $args {
          echo value:$value
      }
}
```

rename   Tcl

Syntax

rename *oldName newName*

Description

This command will rename the command that used to be called *oldName* so that it is now called *newName*. If *newName* is an empty string, *oldName* is deleted. The **rename** command returns an empty string as result.

return   Tcl

Syntax

return [-code *code*] [-errorinfo *info*] [-errorcode *code*] [*string*]

Description

This returns immediately from the current procedure (or top-level command or **source** command), with *string* as the return value. If *string* is not specified, an empty string will be returned as the result.

Exceptional returns

In the usual case where the `-code` option is not specified, the procedure returns normally (with a completion code of TCL_OK). However, the `-code` option may be used to generate an exceptional return from the procedure. *code* may have any of the following values:

`ok`	Normal return: the same as if the option were omitted.
`error`	Error return: the same as if the error command were used to terminate the procedure, except for handling of `errorInfo` and `errorCode` variables (see below).
`return`	The current procedure returns with a completion code of TCL_RETURN, so that the procedure that invoked it returns also.
`break`	The current procedure returns with a completion code of TCL_BREAK, which terminates the innermost-nested loop in the code that invoked the current procedure.
`continue`	The current procedure returns with a completion code of TCL_CONTINUE, which terminates the current iteration of the innermost-nested loop in the code that invoked the current procedure.
value	*value* must be an integer; it is returned as the completion code for the current procedure.

The `-code` option is rarely used. It is provided so that procedures that implement new control structures can reflect exceptional conditions back to their callers.

Two additional options, `-errorinfo` and `-errorcode`, may be used to provide additional information during error returns. These options are ignored unless *code* is error.

The `-errorinfo` option specifies an initial stack trace for the `errorInfo` variable; if it is not specified, the stack trace left in `errorInfo` includes the call to the procedure and to higher levels on the stack, but it does not include any information about the context of the error within the procedure. Typically, the **info** value is supplied from the value left in `errorInfo` after a **catch** command traps an error within the procedure.

If the `-errorcode` option is specified, *code* provides a value for the `errorCode` variable. If the option is not specified, `errorCode` defaults to NONE.

source   **Tcl**

Syntax

source *fileName*

Description

This command reads the file named *fileName* and passes its contents to the Tcl interpreter as a script to evaluate in the normal fashion. The return value from **source** is the return value of the last command executed from the file. If an error occurs in evaluating the contents of the file, the **source** command will return that error. If a **return** command is invoked from within the file, the remainder of the file will be skipped and the **source** command will return normally with the result from the **return** command. (If *fileName* begins with a tilde, it is tilde-substituted, as described in the **glob** manual entry.)

switch   **Tcl**

Syntax

switch [*options*] *string pattern body* [*pattern body ...*]
switch [*options*] *string* {*pattern body* [*pattern body ...*]}

Description

The **switch** command matches its *string* argument against each of the *pattern* arguments, in order. As soon as it finds a pattern that matches *string*, it evaluates the following *body* argument by passing it recursively to the Tcl interpreter, then returns the result of that evaluation. If the last *pattern* argument is default, it matches anything. If no *pattern* argument matches *string* and no default is given, the **switch** command returns an empty string.

If the initial arguments to **switch** begin with a hyphen, they are treated as options. The following options are currently supported:

-exact   Use exact matching when comparing *string* to a pattern. This is the default.

-glob   When matching *string* to the patterns, use glob-style matching
                     (i.e., the same as implemented by the **string** match command).

-regexp   When matching *string* to the patterns, use regular expression-
                     matching (i.e., the same as implemented by the **regexp** command).

--   Marks the end of options. The argument following this one will be
                     treated as *string*, even if it begins with a hyphen.

Two types of syntax are provided for the *pattern* and *body* arguments. The first uses a separate argument for each of the patterns and commands; this form is convenient if substitutions are desired on some of the patterns or commands. The second form places all of the patterns and commands together into a single argument; the argument must have proper list structure, with the elements of the list being the patterns and commands. The second form makes it easy to construct multiline **switch** commands, since the braces around the whole list make it unnecessary to include a backslash at the end of each line. Since the pattern arguments are in braces in the second form, no command or variable substitutions are performed on them; this makes the behavior of the second form different than that of the first form in some cases.

If a *body* is specified with an initial hyphen, it means that the *body* for the next pattern should also be used as the *body* for this pattern (if the next pattern also has a *body* beginning with a hyphen character, then the *body* after that is used, and so on). This feature makes it possible to share a single *body* among several patterns.

Examples

```
switch abc {
      a -
      b { echo 1}
      abc {echo 2}
      default {echo 3}
}
```
➡ 2

```
switch -regexp aaab {
      ^a.*b$ -
      b {echo 1}
      a* {echo 2}
      default {echo 3}
}
```
➡ 1

```
switch xyz {
      a
```

```
        —
   b
        {echo 1}
   a*
        {echo 2}
   default
        {echo 3}
}
```
➡ 3

uplevel   **Tcl**

Syntax

uplevel [*level*] *arg* [*arg* ...]

Description

All of the *arg* arguments are concatenated as if they had been passed to **concat**; the result is then evaluated in the variable context indicated by *level*. **uplevel** returns the result of that evaluation.

If *level* is an integer, it gives a distance (up the procedure-calling stack) to move before executing the command. If *level* consists of # followed by a number, the number gives an absolute level number. If *level* is omitted, it defaults to 1. *level* cannot be defaulted if the first command argument begins with a digit or #.

For example, suppose that a procedure was invoked from top level, and that it called DoJob; and suppose that DoJob called DoAnotherJob. Suppose that DoAnotherJob invokes the **uplevel** command. If *level* is 1 or #2 or omitted, the command will be executed in the variable context of DoJob. If *level* is 2 or #1, the command will be executed in the variable context of DoJob. If *level* is 3 or #0, the command will be executed at top level (only global variables will be visible).

The **uplevel** command causes the invoking procedure to disappear from the procedure-calling stack while the command is being executed. In the above example, suppose DoAnotherJob invokes the command **uplevel** 1 {**set** x 43; DoYetAnotherJob}, where DoYetAnotherJob is another Tcl procedure. The **set** command will modify the variable x in DoJob's context, and DoYetAnotherJob will execute at level 3, as if called from DoJob. If it, in turn, executes the command **uplevel** {**set** x 42}, then the **set** command will modify the same variable x in DoJob's context. The procedure DoAnotherJob does not appear to be on the call stack when DoYetAnotherJob is executing. The command **info** level may be used to obtain the level of the current procedure.

uplevel makes it possible to implement new control constructs as Tcl procedures (for example, **uplevel** could be used to implement the **while** construct as a Tcl procedure).

while   Tcl

Syntax

while *test body*

Description

The **while** command evaluates *test* as an expression (in the same way that **expr** evaluates its argument). The value of the expression must be a proper Boolean value; if it is a true value, *body* is executed by passing it to the Tcl interpreter. Once *body* has been executed, *test* is evaluated again, and the process repeats until eventually *test* evaluates to a false Boolean value. **continue** commands may be executed inside *body* to terminate the current iteration of the loop, and **break** commands may be executed inside *body* to cause immediate termination of the **while** command. The **while** command always returns an empty string.

Debug

Table 25–1 Commands for debugging

Command	Tcl	TclX	Short Description
cmdtrace		✔	Trace Visual Tcl execution
edprocs		✔	Edit named procedures or all procedures
profile		✔	Collect Visual Tcl script performance profile data
profrep		✔	Generate a report of data generated by **profile** command
saveprocs		✔	Save named procedures or all procedures to a file

cmdtrace   TclX

Syntax

```
cmdtrace level | on [noeval] [notruncate] [procs] [fileid]
    | off | depth
```

Description

Prints a trace statement for all commands executed at depth of *level* or below (1 is the top level). If on is specified, all commands at any level are traced.

Options

noeval   Causes arguments to be printed unevaluated. If noeval is specified, the arguments are printed before evaluation. Otherwise, they are printed afterward. If the command line is longer than 60 characters, it is truncated to 60 and "..." is postpended to indicate that there was more output than was displayed. If an evaluated argument contains a space, the entire argument is enclosed within braces, {}, to allow the reader to visually separate the arguments from each other.

`notruncate`	Disables the truncation of commands and evaluated arguments.
`procs`	Enables the tracing of procedure calls only. Commands that are not procedure calls (i.e., calls to commands that are written in C, C++, or some object-compatible language) are not traced if the `procs` option is specified. This option is particularly useful for greatly reducing the output of **cmdtrace** while debugging.
fileid	This is a file identifier as returned by the **open** command. If specified, the trace output will be written to the file rather than to `stdout`. A `stdio` buffer flush is performed after every line is written so that the trace may be monitored externally or provide useful information for debugging problems that cause core dumps.
`off`	Turns off all tracing.
`depth`	Returns the current maximum trace level, or 0 if trace is disabled.

Example

The most common use of this command is to enable tracing to a file during the development. If a failure occurs, a trace is then available when needed. Command tracing will slow down the execution of code, so it should be removed when code is debugged. The following command will enable tracing to a file for the remainder of the program:

```
cmdtrace on [open cmd.log w]
```

To turn command tracing off:

```
cmdtrace off
```

edprocs   TclX

Syntax

edprocs [*proc* ...]

Description

This procedure writes the named procedures—or all currently defined procedures—to a temporary file, then calls an editor on it (as specified by the EDITOR environment variable, or vi if none is specified), then sources the file back in if it was changed.

profile   TclX

Syntax

profile [-commands] on
profile off *arrayVar*

Description

This command is used to collect a performance profile of a Tcl script. It collects data at the Tcl procedure level. The number of calls to a procedure and the amount of real and CPU time are collected. Time is also collected for the global context. The procedure data are collected by bucketing, based on the procedure call stack. This allows determination of how much time is spent in a particular procedure in each of its calling contexts.

The on option enables profile data collection. If the -commands option is specified, data on all commands within a procedure are collected. Multiple occurrences of a command within a procedure are not distinguished, but these data may still be useful for analysis.

The off option turns off profiling and moves the data collected to the array *arrayVar*. The array is addressed by a list containing the procedure call stack. Element 0 is the top of the stack, the procedure for the data. The data in each entry are contained in a list consisting of the procedure call count and the real time and CPU time (in milliseconds) spent in the procedure (and all procedures it called). The list is in the form:

    {count real cpu}

A Tcl procedure **profrep** is supplied for reducing the data and producing a report.

profrep   TclX

Syntax

profrep *profDataVar sortKey stackDepth* [*outFile*]
    [*userTitle*]

Description

This procedure generates a report from data collected from the **profile** command. *profDataVar* is the name of the array containing the data returned by the **profile** command. *sortKey* indicates which data value to sort by. It should be one of calls, cpu, or real. *outFile* is the name of the file to which to write the report. If omitted, stdout is assumed. *userTitle* is an optional title line to add to output.

saveprocs   TclX

Syntax

saveprocs *fileName* [*proc* ...]

Description

This procedure saves the definition of the named procedure, or all currently defined procedures if none is specified, to the named file.

Files

Table 26–1 File commands

Command	Tcl	TclX	Description
bsearch		✔	Search file of sorted lines of text for string
chgrp		✔	Change the UNIX file group
chmod		✔	Set the UNIX file permissions
chown		✔	Change the UNIX file owner and/or group
chroot		✔	Change the root directory
close	✔		Close an open file
copyfile		✔	Copy the remainder of an open file into another
dup		✔	Duplicate an open file
echo		✔	Echo one or more strings to stdout, followed by a newline
eof	✔		Check for end-of-file condition on an open file
fcntl		✔	Get or set file access options for an open file—atime, ctime, dev, gid, ino, mod, mtime, nlink, size, tty, type, uid, remotehost
file	✔		Manipulate file names and attributes—atime, dirname, executable, exists, extension, isdirectory, isfile, lstat, mtime, owned, readable, readlink, rootname, size, stat, tail, type, writable

Table 26–1   File commands (cont.)

Command	Tcl	TclX	Description
flock		✔	Lock all or part of a file
flush	✔		Flush buffered output for a file
for_file		✔	Loop through each line in a file
for_recursive_glob		✔	Loop through each file matching a glob statement
frename		✔	Rename a file
fstat		✔	Obtain status information about an open file
funlock		✔	Remove a lock from part or all of a file
gets	✔		Read a line from a file
glob	✔		Return names of files that match a given pattern
lgets		✔	Read next Tcl list from file and discard terminating newline
link		✔	Create a link to a file
mkdir		✔	Create a new directory
open	✔		Open a file
pipe		✔	Create a pipe
puts	✔		Write a to a file
read	✔		Read from a file
read_file		✔	Read a file into a string
readdir		✔	Read the contents of a directory
recursive_glob		✔	Recursive file name matching
rmdir		✔	Remove directories
seek	✔		Change the access position for an open file
select		✔	Synchronous I/O multiplexing
server_info		✔	Obtain information about a TCP/IP server
server_open		✔	Open a connection to a TCP/IP server
sync		✔	For a file or files to be written to disk

Table 26–1 File commands (cont.)

Command	Tcl	TclX	Description
tell	✔		Return current access position for an open file
unlink		✔	Delete files
write_file		✔	Write strings out to a file

bsearch   TclX

Syntax

bsearch *fileId key* [*retVar*] [*compare_proc*]

Returns

1 : if key found (if *retVar* specified)

0 : if key not found (if *retVar* specified)

line : if key found (if *retVar* not specified)

{ } : if key not found (if *retVar* not specified)

Description

This command searches an opened file *fileId* containing lines of text sorted in ascending order for a match. key contains the string to match. If *retVar* is specified, the matched line is returned in *retVar*.

compare_proc

By default, the key is matched against the first whitespace separated in each line. The field is treated as an ASCII string. If *compare_proc* is specified, it defines the name of a Tcl procedure to evaluate against each line read from the sorted file during execution of **bsearch**. *compare_proc* must take two arguments:

- a key
- a line extracted from the file

The compare routine should return a number of less than 0 if the key is less than the line, 0 if the key matches the line, or greater than 0 if the key is greater than the line. The file must be sorted in ascending order according to the same criteria *compare_proc* uses to compare the key with the line, or erroneous results will occur.

chgrp   TclX

Syntax

chgrp *group filelist*

Description

This will set the group ID of each file in the list *filelist* to *group*, which can be either a group name or a numeric group ID.

Example

    chgrp other {people.dat folks.dat}

chmod   TclX

Syntax

chmod *mode filelist*

Description

This command sets permissions of each file in *filelist* to *mode*, where *mode* is an absolute numeric mode or symbolic permissions, as in the UNIX chmod command. Octal modes should be prefixed with 0 (e.g., 0622).

Example

    chmod 755 /tmp/toys

chown   **TclX**

Syntax

chown *owner*|*{owner group}* *filelist*

Description

This sets owner of each file in *filelist* to *owner*. *owner* can be a user name or a
numeric user ID. If the first parameter is a list, then *owner* is set to the first element of
the list and *group* is set to the second element. *group* can be a group name or a
numeric group ID. If *group* is { }, then the file group will be set to the login group of the
specified user.

Example

    chown {alice prodmkt} /u/alice/inventory.data

chroot   **TclX**

Syntax

chroot *dirname*

Description

This command changes the root directory to *dirname* by invoking the POSIX chroot
system call. This command only succeeds if running as root.

close   **Tcl**

Syntax

close *fileID*

Returns

{ } : if no errors encountered

Description

Closes the file given by *fileID*. *fileID* must be the return value from a previous invocation of the open command. After completion, the value in *fileID* should no longer be referenced. If *fileID* refers to a command pipeline instead of a file, then close waits for the children to complete. The normal result of this command is an empty string, but errors are returned if there are problems in closing the file or in waiting for children to complete.

copyfile   TclX

Syntax

copyfile [-bytes *num* |-maxbytes *num*] *fromFieldId toFieldId*

Returns

Error : if -bytes specified and there are fewer than *num* present.
NONE : if -maxbytes specified and there are fewer than *num* present # of bytes copied.

Description

Copies the rest of the file specified by *fromFieldId*, starting from its current position, to the file specified by *toFieldId*, starting from its current position. The -bytes option is particularly useful for mixing binary data with ASCII commands or data in a data stream.

dup   TclX

Syntax

dup *fileId* [*targetFileId*]

Returns

A new file ID is opened that addresses the same file as *fileId*.

Description

Duplicates an open file. If *targetFileId* is specified, the file is duplicated to this specified file ID. Normally, this is stdin, stdout, or stderr.

echo   TclX

Syntax

echo [*str ...*]

Description

This command writes zero or more strings to standard output, followed by a newline.

Example

```
if {$arg == "-h"} {
      echo "Usage: coolapp [-habcdefghijk]"
}
```

eof   Tcl

Syntax

eof *fileId*

Returns

1: end-of-file condition
0: otherwise

Description

fileId must have been the return value from a previous call to **open**, or it may be stdin, stdout or stderr to refer to one of the standard I/O channels.

Example

```
while { ! [eof $fd]} {
        lgets $fd output
}
```

fcntl   TclX

Syntax

fcntl *fileId attribute* [*value*]

Returns

Current file value: if value specified.
Current attribute value: if no value specified.

Description

This command sets or clears a file option or returns its current value if no value is specified.

Attributes

RDONLY	File is opened for reading only
WRONLY	File is opened for writing only
RDWR	File is opened for reading and writing
READ	If the file is readable
WRITE	If the file is writable
APPEND	File is opened for append-only writes. All writes will be forced to the end of file.
NONBLOCK	File is to be accessed with nonblocking I/O. See read system call for nonblocking I/O behavior.

CLOEXEC   Close the file on a process exec (via **execl** or other mechanism that causes the process to do an exec).

NOBUF   File is not buffered. If set, there is no stdio buffering for the file.

LINEBUF   File output will be line buffered. The buffer will be flushed when newline is written, when the buffer is full, or when input is request.

APPEND, NONBLOCK, CLOEXEC attributes may be set or cleared by specifying the attribute name and a value 1 to set the attribute and 0 to clear it.

NOBUF, LINEBUF attributes only may be set (a value of 1), and only one of the options may be selected. Once set, it may not be changed. These options should be set before any I/O operations are performed. There is a risk of losing data.

file   Tcl

Syntax

file *option* *fileName* [*arg arg ...*]

Description

This command performs an assortment of operations on a file's name or attributes. If *fileName* begins with a tilde, tilde substitution is done before executing the command. *option* indicates what to do with *fileName*. Any unique abbreviation for options is acceptable.

Options

file atime *fileName*   Returns a decimal string giving the time at which *fileName* was last accessed. The time is measured in the standard POSIX fashion as seconds from a fixed starting time (often January 1, 1970). If the file does not exist or if its access time cannot be queried, an error is generated.

file dirname *fileName*   Returns all of the characters in *fileName*, up to but not including the last slash character. If there are no slashes in the name, return is a period. If the last slash in *fileName* is its first character, return is a slash.

file executable *fileName*	Returns 1 if *fileName* is executable by the current user, 0 otherwise.
file exists *fileName*	Returns 1 if *fileName* exists and the current user has search privileges for the directories leading to it, 0 otherwise.
file extension *fileName*	Returns all of the characters in name after and including the last dot in name. Returns empty string if there is no dot in *fileName*.
file isdirectory *fileName*	Returns 1 if *fileName* is a directory, 0 otherwise.
file isfile *fileName*	Returns 1 if *fileName* is a regular file, 0 otherwise.
file lstat *fileName varName*	Same as stat option (below), except this option uses the lstat kernel call instead of stat. This means that if *fileName* refers to a symbolic link, the information returned in *varName* is for the link rather than the file it refers to. On systems that do not support symbolic links, this option behaves exactly the same as the stat option.
file mtime *fileName*	Returns a decimal string giving the time at which *fileName* was last modified. See file atime *fileName*, above.
file owned *fileName*	Returns 1 if *fileName* is owned by the current user, 0 otherwise.
file readable *fileName*	Returns 1 if *fileName* is readable by the current user, 0 otherwise.
file readlink *fileName*	Returns the value of the symbolic link given by *fileName* (i.e., the name of the file it points to). If name is not a symbolic link or its value cannot be read, an error is returned. On systems that do not support symbolic links, this option is undefined.

file rootname *fileName*	Returns all of the characters in *fileName*, up to but not including the last period character in the name. If *fileName* does not contain a period, return is *fileName*.
file size *fileName*	Returns a decimal string giving the size of *fileName* in bytes. If the *fileName* does not exist or its size cannot be queried, an error is generated.
file state *fileName var*	Invokes the stat kernel call on *fileName*, using the variable *var* to hold information returned from the kernel call. *var* is treated as an array variable, and the following elements of that variable are set:
	➡ atime, ctime, dev, gid, ino, mode mtime, nlink size type, uid
file tail *fileName*	Returns all of the characters in *fileName* after the last slash. If *fileName* contains no slashes, *fileName* is returned.
file type *fileName*	Returns a string giving the type of file:
	➡ file, directory, characterSpecial, blockSpecial, fifo, link, socket
file writable *fileName*	Returns 1 if *fileName* is writable by the current user, 0 otherwise.

Example

```
set TmpHistoryFile /u/user/history.dat
if { [file exists $TmpHistoryFile] &&
     [file readable $TmpHistoryFile] } {
    set fd [open $TmpHistoryFile r]
}
```

flock   TclX

Syntax

flock *options fileId* [*start*] [*length*] [*origin*]

Description

This command places a lock on all or part of the file specified by *fileId*. The lock is either advisory or mandatory, depending on the mode bits of the file. The lock is placed beginning at relative byte offset *start* for *length* bytes. If *start* or *length* are omitted or empty, 0 is assumed. If *length* is 0, the lock always extends to end of file (EOF), even if the file grows. If *origin* is the string "start", the offset is relative to the beginning of the file. If it is the string "current", it is relative to the current access position in the file. If it is the string "end", it is relative to the EOF (a negative is before the EOF, positive is after). If origin is omitted, start is assumed.

Options

-read   Place a read lock on the file. Multiple processes may be accessing the file with read locks.

-write   Place a write lock on the file. Only one process may be accessing a file if there is a write lock.

-nowait   If specified, the process will not block if the lock cannot be obtained. With this option, the command returns 1 if the lock is obtained; 0 if it is not.

See your system **fcntl** system call documentation for full details of the behavior of file locking. If locking is being done on ranges of a file, it is best to use unbuffered file access (see the **fcntl** command).

flush   Tcl

Syntax

flush *fileId*

Description

This command flushes any output that has been buffered for *fileId*. *fileId* must have been the return value from a previous call to open, or it may be stdout or stderr to access one of the standard I/O streams. It must refer to a file that was opened for writing.

for_file   TclX

Syntax

for_file *var fileName body*

Description

This procedure implements a loop over the contents of the file named by *fileName*. For each line in *fileName*, **for_file** sets *var* to the line and executes code. The **break** and **continue** commands work as with the **foreach** command.

Example

```
for_file line /etc/passwd {
        ParsePasswordRecord $line
}
```

for_recursive_glob   TclX

Syntax

for_recursive_glob *var dirlist globlist body*

Description

This procedure performs a **foreach**-style loop over recursively matched files. All directories in *dirlist* are recursively searched (breadth-first), comparing each file found against the file glob patterns in *globlist*. For each matched file, the variable *var* is set to the file path, and *body* is evaluated. Symbolic links are not followed.

frename   TclX

Syntax

frename *oldPath newPath*

Description

This command renames *oldPath* to *newPath*. It does not support renaming across file systems unless supported by the rename system call. Renaming across file systems can be accomplished with an exec of the mv command.

fstat   TclX

Syntax

fstat *fileId* [*options*]|[stat *arrayvar*]

Description

This command obtains status information about an open file.

Options

atime	The time of last access.
ctime	The time of last file status change.
dev	The device containing a directory for the file. This value uniquely identifies the file system that contains the file.
gid	The group ID of the file's group.
ino	The inode number. This field uniquely identifies the file in a given file system.
mode	The mode of the file (see the mknodsystem call).
mtime	Time that the data in the file was last modified.

Nlink   The number of links to the file.

Size   The file size in bytes.

tty   If the file is associated with a terminal, 1; otherwise, 0.

type   The type of the file in symbolic form, which is one of the
                 following values:

                 ➡ file, directory, characterSpecial,
                 blockSpecial, fifo, link, socket

uid   The user ID of the file's owner.

If one of these keys is specified as *item*, that data item is returned. If *stat arrayvar* is specified, the information is returned in the array *arrayvar*. Each of the above keys indexes an element of the array containing the data. If only *fileId* is specified, the command returns the data as a keyed list.

The following value may be returned only if explicitly requested. It will not be returned with the array or keyed list forms:

remotehost   If *fileId* is a TCP/IP socket connection, a list is returned, with
                 the first element being the remote host IP address. If the remote
                 host name can be found, it is returned as the second element of the
                 list.

Example

```
set fd [open /tmp/data.dat r]
fstat $fd stat statArray
echo "Information on /tmp/data.dat"
echo "\tSize: $statArray(size)"
echo "\tType: $statArray(type)"
echo "\tPermissions: [format "%o" $statArray(mode)]"
```

funlock   TclX

Syntax

funlock *fileId* [*start*] [*length*] [*origin*]

Description

This command removes a lock from a file that was previously placed with the **flock** command. The arguments are the same as for the **flock** command.

gets   Tcl

Syntax

gets *fileId* [*varName*]

Returns

number of bytes read (if *varName* specified)

-1 : if EOF reached (if *varName* specified)

string of data read (if *varName* not specified)

{ } : if EOF reached (if *varName* not specified)

Description

This command reads the next line from the file given by *fileId*, discarding the terminating newline character. If *varName* is specified, the line is placed in the variable by that name, and the return value is the count of the number of characters read (minus the newline). If the EOF is reached before reading any characters, -1 is returned and *varName* is set to an empty string.

If *varName* is not specified, the return value will be the line (minus the newline) or an empty string, if the EOF is reached. An empty string will also be returned if the line contains no characters except the newline, so the **eof** command may have to be used to determine what really happened. If the last character in the file is not a newline character, **gets** behaves as if there were an additional newline character at the EOF. *fileId* must be stdin or the return value from a previous call to **open**; it must refer to a file that was opened for reading. Any existing EOF or error condition on the file is cleared at the beginning of the **gets** command.

Example

```
set fd [open /etc/passwd r]
# read each record and pass it to a fictitious
procedure.
```

```
while { [lgets $fd record] != -1 } {
      ProcessPassword $record
}
close $fd
```

glob   Tcl

Syntax

glob [*switches*] *pattern* [*pattern* ...]

Description

This command performs file name *globbing* in a fashion similar to the csh shell. It returns a list of the files whose names match any of the *pattern* arguments. If the initial arguments to **glob** begin with a hyphen, they are treated as *switches*. The following switches are currently supported:

-nocomplain	Allows an empty list to be returned without error. Without this switch, an error is returned if the result list would be empty.
--	Marks the end of *switches*. The argument following this one will be treated as *pattern*, even if it begins with a hyphen.

The *pattern* arguments may contain any of the following special characters:

?	Matches any single character.
*	Matches any sequence of 0 or more characters.
[*chars*]	Matches any single character in *chars*. If *chars* contains a sequence of the form a-b, any character between a and b (inclusive) will match.
\x	Matches the character x.
{a,b,...}	Matches any of the strings a, b, etc.

As with csh, a period at the beginning of a file's name or just after a slash must be matched explicitly or with a {} construct. In addition, all slash characters must be matched explicitly. If the first character in a pattern is a tilde, it refers to the home directory for the user whose name follows the tilde. If the tilde is followed immediately by slash, the value of the HOME environment variable is used.

The **glob** command differs from csh globbing in two ways. Firstly, it does not sort its result list. (Use the **lsort** command if you want the list sorted.) Secondly, **glob** returns only the names of files that actually exist. In csh no check for existence is made unless a pattern contains a ?, *, or [ ] construct.

lgets   TclX

Syntax

lgets *fileId* [*varName*]

Description

This command reads the next Tcl list from the file given by *fileId* and discards the terminating newline character. This command differs from the **gets** command, in that it reads Tcl lists rather than lines. If the list contains a newline, that newline will be returned as part of the result. Only a newline not quoted as part of the list indicates the end of the list. There is no corresponding command for outputting lists, as puts will do this correctly.

If *varName* is specified, then the line is placed in the variable by that name, and the return value is a count of the number of characters read (not including the newline).

If the end of the file is reached before reading any characters, -1 is returned and *varName* is set to an empty string.

If *varName* is not specified, the return value will be the line (minus the newline character) or an empty string if the EOF is reached before reading any characters. An empty string will also be returned if a line contains no characters except the newline, so **eof** may have to be used to determine what really happened.

link   TclX

Syntax

link [-sym] *srcpath destpath*

Description

This command creates a directory entry, *destpath*, linking it to the existing file, *srcpath*. If -sym is specified, a symbolic link, rather than a hard link, is created. The -sym option is available only on systems that support symbolic links.

mkdir   TclX

Syntax

mkdir [-path] *dirList*

Description

This command creates each of the directories in the list *dirList*. The mode on the new directories is 777, modified by the system umask. If -path is specified, any nonexistent parent directories in the specified path or paths are also created.

open   Tcl

Syntax

open *fileName* [*access*] [*permissions*]

Description

This command opens a file and returns an identifier that may be used in future invocations of commands like **read**, **puts**, **gets**, **lgets**, and **close**. *fileName* gives the name of the file to open. If it starts with a tilde, tilde substitution is performed, as described for Tcl_TildeSubst. If the first character of *fileName* is a pipe character, |, the remaining characters of *fileName* are treated as a command pipeline to invoke, in the same style as **exec**. For example,

    set fd [open "|df" r]

returns a file descriptor that can be read by commands like **read** for the file system information provided by the UNIX df command. This same approach can also be used to write to the command's input pipe.

The *access* argument indicates the way in which the file (or command pipeline) is to be accessed. It may take two forms, either a string in the form that would be passed to the fopen library procedure or a list of POSIX access flags. It defaults to "r". In the first form, access may have any of the following values:

r   Opens the file for reading only; the file must already exist.

r+   Opens the file for both reading and writing; the file must already exist.

w   Opens the file for writing only; truncates it if it exists. If it does not exist, creates a new file.

w+   Opens the file for reading and writing; truncate it if it exists. If it does not exist, creates a new file.

a   Opens the file for writing only. The file must already exist, and the file is positioned so that new data are appended to the file.

a+   Opens the file for reading and writing. If the file does not exist, creates a new empty file. Sets the initial access position to the end of the file.

In the second form, *access* consists of a list of any of the following flags, all of which have the standard POSIX meanings. One of the flags must be RDONLY, WRONLY, or RDWR.

RDONLY   Opens the file for reading only.

WRONLY   Opens the file for writing only.

RDWR   Opens the file for both reading and writing.

APPEND   Sets the file pointer to the end of the file prior to each write.

CREAT   Creates the file if it does not already exist.

EXCL   If CREAT is specified and the file already exists, an error is returned.

NOCTTY   If the file is a terminal device, prevents the file from becoming the controlling terminal of the process.

NONBLOCK   Prevents the process from blocking while opening the file. For details on the O_NONBLOCK flag, refer to open(S).

TRUNC   If the file exists, truncates it to zero length.

If a new file is created as part of opening it, *permissions* (an integer) is used to set the permissions for the new file, in conjunction with the process's file mode creation mask. *permissions* defaults to 0666.

If a file is opened for both reading and writing, **seek** must be invoked between a read and a write. If for writing or reading, **seek** must be invoked before the write or the read. This restriction does not apply to command pipelines opened with **open**. When *fileName* specifies a command pipeline and a write-only access is used, standard output from the pipeline is directed to the current standard output unless overridden by the command. When *fileName* specifies a command pipeline and a read-only access is used, standard input from the pipeline is taken from the current standard input unless overridden by the command.

pipe   **TclX**

Syntax

pipe [*fileId_var_r fileId_var_w*]

Description

The **pipe** command creates a pipe. If *fileId_var_r* and *fileId_var_w* are specified, **pipe** will set the variable named *fileId_var_r* to contain the file ID of the side of the pipe that was opened for reading, and set *fileId_var_w* to contain the file ID of the side of the pipe that was opened for writing. If the file ID variables are not specified, a list containing the read and write file IDs is returned as the result of the command.

puts   **Tcl**

Syntax

puts [-nonewline] [*fileId*] *string*

Description

This command writes the characters given by string to the file given by *fileId*. *fileId* must be the return value from a previous call to **open**, or it may be stdout or stderr, to refer to one of the standard I/O channels; it must refer to a file that was opened for writing. If no *fileId* is specified, it defaults to stdout. **puts** normally outputs a newline character after *string*, but this feature may be suppressed by specifying the -nonewline switch. Output to files is buffered internally by Tcl; the **flush** command may be used to force buffered characters to be output.

read   **Tcl**

Syntax

read [-nonewline] *fileId*
read *fileId numBytes*

Description

In the first form, all of the remaining bytes are read from the file given by *fileId*; they are returned as the result of the command. If the -nonewline switch is specified, the last character of the file is discarded if it is a newline. In the second form, the extra argument specifies how many bytes to read; exactly this many bytes will be read and returned, unless there are fewer than numBytes bytes remaining in the file. In this case, all the remaining bytes are returned. *fileId* must be stdin or the return value from a previous call to **open**; it must refer to a file that was opened for reading. Any existing EOF or error condition on the file is cleared at the beginning of the **read** command.

read_file   Tcl

Syntax

read_file [-nonewline] *fileName*
read_file *fileName numBytes*

Description

This procedure reads the file *fileName* and returns the contents as a string. If -nonewline is specified, the last character of the file is discarded if it is a newline. The second form specifies exactly how many bytes will be read and returned, unless there are fewer than *numBytes* bytes left in the file; in this case, all the remaining bytes are returned.

readdir   TclX

Syntax

readdir *dirpath*

Description

This command returns a list containing the contents of the directory *dirpath*. The directory entries "." and ".." are not returned.

recursive_glob   **TclX**

Syntax

recursive_glob *dirlist globlist*

Description

This procedure returns a list of recursively matched files. All directories in *dirlist* are recursively searched (breadth-first), comparing each file found against the file glob patterns in *globlist*. Symbolic links are not followed.

rmdir   **TclX**

Syntax

rmdir [-nocomplain] *dirList*

Description

This removes each of the directories in the list *dirList*. If -nocomplain is specified, errors will be ignored.

seek   **Tcl**

Syntax

seek *fileId offset* [*origin*]

Description

This command changes the current access position for *fileId*. *fileId* must have been the return value from a previous call to open, or it may be stdin, stdout, or stderr to refer to one of the standard I/O channels. The offset and origin arguments specify the position at which the next read or write will occur for *fileId*. *offset* must be an integer (which may be negative), and *origin* must be one of the following:

start   The new access position will be *offset* bytes from the start of the file.

current   The new access position will be *offset* bytes from the current access position; a negative offset moves the access position backward in the file.

end   The new access position will be *offset* bytes from the EOF. A negative offset places the access position before the EOF, and a positive offset places the access position after the EOF.

The origin argument defaults to start. This command returns an empty string.

select   **TclX**

Syntax

select *readfileIds* [*writefileIds*] [*exceptfileIds*] [*timeout*]

Description

This command allows an TclX program to wait for zero or more files to become available for reading, writing, to have an exceptional condition pending, or for a timeout period to expire. *readFileIds*, *writeFileIds*, and *exceptFileIds* are each lists of file IDs, as returned from open, to query. An empty list, {}, may be specified if a category is not used.

The files specified by the *readFileIds* list are checked to see if data are available for reading. The *writeFileIds* are checked if the specified files are clear for writing. The *exceptFileIds* are checked to see if an exceptional condition has occurred (typically, an error). The write and exception checking are most useful on devices, however, the read checking is very useful when communicating with multiple processes through pipes. **select** considers data pending in the stdio input buffer for read files as being ready for reading. The files do not have to be unbuffered.

timeout is a floating point timeout value, in seconds. If an empty list is supplied (or the parameter is omitted), no *timeout* is set. If the value is zero, the **select** command functions as a poll of the files, returning immediately, even if none are ready. If the timeout period expires with none of the files becoming ready, the command returns an empty list. Otherwise, the command returns a list of three elements. Each of those elements is a list of the file IDs that are ready in the read, write, and exception classes. If no IDs are ready in a class, that element will be the null list. For example:

```
select {file3 file4 file5} {file6 file7} {} 10.5
```

could return
➡ {file3 file4} {file6} {}

or perhaps
➡ file3 {} {}

server_info   TclX

Syntax

server_info *option hostname*

Description

This command obtains information about a TCP/IP server. The options are as follows:

address   Returns the list of IP addresses for the server.

official_name   Returns the official name for *hostname*.

aliases   Returns the list of aliases for *hostname*.

server_open   TclX

Syntax

server_open [*option*] *host service*

Description

This command opens a TCP/IP connection to a server of *host* on the port specified by *service*. The server is then accessed using the standard Tcl file I/O commands. *host* may be a host name or an IP address. *port* may be a port number of a service name. *option* is -buf or -nobuf. If no options are specified, -buf is the default.

If -buf is specified, the file is buffered. In this case, a pair of Tcl file IDs are returned in a list. The first ID is open for read access, the second for write. When writing to the file, the **flush** command must be used to force data in the buffer to be sent to the server. The **close** command must be called against both file IDs when through with the socket. Buffered access will result in significantly better performance when reading data and will also improve a series of writes being done without intermixed reads. The **fcntl** command may be used to make one of these files unbuffered.

If -nobuf is specified, the file is unbuffered and a single file ID, open for both reading and writing, is returned.

If a host name is supplied and more than one address is valid for the host, the addresses are tried iteratively until a connection is established. Use **server_info** to obtain the list of valid addresses.

sync   TclX

Syntax

sync [*fileId*]

Description

If *fileId* is not specified, or if it is specified and this system does not support the **fsync** system call, this issues a **sync** system call to flush all pending disk output. If *fileId* is specified and the system does support the **fsync** system call, it issues an **fsync** on the file corresponding to the specified Tcl file ID to force all pending output to that file out to the disk.

If *fileId* is specified, the file must be writable. A flush is issued against *fileId* before the **sync**.

The command

    infox have_fsync

can be used to determine whether **sync** *fileId* will do a **sync** or an **fsync**.

tell   Tcl

Syntax

tell *fileId*

Description

This command returns a decimal string giving the current access position in *fileId*. *fileId* must have been the return value from a previous call to **open**, or it may be stdin, stdout, or stderr to refer to one of the standard I/O channels.

unlink   TclX

Syntax

unlink [-nocomplain] *filelist*

Description

This command deletes (unlinks) the files whose names are in the list *filelist*. If -nocomplain is specified, errors are ignored.

write_file   TclX

Syntax

write_file *fileName string [string ...]*

Description

This procedure writes the specified strings to the named file.

File Scan

*T*hese commands provide a facility to scan files, matching lines of a file against regular expressions and executing Tcl code on a match. With this facility you can use Tcl to do the sort of file processing that is traditionally done with awk (C). Because the Tcl language is more declarative, some of the scripts that can be difficult to write in awk are simple to code in Tcl.

File scanning in Tcl centers around the concept of a "scan context." A scan context contains one or more match statements, with associated regular expressions to scan for and Tcl code to be executed when the expressions are matched.

Table 27–1 File scan commands

Command	Tcl	TclX	Short Description
scancontext		✔	Manage file scan contexts
scanfile		✔	Scan a file, executing match code when patterns are matched
scanmatch		✔	Specific Visual Tcl code to execute when match occurs

scancontext   TclX

Syntax

scancontext [*option*]

Description

This command manages file scan contexts. A scan context is a collection of regular expressions and commands to execute when that regular expression matches a line of the file. A context may also have a single default match, to be applied against lines that do not match any of the regular expressions.

Multiple scan contexts may be defined, and they may be reused on multiple files. A scan context is identified by a context handle. The **scancontext** command takes the following forms:

scancontext *create*

This form creates a new scan context. The **scanmatch** command is used to define patterns in the context. A context handle is returned, which the Tcl programmer uses to refer to the newly created scan context in calls to the Tcl file scanning commands.

scancontext *delete contexthandle*

This form deletes the scan context identified by *contexthandle* and frees all of the match statements and compiled regular expressions associated with the specified context.

scanfile   TclX

Syntax

scanfile [-copyfile *copyFileId*] *contexthandle fileId*

Description

This command scans the file specified by *fileId*, starting from the current file position, and checks all patterns in the scan context specified by *contexthandle* against it, executing the match commands corresponding to patterns matched. If the optional -*copyfile* argument is specified, the next argument is a file ID to which all lines not matched by any pattern (excluding the default pattern) are to be written.

scanmatch   **TclX**

Syntax

scanmatch [-nocase] *contexthandle* [*regexp*] *commands*

Description

This command specifies Tcl commands, to be evaluated when *regexp* is matched by a **scanfile** command. The match is added to the scan context specified by **contexthandle**. Any number of match statements may be specified for a given context. *regexp* is a regular expression (see the **regexp** command). If -nocase is specified as the first argument, the pattern is matched regardless of alphabetic case.

If *regexp* is not specified, a default match is specified for the scan context. The default match will be executed when a line of the file does not match any of the regular expressions in the current scan context.

The array matchInfo is available to the Tcl code, executed when an expression matches (or defaults). It contains information about the file being scanned and where within it the expression was matched.

matchInfo is local to the top level of the match command unless declared global at that level by the Tcl **global** command. If it is to be used as a global, it must be declared global before **scanfile** is called (since **scanfile** sets matchInfo before the match code is executed, a subsequent global will override the local variable). The following array entries are available:

matchInfo(line)	The text of the line of the file that was matched.
matchInfo(offset)	The byte offset into the file of the first character of the line that was matched.
matchInfo(linenum)	The line number of the line that was matched. This is relative to the first line scanned, which is usually, but not necessarily, the first line of the file. The first line is line number 1.
matchInfo(handle)	The file ID (handle) of the file currently being scanned.
matchInfo(copyHandle)	The file ID (handle) of the file specified by the -copyfile option. The element does not exist if -copyfile was not specified.
matchInfo(submatch0)	The characters matching the first parenthesized subexpression. The second will be contained in submatch1, etc.

`matchInfo(subindex0)` The list of the starting and ending indices of the string matching the first parenthesized subexpression. The second will be contained in `subindex1`, etc.

All **scanmatch** patterns that match a line will be processed in the order in which their specifications were added to the scan context. The remainder of the **scanmatch** pattern-command pairs may be skipped for a file line if a continue is executed by the Tcl code of a preceding, matched pattern.

If a return is executed in the body of the match command, the **scanfile** command currently in progress returns, with the value passed to return as its return value.

International

Table 28–1 International Commands

Command	Tcl	TclX	Short Description
catclose		✔	Close a message catalog
catgets		✔	Retrieve a message from a message catalog
catopen		✔	Open a message catalog

These commands provide a Tcl interface to message catalogs that are compliant with XPG/3. Tcl programmers can use message catalogs to create applications that are language-independent. Through the use of message catalogs, prompts, messages, menus, and so forth can exist for any number of languages; they can be altered, and new languages can be added without affecting any Tcl or C source code, greatly easing the maintenance difficulties incurred by supporting multiple languages.

A default text message is passed to the command that fetches entries from message catalogs. This allows the Tcl programmer to create message catalogs containing messages in various languages, retaining a set of default messages available, regardless of the presence of any message catalogs, and allowing the programs to press on without difficulty when no catalogs are present.

The normal approach to using message catalogs is to ignore errors on **catopen**, in which case **catgets** will return the default message that was specified in the call.

The Tcl message catalog commands normally ignore most errors. If it is desirable to detect errors, a special option is provided. This is normally used only during debugging, to ensure that message catalogs are being used. If your UNIX implementation does not have XPG/3 message catalog support, stubs will be compiled that will create a version of **catgets** that always returns the default string. This allows for easy porting of software to environments that do not have support for message catalogs.

Message catalogs are global to the process. An application with multiple Tcl interpreters within the same process may pass and share message catalog handles.

catclose   TclX

Syntax

catclose [-fail|-nofail] *cathandle*

Description

This command closes the message catalog specified by *catHandle*. Normally, errors are ignored. If -fail is specified, any errors closing the message catalog file are returned. The option -nofail specifies the default behavior of not returning an error. The use of -fail makes sense only if it was also specified in the call to **catopen**.

catgets   TclX

Syntax

catgets *catHandle setnum msgnum defaultstr*

Description

This command retrieves a message from a message catalog. *catHandle* should be a Tcl message catalog handle that was returned by **catopen**. *setnum* is the message set number, and *msgnum* is the message number. If the message catalog was not opened, or if the message set or message number cannot be found, the default string, *defaultStr*, is returned.

catopen   TclX

Syntax

catopen [-fail|-nofail] *catname*

Description

This command opens the message catalog *catname*. This may be a relative pathname, in which case the NLSPATH environment variable is searched to find an absolute path to the message catalog. A handle in the form msgcatN is returned. Normally, errors are ignored, and in the case of a failed call to **catopen**, a handle is returned to an unopened message catalog. This handle may still be passed to **catgets** and **catclose**, causing **catgets** to simply return the default string, as described above. If the -fail option is specified, an error is returned if the open fails. The option -nofail specifies the default behavior of not returning an error when **catopen** fails to open a specified message catalog. If the handle from a failed **catopen** is passed to **catgets**, the default string is returned.

## CHAPTER 29

Keyed Lists

Table 29–1 Keyed list commands

Command	Tcl	TclX	Short Description
keyldel		✔	Delete a field in a keyed list
keylget		✔	Retrieve a value of a field in a keyed list
keylkeys		✔	Retrieve the list of keys in a keyed list
keylset		✔	Assign a value of a field in a keyed list

keyldel   TclX

Syntax

keyldel *listVar key*

Description

This command deletes the field specified by *key* from the keyed list in the variable *listVar*. This removes both the key and the value from the keyed list.

Keylget   TclX

Syntax

keylget *listVar* [*key*] [*retVar* | {}]

Description

This returns the value associated with *key* from the keyed list in the variable *listVar*. If *retVar* is not specified, the value will be returned as the result of the command. In this case, if *key* is not found in the list, an error will result.

If *retVar* is specified and *key* is in the list, the value is returned in the variable *retVar*, and the command returns 1 if *key* was present within the list. If *key* is not in the list, the command will return 0, and *retVar* will be left unchanged. If { } is specified for *retVar*, the value is not returned, allowing the Tcl programmer to determine whether a key is present in a keyed list without setting a variable as a side effect. If *key* is omitted, a list of all the keys in the keyed list is returned.

Keylkeys   TclX

Syntax

keylkeys *listVar* [*key*]

Description

This returns a list of the keys in the keyed list in the variable *listVar*. If *key* is specified, it is the name of a key field whose subfield keys are to be retrieved.

Keylset   TclX

Syntax

keylset *listVar key value* [*key2 value2 ...*]

Description

This command sets the value associated with *key*, in the keyed list contained in the variable *listVar*, to *value*. If *listVar* does not exist, it is created. If *key* is not currently in the list, it will be added. If it already exists, *value* replaces the existing value. Multiple keywords and values may be specified, if desired.

Package Library

Table 30–1 Package library commands

Command	Tcl	TclX	Short Description
auto_commands		✔	List names of loadable library commands and procedures
auto_load		✔	Force an automatic load of a command
auto_load_file		✔	Search the auto_path for a file to source
auto_packages		✔	List all packages
buildpackageindex		✔	Build index files for package libraries
convert_lib		✔	Convert an Ousterhout-style tclIndex file to a package library
loadlibindex		✔	Load the index of a package library
searchpath		✔	Search a path list for a file
unknown	✔		Handle attempts to use nonexistent commands

auto_commands   TclX

Syntax

```
auto_commands [-loaders]
```

Description

This command lists the names of all known loadable procedures and command procedures. If -loaders is specified, the command that will be executed to load the command will be returned also.

auto_load   TclX

Syntax

auto_load [*command*]

Description

This command attempts to load the specified command from a loadable library, loading the package containing the procedure. If the package indexes have not been loaded for all package libraries in auto_path, they are loaded. Out-of-date library indexes are rebuilt if they are writable. The procedure returns 1 if the command was successfully loaded, or 0 if it was not.

Duplicated package names are skipped; the first package of a given name found in the path is loaded. If the auto_path has changed since the last load, indexes are reloaded (duplicate packages are not redefined).

If *command* is not specified, the indexes are loaded if they have not already been loaded or if the auto_path variable has changed, but no command is loaded.

This command overrides the standard Tcl procedure of the same name.

auto_load_file   TclX

Syntax

auto_load_file *fileName*

Description

This sources a file specified in *fileName*, as with the **source** command, except that it searches auto_path for the file in which to source.

auto_packages   TclX

Syntax

auto_packages [-files]

Description

This returns a list of the names of all defined packages. If -files is specified, **auto_packages** returns a list containing pairs of values. The first value in each pair is the package name; the second is its corresponding .tlib pathname, offset, and length (within the .tlib file).

buildpackageindex   TclX

Syntax

buildpackageindex *libfilelist*

Description

This command builds index files for package libraries. The argument *libfilelist* is a list of package libraries. Each name must end with the suffix .tlib. A corresponding .tndx file is built. The user must have write access to the directory containing each library.

convert_lib   TclX

Syntax

convert_lib *tclIndex packagelib* [ignore]

Description

This converts an Ousterhout-style *tclIndex* index file and associated source files into a package library *packagelib*. If *packagelib* does not have a .tlib extension, one is added. Any files specified in *tclIndex* that are in the list `ignore` are skipped. Files listed in `ignore` should be just the base file names, not full paths.

loadlibindex   TclX

Syntax

loadlibindex *libfile*.tlib

Description

This will load the package library index of the library file *libfile* (which must have the suffix `.tlib`). Package library indexes along the `auto_path` are loaded automatically on the first `demand_load`; this command is provided to explicitly load libraries that are not in the path. If the index file (with a `.tndx` suffix) does not exist or is out of date, it is rebuilt if the user has directory permissions to create it. If a package with the same name as a package in *libfile*.tlib has already been loaded, its definition is overridden by the new package. However, if any procedure has actually been used from the previously defined package, the procedures from *libfile*.tlib are not loaded.

This command also loads an index built by the `mkindex.tcl` program supplied with standard Tcl. This file must be named `tclIndex`.

searchpath   TclX

Syntax

searchpath *path file*

Description

This will search all directories in the specified path, which is a Tcl list, for the specified file. Returns the full pathname of the file, or an empty string if the requested file cannot be found.

unknown   **Tcl**

Syntax

unknown *cmdName* [*arg arg ...*]

Description

This command is not a core part of Tcl, but Tcl will invoke it if it does exist (that is, if a function called unknown has been written and linked to Tcl in the current application). If the Tcl interpreter encounters a command name for which there is not a defined command, Tcl checks for the existence of a command named **unknown**. If there is no such command, the interpreter returns an error. If the **unknown** command exists, it is invoked with arguments consisting of the fully substituted name and arguments for the original nonexistent command.

The **unknown** command typically does things like searching through library directories for a command procedure with the name *cmdName*, expanding abbreviated command names to full length or automatically executing **unknown** commands as subprocesses. In some cases (such as expanding abbreviations) **unknown** will change the original command slightly and then (re-)execute it. The result of the **unknown** command is used as the result for the original, nonexistent command.

Lists

Table 31–1   List Commands

Command	Tcl	TclX	Short Description
concat	✔		Join lists into a single list
intersect		✔	Return list of elements that occur in both lists
intersect3		✔	Return three lists from an intersection of two lists
join	✔		Create new string from joining list elements
lappend	✔		Append list elements onto a list variable
lassign		✔	Assign successive elements of a list to specified variables
lempty		✔	Determine whether a list is empty
lindex	✔		Retrieve an element by position within a list
linsert	✔		Insert elements into a list by position
list	✔		Create a list
llength	✔		Return the number of elements in a list
lmatch		✔	Return a list of elements from a list that match a pattern
lrange	✔		Return one or more adjacent elements from a list
lreplace	✔		Replace elements in a list with new elements

Table 31–1   List Commands (cont.)

Command	Tcl	TclX	Short Description
lrmdups		✔	Removal all duplicate elements in a list
lsearch	✔		Determine whether a list contains a particular element
lsort	✔		Sort the elements in a list
lvarcat		✔	Concatenate the contents of a list or string into a variable
lvarpop		✔	Pop or replace an element from a list
lvarpush		✔	Push or insert an element into a list
split	✔		Split a string at one or more delimiters into a Tcl list
union		✔	Return the logical union of two lists

concat   Tcl

Syntax

```
concat [arg arg ...]
```

Description

This command treats each argument as a list and concatenates argument lists into a single list. It also eliminates leading and trailing spaces in the *args* and adds a single separator space between *args*. It permits any number of arguments. For example, the command

```
concat a b {c d e} {f {g h}}
```

will return

```
a b c d e f {g h}
```

as its result. If no *args* are supplied, the result is an empty string.

intersect   TclX

Syntax

`intersect` *lista listb*

Description

This returns the logical intersection of two lists. The returned list will be sorted.

intersect3   TclX

Syntax

`intersect3` *lista listb*

Description

This command intersects two lists, returning a list containing three lists. The first list returned is everything in *lista* that was not in *listb*. The second list contains the intersection of the two lists. The third list contains all the elements that were in *listb* but were not in *lista*. The returned lists will be sorted.

join   Tcl

Syntax

`join` *list* [joinString]

Description

The `list` argument must be a valid Tcl list. This command returns the string formed by joining all of the elements of `list`, with `joinString` separating each adjacent pair of elements. The `joinString` argument defaults to a space character.

lappend   Tcl

Syntax

lappend *varName* [*value value* ...]

Description

This command treats the variable given by *varName* as a list and appends each value argument to that list as a separate element, with spaces between elements. If *varName* does not exist, it is created as a list with elements given by the value arguments. **lappend** is similar to **append**, except that the values are appended as list elements rather than as raw text. This command provides a relatively efficient way to build up large lists.

Example

For example,

    lappend a $b

is much more efficient than

    set a [**concat** $a [**list** $b]]

when $a is long.

lassign   TclX

Syntax

lassign *list var* [*var* ...]

Description

This command assigns successive elements of a list to specified variables. If there are more variable names than there are fields, the remaining variables are set to the empty string. If there are more elements than there are variables, a list of the unassigned elements is returned.

Example

For example

lassign {dave 100 200 {Dave Foo}} name uid gid longName

assigns name to dave, uid to 100, gid to 200, and longName to Dave Foo.

lempty   TclX

Syntax

lempty *list*

Description

This command determines whether the specified list is empty. If empty, 1 is returned, otherwise, 0 is returned. This command is an alternative to comparing a list to an empty string.

lindex   Tcl

Syntax

lindex *list index*

Description

This command treats *list* as a Tcl list and returns the element which is *index* elements from the beginning of the list (for example, 0 refers to the first element, 1 to the second, and so on). In extracting the element, **lindex** observes the same rules concerning braces, quotes, and backslashes as does the Tcl command interpreter; however, variable substitution and command substitution do not occur. If *index* is negative, or greater than or equal to the number of elements in *value*, an empty string is returned.

If *index* has the value end, it refers to the last element in the list.

linsert   Tcl

Syntax

linsert *list index element* [*element element* ...]

Description

This command produces a new list from *list* by inserting all of the *element* arguments into *list*, after *index* elements of the current list. Each *element* argument will become a separate element of the new list. If *index* is less than or equal to 0, the new elements are inserted at the beginning of the list.

If *index* has the value end, or if it is greater than or equal to the number of elements in the list, the new elements are appended to the list.

list   Tcl

Syntax

list [*arg arg* ...]

Description

This command returns a list comprised of all the *arg*s, or an empty string if no *arg*s are specified. Braces and backslashes are added as necessary, so that the **lindex** command may be used on the result to re-extract the original arguments, and also so that **eval** may be used to execute the resulting list (with *arg1* comprising the command's name and the other *arg*s comprising its arguments). **list** produces slightly different results from **concat**. **concat** removes one level of grouping before forming the list, while **list** works directly from the original arguments.

Example

For example, the command

    list a b {c d e} {f {g h}}

will return

    a b {c d e} {f {g h}}

while **concat** with the same arguments will return

```
a b c d e f {g h}
```

llength   Tcl

Syntax

llength *list*

Description

This command treats *list* as a list and returns a decimal string giving the number of its elements.

lmatch   TclX

Syntax

lmatch [*mode*] *list pattern*

Description

This will search the elements of *list* and return a list of all elements matching *pattern*. If there are no matches, an empty list is returned. The *mode* argument indicates how the elements of the list are to be matched against *pattern*, and it must have one of the following values:

-exact   The list element must contain exactly the same string as *pattern*.

-glob   *pattern* is a glob-style pattern that is matched against each list element using the same rules as the **string** match command.

-regexp   *pattern* is treated as a regular expression and matched against each list element, using the same rules as the **regexp** command.

If *mode* is omitted, it defaults to -glob.

lrange   Tcl

Syntax

```
lrange list first last
```

Description

list must be a valid Tcl list. This command returns a new list consisting of elements *first* through *last*, inclusive. *first* or *last* may be end (or any abbreviation of it) to refer to the last element of the list. If *first* is less than 0, it is treated as if it were 0. If *last* is greater than or equal to the number of elements in the list, it is treated as if it were end. If *first* is greater than *last*, an empty string is returned.
NOTE:

```
lrange list first first
```

does not always produce the same result as does

```
lindex list first
```

(although it often does for simple fields that are not enclosed in braces). It does, however, produce exactly the same result as does

```
list [lindex list first].
```

lreplace   Tcl

Syntax

```
lreplace list first last [element element ...]
```

Description

lreplace returns a new list formed by replacing one or more elements of *list* with the *element* arguments. *first* gives the index in *list* of the first element to be replaced (0 refers to the first element). If *first* is less than 0, it refers to the first element of *list*; the element indicated by *first* must exist in the list. *last* gives the index in *list* of the last element to be replaced. It must be greater than or equal to *first*. *first* or *last* may be end (or any abbreviation of it) to refer to the last element of the list. The *element* arguments specify 0 or more new arguments to be added to the list in place of those that were deleted. Each *element* argument will become a separate element of the list. If no *element* arguments are specified, the elements between *first* and *last* are simply deleted.

lrmdups   **TclX**

Syntax

lrmdups *list*

Description

This command removes duplicate elements from a list. The returned list will be sorted.

Example

    set people {John Pete Alice Ann Alice Pete Bob George}
    echo [**lrmdups** $people]
➡   {Alice Ann Bob George John Pete}

lsearch   **Tcl**

Syntax

lsearch [*mode*] *list pattern*

Description

This command searches the elements of *list* to see if one of them matches *pattern*. If so, the command returns the index of the first matching element. If not, the command returns −1. The *mode* argument indicates how the elements of the list are to be matched against *pattern*. *mode* must have one of the following values:

-exact   The *list* element must contain exactly the same string as *pattern*.

-glob   *pattern* is a glob-style pattern that is matched against each *list* element using the same rules as the **string** match command.

-regexp   *pattern* is treated as a regular expression and matched against each *list* element using the same rules as the **regexp** command.

If *mode* is omitted, it defaults to -glob.

lsort   Tcl

Syntax

lsort [*switches*] *list*

Description

This command sorts the elements of *list*, returning a new list in sorted order. By default, ASCII sorting is used, with the result returned in increasing order. However, any of the following switches may be specified before *list* to control the sorting process (unique abbreviations are accepted):

-ascii   Use string comparison with ASCII collation order. This is the default.

-integer   Convert *list* elements to integers and use integer comparison.

-real   Convert *list* elements to floating-point values and use floating-point comparison.

-command *command*   Use *command* as a comparison command. To compare two elements, evaluate a Tcl script consisting of *command* with the two elements appended as additional arguments. The script should return an integer less than, equal to, or greater than 0 if the first element is to be considered less than, equal to, or greater than the second, respectively.

-increasing   Sort the list in increasing order (smallest items first). This is the default.

-decreasing   Sort the list in decreasing order (largest items first).

lvarcat   **TclX**

Syntax

`lvarcat` *listName string* [*string ...*]

Description

This command treats each *string* argument as a list and concatenates them to the end of the contents of *listName*, forming a single list. The list is stored back into *listName* and also returned as the result. If *listName* does not exist, it is created.

lvarpop   **TclX**

Syntax

`lvarpop` *listName* [*indexExpr*] [*string*]

Description

The **lvarpop** command pops (returns and removes) the element indexed by the expression *indexExpr* from the list contained in the variable *listName*. If *indexExpr* is omitted, then 0 is assumed. If *string* is specified, the deleted element is replaced by *string*. The replaced or deleted element is returned. Thus,

> `lvarpop` argv

returns the first element of argv, setting argv to contain the remainder of the string.

If the expression *indexExpr* begins with the string end, then end is replaced with the index of the last element in the list. If the expression begins with len, then len is replaced with the length of the list.

lvarpush   **TclX**

Syntax

`lvarpush` *listName string* [*indexExpr*]

Description

The **lvarpush** command pushes (inserts) *string* as an element in the list contained in the variable *listName*. The element is inserted before position *indexExpr* in the list. If *indexExpr* is omitted, 0 is assumed. If *listName* does not exist, it is created.

If the expression *indexExpr* starts with the string end, then end is replaced with the index of the last element in the list. With end, the string is inserted before the last element. If the expression starts with len, then len is replaced with the length of the list.

split   Tcl

Syntax

split *string* [*splitChars*]

Description

This command returns a list created by splitting *string* at each character that is specified in the *splitChars* argument. Each element of the resulting list will consist of the characters from *string* that lie between instances of the characters in *splitChars*. Empty list elements will be generated if *string* contains adjacent characters in *splitChars*, or if the first or last character of *string* is in *splitChars*. If *splitChars* is an empty string, each character of *string* becomes a separate element of the resulting list. *splitChars* defaults to the standard whitespace characters.

Example

For example,

```
    split "comp.unix.misc" .
```
➡ comp unix misc

```
    # split everything into individual list items
    split "Hello world" {}
```
➡ H e l l o { } w o r l d.

union   **TclX**

Syntax

union *lista listb*

Description

The **union** command returns the logical union of the two specified lists. Any duplicate
elements are removed.

## CHAPTER 32

Math

Table 32–1 Math commands

Command	Tcl	TclX	Short Description
expr	✔		Evaluate an expression
fmathcmds		✔	**expr** math functions: sin, cos, tan
incr	✔		Increment the value of a variable
max		✔	Return the argument that has the highest numeric value
min		✔	Return the argument that has the lowest numeric value
random		✔	Return a pseudorandom integer or set the seed

expr   Tcl

Syntax

expr *arg* [*arg* ...]

Description

This command concatenates *arg*s (adding separator spaces between them), evaluates the result as a Tcl expression, and returns the value. The operators permitted in Tcl expressions are a subset of the operators permitted in C expressions, and they have the same meaning and precedence as do the corresponding C operators. Expressions almost always yield numeric results (integer or floating-point values). For example, the expression

expr 8.2 + 6

evaluates to 14.2. Tcl expressions differ from C expressions in the way that operands are specified. Also, Tcl expressions support nonnumeric operands and string comparisons.

Operands

A Tcl expression consists of a combination of operands, operators, and parentheses. Whitespace may be used between the operands and operators and parentheses; it is ignored by the expression processor. Where possible, operands are interpreted as integer values. Integer values may be specified in decimal (the normal case), octal (if the first character of the operand is 0), or hexadecimal (if the first two characters of the operand are 0 and x) format. If an operand does not have one of the integer formats given above, it is treated as a floating-point number if that is possible.

Floating-point numbers may be specified in any of the ways accepted by an ANSI-compliant C compiler (except that the f, F, 1, and L suffixes will not be permitted in most installations). For example, all of the following are valid floating-point numbers: 2.1, 3., 6e4, 7.91e+16. If no numeric interpretation is possible, then an operand is left as a string (and only a limited set of operators may be applied to it).

Operands may be specified in any of the following ways:

1. As a numeric value, either integer or floating-point.
2. As a Tcl variable, using standard $ notation. The variable's value will be used as the operand.
3. As a string enclosed in double quotes. The expression parser will perform backslash, variable, and command substitutions on the information between the quotes and will use the resulting value as the operand.
4. As a string enclosed in braces. The characters between the open brace and matching close brace will be used as the operand without any substitutions.
5. As a Tcl command enclosed in brackets. The command will be executed, and its result will be used as the operand.
6. As a mathematical function whose arguments have any of the above forms for operands, such as sin($x). See below for a list of defined functions.

Where substitutions occur above (for example, inside quoted strings), they are performed by the expression processor. However, an additional layer of substitution may already have been performed by the command parser before the expression processor was called. As discussed below, it is usually best to enclose expressions in braces to prevent the command parser from performing substitutions on the contents.

For some examples of simple expressions, suppose that the variable a has the value 3 and that the variable b has the value 6. The command on the left, below, will produce the value on the right.

```
expr 3.1 + $a 6.1
expr 2 + "$a.$b" 5.6
expr 4*[llength "6 2"] 8
expr {{word one} < "word $a"} 0
```

Operators

The valid operators are listed below, grouped in decreasing order of precedence:

`- ~ !`	Unary minus, bitwise NOT, logical NOT. None of these operands may be applied to string operands, and bitwise NOT may be applied only to integers.
`* / %`	Multiply, divide, remainder. None of these operands may be applied to string operands, and remainder may be applied only to integers. The remainder will always have the same sign as the divisor and an absolute value smaller than the divisor.
`+ -`	Add and subtract. Valid for any numeric operands.
`<< >>`	Left and right shift. Valid for integer operands only.
`< > <= >=`	Boolean less, greater, less or equal, and greater or equal. Each operator produces 1 if the condition is true, 0 otherwise. These operators may be applied to strings as well as numeric operands, in which case string comparison is used.
`== !=`	Boolean equal and not equal. Each operator produces 1 if the condition is true, otherwise. Valid for all operand types.
`&`	Bitwise AND. Valid for integer operands only.
`^`	Bitwise exclusive OR. Valid for integer operands only.
`|`	Bitwise OR. Valid for integer operands only.
`&&`	Logical AND. Produces a 1 result if both operands are non-zero, 0 otherwise. Valid for numeric operands only (integers or floating-point).
`||`	Logical OR. Produces a 0 result if both operands are zero, 1 otherwise. Valid for numeric operands only (integers or floating-point).
`x?y:z`	IF-THEN-ELSE, as in C. If x evaluates to non-zero, then the result is the value of y. Otherwise, the result is the value of z. The x operand must have a numeric value.

Results produced by each operator correspond to the equivalent operators in the C programming language. All of the binary operators group left to right within the same precedence level. For example, the command

expr 4*2 < 7

returns 0. The &&, ||, and ?: operators have "lazy evaluation," just as in C, which means that operands are not evaluated if they are not needed to determine the outcome. For example, in the command

expr {$v ? [a] : [b]}

only one of [a] or [b] will actually be evaluated, depending on the value of $v. Note, however, that this is true only if the entire expression is enclosed in braces; otherwise the Tcl parser will evaluate both [a] and [b] before invoking the **expr** command.

Math functions

Tcl supports the following mathematical functions in expressions:

acos	cos	hypot	sinh
asin	cosh	log	sqrt
atan	exp	log10	tan
atan2	floor	pow	tanh
ceil	fmod	sin	

Each of these functions invokes the math library function of the same name; see the manual entries for the library functions for further details. Tcl also implements the following functions for conversion between integers and floating-point numbers:

abs(*arg*)   Returns the absolute value of *arg*. *arg* may be either integer or floating-point, and the result is returned in the same form.

double(*arg*)   If *arg* is a floating-point value, returns *arg*; otherwise, converts *arg* to floating-point and returns the converted value.

int(*arg*)   If *arg* is an integer value, returns *arg*; otherwise, converts *arg* to integer by truncation and returns the converted value.

round(*arg*)   If *arg* is an integer value, returns *arg*; otherwise, converts *arg* to integer by rounding and returns the converted value.

In addition to these predefined functions, applications may define additional functions using Tcl_CreateMathFunc().

Types, overflow, and precision

All internal computations involving integers are done with the C-type `long`, and all internal computations involving floating-point are done with the C-type `double`. When converting a string to floating-point, exponent overflow is detected and results in a Tcl error. For conversion to integer from string, detection of overflow depends on the behavior of some routines in the local C library, so it should be regarded as unreliable. In any case, integer overflow and underflow are generally not detected reliably for intermediate results. Floating-point overflow and underflow are detected to the degree supported by the hardware, which is generally reliable.

Conversion among internal representations for integer, floating-point, and string operands is done automatically as needed. For arithmetic computations, integers are used until some floating-point number is introduced, after which floating-point is used. For example,

expr 5 / 4

returns 1, while

expr 5 / 4.0

and

expr 5 / ([**string** length "abcd"] + 0.0)

both return 1.25. Floating-point values are always returned with a period character or with an e, so that they will not look like integer values. For example,

expr 20.0/5.0

returns 4.0, not 4. The global variable `tcl_precision` determines the number of significant digits that are retained when floating values are converted to strings (except that trailing zeroes are omitted). If `tcl_precision` is unset, then 6 digits of precision are used. To retain all of the significant bits of an IEEE floating-point number, set `tcl_precision` to 17; if a value is converted to a string with 17 digits of precision and then converted back to binary for some later calculation, the resulting binary value is guaranteed to be identical to the original one.

String operations

String values may be used as operands of the comparison operators, although the expression evaluator tries to do comparisons as integer or floating-point when it can. If one of the operands of a comparison is a string and the other has a numeric value, the numeric operand is converted back to a string using the C `sprintf` format specifier `%d` for integers and `%g` for floating-point values.

For example, the commands

expr {"0x03" > "2"}

and

expr {"0y" < "0x12"}

both return 1. The first comparison is done using integer comparison, and the second is done using string comparison after the second operand is converted to the string "18".

`fmathcmds`   **TclX**

Syntax

<mathcmd> arg [arg ...]

Description

The following procedures provide command interfaces to the **expr** math functions. They take the same arguments as do the **expr** functions and may take expressions as arguments.

abs	acos	asin	atan2
atan	ceil	cos	cosh
double	exp	floor	fmod
hypot	int	log10	log
pow	round	sin	sinh
sqrt	tan	tanh	

Example

round 3.34

➡   3

incr   Tcl

Syntax

incr *varName* [*increment*]

Description

This command increments the value stored in the variable whose name is *varName*. The value of the variable must be an integer. If *increment* is supplied, its value (which must be an integer) is added to the value of variable *varName*; otherwise, 1 is added to *varName*. The new value is stored as a decimal string in variable *varName* and also returned as result.

max   TclX

Syntax

max *num1 num2* [...*numN*]

Description

This command returns the argument that has the highest numeric value. The arguments *numN* may be any integer or floating-point values.

min   TclX

Syntax

min *num1 num2* [...*numN*]

Description

This returns the argument that has the lowest numeric value. The arguments *numN* may be any integer or floating-point values.

random   **TclX**

Syntax

random *limit* | seed [*seedval*]

Description

This command generates a pseudorandom integer number greater than or equal to zero and less than *limit*. If seed is specified, the command resets the random number generator to a starting point derived from *seedval*. This allows you to reproduce pseudorandom number sequences for testing purposes. If *seedval* is omitted, the seed is set to a value based on current system state and the current time, providing a reasonably interesting and ever-changing seed.

Process and Signals

Table 33–1 Process and signal commands

Command	Tcl	TclX	Short Description
exec	✔		Invoke one or more subprocesses
execl		✔	Perform a process exec, executing a file
exit	✔		End the application
fork		✔	Fork the current Visual Tcl process
kill		✔	Send a signal to the specified process
nice		✔	Change or return the process priority
pid		✔	Retrieve one or more process IDs
signal		✔	Specify action to take when a signal is received
system		✔	Execute command via system(S) call
wait		✔	Wait for a child process to terminate

exec   Tcl

Syntax

exec [*switches*] *arg* [*arg* ...]

Description

This command treats its arguments as the specification of one or more subprocesses to execute. The arguments take the form of a standard shell pipeline where each *arg* becomes one word of a command, and each distinct command becomes a subprocess.

If the initial arguments to **exec** begin with a hyphen character, they are treated as command-line switches and are not part of the pipeline specification. The following switches are currently supported:

-keepnewline	Retains a trailing newline in the pipeline's output. Normally, a trailing newline will be deleted.
--	Marks the end of switches. The argument following this one will be treated as the first *arg* even if it begins with a hyphen.

If an *arg* (or pair of *arg*s) has one of the forms described below, it is used by **exec** to control the flow of input and output among the subprocess(es). Such arguments will not be passed to the subprocess(es). In forms such as < *fileName*, *fileName* may either be in a separate argument from < or in the same argument with no intervening space (i.e., <*fileName*).

|	Separates distinct commands in the pipeline. The standard output of the preceding command will be piped into the standard input of the next command.
|&	Separates distinct commands in the pipeline. Both standard output and standard error of the preceding command will be piped into the standard input of the next command. This form of redirection overrides forms such as 2> and >&.
< *fileName*	The file named by *fileName* is opened and used as the standard input for the first command in the pipeline.
<@ fileId	fileId must be the identifier for an open file, such as the return value from a previous call to **open**. It is used as the standard input for the first command in the pipeline. fileId must have been opened for reading.
<< value	value is passed to the first command as its standard input.
> *fileName*	Standard output from the last command is redirected to the file named *fileName*, overwriting its previous contents.
2> *fileName*	Standard error from all commands in the pipeline is redirected to the file named *fileName*, overwriting its previous contents.

`>& fileName`	Both standard output from the last command and standard error from all commands are redirected to the file named *fileName*, overwriting its previous contents.
`>> fileName`	Standard output from the last command is redirected to the file named *fileName*, appending to it, rather than overwriting it.
`2>> fileName`	Standard error from all commands in the pipeline is redirected to the file named *fileName*, appending to it, rather than overwriting it.
`>>& fileName`	Both standard output from the last command and standard error from all commands are redirected to the file named *fileName*, appending to it, rather than overwriting it.
`>@ fileId`	`fileId` must be the identifier for an open file, such as the return value from a previous call to **open**. Standard output from the last command is redirected to `fileId`'s file, which must have been opened for writing.
`2>@fileId`	`fileId` must be the identifier for an open file, such as the return value from a previous call to **open**. Standard error from all commands in the pipeline is redirected to `fileId`'s file. The file must have been opened for writing.
`>&@ fileId`	`fileId` must be the identifier for an open file, such as the return value from a previous call to **open**. Both standard output from the last command and standard error from all commands are redirected to `fileId`'s file. The file must have been opened for writing.

If standard output has not been redirected, the **exec** command returns the standard output from the last command in the pipeline. If any of the commands in the pipeline exit abnormally or are killed or suspended, **exec** will return an error, and the error message will include the pipeline's output, followed by error messages describing the abnormal terminations; the `errorCode` variable will contain additional information about the last abnormal termination encountered. If any of the commands writes to its standard error file and that standard error isn't redirected, **exec** will return an error; the error message will include the pipeline's standard output, followed by messages about abnormal terminations (if any), followed by the standard error output.

If the last character of the result or error message is a newline, that character is normally deleted from the result or error message. This is consistent with other Tcl return values, which don't normally end with newlines. However, if `-keepnewline` is specified, the trailing newline is retained.

If standard input isn't redirected with symbols <, <<, or <@, the standard input for the first command in the pipeline is taken from the application's current standard input.

If the last *arg* is & then the pipeline will be executed in background. In this case, the **exec** command will return a list whose elements are the process identifiers for all of the subprocesses in the pipeline. The standard output from the last command in the pipeline will go to the application's standard output if it hasn't been redirected, and error output from all of the commands in the pipeline will go to the application's standard error file unless redirected.

The first word in each command is taken as the command name; tilde-substitution is performed on it, and if the result contains no slashes, the directories in the PATH environment variable are searched for an executable with the given name. If the name contains a slash, it must refer to an executable reachable from the current directory. No "glob" expansion or other shell-like substitutions are performed on the arguments to commands.

execl   TclX

Syntax

execl [-argv0 *argv0*] *prog* [*arglist*]

Description

This command does an **execl**, replacing the current program (either TclX or an application with TclX embedded into it) with *prog* and passing the arguments in the list *arglist*.

The -argv0 option specifies that *argv0* is to be passed to the program as *argv[0]* rather than *prog*.

exit   Tcl

Syntax

exit [*returnCode*]

Description

This terminates the process, returning *returnCode* to the system as the exit status. If *returnCode* isn't specified, it defaults to 0.

fork   TclX

Syntax

fork

Description

The **fork** command forks the current Tcl process. **fork** returns zero to the child process and the process number of the child to the parent process. If the fork fails, a Tcl error is generated.

If an **execl** is not going to be performed before the child process does output, or if a close and dup sequence is going to be performed on stdout or stderr, a flush should be issued against stdout, stderr, and any other open output file before doing the fork. Otherwise, characters from the parent process pending in the buffers will be output by both the parent and child processes.

kill   TclX

Syntax

kill [-pgroup] [*signal*] *idlist*

Description

This command sends a signal to each process in the list *idlist*, if permitted. *signal*, if present, is the signal number or the symbolic name of the signal; see signal(S) for details. The leading SIG is optional when the signal is specified by its symbolic name. The default for *signal* is 15, SIGTERM.

If -pgroup is specified, the numbers in *idlist* are taken as process group IDs, and the signal is sent to all of the processes in that process group. A process group ID of 0 specifies the current process group.

nice   TclX

Syntax

nice [*priorityincr*]

Description

This command changes or returns the process priority. If *priorityincr* is omitted, the current priority is returned. If *priorityincr* is positive, it is added to the current priority level, up to a system-defined maximum (normally 19).

Negative *priorityincr* values cumulatively increase the program's priority, down to a system-defined minimum (normally 19); increasing priority with negative niceness values will work only for the superuser.

pid   TclX

Syntax

pid [*fileId*]

Description

If the *fileId* argument is given, it should normally refer to a process pipeline created with the **open** command. In this case, the **pid** command will return a list whose elements are the process identifiers of all the processes in the pipeline, in order. The list will be empty if *fileId* refers to an open file that isn't a process pipeline. If no *fileId* argument is given, **pid** returns the process identifier of the current process. All process identifiers are returned as decimal strings.

signal   TclX

Syntax

signal *action siglist* [*command*]

Description

This command specifies the action to take when a UNIX signal is received by Visual Tcl. `siglist` is a list of either the symbolic or numeric UNIX signal (the SIG prefix is optional). `action` is one of the following actions to be performed on receipt of the signal. To specify all modifiable signals, use the asterisk character (this does not include SIGKILL or SIGSTOP, as these cannot be modified).

default	Performs system default action when signal is received (see signal system call documentation).
ignore	Ignores the signal.
error	Generates a catchable Tcl error as if the command that was running returned an error. The error code is in the form: POSIX SIG *signame* For the death of child signal, *signame* is always SIGCHLD, rather than SIGCLD, to allow writing portable code.
trap	When the signal occurs, executes *command* and continues execution if an error is not returned by *command*. *command* will be executed in the global context. The command is edited before execution, replacing occurrences of %S with the signal name. Occurrences of %% result in a single %. This editing occurs just before the **trap** command is evaluated. If an error is returned, follow the standard Tcl error mechanism. Often, command simply exits.
get	Retrieves the current settings of the specified signals. A keyed list is returned where the keys are one of the specified signals. The values are a list consisting of the action associated with the signal: a 0 value if the signal may be delivered (not blocked) and a 1 if it can be blocked. The actions may be one of default, ignore, error, or trap. For example, if the action is trap, the third element is the command associated with the action.
set	Sets the signals from a keyed list in the format returned by the **get** command. For this action, *siglist* is the keyed list of signal states. Signals with an action of unknown are not modified.
block	Blocks the specified signals from being received. (POSIX systems only).
unblock	Allows the specified signal to be received. Pending signals do not occur. (POSIX systems only.)

The signal action is enabled after the specified signal has occurred. The exception to this is SIGCHLD on systems without POSIX signals. For these systems, SIGCHLD is not automatically re-enabled. After a SIGCHLD signal is received, a call to **wait** must be performed to retrieve the exit status of the child process before issuing another signal SIGCHLD command. For code that is to be portable between both types of systems, use this approach.

Signals are not processed until after the completion of the Tcl command that is executing when the signal is received. If an interactive Tcl shell is running, the SIGINT is set to error; noninteractive Tcl sessions leave SIGINT unchanged from when the process started (normally default for foreground processes and ignore for processes in the background system).

system   TclX

Syntax

system *command*

Description

This command executes *command* via the system(S) call. It differs from **exec** in that **system** does not return the executed command's standard output as the result string, and **system** goes through the UNIX shell to provide wildcard expansion, redirection, etc., as is normal from an sh(C) command line. The exit code of the command is returned.

wait   TclX

Syntax

wait [-nohang] [-untraced] [-pgroup] [*pid*]

Description

This command waits for a process created with the **execl** command to terminate, due either to an untrapped signal or to a call to an exit system call. If the process ID *pid* is specified, it waits for that process, otherwise it waits for any child process to terminate.

If -nohang is specified, waiting for a process to terminate is not blocked. If no process is immediately available, it returns an empty list. If -untraced is specified, the status of child processes that are stopped and whose status has not yet been reported since they stopped, is also returned. If -pgroup is specified and *pid* is not specified, it waits on any child process whose process group ID is the same as the calling process. If *pid* is specified with -*pgroup*, it is taken as a process group ID, waiting on any process in that process group to terminate.

wait returns a list containing three elements. The first element is the process ID of the process that terminated. If the process exited normally, the second element is EXIT, and the third contains the numeric exit code. If the process terminated due to a signal, the second element is SIG, and the third contains the signal name. If the process is currently stopped (on systems that support SIGSTP), the second element is STOP, followed by the signal name.

It is possible to wait on processes that were created in the background with the **exec** command to terminate. However, if any other **exec** command is executed after the process terminates, the process status will be reset by the **exec** command and will not be available to the **wait** command.

Status

Table 34–1   Status commands

Command	Tcl	TclX	Short Description
cd	✔		Change working directory
dirs		✔	List directories in directory stack
history	✔		Manipulate the history list
id		✔	Get, set, convert user, group, process IDs
info	✔		Return information about the status of the Tcl interpreter
infox		✔	Return info on application or TclX
popd		✔	Pop top directory from directory stack to current directory
pushd		✔	Push current directory onto directory stack and change working directory to specified directory
pwd	✔		Return the current working directory
showproc		✔	List definitions of named procedures
umask		✔	Set file creation mode

cd   TclX

Syntax

cd [*dirName*]

Description

The **cd** command changes the current working directory to *dirName*, or to the home directory (as specified in the HOME environment variable) if *dirName* is not given. If *dirName* begins with a tilde, tilde expansion is done as described for Tcl_TildeSubst. Returns an empty string.

dirs   **TclX**

Syntax

```
dirs
```

Description

This procedure lists the directories in the directory stack.

history   **Tcl**

Syntax

```
history [option] [arg arg ...]
```

Description

The **history** command performs one of several operations related to recently executed commands recorded in a history list. Each of these recorded commands is referred to as an *event*. When specifying an event to the **history** command, the following forms may be used:

A number: if positive, it refers to the event with that number (all events are numbered beginning at 1). If the number is negative, it selects an event relative to the current event (-1 refers to the previous event, -2 to the one before that, and so on).

A string: selects the most recent event that matches the string. An event is considered to match the string if the string is the same as the first characters of the event, or if the string matches the event in the sense of the **string** match command. The history command can take any of the following forms:

```
history
```

Same as **history** info, described below.

    history add *command* [exec]

Adds the *command* argument to the history list as a new event. If exec is specified (or abbreviated), the command is also executed and its result is returned. If exec isn't specified, an empty string is returned as the result.

    history change *newValue* [event]

Replaces the value recorded for an event with *newValue*. event specifies the event to replace and defaults to the current event (not event -1). This command is intended for use in commands that implement new forms of history substitution and wish to replace the current event (which invokes the substitution) with the command created through substitution. The return value is an empty string.

    history event [event]

Returns the value of the event given by event. event defaults to -1. This command causes history revision to occur. See below for details.

    history info [count]

Returns a formatted string (intended for humans to read) giving the event number and contents for each of the events in the history list except the current event. If count is specified, only the most recent count events are returned.

    history keep *count*

This command may be used to change the size of the history list to count events. Initially, 20 events are retained in the history list. This command returns an empty string.

    history nextid

Returns the number of the next event to be recorded in the history list. It is useful for things like printing the event number in command-line prompts.

    history redo [event]

Re-executes the command indicated by event and return its result. event defaults to -1. This command results in history revision. See below for details.

    history substitute *old new* [event]

Retrieves the command given by event (-1 by default), replaces any occurrences of *old* by *new* in the command (only simple character equality is supported; no wild cards), executes the resulting command, and returns the result of that execution. This command results in history revision. See below for details.

    history words *selector* [event]

Retrieves from the command given by event (-1 by default) the words given by *selector* and returns those words in a string separated by spaces. The selector argument has three forms: If it is a single number, it selects the word given by that number (0 for the command name, 1 for its first argument, and so on). If it consists of two numbers separated by a dash, then it selects all the arguments between those two. Otherwise, *selector* is treated as a pattern; all words matching that pattern (in the sense of string match) are returned. In the numeric forms, $ may be used to select the last word of a command. For example, suppose the most recent command in the history list is

format {%s is %d years old} Alice [**expr** $ageInMonths/12]

Below are some **history** commands (executed inside a vtcl session) and the results they would produce:

history words $ [expr $ageInMonths/12]
history words 1-2   {%s is %d years old} Alice
history words *a*o*   {%s is %d years old} [expr $ageInMonths/12]
history words

These commands generate "history revision." See below for details.

History revision

The **history** options event, redo, substitute, and words result in "history revision." When one of these options is invoked, the current event is modified to eliminate the **history** command and replace it with the result of the **history** command. For example, suppose that the most recent command in the history list is

set a [**expr** $b+2]

and suppose that the next command invoked is one of the ones on the left side of the list below. The command actually recorded in the history event will be the corresponding one on the right side of the list.

history redo   **set** a [**expr** $b+2]

history s a b   **set** b [**expr** $b+2]

set c [**history** w 2]   **set** c [**expr** $b+2]

History revision is needed because event specifiers like -1 are valid only at a particular time: Once more events have been added to the history list, a different event specifier would be needed. History revision occurs even when history is invoked indirectly from the current event (for example, a user types a command that invokes a Tcl procedure that invokes history): The top-level command whose execution eventually resulted in a **history** command is replaced. If you wish to invoke commands like **history** words without history revision, you can use **history** event to save the current history event and then use **history** change to restore it later.

id   **TclX**

Syntax

id *options*

Description

This command provides a means of getting, setting, and converting user, group, and process IDs.

Options

id user [*name*] **id** userid [*uid*]	Sets the real and effective user ID to *name* or *uid*, if the *name* or *uid* is valid and permissions allow it. If the *name* or *uid* is not specified, the current name or user ID is returned.
id convert userid *uid* **id** convert user *name*	Converts a user ID number to a user name or vice versa.
id group [*name*] **id** groupid [*gid*]	Sets the real and effective group ID to *name* or *gid*, if the *name* or *gid* is valid and permissions allow it. If the group *name* or *gid* is not specified, the current group name or gid is returned.
id convert groupid *gid* **id** convert group *name*	Converts a group ID number to a group name or vice versa.
id effective user **id** effective userid	Returns the effective user name or effective user ID number, respectively.
id effective group **id** effective groupid	Returns the effective group name or effective group ID number, respectively.
id process	Returns the process ID of the current process.
id process parent	Returns the process ID of the parent of the current process.
id process group	Returns the process group ID of the current process.
id process group set	Sets the process group ID of the current process to its process ID.

info   **Tcl**

Syntax

info *option* [*arg arg ...*]

Description

This command provides information about various internals of the Tcl interpreter. The legal options (which may be abbreviated) are:

info *args procName*

Returns a list containing the names of the arguments to procedure *procName*, in order. *procName* must be the name of a Tcl command procedure.

info body *procName*

Returns the body of procedure *procName*. *procName* must be the name of a Tcl command procedure.

info cmdcount

Returns a count of the total number of commands that have been invoked in this interpreter.

info commands [*pattern*]

If *pattern* isn't specified, returns a list of names of all the Tcl commands, including both the built-in commands written in C and the command procedures defined using the **proc** command. If *pattern* is specified, only those names matching *pattern* are returned. Matching is determined using the same rules as for string match.

info complete *command*

Returns 1 if command is a complete Tcl command in the sense of having no unclosed quotes, braces, brackets, or array element names: If the command does not appear to be complete, 0 is returned. This command is typically used in line-oriented input environments to allow users to type in commands that span multiple lines; if the command isn't complete, the script can delay evaluating it until additional lines have been typed to complete the command.

info default *procName arg varName*

ProcName must be the name of a Tcl command procedure and *arg* must be the name of an argument to that procedure. If *arg* does not have a default value, the command returns 0. Otherwise, it returns 1 and places the default value of *arg* into variable *varName*.

info exists *varName*

Returns 1 if the variable named *varName* exists in the current context (as either a global or local variable), returns 0 otherwise.

info globals [*pattern*]

If *pattern* isn't specified, returns a list of all the names of currently defined global variables. If *pattern* is specified, only those names matching *pattern* are returned. Matching is determined using the same rules as for string match.

info level [number]

If number is not specified, this command returns a number giving the stack level of the invoking procedure, or 0 if the command is invoked at top level. If number is specified, the result is a list consisting of the name and arguments for the procedure call at level number on the stack. If number is positive, it selects a particular stack level (1 refers to the topmost active procedure, 2 to the procedure it called, and so on); otherwise, it gives a level relative to the current level (0 refers to the current procedure, -1 to its caller, and so on). See the **uplevel** command for more information on what stack levels mean.

info library

Returns the name of the library directory in which standard Tcl scripts are stored. The default value for the library is compiled into Tcl, but it may be overridden by setting the TCL_LIBRARY environment variable. If there is no TCL_LIBRARY variable and no compiled-in value, an error is generated. See the library(TCL) manual entry for details of the facilities provided by the Tcl script library. Normally, each application will have its own application-specific script library in addition to the Tcl script library. Each application should consider setting a global variable with a name like $app_library (where app is the application's name) to hold the location of that application's library directory.

info locals [*pattern*]

If *pattern* isn't specified, returns a list of all the names of currently defined local variables (including arguments to the current procedure, if any). Variables defined with the **global** and **upvar** commands will not be returned. If *pattern* is specified, only those names matching pattern are returned. Matching is determined using the same rules as for string match.

info patchlevel

Returns a decimal integer giving the current patch level for Tcl. The patch level is incremented for each new release or patch, and it uniquely identifies an official version of Tcl.

info procs [*pattern*]

If *pattern* isn't specified, returns a list of all the names of Tcl command procedures. If *pattern* is specified, only those names matching pattern are returned. Matching is determined using the same rules as for string match.

>   **info** script

If a Tcl script file is currently being evaluated (that is, there is a call to Tcl_EvalFile active or there is an active invocation of the **source** command), this command returns the name of the innermost file being processed. Otherwise, the command returns an empty string.

>   **info** tclversion

Returns the version number for this version of Tcl in the form $x.y$, where changes to x represent major changes with probable incompatibilities and changes to y represent small enhancements and bug fixes that retain backward compatibility.

>   **info** vars [*pattern*]

If *pattern* isn't specified, returns a list of all the names of currently visible variables, including both locals and currently visible globals. If *pattern* is specified, only those names matching *pattern* are returned. Matching is determined using the same rules as for string match.

infox   TclX

Syntax

infox *option*

Description

Returns information about TclX or the current application.

Options

version	Returns the version number of TclX. The version number for TclX is generated by combining the base version of the standard Tcl code with a letter indicating the version of TclX being used. This is the documentation for version 7.3b.

`patchlevel`	Returns the patch level for TclX.
`have_flock`	Returns 1 if the **flock** command is defined, otherwise 0.
`have_fsync`	Returns 1 if the `fsync` system call is available and the **sync** command will sync individual files, 0 if it is not available and the **sync** command will always sync all file buffers.
`have_msgcats`	Returns 1 if XPG message catalogs are available, 0 if they are not. The **catgets** command is designed to continue to function without message catalogs, always returning the default string.
`have_posix_signals`	Returns 1 if POSIX signals are available (`block` and `unblock` options available for the **signal** command). 0 is returned if POSIX signals are not available.
`have_sockets`	Returns 1 if sockets are available (**server_open, server_info** commands and **fstat** removehost option). 0 is returned if sockets are not available.
`appname`	Returns the symbolic application name of the current application linked with the TclX library. The C variable *tclAppName* must be set by the application to return an application-specific value for this variable.
`applongname`	Returns a natural language name for the current application. The C variable *tclLongAppName* must be set by the application to return an application-specific value for this variable.
`appversion`	Returns the version number for the current application. The C variable *tclAppVersion* must be set by the application to return an application-specific value for this variable.
`apppatchlevel`	Returns the patch level for the current application. The C variable *tclAppPatchlevel* must be set by the application to return an application-specific value for this variable.

popd   TclX

Syntax

`popd`

Description

This procedure pops the top directory entry from the directory stack and makes it the current directory.

pushd   TclX

Syntax

`pushd` `[dir]`

Description

This procedure pushes the current directory onto the directory stack and changes the working directory to the specified directory. If the directory is not specified, the current directory is pushed but remains unchanged.

pwd   Tcl

Syntax

`pwd`

Description

This command returns the pathname of the current working directory.

showproc   **TclX**

Syntax

showproc [*procName* ...]

Description

This procedure lists the definition of the named procedures, loading them if they are not already loaded. If no procedure names are supplied, the definitions of all currently loaded procedures are returned.

umask   **TclX**

Syntax

umask [*octalmask*]

Description

This command sets the file-creation mode mask to the octal value of *octalmask*. If *octalmask* is omitted, the current mask is returned.

Strings

Table 35–1   String commands

Commands	Tcl	TclX	Short Description
append	✔		Append to a variable
cequal		✔	String equality convenience command
cexpand		✔	Expand backslash sequences in a character string
cindex		✔	Return indexed character from a string
clength		✔	Return length of specified string
crange		✔	Return range of characters from a string
csubstr		✔	Return a substring from within a string
ctoken		✔	Parse a token from a character string
ctype		✔	Determine whether a string has various characteristics
format	✔		Format a string in the style of `sprintf`
regexp	✔		Match a regular expression against a string
regsub	✔		Perform substitutions based on regular expression pattern matching
replicate		✔	Replicate string a number of times
scan	✔		Parse string using conversion specifiers in the style of `sscanf`
string	✔		Manipulate strings
translit		✔	Translate characters in a string according to patterns

append   Tcl

Syntax

append *varName* [*value value value ...*]

Description

This appends all of the *value* arguments to the current value of variable *varName*. If *varName* does not exist, it is given a value equal to the concatenation of all the value arguments. This command provides an efficient way to build up long variables incrementally. For example, if $a is long, then

    append a $b

is much more efficient than

    set a ab

cequal   TclX

Syntax

cequal *string1 string2*

Description

This command compares two strings for equality. Returns 1 if *string1* and *string2* are identical and 0 if they are not. This command is a shortcut for **string** compare and avoids the problems with string expressions being treated unintentionally as numbers.

cexpand   TclX

Syntax

cexpand *string*

Description

This command expands backslash sequences in *string* to their actual characters. No other substitution takes place.

cindex   **TclX**

Syntax

cindex *string indexExpr*

Description

This command returns the character indexed by the expression *indexExpr* from *string*.

If the expression *indexExpr* begins with the string end, then end is replaced with the index of the last character in the string. If the expression begins with len, then len is replaced with the length of the string.

Example

```
echo The last character in \"Computer\" \
     is \"[cindex Computer end]\"
```
➡ The last character in "Computer" is "r"

clength   **TclX**

Syntax

clength *string*

Description

The **clength** command returns the length of *string*, in characters. This command is a shortcut for:

```
string length string
```

Example

```
set nameOfDept "Accounting"
set length [clength $nameOfDept]
echo "$nameOfDept is $length characters long"
```

➡ Accounting is 10 characters long

crange   TclX

Syntax

crange *string firstExpr lastExpr*

Description

This command returns a range of characters from *string*, starting at the character indexed by the expression *firstExpr* , up to the character indexed by the expression *lastExpr*.

If the expressions *firstExpr* or *lastExpr* begins with the string end, then end is replaced with the index of the last character in the string. If the expression begins with len, then len is replaced with the length of the string.

csubstr   TclX

Syntax

csubstr *string firstExpr lengthExpr*

Description

This returns a range of characters from *string*, starting at the character indexed by the expression *firstExpr*, for *lengthExpr* characters. If the expressions *firstExpr* or *lengthExpr* begin with the string end, then end is replaced with the index of the last character in the string. If the expression begins with len, then len is replaced with the length of the string.

ctoken   **TclX**

Syntax

ctoken *strName separators*

Description

This will parse a token out of a character string. *strName* contains the string to be parsed. *separators* contains all of the valid separator characters for tokens in the string. Leading separators are skipped, and the first token is returned. The variable *strName* will be modified to contain the remainder of the string following the token.

ctype   **TclX**

Syntax

ctype [-failindex *var*] *class string*

Description

ctype determines whether all characters in *string* are of the specified *class*. It returns 1 if they are all of *class* and 0 if they are not or if *string* is empty. If -failindex is specified, the index into *string* of the first character that did not match the class is returned in *var*.

   This command also provides another method (besides **format** and **scan**) of converting between an ASCII character and its numeric value. The two conversion commands are:

ctype char *number*	Converts the numeric value, *number*, to an ASCII character. *number* must be in the range 0 through 255.
ctype ord *character*	Converts a character to its decimal numeric value. The first character of the *string* is converted.

   The following **ctype** classes are supported.

`alnum`	Tests that all characters are alphabetic or numeric characters, as defined by the character set.
`alpha`	Tests that all characters are alphabetic characters, as defined by the character set.
`ascii`	Tests that all characters are ASCII characters (nonnegative numbers less than 0200).
`cntrl`	Tests that all characters are control characters, as defined by the character set.
`digit`	Tests that all characters are valid decimal digits, i.e., 0–9.
`graph`	Tests that all characters are characters for which **ctype** `print` is true, except for space characters.
`lower`	Tests that all characters are lowercase letters, as defined by the character set.
`space`	Tests that all characters are spaces, horizontal tabs, carriage returns, newlines, vertical tabs, or form feeds.
`print`	Tests that all characters are spaces, characters for which **ctype** `alnum` or **ctype** `punct` is true, or other printing characters, as defined by the character set.
`punct`	Tests that all characters are characters other than the ones for which `alnum`, `cntrl`, or `space` is true.
`upper`	Tests that all characters are uppercase letters, as defined by the character set.
`xdigit`	Tests that all characters are valid hexadecimal digits, i.e., 0–9, a–f, or A–F.

format   Tcl

Syntax

format *formatString* [*arg arg ...*]

Description

The **format** command returns a formatted string by the same method as the ANSI C sprintf procedure (it uses sprintf in its implementation). *formatString* indicates how to format the result, using % conversion specifiers as in sprintf, and the additional arguments, if any, provide values to be substituted into the result.

The command operates by scanning *formatString* from left to right. Each character from the format string is appended to the result string, unless it is a percent symbol; if so, it is not copied to the result string. Instead, the characters following the % character are treated as a conversion specifier. The conversion specifier controls the conversion of the next successive *arg* to a particular format, and the result is appended to the result string in place of the conversion specifier. If there are multiple conversion specifiers in the format string, each one controls the conversion of one additional *arg*. The format command must be given enough *arg*s to meet the needs of all of the conversion specifiers in *formatString*.

Each conversion specifier may contain up to six different parts: an XPG/3 position specifier, a set of flags, a minimum field width, a precision specifier, a length modifier, and a conversion character. Any of these fields may be omitted, except for the conversion character. The fields that are present must appear in the order given above. The paragraphs below discuss each of these fields in turn.

If the % is followed by a decimal number and a $, as in %2$d, then the value to convert is not taken from the next sequential argument. Instead, it is taken from the argument indicated by the number, where 1 corresponds to the first *arg*. If the conversion specifier requires multiple arguments because of asterisk characters in the specifier, successive arguments are used, starting with the argument given by the number. This follows the XPG/3 conventions for positional specifiers. If there are any positional specifiers in *formatString*, all of the specifiers must be positional.

The second portion of a conversion specifier may contain any of the following flag characters, in any order:

−	Specifies that the converted argument should be left-justified in its field (numbers are normally right-justified, with leading spaces if needed).
+	Specifies that a number should always be printed with a sign, even if positive.
space	Specifies that a space should be added to the beginning of the number if the first character is not a sign.
0	Specifies that the number should be padded on the left with zeroes instead of spaces.

Requests an alternate output form. For o and O conversions, it
              guarantees that the first digit is always 0. For x or X conversions, 0x or
              0X (respectively) will be added to the beginning of the result, unless it
              is 0. For all floating-point conversions (e, E, f, g, and G), it guarantees
              that the result always has a decimal point. For g and G conversions, it
              specifies that trailing zeros should not be removed.

The third portion of a conversion specifier is a number giving a minimum field
width for the conversion. It is typically used to make columns line up in tabular printouts.
If the converted argument contains fewer characters than the minimum field width, it will
be padded so that it is as wide as the minimum field width. Padding normally occurs by
adding extra spaces on the left of the converted argument, but the 0 and hyphen flags may
be used to specify padding with zeros on the left or with spaces on the right, respectively.
If the minimum field width is specified by an asterisk rather than by a number, the next
argument to the **format** command determines the minimum field width; it must be a
numeric string.

The fourth portion of a conversion specifier is a precision, which consists of a
period followed by a number. The number is used in different ways for different
conversions. For e, E, and f conversions, it specifies the number of digits to appear to the
right of the decimal point. For g and G conversions it specifies the total number of digits
to appear, including those on both sides of the decimal point (however, trailing zeros after
the decimal point will still be omitted unless the # flag has been specified). For integer
conversions, it specifies a minimum number of digits to print (leading zeros will be added
if necessary). For s conversions, it specifies the maximum number of characters to be
printed; if the string is longer than this, the trailing characters will be dropped. If the
precision is specified with an asterisk rather than with a number, the next argument to the
format command determines the precision; it must be a numeric string.

The fourth part of a conversion specifier is a length modifier, which must be h or l.
The h modifier specifies that the numeric value should be truncated to a 16-bit value
before converting. This option is rarely useful. The l modifier is ignored.

The last thing in a conversion specifier is an alphabetic character that determines
what kind of conversion to perform. The following conversion characters are currently
supported:

%   No conversion: just insert %.

c   Convert integer to the 8-bit character it represents.

d   Convert integer to signed decimal string.

e or E	Convert floating-point number to scientific notation in the form x.yyye±zz, where the number of ys is determined by the precision (default: 6). If the precision is 0, no decimal point is output. If the E form is used, E is printed instead of e.
f	Convert floating-point number to signed decimal string of the form xx.yyy, where the number of ys is determined by the precision (default: 6). If the precision is 0, no decimal point is output.
g or G	If the exponent is less than -4 or greater than or equal to the precision, convert floating-point number as for %e or %E. Otherwise, convert as for %f. Trailing zeroes and a trailing decimal point are omitted.
I	Convert integer to signed decimal string; the integer may be in decimal, octal (with a leading 0), or hexadecimal (with a leading 0x) format.
o	Convert integer to unsigned octal string.
s	No conversion; just insert string.
u	Convert integer to unsigned decimal string.
x or X	Convert integer to unsigned hexadecimal string, using digits 0123456789abcdef for x and 0123456789ABCDEF for X).

For the numerical conversions, the argument being converted must be an integer or a floating-point string; **format** converts the argument to binary and then converts it back to a string, according to the conversion specifier.

Differences from ANSI sprintf

The behavior of the **format** command is the same as that of the ANSI C sprintf procedure, except for the following differences:

1. %p and %n specifiers are not currently supported.
2. For %c conversions, the argument must be a decimal string, which will then be converted to the corresponding character value.
3. The l modifier is ignored; integer values are always converted as if there were no modifier present, and real values are always converted as if the l modifier were present (that is, type double is used for the internal representation). If the h modifier is specified, integer values are truncated to short before conversion.

Example

```
echo "Today's date is [format "%s/%s/%s" 12 15 96]"
```
➡ Today's date is 12/15/96

regexp   Tcl

Syntax

regexp [*switches*] *exp string* [*matchVar*] [*subMatchVar*
    subMatchVar ...]

Description

regexp determines whether the regular expression *exp* matches part or all of *string* and returns 1 if it does, 0 if it does not.

If additional arguments are specified after *string*, they are treated as the names of variables in which to return information about which parts of *string* match *exp*. *matchVar* is set to the range of *string* that matched all of *exp*. The first *subMatchVar* contains the characters in *string* that match the leftmost parenthesized subexpression within *exp*, the next *subMatchVar* contains the characters that match the next parenthesized subexpression to the right in *exp*, and so on.

If the initial arguments to **regexp** begin with a hyphen, they are treated as switches. The following switches are currently supported:

-nocase	Causes uppercase characters in *string* to be treated as lowercase during the matching process.
-indices	Changes what is stored in the *subMatchVars*. Instead of storing the matching characters from *string*, each variable contains a list of two decimal strings giving the indices in *string* of the first and last characters in the matching range of characters.
--	Marks the end of *switches*. The argument following this one is treated as *exp*, even if it begins with a hyphen.

If there are more *subMatchVars* than parenthesized subexpressions within *exp*, or if a particular subexpression in *exp* does not match the string (for example, because it was in a portion of the expression that was not matched), the corresponding *subMatchVar* is set to -1 if -indices has been specified, or to an empty string otherwise.

Regular expressions

Regular expressions are implemented using the public-domain Henry Spencer package; the standard SCO regular expression syntax does not apply. The following regular expressions are recognized by Tcl:

A regular expression is zero or more branches, separated by a pipe character (|). It matches anything that matches one of the branches. A branch is 0 or more pieces, concatenated. It matches a match for the first, followed by a match for the second, and so on.

A piece is an atom possibly followed by *, +, or ?. An atom followed by * matches a sequence of zero or more matches of the atom. An atom followed by + matches a sequence of one or more matches of the atom. An atom followed by ? matches a match of the atom, or the null string.

An atom is a regular expression in parentheses (matching a match for the regular expression), a range (see below), a period (matching any single character), a caret symbol (matching the null string at the beginning of the input string), a dollar sign (matching the null string at the end of the input string), a backslash followed by a single character (matching that character), or a single character with no other significance (matching that character).

A range is a sequence of characters enclosed in square brackets. It normally matches any single character from the sequence. If the sequence begins with a caret symbol, it matches any single character not from the rest of the sequence. If two characters in the sequence are separated by a hyphen, this is shorthand for the full list of ASCII characters between them (for example, [0-9] matches any decimal digit). To include a literal square bracket in the sequence, make it the first character (following a possible caret symbol). To include a literal hyphen, make it the first or last character.

Choosing among alternative matches

In general, there may be more than one way to match a regular expression to an input string. For example, consider the command:

regexp (a*)b* aabaaabb x y

Considering only the rules given so far, x and y could end up with the values aabb and aa, aaab and aaa, ab and a, or any of several other combinations. To resolve this potential ambiguity, **regexp** chooses among alternatives using the rule "first then longest." In other words, it considers the possible matches in order, working from left to right across the input string and the pattern, and it attempts to match longer pieces of the input string before shorter ones. More specifically, the following rules apply in decreasing order of priority:

1. If a regular expression can match two different parts of an input string, it matches the one that begins earliest.

2. If a regular expression contains | operators, the leftmost matching subexpression is chosen.

3. In *, +, and ? constructs, longer matches are chosen in preference to shorter ones.

4. In sequences of expression components, the components are considered from left to right.

In the example above, (a*)b* matches aab. The (a*) portion of the pattern is matched first and it consumes the leading aa; then the b* portion of the pattern consumes the next b. Or, consider the following example:

regexp (ab|a)(b*)c abc x y z

After this command, x will be abc, y will be ab, and z will be an empty string. Rule 4, above specifies that (ab|a) is checked for a match against the input string first, and Rule 2 specifies that the ab subexpression is checked before the a subexpression. Thus, the b has already been claimed before the (b*) component is checked, and (b*) must match an empty string.

The regular expression package used in Tcl is not part of any currently supported standard; it was developed at the University of Toronto by Dr. Henry Spencer, was incorporated into Tcl at the University of California at Berkeley by Dr. John Ousterhout, and is used by permission.

regsub   Tcl

Syntax

regsub [*switches*] *exp string subSpec varName*

Description

This command matches the regular expression *exp* against *string*, and copies *string* to the variable whose name is given by *varName*. The command returns 1 if there is a match and 0 if there isn't. If there is a match, then while copying *string* to *varName*, the portion of *string* that matches *exp* is replaced with *subSpec*. If *subSpec* contains & or \0, it is replaced in the substitution with the portion of *string* that matches *exp*. If *subSpec* contains \n, where n is a digit between 1 and 9, it is replaced in the substitution with the portion of *string* that matches the nth parenthesized subexpression of *exp*.

Additional backslashes may be used in *subSpec* to prevent special interpretation of &, \0, \n, or of a backslash. The use of backslashes in *subSpec* tends to interact badly with the Tcl parser's use of backslashes, so it is generally safest to enclose *subSpec* in braces if it includes backslashes.

If the initial arguments to **regexp** begin with a hyphen, they are treated as switches. The following switches are currently supported:

-all
: All ranges in string that match *exp* are found, and substitution is performed for each of these ranges. Without this switch, only the first matching range is found and substituted. If -all is specified, & and \n sequences are handled for each substitution, using the information from the corresponding match.

-nocase
: Uppercase characters in *string* are converted to lowercase before matching against *exp*; however, substitutions specified by *subSpec* use the original unconverted form of *string*.

--
: Marks the end of *switches*. The argument following this one is treated as *exp*, even if it begins with a hyphen.

See the manual entry for **regexp** for details on the interpretation of regular expressions.

replicate   TclX

Syntax

replicate *string countExpr*

Description

This command returns *string*, replicated the number of times indicated by the expression *countExpr*.

Example

```
echo "The dog growled, \"Gr[replicate "r" 8]....\""
```
➨ The dog growled, "Grrrrrrrr...."

scan   **Tcl**

Syntax

scan *string formatString varName* [*varName* ...]

Description

This command parses fields from an input string in the same fashion as the ANSI C
sscanf procedure and returns a count of the number of fields successfully parsed.
string gives the input to be parsed and *formatString* indicates how to parse it,
using % conversion specifiers as in sscanf. When a field is scanned from *string*, the
result is converted back into a string and assigned to the corresponding variable,
varName.

Details on scanning

scan operates by scanning *string* and *formatString* together. If the next
character in *formatString* is a space or tab, it is ignored. Otherwise, if it isn't a %
character, it must match the next non-whitespace character of *string*. When a % is
encountered in *formatString*, it indicates the start of a conversion specifier. A
conversion specifier contains three fields after the %: an asterisk, which indicates that the
converted value is to be discarded instead of assigned to a variable; a number, indicating
a maximum field width; and a conversion character. All of these fields are optional except
for the conversion character.

When **scan** finds a conversion specifier in *formatString*, it first skips any
whitespace characters in *string*. Then it converts the next input characters according to
the conversion specifier and stores the result in the variable given by the next argument to
scan. The following conversion characters are supported:

d   The input field must be a decimal integer. It is read in and the value
           is stored in the variable as a decimal string.

o   The input field must be an octal integer. It is read in and the value is
           stored in the variable as a decimal string.

x   The input field must be a hexadecimal integer. It is read in and the
           value is stored in the variable as a decimal string.

c   A single character is read in and its binary value is stored in the
           variable as a decimal string. Initial whitespace is not skipped in this
           case, so the input field may be a whitespace character. This
           conversion is different from the ANSI standard in that the input field

always consists of a single character, and no field width may be specified.

s   The input field consists of all the characters up to the next whitespace character; the characters are copied to the variable.

e or f or g   The input field must be a floating-point number consisting of an optional sign, a string of decimal digits possibly containing a decimal point, and an optional exponent consisting of an e or E, followed by an optional sign and a string of decimal digits. It is read in and stored in the variable as a floating-point string.

[chars]   The input field consists of any number of characters in chars. The matching string is stored in the variable. If the first character between the brackets is], it is treated as part of chars, rather than as the closing bracket for the set.

[^chars]   The input field consists of any number of characters not in chars. The matching string is stored in the variable. If the character immediately following the ^ is], it is treated as part of the set rather than as the closing bracket for the set.

The number of characters read from the input for a conversion is the largest number that makes sense for that particular conversion (for example, as many decimal digits as possible for %d, as many octal digits as possible for %o, and so on). The input field for a given conversion terminates either when a whitespace character is encountered or when the maximum field width has been reached, whichever comes first. If an asterisk is present in the conversion specifier, no variable is assigned and the next **scan** argument is not consumed.

Differences from ANSI sscanf

The behavior of the **scan** command is the same as the behavior of the ANSI C sscanf procedure, except for the following differences:

1. %p and %n conversion specifiers are not currently supported.

2. For %c conversions, a single character value is converted to a decimal string, which is then assigned to the corresponding varName; no field width may be specified for this conversion.

3. The l, h, and L modifiers are ignored; integer values are always converted as if there were no modifier present, and real values are always converted as if the l modifier were present (i.e., type double is used for the internal representation).

string   Tcl

Syntax

string option *arg* [*arg* ...]

Description

This command performs one of several string operations, depending on option. The legal options (which may be abbreviated) are:

string compare *string1* *string2*

This performs a character-by-character comparison of strings *string1* and *string2* in the same way as the C strcmp procedure. It returns -1, 0, or 1, depending on whether *string1* is lexicographically less than, equal to, or greater than *string2*.

string first *string1* *string2*

Searches *string2* for a sequence of characters that exactly matches the characters in *string1*. If found, it returns the index of the first character in the first such match within *string2*. If not found, it returns -1.

string index *string* *charIndex*

Returns the *charIndex*th character of the *string* argument. A *charIndex* of 0 corresponds to the first character of the string. If *charIndex* is less than 0 or greater than or equal to the length of the string, an empty string is returned.

string last *string1* *string2*

Searches *string2* for a sequence of characters that exactly match the characters in *string1*. If found, it returns the index of the first character in the last such match within *string2*. If there is no match, it returns -1.

string length *string*

Returns a decimal string giving the number of characters in *string*.

string match *pattern* *string*

Checks whether *pattern* matches *string*; returns 1 if it does, 0 if it does not. Matching is done in a fashion similar to that used by the C-shell. For the two strings to match, their contents must be identical, except that the following special sequences may appear in *pattern*:

*	Matches any sequence of characters in *string*, including a null string.
?	Matches any single character in *string*.
[*chars*]	Matches any character in the set given by *chars*. If a sequence of the form x-y appears in *chars*, then any character between x and y, inclusive, will match.
\x	Matches the single character x. This provides a way of avoiding the special interpretation of the characters * ? [ ] \ in *pattern*.

string range *string* first last

Returns a range of consecutive characters from *string*, starting with the character whose index is first and ending with the character whose index is last. An index of 0 refers to the first character of the string. last may be end (or any abbreviation of it) to refer to the last character of the string. If first is less than 0, it is treated as if it were 0, and if last is greater than or equal to the length of the string, it is treated as if it were end. If first is greater than last, an empty string is returned.

string tolower *string*

Returns a value equal to *string*, except that all uppercase letters have been converted to lower case.

string toupper *string*

Returns a value equal to *string*, except that all lowercase letters have been converted to upper case.

string trim *string* [*chars*]

Returns a value equal to *string*, except that any leading or trailing characters from the set given by *chars* are removed. If *chars* is not specified, whitespace is removed (spaces, tabs, newlines, and carriage returns).

string trimleft *string* [*chars*]

Returns a value equal to *string*, except that any leading characters from the set given by *chars* are removed. If *chars* is not specified, whitespace is removed (spaces, tabs, newlines, and carriage returns).

string trimright *string* [chars]

Returns a value equal to *string*, except that any trailing characters from the set given by *chars* are removed. If *chars* is not specified, whitespace is removed (spaces, tabs, newlines, and carriage returns).

translit   TclX

Syntax

translit *inrange outrange string*

Description

This command translates characters in *string*, changing characters occurring in *inrange* to the corresponding characters in *outrange*. *inrange* and *outrange* may be a list of characters or a range, such as in the form A-M.

Example

    translit a-z A-Z foobar
➡ FOOBAR

Time

Table 36–1 Time Commands

Command	Tcl	TclX	Short Description
alarm		✔	Set a process alarm clock
convertclock		✔	Parse and convert a date and time string to an integer clock value
fmtclock		✔	Convert an integer time value to human-readable format
getclock		✔	Return current date and time as an integer value
sleep		✔	Sleep for a specified number of seconds
time	✔		Time the execution of a script
times		✔	Get process and child execute times

alarm　　　　　　　　　　　　　　　　　　　　TclX

Syntax

`alarm` *seconds*

Description

This command instructs the system to send a SIGALRM signal in the specified number of *seconds*. This is a floating-point number, so fractions of a second may be specified. If *seconds* is 0.0, any previous alarm request is canceled. Only one alarm at a time may be active. The command returns the number of seconds left in the previous alarm. On systems without the `setitimer` system call, *seconds* is rounded up to an even number of seconds.

Example

```
proc CatchTheAlarm {} {
       echo sig alarm caught!
}
alarm 5
signal trap SIGALRM CatchTheAlarm
while {1} {sleep 1; echo hello}

hello
hello
hello
hello
hello
sig alarm caught!
...
```

convertclock   TclX

Syntax

convertclock *dateString* [GMT|{}] [*baseClock*]

Description

This command converts *dateString* to an integer clock value (see **getclock**). This command can parse and convert virtually any standard date and/or time string, which can include standard time zone mnemonics. If only a time is specified, the current date is assumed. If the string does not contain a time zone mnemonic, the local time zone is assumed, unless the GMT argument is specified, in which case the clock value is calculated assuming that the specified time is relative to Greenwich Mean Time. If *baseClock* is specified, it is taken as the current clock value. This is useful for determining the time on a specific day.

The character string consists of 0 or more specifications of the following form:

time   A time of day, which is of the form **hh[:mm[:ss]] [meridian] [zone]**
                or **hhmm [meridian] [zone]**. If no meridian is specified, **hh** is
                interpreted on a 24-hour clock.

date   A specific month and day with optional year. The acceptable formats are **mm/dd[/yy], yyyy/mm/dd, monthname dd[, yy], dd monthname [yy]**, and **day, dd monthname yy**. The default year is the current year. If the year is less than 100, then 1900 is added to it.

relative time   A specification relative to the current time. The format is **number unit**; acceptable units are `year`, `fortnight`, `month`, `week`, `day`, `hour`, `minute` (or `min`), and `second` (or `sec`). The unit can be specified as a singular or plural, as in 3 `weeks`. These modifiers may also be specified: `tomorrow`, `yesterday`, `today`, `now`, `last`, `this`, `next`, `ago`.

The actual date is calculated according to the following steps. First, any absolute date and/or time is processed and converted. Using that time as the base, day-of-week specifications are added. Next, relative specifications are used. If a date or day is specified and no absolute or relative time is given, midnight is used. Finally, a correction is applied so that the correct hour of the day is produced after allowing for daylight saving time differences.

convertclock ignores case when parsing all words. The names of the months and days of the week can be abbreviated to their first three letters, with optional trailing period. Periods are ignored in any time zone or meridian values.

Examples

```
convertclock "14 Feb 92"
convertclock "Feb 14, 1992 12:20 PM PST"
convertclock "12:20 PM Feb 14, 1992"
```

fmtclock   TclX

Syntax

fmtclock *clockval* [*format*] [GMT|{}]

Description

This command converts a UNIX integer time value represented by *clockval*. *clockval* is typically provided by **getclock**, **convertclock**, or the `atime`, `mtime`, or `ctime` options of the **file** command, to human-readable form. The *format* argument is a string that describes how the date and time are to be formatted.

Field descriptors consist of `%` followed by a field descriptor character. All other characters are copied into the result. Valid field descriptors are:

`%%`	Insert a `%`
`%a`	Abbreviated weekday name
`%A`	Full weekday name
`%b`	Abbreviated month name
`%B`	Full month name
`%d`	Day of month (01 – 31)
`%D`	Date as `%m/%d/%y`
`%e`	Day of month (1 – 31), no leading zeros
`%h`	Abbreviated month name
`%H`	Hour (00 – 23)
`%I`	Hour (00 – 12)
`%j`	Day number of year (001 – 366)
`%m`	Month number (01 – 12)
`%M`	Minute (00 – 59)
`%n`	Insert a new line
`%p`	AM or PM
`%r`	Time as `%I:%M:%S %p`
`%R`	Time as `%H:%M`
`%S`	Seconds (00 – 59)
`%t`	Insert a tab
`%T`	Time as `%H:%M:%S`
`%U`	Week number of year (01 – 52); Sunday is the first day of the week
`%w`	Weekday number (Sunday = 0)
`%W`	Week number of year (01 – 52); Monday is the first day of the week

%x   Local specific date format

%X   Local specific time format

%y   Year within century (00 – 99)

%Y   Year as **ccyy** (for example, 1990)

%Z   Time zone name

If format is not specified, %a %b %d %H:%M:%S %Z %Y is used. If GMT is specified, the time will be formatted as Greenwich Mean Time. If the argument is not specified or is empty, then the local time zone will be used, as defined by the TIMEZONE environment variable.

Example

```
echo "Today is [fmtclock [getclock] %A]"
```
➡ Today is Sunday

getclock   TclX

Syntax

```
getclock
```

Description

This will return the current date and time as a system-dependent integer value. The unit of the value is seconds, allowing it to be used for relative time calculations.

sleep   TclX

Syntax

sleep *seconds*

Description

This command puts the Tcl interpreter process to sleep for *seconds* seconds.

time   Tcl

Syntax

time *script count*

Description

This command will call the Tcl interpreter *count* times to evaluate script (or once if *count* isn't specified). It will then return a string of the form
➡ 503 microseconds per iteration

which indicates the average amount of time required per iteration, in microseconds. Time is measured in elapsed time, not CPU time.

times   TclX

Syntax

times

Description

This command returns a list containing the process and child execution times in the form:
utime stime cutime cstime. The values are in milliseconds.

Variables

Table 37–1 Variables commands

Command	Tcl	TclX	Short Description
array	✔		Manipulate array variables
for_array_keys		✔	Loop through each key in an array
global	✔		Access global variables
set	✔		Read and write variables
trace	✔		Monitor variable accesses
unset	✔		Delete variables
uplevel	✔		Execute a script in a different stack frame
upvar	✔		Create link to variable for call-by-reference

array   Tcl

Syntax

array *option arrayName* [*arg arg ...*]

Description

This command performs one of several operations on the variable given by *arrayName*. *arrayName* must be the name of an existing array variable. The *option* argument determines what action is carried out by the command. The legal options (which may be abbreviated) are:

array anymore *arrayName* searchId

Returns 1 if there are any more elements left to be processed in an array search, 0 if all elements have already been returned. searchId indicates which search on *arrayName* to check, and must have been the return value from a previous invocation of **array** startsearch. This option is particularly useful if an array has an element with an empty name, since the return value from **array** nextelement won't indicate whether the search has been completed.

array donesearch *arrayName* searchId

This command terminates an array search and destroys all the state associated with that search. searchId indicates which search on *arrayName* to destroy and must have been the return value from a previous invocation of **array** startsearch. Returns an empty string.

array names *arrayName*

Returns a list containing the names of all of the elements in the array. If there are no elements in the array, an empty string is returned.

array nextelement *arrayName* searchId

Returns the name of the next element in *arrayName*, or an empty string if all elements of *arrayName* have already been returned in this search. The searchId argument identifies the search and must have been the return value of an **array** startsearch command.

> **Warning:**   If elements are added to or deleted from the array, then all searches are automatically terminated, just as if **array** donesearch had been invoked; this will cause **array** nextelement operations to fail for those searches.

array size *arrayName*

Returns a decimal string giving the number of elements in the array.

array startsearch *arrayName*

This command initializes an element-by-element search through the array given by *arrayName*, such that invocations of the **array** nextelement command will return the names of the individual elements in the array.

When the search has been completed, the **array** donesearch command should be invoked. The return value is a search identifier that must be used in **array** nextelement and **array** donesearch commands; it allows multiple searches to be underway simultaneously for the same array.

for_array_keys   TclX

Syntax

for_array_keys *var array_name code*

Description

This procedure performs a **foreach**-style loop for each key in the named array, *array_name*. The **break** and **continue** statements work as with **foreach**.

Example

```
set planetsArray(jupiter) {big swirly}
set planetsArray(saturn) {big swirly rings}
set planetsArray(mercury) {small hot}
for_array_keys key planetsArray {
      echo $key is $planetsArray($key)
}
```

➡ jupiter is big swirly
   saturn is big swirly rings
   mercury is small hot

global   Tcl

Syntax

global *varName* [*varName* ...]

Description

This command is ignored unless a Tcl procedure is being interpreted. If so, then it declares the given variable names, *varName*, to be global variables rather than local ones. For the duration of the current procedure (and only while executing in the current procedure), any reference to any of the *varName*s will refer to the global variable by the same name.

set   **Tcl**

Syntax

set *varName* [*value*]

Description

This command returns the value of variable *varName*. If *value* is specified, it sets the value of *varName* to *value*, creating a new variable if one does not already exist, and returns its value. If *varName* contains an open parenthesis and ends with a close parenthesis, it refers to an array element: The characters before the first open parenthesis are the name of the array and the characters between the parentheses are the index within the array. Otherwise, *varName* refers to a scalar variable. If no procedure is active, *varName* refers to a global variable. If a procedure is active, *varName* refers to a parameter or local variable of the procedure unless the **global** command has been invoked to declare *varName* to be global.

trace   **Tcl**

Syntax

trace *option* [*arg arg* ...]

Description

This command causes Tcl commands to be executed whenever certain operations are invoked. At present, only variable tracing is implemented. The legal options (which may be abbreviated) are:

  trace *variable name ops command*

Arranges for *command* to be executed whenever *variable name* is accessed in one of the ways given by *ops*. *name* may refer to a normal variable, an element of an array, or to an array as a whole (i.e., *name* may be just the name of an array, with no parenthesized index). If *name* refers to a whole array, *command* is invoked whenever any element of the array is manipulated. *ops* indicates which operations are of interest and consists of one or more of the following letters:

  r   Invoke *command* whenever the variable is read.

w   Invoke *command* whenever the variable is written.

u   Invoke *command* whenever the variable is unset. Variables can be unset
                 explicitly with the **unset** command, or implicitly when procedures return
                 (all of their local variables are unset). Variables are also unset when
                 interpreters are deleted, but traces will not be invoked because there is no
                 interpreter in which to execute them.

When the trace triggers, three arguments are appended to *command* so that the actual
command is as follows:

```
command name1 name2 op
```

name1 and *name2* give the name(s) for the variable being accessed: If the variable is a
scalar, *name1* gives the variable's name and *name2* is an empty string; if the variable is
an array element, *name1* gives the name of the array and *name2* gives the index into the
array; if an entire array is being deleted and the trace was registered on the overall array,
rather than a single element, *name1* gives the array name and *name2* is an empty string.
op indicates what operation is being performed on the variable, and is one of r, w, or u,
as defined above.

   command executes in the same context as the code that invoked the traced
operation: if the variable was accessed as part of a Tcl procedure, *command* has access to
the same local variables as code in the procedure. This context may be different than the
context in which the trace was created. If *command* invokes a procedure (which it
normally does), the procedure uses **upvar** or **uplevel** if it wishes to access the traced
variable. Note also that *name1* may not necessarily be the same as the name used to set
the trace on the variable; differences can occur if the access is made through a variable
defined with the **upvar** command.

   For read and write traces, *command* can modify the variable to affect the result of
the traced operation. If *command* modifies the value of a variable during a read or write
trace, the new value is returned as the result of the traced operation. The return value
from *command* is ignored except that if it returns an error of any sort, the traced
operation also returns an error with the same error message returned by the **trace**
command (this mechanism can be used to implement read-only variables, for example).
For write traces, *command* is invoked after the variable's value has been changed; it can
write a new value into the variable to override the original value specified in the write
operation. To implement read-only variables, *command* restores the old value of the
variable.

   While *command* is executing during a read or write trace, traces on the variable are
temporarily disabled. This means that reads and writes invoked by *command* occur
directly, without invoking *command* (or any other traces) again. However, if *command*
unsets the variable, unset traces are invoked.

   When an unset trace is invoked, the variable has already been deleted: it appears to
be undefined with no traces. If an unset occurs because of a procedure return, the trace is

invoked in the variable context of the procedure being returned to: The stack frame of the returning procedure no longer exists. Traces are not disabled during unset traces, so if an unset **trace** command creates a new trace and accesses the variable, the trace is invoked. Any errors in unset traces are ignored.

If there are multiple traces on a variable, they are invoked in order of creation, the most recent first. If one trace returns an error, then no further traces are invoked for the variable. If an array element has a trace set, and there is also a trace set on the array as a whole, the trace on the overall array is invoked before the one on the element.

Once created, the trace remains in effect either until the trace is removed with the **trace** vdelete command (described below) until the variable is unset, or until the interpreter is deleted. Unsetting an element of the array removes any traces on that element, but traces on the overall array are not removed.

This command returns an empty string.

    trace vdelete *name ops command*

If there is a trace set on variable *name* with the operations and command given by *ops* and *command*, the trace is removed, so that *command* is never again invoked. This command returns an empty string.

    trace vinfo *name*

Returns a list containing one element for each trace currently set on variable *name*. Each element of the list is itself a list containing two elements, which are the *ops* and *command* associated with the trace. If *name* does not exist or does not have any traces set, the result of the command is an empty string.

unset   Tcl

Syntax

unset *name* [*name name* ...]

Description

This command removes one or more variables. Each *name* is a variable name, specified in any of the ways acceptable to the **set** command. If a name refers to an element of an array, that element is removed without affecting the rest of the array. If a name consists of an array name with no parenthesized index, the entire array is deleted. The **unset** command returns an empty string. An error occurs if any of the variables does not exist, and any variables after the nonexistent one are not deleted.

upvar   **Tcl**

Syntax

upvar [*level*] *otherVar myVar* [*otherVar myVar* ...]

Description

This command arranges for one or more local variables in the current procedure to refer
to variables in an enclosing procedure call or to global variables. *level* may have any of
the forms permitted for the **uplevel** command, and may be omitted if the first letter of
the first *otherVar* isn't # or a digit (it defaults to 1). For each *otherVar* argument,
upvar makes the variable by that name in the procedure frame given by *level* (or at
global level, if *level* is #0) accessible in the current procedure by the name given in the
corresponding *myVar* argument. The variable named by *otherVar* need not exist at the
time of the call; it will be created the first time *myVar* is referenced, just like an ordinary
variable. **upvar** may be invoked only from within procedures. *myVar* may not refer to
an element of an array, but *otherVar* may refer to an array element. **upvar** returns an
empty string.

The **upvar** command simplifies the implementation of call-by-name procedure
calling and also makes it easier to build new control constructs as Tcl procedures. For
example, consider the following procedure:

```
proc Add2 name {
        upvar $name x
        set x [expr $x+2]
}
```

Add2 is invoked with an argument giving the name of a variable, and it adds 2 to the
value of that variable. Although Add2 could have been implemented using **uplevel**,
upvar makes it simpler for Add2 to access the variable in the caller's procedure frame.

If an **upvar** variable is unset (e.g., x in Add2, above), the unset operation affects
the variable to which it is linked, not the **upvar** variable. There is no way to unset an
upvar variable except by exiting the procedure in which it is defined. However, it is
possible to retarget an **upvar** variable by executing another **upvar** command.

Vt Options Classes

Table 38–1   Vt Options Classes

Class Name	*Short Description*
Dialog class	Options that represent resources and widgets typical of common dialogs.
Form class	Options that affect the way that widgets/objects are positioned in a form.
Geometry class	Options that are used by a widget/object in pursuit of being arranged in a form.
Label class	Options that manage how a label is aligned, how it appears as a simple label, or how it appears as a label in a push button.
Object class	A collection of options used by all widgets/objects.

Dialog Class

Description

Dialogs contain standard widgets—such as OK or APPLY push buttons—and associated callbacks that carry out a specific task—such as applying the data provided by the user via the dialog to some operation. The Dialog class provides options that are common to dialogs, such as the automatic handling of OK or APPLY buttons. Manipulation of the window manager is also provided by this class.

Options

The attributes of each Visual Tcl graphical object can often be manipulated, whether by changing the color of the foreground or by updating a label with a new string. In many other cases, the current value of the object's attribute can be retrieved for examination, as well.

The chart below provides symbols to indicate when an option can be set and/or retrieved. These symbols will also be used in Chapter 38, **Vt** *Commands*, where these commands will be discussed in more detail.

Symbol   Meaning

▼   The option can be set after the object is created, using **VtSetValues**.

▲   The value associated with the option can be retrieved after the object is created, using **VtGetValues**.

▼▲   The option can both be set and retrieved by **VtSetValues** and **VtGetValues**, respectively.

`-apply`

Specifies that an Apply button should appear on the form. Also signifies that only the buttons specified with a button, callback, or label reference will be used on the dialog (as opposed to the default buttons for the dialog). If no buttons are specified, the default buttons for that dialog will appear. (This is not applicable to Message dialogs, since there is no Apply button.)

`-applyCallback` *cmd*

Command *cmd* to call when Apply button is pressed.

`-applyLabel` *string*   ▼

Label for the Apply button.

`-autoDestroy` *boolean*   ▼

If boolean is true, the dialog is automatically destroyed after the user hits either the OK button or the Cancel button on the dialog box. The default is true. If false, the dialog must be destroyed with **VtDestroy**. This option is valid only in Selection, File Selection, and Message dialogs.

`-autoHide` *boolean*   ▼

If true, the dialog is automatically hidden after the user hits either the OK button or the Cancel button on the dialog box. The default is true. If false, the dialog must be destroyed with **VtHide**. This option is valid only in Selection, File Selection, and Message dialogs.

`-cancel`

Sets a Cancel button on the form. Also signifies that only the buttons specified with a button, callback, or label reference will be used on the dialog (as opposed to the default buttons for the dialog). If no buttons are specified, the default buttons for that dialog will appear.

`-cancelCallback` *cmd*

Callback *cmd* to call when the Cancel button is pressed in a dialog.

`-cancelLabel` *string*   ▼

Sets the Cancel button label string.

`-defaultButton` OK | APPLY | RESET | CANCEL | HELP | *widgetName*   ▼

Sets the default button for a dialog. (The default button is the one that is selected by default.) For dialog boxes that have predefined buttons you specify the tokens OK or APPLY, and so on. If the user creates a form dialog, the default button is specified by passing in the *widgetName*. This option does not apply to File Selection dialogs.

`-help`

Specifies that a Help button should appear on the form. Also signifies that only the buttons specified with a button, callback, or label reference will be used on the dialog (as opposed to the default buttons for the dialog). If no buttons are specified, the default buttons for that dialog will appear.

`-helpLabel` *string*

Sets the label for the Help button.

`-modeless`   ▼

Sets the dialog to be modeless. This means that input can go to any window (as opposed to modal behavior, which means that only the topmost dialog can accept input).

`-ok`

Specifies that an OK button should appear on the form. Also signifies that only the buttons specified with a button, callback, or label reference will be used on the dialog (as opposed to the default buttons for the dialog). If no buttons are specified, the default buttons for that dialog will appear.

`-okCallback` *cmd*

Sets *cmd* to be the command to call when the OK button in a dialog is pressed. Selection and File Selection dialogs will pass the user's selection as part of the callback data (which is a keyed list). The key to reference is selection.

Additional callback keys

`selection`

>   Selection in the selection dialog

`-okLabel` *string*   ▼

>   Labels the OK button with string.

`-reset`

>   Specifies that a Reset button should appear on the form.

`-resetCallback` *cmd*

>   Sets the callback command *cmd* for the Reset button.

`-resetLabel` *string*

>   Sets the label *string* for the Reset button.

`-wmDecoration ALL |RESIZE |TITLE |BORDER |MENU |MINIMIZE |MAXIMIZE`

>   Sets the window manager window decoration. This applies only in the graphical environment under an OSF/Motif-based window manager. You can combine more than one option; `MINIMIZE` and `MAXIMIZE` apply only on the first dialog created. For example:

>   **VtFormDialog** `$ap.form \`
>   `-wmDecoration {TITLE RESIZE MENU}`

`-wmShadowThickness` *integer*   ▼

>   Works only in character mode. Indicates how much of a shadow to put around dialogs. Zero is no shadow, 1 is the default of a single space on the top and left and a single shadow character on the bottom and right. Numbers above 1 work, but are not optimally designed for visual appearance. Normal setting would be `-wmShadowThickness 0` on the main form dialog and on any subsequent dialogs requiring the full width or height of the screen.

Form Class

Description

Forms provide the "canvas" upon which widgets are placed. The options provided by the Form class address some of the calculations made in the display of the form, as well as the spacing of widgets placed in the form.

Options

`-fractionBase` *integer*

> Specifies the denominator used in calculating the relative position of an object within a form. The numerator is the "distance" given when specifying options such as `-topSide,` `-rightSide,` `-leftSide,` and `-bottomSide.` The default value is 100.

`-horizontalSpacing` *integer*   ▼

> Sets the space between the left and right sides of the objects inside a form. The default value is 5 pixels in graphical mode, 1 character in character mode.

`-marginHeight` *int*   ▼

> Sets the margin between the top or bottom of the objects inside a form. The default value is 10 pixels in graphical mode, 0 in character mode.

`-marginWidth` *int*   ▼

> Sets the margin between the left and right of the objects inside a form. The default value is 10 pixels in graphical mode, 0 in character mode.

`-resizable` *boolean*   ▼

> Specifies whether or not the form will resize if one of the widgets inside it grows or shrinks. The default is true.

`-verticalSpacing` *integer*   ▼

> Sets the space between the top and bottom of objects inside a form. The default value is 5 pixels in graphical mode, 0 in character mode.

If you have a label that is going to have several different length strings displayed in it, you may want to use `-recomputeSize FALSE`. This option (described with Label Class options) will ensure that the label does not resize every time a different length string is displayed. If you allow the label to resize, the form will also resize around it unless you have specified the `-resizable FALSE` option on your form. When you use `-recomputeSize FALSE` on your label, make sure that your label is the size you want it to be when it is created. You can do this by using attachments to the form or other widgets, or you can specify the width of the label.

Geometry Class

Description

The Geometry class options are used to determine the placement of a widget in a form. Within a form, widgets are located relative to each other as well to the edges of the parent form itself.

Options

-above widgetName   ▼

> Used for widget placement. Puts the object above *widgetName*. For example, to create two push buttons, with button b above button a:

```
set a [VtPushButton $fn.a \
    -label "button a" \
    -topSide NONE \
    -bottom FORM]
set b [VtPushButton $fn.b \
    -label "button b" \
    -above $a]
```

Be careful not to put widgets into negative space. In the above example, button a is explicitly attached to the bottom of the form. If it were not, button b would exist outside the viewing form area.

-alignBottom *widgetName*   ▼

> Aligns the bottom of the source object with the bottom side of the target object.

-alignLeft *widgetName*   ▼

> Aligns the left side of the source object with the left side of the target object.

-alignRight *widgetName*   ▼

> Aligns the right side of the source object with the right side of the target object.

-alignTop *widgetName*   ▼

> Aligns the top of the source object with the top side of the target object.

-below widgetName   ▼

> Puts the source object below the target object.

-bottomSide *widgetName* |FORM | distance | NONE   ▼

> Attaches the bottom side of the source object to one of:

the top of the target object

the bottom of the FORM

a distance % of the height of the form from the bottom of the form.

Alternatively, if NONE is specified, any attachment is removed.

-bottomOffset integer   ▼

integer is the amount to offset the bottomSide attachment by (in character widths under character mode, or in pixels under graphical mode).

-leftSide *widgetName* | FORM | distance | NONE   ▼

Attaches the left side of the source object to one of:

the right side of the target object

the left side of the FORM

a distance % of the width of the form from the left side of the form.

Alternatively, if NONE is specified, any attachment is removed.

-leftOffset integer   ▼

integer is the amount to offset the leftOffset attachment by (in character widths under character mode, or in pixels under graphical mode).

-rightSide *widgetName* | FORM | distance | NONE

Attaches the right side of the source object to one of:

the left side of the target object

the right side of the FORM

a distance % of the width of the form from the right side of the form.

Alternatively, if NONE is specified, any attachment is removed.

-rightOffset integer   ▼

integer is the amount to offset the rightOffset attachment by (in character widths under character mode, or in pixels under graphical mode).

-topSide *widgetName* | FORM | distance | NONE   ▼

Attaches the top of the source object to one of:

the bottom of the target object

the top of the FORM

a distance % of the height of the form from the top of the form.

Alternatively, if NONE is specified, any attachment is removed.

-topOffset integer   ▼

>   integer is the amount to offset the topOffset attachment by (in
>   character widths under character mode, or in pixels under graphical mode).

Fractional distances in the options bottomSide, leftSide, rightSide, and topSide are defined in terms of the defined fractionBase value of the form. See the Form class for details.

Object Class

Description

The Object class is an assortment of widget attributes inherited by all Visual Tcl widgets, ranging from the widget's color to user-defined data that can be stored in the widget's data structure, to the callback that is invoked when the user's cursor crosses over the widget's face.

Options

-allowDuplicateName

>   Creates objects with duplicated names. Use this option only if you do not
>   intend to reference the object. A typical use of this option could be in a menu
>   routine where references to the separators are not needed. Referencing an
>   object with duplicated names is undefined and not supported.

-autoLock list_of_callback_procedure_names

>   Locks the server process before calling a callback. The server will lock itself
>   (i.e., not accept any more input) before calling any of the callbacks specified
>   in the list. The lock is exactly the same as calling **VtLock**. The programmer
>   must remember to unlock the application by calling **VtUnLock**. For
>   example:

```
proc lockCB {cbs} {
    sleep 5
    VtUnLock
} . . .

set ap [VtOpen Lock]
set dlog [VtFormDialog $ap.form ]
VtPushButton $dlog.Lock  -callback lockCB -autoLock lockCB
VtShow $dlog
VtMainLoop
```

autoLock is typically used in cases where you are changing the current form and do not want the user to be able to access the form while those changes are being made (for example, if you are stippling fields in the current form).

-background

Sets the background color of the widget to one of the symbolic color names defined in the Visual Tcl application resource file. Predefined symbols are:

urgentColor

highlightColor

foregroundColor

backgroundColor

altBackgroundColor

-baseLineList

Gets the list of baselines for a widget. In character mode this always returns 0. The baseline is the distance from the top of the widget to the baseline of the font for the text within the widget.

-borderWidth *integer*   ▼

Sets the width of the border in pixels. In character mode: If the borderWidth is 0, the border is turned off; if 1, the border is single-lined; if > 1, the border is double-lined.

-errorCallback *cmd*

Sets command *cmd* as the handler to be called when an error occurs in a callback. When an error occurs, Visual Tcl will go up the object tree until it finds an error callback to handle the error.

Additional callback keys

result	Tcl return string
callback	Callback that encountered the error
returnCode	Tcl return code

-font *string*   ▼

Sets the fontList of an object to symbolic font names defined in the Visual Tcl application resource file. Predefined symbols are:

smallPlainFont
smallBoldFont
smallItalicFont
medPlainFont

```
medBoldFont
medItalicFont
largePlainFont
largeBoldFont
largeItalicFont
monoNormalFont
monoBoldFont
monoItalicFont
```

For example:

VtPushButton $parent.button -font largePlainFont

-foreground

Sets the foreground color of the widget to one of the symbolic color names defined in the Visual Tcl application resource file. Predefined symbols are:

```
urgentColor
highlightColor
foregroundColor
backgroundColor
altBackgroundColor
```

-height *integer*   ▼

Sets the height of the object. In graphical mode, integer is the height in pixels. In character mode, *integer* sets the height of the object in character units. The widget must be "managed" before this value can be retrieved with **VtGetValues**. (If the object has -rows as an option, this may be a more convenient way of setting its height.)

-helpCallback *cmd*

Sets the help callback for an object. This callback is called when the <F1> keypress is received by the object. The callback structure returns a keyed list.

Additional callback keys:
tree   Widget tree token (used by help system)

-hidden *boolean*

Specifies whether the object is displayed or not displayed after creation. By default, all nondialog objects are displayed when created.

-sensitive *boolean*   ▼▲

Determines whether the widget receives input events. If set to false, the widget will be grayed and will not accept events. The default is true.

-shortHelpCallback *cmd*   ▼

Sets the *cmd* to call when the mouse button enters or leaves a widget.

Additional callback keys
```
helpString   shortHelpString
             set for the widget
```

`-shortHelpString` *string*   ▼

Sets the string that is sent to the short help callback.

`-width` *integer*   ▼▲

In the graphical environment this sets the width of the widget in pixels. In character mode, it sets the width in characters. The widget must be "managed" before this value can be obtained by **VtGetValues**.

`-userData` *string*   ▼▲

Sets any string that you want to attach to any widget. (This is typically used to attach comment information to widgets that can be retrieved later, using **VtGetValues**.) See also: **VxSetVar** and **VxGetVar**.

`-xmArgs` list_of_string_pairs   ▼

This is a "back-door" routine for setting OSF/Motif resources that have not been implemented. The OSF/Motif resources specified with xmArgs are passed to the widget creation and manipulation commands, as described in the Motif reference manual. For example, this changes the background of the button to blue and the foreground to red:

```
VtPushButton $fn.but \
    -xmArgs {XmNbackground blue XmNforeground red}
```

Note!   Visual Tcl allows you to drop the XmN prefix for Motif resource names. Therefore, background is equivalent to XmNbackground.

Label Class

Description

The Label class supports options that the label widget, commonly used by push buttons, supports. This includes justification of the label, as well as accelerators and mnemonics associated with a push button.

Options

-accelerator *string*   ▼

> Sets the button widget's accelerator. (Accelerators are keystroke
> combinations, usually involving <Ctrl> or <Alt> keys to distinguish them
> from ordinary keypresses to be sent to the application, that invoke a menu or
> a menu item, even when the menu is not displayed.) The accelerator string
> format is like that of a translation, but allows only a single keypress event to
> be specified. For example, to specify the accelerator <Ctrl>N, the string
> Ctrl<Key>N is used.

-acceleratorString *string*   ▼

> Sets the text that is displayed for the accelerator. The string is displayed
> adjacent to the label string or pixmap. For example, the string used to specify
> that <Ctrl>N is the accelerator is Ctrl+N. Accelerator text for buttons is
> displayed only for push buttons and toggle buttons in pulldown and popup
> menus.

-insensitivePixmap *filename*   ▼

> Sets the pixmap to use when the object is insensitive. Do not set this if you
> want it generated for you.

-label *string*   ▼▲

> String that is to be displayed in the widget.

-labelCenter   ▼

> Centers the label within the widget.

-labelLeft   ▼

> Left-aligns the label within the widget.

-labelRight   ▼

> Right-aligns the label within the widget.

-mnemonic *char*   ▼

> To make menu functions even more convenient, menus can have mnemonics
> associated with them. A mnemonic is a letter in a menu button label that can
> be pressed to activate the button. The first character in the label string that
> exactly matches the mnemonic is underlined when the button is displayed.
> When you specify a mnemonic for a pulldown, both the character and
> graphical servers automatically add <Alt>mnemonic as an accelerator for the
> menu.

-pixmap *filename*   ▼

> Sets the pixmap to use in a label or subclass of a label. If you just specify this without specifying -insensitivePixmap or -armedPixmap, those two pixmaps will be automatically generated for you.

-recomputeSize *boolean*   ▼

> Sets whether the widget shrinks or expands to accommodate its content (label or pixmap). This option is recognized only by the graphical server. The default is true. If true, the widget shrinks or expands to exactly fit the label string or pixmap. If false, the widget never attempts to change size on its own.

> If you have a label that is going to have several different length strings displayed in it, you may want to use the -recomputeSize FALSE option. This ensures that the label does not resize every time a different length string is displayed. If you allow the label to resize, the form will also resize around it, unless you specified the -resizable FALSE option on your form. When you use -recomputeSize FALSE on your label, make sure that your label is the size you want it to be when it is created. You can do this by using attachments to the form or other widgets, or you can specify the width of the label.

Vt Commands

There are references here and there to "character" behavior. The version of Visual Tcl that is part of the core SCO OpenServer Release 3 and 5 environments supports a curses-based, character display engine in parallel with the Motif display engine. Because this technology is not supported cross-platform, this book does not give the character personality of Visual Tcl a lot of attention.

The commands below are built on top of the text from the SCO Visual Tcl man pages. As a result, some places contain character references that can be ignored.

Table 39–1 Vt Commands

Command	Short Description
VtAddInput	Add a callback on file activity (read, write, error)
VtAddTimeOut	Add a timeout callback
VtBeep	Ring the terminal bell
VtCheckBox	Create a check box widget and return widget name
VtClose	Close connection to Visual Tcl server and destroy current widgets
VtComboBox	Create a combo box widget and return widget name
VtControl	Bring server into and out of curses raw/cooked mode

Table 39–1   Vt Commands (cont.)

Command	Short Description
VtDestroy	Destroy a widget and its descendants
VtDestroyDialog	Destroy the specified dialog and its descendants
VtDisplayHelp	Display a hard-coded topic name for a widget
VtDrawnList	Create a drawn list object and return the widget name
VtDrawnListAddItem	Add an item to a drawn list
VtDrawnListDeleteItem	Delete an item from a drawn list
VtDrawnListDeselectItem	Deselect an item from a drawn list
VtDrawnListGetItem	Get record(s) from a drawn list
VtDrawnListGetSelectedItem	Return the position of selected items from drawn list
VtDrawnListSelectItem	Select items in a drawn list
VtDrawnListSetItem	Replace contents of item in drawn list
VtDrawnListSetItemValues	Set values of item in drawn list, given specified options
VtErrorDialog	Create error message dialog, return widget name
VtFileSelectionDialog	Create file selection dialog for current directory
VtForm	Create a form, return widget name
VtFormDialog	Create form dialog using form class options
VtFrame	Create frame around single child, return widget name
VtGetValues	Return value of specified option for given widget
VtHide	Hide but do not destroy object
VtHideDialog	Hide but do not destroy dialog box
VtInfo	Return information about Visual Tcl

Table 39–1   Vt Commands (cont.)

Command	Short Description
VtInformationDialog	Create message dialog containing information icon, return widget name
VtLabel	Create label, return widget name
VtList	Create list widget with or without scrollbar, return widget name
VtListAddItem	Add item(s) to list
VtListDeleteItem	Delete item(s) from list
VtListDeselectItem	Deselect item(s) from list
VtListGetItem	Return item(s) from list
VtListGetSelectedItem	Return positions of selected items in a list
VtListSelectItem	Select item(s) in list
VtListSetItem	Set a list item to a specified value
VtLock	Set cursor to watch cursor, lock out user input
VtMenuBar	Create menu bar, return widget name
VtMessageDialog	Create Message dialog, return widget name
VtOpen	Establish connection to Visual Tcl server
VtOptionMenu	Create an option menu widget, return widget name
VtPullDown	Create pulldown menu, return widget name
VtPushButton	Create push button, return widget name
VtQuestionDialog	Create Message dialog containing question icon, return widget name
VtQuitServer	Kill all Visual Tcl applications connected to server, then kill server
VtRadioBox	Create radio box, return widget name
VtRaiseDialog	Raise specified dialog above all others
VtRemoveInput	Remove add input command for fileID
VtRemoveTimeOut	Remove timeout callback

Table 39–1   Vt Commands (cont.)

Command	Short Description
VtRemoveWorkProc	Remove working procedure
VtRowColumn	Create a row column widget
VtScale	Create graphical scale based on current value of field, return widget name
VtSelectionDialog	Create selection dialog, return widget name
VtSeparator	Create horizontal or vertical line, return widget name
VtSetAppValues	Set options for script
VtSetFocus	Set focus to an object
VtSetSensitive	Set sensitivity of an object
VtSetValues	Set value of a widget option
VtShow	Display a previously hidden object
VtShowDialog	Display a previously hidden dialog
VtText	Create text object, return widget name
VtToggleButton	Create toggle button, return widget name
VtUnLock	Unlock specified application
VtWarningDialog	Create Message dialog containing warning icon, return widget name
VtWorkingDialog	Create Message dialog containing working icon, return widget name

VtAddInput

Syntax

VtAddInput *fileID callback*

Description

This command registers a command or procedure callback that is called when an I/O stream is ready for file activity. When the stream referenced by *fileID* becomes readable, writable, or in error, the indicated *callback* command registered is called with the *fileID* as its argument. You can then read and write to the stream without fear of the interpreter blocking.

You must execute **VtMainLoop** to allow the callback to be called.

Example

The following code fragment illustrates the use of **VtAddInput** to filter the output of a UNIX system command, in this case, find.

```
proc DumpFoundCB {fid} {
      set count 1

      while { $count > 0 } {
          set count [gets $fid line];  # read a line of input
          puts stdout ">> $line"
      }

      if { $count == -1 } { ;# end of file
          echo "\n\nFinished"
          exit 0
      }
}; end of DumpFoundCB

set cmd {| /bin/find /usr -name "*" -print}

# open the pipe
if [catch {set f [open  $cmd ] } msg ] {
      echo "open failed"
      exit 1
}

# setup read handler on it..
VtAddInput $f DumpFoundCB
VtMainLoop
```

VtAddTimeOut

Syntax

VtAddTimeOut [*options*]

Description

This command adds a timeout callback. This callback gets called only once. If you want periodic events you must reset the timeout in your callback. This command returns an ID; you will need the ID if you want to remove the timeout with **VtRemoveTimeOut**.

Options

-callback *cmd*   Sets the callback to call after the timeout interval has elapsed.

-interval *integer*   Sets the timeout interval to integer milliseconds. For example, 1000 = 1 second.

VtBeep

Syntax

VtBeep [*options*]

Description

This command rings the terminal bell.

Options

-duration *integer*   On bitmapped terminals, specifies the number of milliseconds that the bell rings. On character terminals, specifies 100 times the number of times the terminal bell rings. For example, -duration 500 will ring the bell for half of a second on a bitmapped terminal, or will ring the bell five times in succession on a character terminal.

-pitch *integer*   Sets the frequency of the bell in Hz. This defaults to the server default pitch. It is ignored when in character mode.

-volume *integer*   Sets the maximum volume *integer* at which to ring the bell (as for XBell(); the range is -100 to +100). The default is 50.

VtCheckBox

Syntax

VtCheckBox *widgetName* [*options*]

Description

This command creates a check box widget. Returns the widget name. This command is used in conjunction with **VtPushButton** to get the full check box effect.

Options

`-callback` *cmd*

Specifies that *cmd* is called when a toggle button in the check box is selected (using the space bar, <Enter> key, or mouse button). This overrides any individual callback set for the contained toggle buttons.

Additional callback keys

`selectedWidget`	List of selected toggle buttons
`value`	List of selected toggle buttons

`-horizontal`   ▼

Sets the orientation to horizontal.

`-numColumns` *integer*   ▼

Sets the number of columns of objects in a row column, check box, or radio box.

`-spacing` *integer*   ▼

Sets the spacing between objects inside a row column. Useful for a toolbar.

`-value` *widgetName*   ▼

Turns on the passed-in toggle button (unsetting all the rest). To set more than one button, use `-valueList`.

-valueList *list*   ▼▲

Takes a list of toggle button widget names and turns those toggle buttons on (unsetting all the rest).

-vertical   ▼

Sets the orientation to vertical.

Inherited Classes

- Object class
- Geometry class

VtClose

Syntax

VtClose

Description

This command closes your connection to the Visual Tcl server and destroys all widgets associated with the current application.

VtComboBox

Syntax

VtComboBox *widgetName* [*options*]

Description

This command creates a combo box widget. Returns the widget name.

Options

-callback *cmd*

Specifies the callback *cmd*. This is called when one of two conditions occurs:

The value changed and the widget lost focus.

The <Enter> keypress was received in the combo box text.

Additional callback keys:

`value`   value in text field of the
combo box

`-columns` *`integer`*   ▼

Makes the object *`integer`* columns wide. This means that *`integer`* characters are shown. In the graphical environment, this will make the width of the object *`integer`* * `MaxCharwidth` wide (where `MaxCharwidth` is the width of the largest character in the current character set).

`-dropListCallback` *`cmd`*

Sets the callback *`cmd`*, called when the droplist on the combo box is opened.

Additional callback keys:

`value`   value in text field of
combo box

`-itemList` *`list`*

Sets a list of items for the combo box object.

`-rows integer`   ▼

Makes the object display *`integer`* rows of text. If there are more than *`integer`* rows, the object will provide a vertical scrollbar (to permit scrolling over the entire list). If there are less than *`integer`* rows, only that number of items will be shown. The default value for *`integer`* is 6.

`-value` *`string`*   ▼

Sets the string to put in the text field in the combo box.

`-valueChangedCallback` *`cmd`*   ▼

Sets the callback *`cmd`* called after text is deleted from or inserted into the widget.

Additional callback keys:

`value`   value in text field of the
combo box

Inherited Class Options

- Objects class
- Geometry class

VtControl

Syntax

`VtControl` [*options*]

Description

This command is used only in the character mode server. It is used to bring the server in and out of curses raw/cooked mode. (In cooked mode, the server preprocesses keyboard input to the application process; in raw mode, all keypresses are transmitted directly.)

Options

`-resume`   Resumes the character mode server and sets curses to raw mode.

`-suspend`   Suspends the character mode server and sets curses to cooked mode.

VtDestroy

Syntax

`VtDestroy` *widgetName*

Description

This command destroys an object (and all its descendants).

VtDestroyDialog

Syntax

`VtDestroyDialog` *widgetName*

Description

This destroys the dialog that is the parent of the *widgetName*. As a convenience you can pass the name of any descendants of the dialog. That way, you can destroy the dialog from a callback without needing to know the name of the dialog.

Example

```
proc pushButtonCB {cbs} {
        set w [keylget cbs widget]
        # w is a reference to the push button
        VtDestroyDialog $w
}
```

VtDisplayHelp

Syntax

VtDisplayHelp *widgetName* [*options*]

Description

This displays a hard-coded topic for *widgetName*.

Options

-book *string*   *string* specifies the help book to search for the topic.

-topic *string*   *string* specifies the help topic to send to the help server.

VtDrawnList

Syntax

VtDrawnList *widgetName* [*options*]

Description

This command creates a drawn list object. Returns the widget name.

Options

-autoSelect *boolean*   ▼

> In character mode, combining this option with -selection BROWSE (which is the default) will automatically select each item as the user arrows down the list. This option has no effect in graphical mode.

-callback *cmd*

> Sets the callback *cmd* to call when you select items in the list (using space bar, <Enter> key, or single mouse click).
>
> *Additional callback keys:*
> itemPosition   selected item
>   position

-columns *integer*   ▼

> In the graphical environment, this will make the width of object *integer* * (the average character width of the font) wide. See the -columnWidth option of **VtSetAppValues** if the maximum character width of the font is needed instead. In character mode, this option makes the object *integer* columns wide.

-defaultCallback *cmd*

> Callback called when the user double-clicks (graphical mode) or presses <Enter> (character mode) on a list item.
>
> *Additional callback keys:*
> itemPosition   selected item
>   position
> valueselected   item position

-fieldList *list*

> Sets a row of data for the drawn list. The default formatting is used on the list if you do not specify -formatList in the command. For example:
>
> ```
> -formatList {{ICON 2} {STRING 20} {STRING 15}}\
> -fieldList [list 1 "John Doe" "555-1212"]
> ```
>
> See the note below.

-formatList *list*   ▼

Describes the columns used in the drawn list. This field contains a list of column descriptions. Each column description, in turn, is a list containing the column type, the column width, and the column's left and right margins. The syntax is:

```
{ TYPE WIDTH [Left Margin, Right Margin] }
```

The left and right margins are optional parameters. The following specifies a column that is of type ICON, with a width of 1 icon and left and right margins of 5 pixels.

```
{ ICON 1 5 5 }
```

Valid types are ICON, STRING, and DATA. DATA does not display on the screen; it is used to store item-specific data. For example:

```
-formatList { {ICON 3} {STRING 20 5} {DATA} }
```

The first column is an icon field with a width of 3, the second column contains a string with a width of 20 and a left margin of 5, and the third column contains hidden data.

-horizontalScrollBar *boolean*   ▼

Sets whether or not a horizontal scroll bar is drawn. You should set the boolean value to true if you want a horizontal scroll bar, false if not. The default value is false. This is ignored in character mode. The maximum size is the width of formatList. If formatList changes, the maximum size will change, too.

-iconList pixmap_filename_list

Sets a list of pixmap filenames to use in the drawn list on graphical systems. On character systems, specify characters to display instead of pixmap file names. Options specific to character displays should be prefixed with CHARM_. For example:

```
-CHARM_iconList {a b c}
-MOTIF_iconList {a.px b.px c.px}
```

(In this example, graphical systems load the pixmaps a.px, b.px, and c.px; character systems load no pixmaps, but display instead the letters a, b, and c.)

-labelFormatList *list*   ▼

> Similar to -formatList but applies to the label. (This option is not
> available in character mode.) Type ICON may be used as a format identifier,
> but currently icons are not supported in drawn list labels.

-labelList *list*   ▼

> Sets the label above the drawn list. (Similar to -fieldList, except that it
> applies to the label.) The format used in -labelFormatList is used.
> This feature is not available in character mode. Note that icons are not
> currently supported in drawn list labels.

-recordList list_of_lists

> Sets one or more rows of data for a drawn list. For example:

```
{ \
{ 0 1 "field one" "field two"} \
{ 1 1 "field one" "field two"} \
{ 1 3 "field one" "field two"} \
}
```

> See the note below.

-rows integer   ▼▲

> Sets the number of rows visible in the drawn list to *integer*.

-selection SINGLE | MULTIPLE   ▼

> (Graphical mode)

> | | |
> |---|---|
> | SINGLE | (This method is used by default.) A single item is always selected. It is possible to select a different item, but not to deselect an item. |
> | MULTIPLE | An item is always selected. It is possible to drag-select on a different item, or to select more than one item, but not to deselect an item. |

-topItemPosition *integer*   ▼▲

> Sets *integer* to be the position of the item shown at the top of the list.

Note: When specifying an icon index in -fieldList or -recordList, the following
indexes can be used to reference connection icons or no icons.

```
CONNECT_L
CONNECT_I
CONNECT_T
NO_ICON
```

Inherited Class Options

- Object class
- Geometry class

VtDrawnListAddItem

Syntax

VtDrawnListAddItem *widgetName* [*options*]

Description

This command adds an item to a drawn list. If you do not specify a position **VtDrawnListAddItem** will append it to the end of the list.

Options

`-fieldList` *list*

Sets a row of data for the drawn list. The default formatting is used on the list if you do not specify `-formatList` in the command. For example:

```
-formatList {{ICON 2} {STRING 20} {STRING 15}}    \
-fieldList  [list 1 "John Doe" "555-1212"]
```

`-formatList` *list*

Describes the columns used in the drawn list. This field contains a list of column descriptions. Each column description, in turn, is a list containing the column type, the column width, and the column's left and right margins. The syntax is:

```
{ TYPE WIDTH [Left_Margin, Right_Margin] }
```

The left and right margins are optional parameters. The following specifies a column that is of type ICON, with a width of 1 icon width and left and right margins of 5 pixels:

```
{ ICON 1 5 5 }
```

Valid types are ICON, STRING, and DATA. DATA is not displayed on the screen; it is used to store item-specific data. An example of a `formatList` is:

```
-formatList { {ICON 3} {STRING 20 5} {DATA} }
```

The first column is an icon field with a width of 3, the second column contains a string with a width of 20 and a left margin of 5, the third column contains hidden data.

-itemBorder NONE | ONOFFDASH | DOUBLEDASH | SOLID   ▼

Used to set a border around a drawn list item. This option applies only to the graphical environment.

-overrideFont *string*   ▼

Sets the font of the drawn list item to one of the symbolic font names defined in the Visual Tcl application resource file. Predefined symbols are:

```
smallPlainFont
smallBoldFont
smallItalicFont
medPlainFont
medBoldFont
medItalicFont
largePlainFont
largeBoldFont
largeItalicFont
monoNormalFont
monoBoldFont
monoItalicFont
```

This option applies only to the graphical environment.

-position *integer*

Sets the position of the item to select in a list or a drawn list. (The base position is 1. To indicate the last item on the list, use 0.)

-recordList list_of_lists

Sets one or more rows of data.

```
{
{ 0 1 "field one"  "field two"}
{ 1 1 "field one"  "field two"}
{ 1 3 "field one"  "field two"}
}
```

When specifying an icon index in -fieldList or -recordList, the following indexes can be used to reference connection icons or no icons:

```
CONNECT_L
CONNECT_I
CONNECT_T
NO_ICON
```

For example:

```
VtDrawnListAddItem $lst \
       -formatList {{ICON 5} {STRING 20 5}} \
       -fieldList {"CONNECT_I NO_ICON 1 CONNECT_H  2"
"Multiple icons" }
```

VtDrawnListDeleteItem

Syntax

VtDrawnListDeleteItem *widgetName* [*options*]

Description

This command deletes an item from a drawn list. It is an error if the position or the field options do not match something in the list.

Options

`-all`

Specifies the entire list.

`-field column matchStr`

Deletes the item whose field column matches the string `matchStr`. For example, if your list contains:

```
{0 1 "String one"}{0 1 "String two"} {0 1 "String three"}
```

specifying

```
-field 2 "String one"
```

would match item 1.

`-position integer`

Specifies a list item by position. The base position is 1. To indicate the last item on the list, use 0.

`-positionList integer_list`

Specifies a list of items to delete by position.

VtDrawnListDeselectItem

Syntax

VtDrawnListDeselectItem *widgetName* [*options*]

Description

This deselects an item from a drawn list. It is an error if the position or the field options do not match something in the list.

Options

-all

>   Deselects the entire list.

-field column matchStr

>   Deselects the item whose field column matches matchStr. For example, if your list contains:
>
>   {0 1 "String one"}{0 1 "String two"} {0 1 "String three"}
>
>   specifying
>
>   -field 2 "String one"
>
>   would match item 1 (i.e., the second item in the list).

-position *integer*

>   Sets the position of an item to deselect.

-positionList *integer_list*

>   Sets a list of positions to deselect.

VtDrawnListGetItem

Syntax

VtDrawnListGetItem *widgetName* [*options*]

Description

This command gets the records from the list and returns a list of lists; a two-dimensional list of the items in the drawn list.

```
{ \
        { 0 {string} {data}} \
        { 0 {string} {data}} \
}
```

Options

`-all`

Gets the entire list.

`-field column matchStr`

Gets fields on the basis of a match on columns of data. For example, if your list contains:

```
{0 1 "String one"}
{0 1 "String two"}
{0 1 "String three"}
```

specifying

`-field 2 "String two"`

matches item 2.

`-position integer`

Sets an item to get by position. The base position is 1. To indicate the last item on the list, use 0.

`-positionList integer_list`

Sets a list of item positions to get. If this option is selected, **VtDrawnListGetSelectedItem** returns a list of positions instead of the normal return value.

VtDrawnListGetSelectedItem

Syntax

VtDrawnListGetSelectedItem *widgetName* [*options*]

Description

This command returns the selected items in the drawn list, returns byPositionList if you do not specify any options.

Options

-byPositionList

Returns items by position list.

-byRecordList

For the drawn list, returns a list of lists of fields; for example:

```
{ { 0 1 "field one" "field two"}
{ 1 1 "field one" "field two"}
{ 1 3 "field one" "field two"}}
```

VtDrawnListSelectItem

Syntax

VtDrawnListSelectItem *widgetName* [*options*]

Description

This command selects the items in a drawn list.

Options

-all

Selects the entire list.

-field *column matchStr*

Selects all items that contain matchStr in column. For example, if your list contains:

```
{0 1 "String one"}
{0 1 "String two"}
{0 1 "String three"}
```

specifying

```
-field 2 "String one"
```

would match item 1.

`-next`

Selects the next item.

`-position` *integer*

Selects an item by list position. The base position is 1. To indicate the last item on the list, use 0.

`-positionList` *integer_list*

Selects a list of items by position.

`-previous`

Selects the previous item.

VtDrawnListSetItem

Syntax

VtDrawnListSetItem *widgetName* [*options*]

Description

This replaces the contents of an item in a drawn list (specified with either `-field` or `-position`) with the new item given in `-fieldList`.

Options

`-field` *column matchStr*

Selects a field to set, based on a match of columns of data. For example, if your list contains:

{0 1 "String one"}{0 1 "String two"} {0 1 "String three"}

specifying

`-field 2 "String one"`

would match item 1.

`-fieldList` *list*

Sets a row of data for the drawn list. The default formatting is used on the list if you do not specify `-formatList` in the command. For example:

```
-formatList {{ICON 2} {STRING 20} {STRING 15}} \
-fieldList  [list 1 "John Doe" "555-1212"]
```

-formatList *list*   ▼

Describes the columns used in the drawn list. This field contains a list of
column descriptions. Each column description in turn is a list containing the
column type, the column width, and the column's left and right margins. The
syntax is:

```
{ TYPE WIDTH [Left Margin, Right Margin] }
```

The left and right margins are optional parameters. The following specifies a
column that is of type ICON, with a width of 1 icon and left and right margins
of 5 pixels:

```
{ ICON 1 5 5 }
```

Valid types are ICON, STRING, and DATA. DATA does not display on the
screen; it is used to store item-specific data.

-position *integer*

Sets an item by list position. The base position is 1. To indicate the last item
on the list, use 0.

When specifying an icon index in -fieldList or -recordList, the following
indexes can be used to reference connection icons or no icons:

```
CONNECT_L
CONNECT_I
CONNECT_T
NO_ICON
```

VtDrawnListSetItemValues

Syntax

VtDrawnListSetItemValues *widgetName* [*options*]

Description

Given an item in a drawn list (via position or field option), this command sets the options
passed in. Currently, -overrideFont and -itemBorder are the only options
available to set. These options work only in the graphical environment.

Options

`-field` *column matchStr*

> Specifies a match string for a column of data in the drawn list. The value of `matchStr` is compared to each field in the named column, and the appropriate records are matched. For example, if your list contains:
>
> `{0 1 "String one"}{0 1 "String two"}  {0 1 "String three"}`
>
> specifying
>
> `-field 2 "String one"`
>
> would match item 1 (i.e., the second item in the list).

`-itemBorder NONE | ONOFFDASH | DOUBLEDASH | SOLID`   ▼

> Used to set a border around a drawn list item. This option applies only to the graphical environment.

`-overrideFont` *string*   ▼

> Sets the font of a drawn list item to one of the symbolic font names defined in the Visual Tcl application resource file. This option applies only to the graphical environment.

`-position` *integer*

> Sets the position of the item whose value is to be set. The base position is 1. To indicate the last item on the list, use 0.

VtErrorDialog

Syntax

VtErrorDialog *widgetName* [*options*]

Description

This command creates a Message dialog that has an "error" icon in it. Returns the widget name. This dialog box comes up with the default push buttons OK, Cancel, and Help. To override the default buttons, the options `-ok`, `-cancel`, `-help`, and `-apply` can be used to specify which buttons go in the dialog. If any one of these options is used, it is assumed that only buttons that have been individually specified or referenced via either a label or a callback option will be put in the dialog.

If the user chooses the OK or Cancel button, the dialog is automatically popped down and destroyed. The `-autoHide` and `-autoDestroy` options can be used to override this default behavior.

Options

`-message` *string*   ▼▲

Sets the text of the message (in *string*). Use \n to separate lines.

Inherited Class Options

- Dialog class
- Object class
- Geometry class

VtFileSelectionDialog

Syntax

VtFileSelectionDialog *widgetName* [*options*]

Description

This command creates a File Selection dialog that displays a list of directories and files for the current directory. The user can select a file from the list or type in the text area. It also allows the user to switch to other directories. The lists are automatically updated to show the list of files and directories in the current directory. Returns the widget name.

By default, File Selection dialogs have OK, Cancel, Help and Filter buttons. The Filter button is used to switch directories. You can choose whether you want the OK, Cancel, and Help buttons by using the options `-ok`, `-cancel`, and `-help` (see Message dialog). The Filter button is always present.

If the user chooses either the OK or Cancel button, the dialog is automatically popped down and destroyed, and the user's selection is passed as a parameter to the OK callback. To override this default, `-autoHide` and `-autoDestroy` options can be used.

Options

-dirListLabel *string*   ▼

>   Sets the label of the directory list box to *string*.

-fileListLabel *string*   ▼

>   Sets the label of the file list box to *string*.

-filter *string*   ▼

>   Sets the pattern used for filtering files (for example, */etc/default/**).

-filterLabel *string*   ▼

>   Sets the label over the box where the user can type in a filter to *string*.

-hideDirList

>   Does not display the directory list.

-hideFilter

>   Does not display the filter text.

-selection *string*   ▼

>   Sets the value of the file name in the file name text widget to *string*.

-selectionLabel *string*   ▼

>   Sets the label over the box where the user can type in a selection.

Inherited Class Options

- Dialog class
- Object class
- Geometry class

VtForm

Syntax

VtForm *widgetName* [*options*]

Description

This command creates a form. Returns the widget name.

Inherited Class Options

- Form class

VtFormDialog

Syntax

VtFormDialog *widgetName* [*options*]

Description

This command creates a Form dialog, using all the standard Form class options. You can specify the buttons across the bottom of the dialog by using the -ok, -okLabel, -okCallback, -cancel, and -help options. The command returns the name of the Form dialog. Buttons are created left to right, in the following order: OK APPLY RESET CANCEL HELP.

Note that when creating a form, it is advisable to make the form the child of another form. This enables the new form to inherit attributes, such as fonts, from the dialog where it was launched. (If the form's parent is a button, it cannot inherit such attributes.)

Note also that you should use **VtGetValues** to get the widget name of any of the buttons on the bottom of the form and the option used to get the button. For example, to get the widget name of the OK button:

    set okButton [**VtGetValues** -ok]

For the Cancel button:

    set cancelButton [**VtGetValues** -cancel]

Options

-cancelButton OK | APPLY | RESET | CANCEL | HELP | *widgetName*   ▼

Sets the widget that is the Cancel button for a dialog (that is, the button that is activated in response to an <Esc> keypress). For dialog boxes that have predefined buttons, you can specify one of the tokens OK, APPLY, CANCEL, or HELP to select the default buttons created by the Form dialog. If you create the Form dialog buttons yourself, you can specify the widget name of the button you have created that you want to be treated as the Cancel button.

-wmCloseCallback *cmd*

>   Registers a callback for the window manager Close menu item.

Inherited Class Options

- Dialog class
- Form class
- Object class
- Geometry class

VtFrame

Syntax

VtFrame *widgetName* [*options*]

Description

This command creates a frame widget that places a three-dimensional border around a single child. Returns the widget name of the frame. The border can have different shadow types in the graphical environment, but in the character mode server it is just a single line.

>   For example, to create an empty box:

```
set frame [VtFrame $form.frame -shadowType ETCHED_IN]
set rowcol [VtRowColumn $frame.rowcol ]
VtLabel $rowcol.lab1 -label "   "
```

Options

-shadowType IN | OUT | ETCHED_IN | ETCHED_OUT   ▼▲

>   Sets the shadow type of the frame.

-title *string*

>   Puts the title at the top of the frame widget. This is not supported in character mode.

Inherited Class Options

- Object class
- Geometry class

VtGetValues

Syntax

VtGetValues *widgetName* [*option*]

Description

This command returns the value of the specified option for the given widget. Only options which have a ▲ symbol next to the option name in the command reference can be retrieved with **VtGetValues**. Only one option can be retrieved at a time. See also: **VtSetValues**.

Options

Valid option for the particular widget. For example:

```
set label [VtGetValues $myLabel -label]
```

Returns the label string for the widget $myLabel.

VtHide, VtHideDialog

Syntax

VtHide *widgetName*
VtHideDialog *widgetName*

Description

VtHide hides but does not destroy an object. This is used to hide the object for later retrieval. Useful if you need to hide a dialog containing information that should not be destroyed. Use **VtShow** to redisplay the object.

VtHideDialog works similarly to **VtHide** but is able to walk up the object tree until it finds a dialog to hide.

VtInfo

Syntax

VtInfo [*options*]

Description

This will return some information about Visual Tcl.

Options

`-charm`

> This is a flag; it returns 1 if running in character mode, otherwise 0.

`-colors`

> This is a flag; it returns the maximum number of colors that can be displayed on the X server. This does not mean that you have that many colors free. The character mode environment always returns 2 (foreground and background).

`-displayHeight`

> Returns the height of the display. In character mode, it returns the number of rows for the terminal; in graphical mode, it returns the number of pixels.

`-displayWidth`

> Returns the width of the display. In character mode, it returns the number of columns for the terminal; in graphical mode, it returns the number of pixels.

`-version`

> Returns the Visual Tcl version.

VtInformationDialog

Syntax

VtInformationDialog *widgetName* [*options*]

Description

This command creates a Message dialog that has an "information" icon in it. Returns the widget name.

Options

```
-message string
```
▼▲

>   Text of the message. Use \n to separate lines.

Inherited Class Options

- Dialog class

VtLabel

Syntax

VtLabel *widgetName* [*options*]

Description

This will create a label. Returns the widget name.

Options

All the Label class options are available.

Inherited Class Options

- Object class
- Geometry class
- Label class

VtList

Syntax

VtList *widgetName* [*options*]

Description

VtList creates a list object. Note that the list object may exist with or without scrollbars; see the `-scrollBar` option for details. Returns the list widget name.

Options

`-autoSelect` *boolean*   ▼

In character mode, combining this option with `-selection` BROWSE will automatically select each item as the user arrows down the list. The default is false. In graphical mode, combining this option with `-selection` BROWSE will cause three callbacks to happen when the mouse is pressed over one item and dragged to the next item (two from the first item, when selecting and deselecting, and one from the second). Consequently, this option is normally only used in character mode (i.e., passed as CHARM_autoSelect).

`-callback` *cmd*

Sets the callback *cmd* to call when you select items in the list (by pressing the space bar, <Enter> key, or a single mouse click).

Additional callback keys:
selectedItemList   List of items
                     selected

`-columns` *integer*   ▼

In the graphical environment this makes the width of the object *integer* * (average character width) wide. See the `-columnWidth` option of **VtSetAppValues**. In character mode, this makes the object integer -2 characters wide (because the boundary line characters are included in the width).

`-defaultCallback` *cmd*

Callback to handle double-click events (in graphical mode) or when <Enter> is pressed on a list item (character mode).

Additional callback keys
selectedItemList   List of items
                     selected.
value   List of items selected.

`-itemList` *list*

Sets a list of items for the list object.

-selection SINGLE | EXTENDED | MULTIPLE | BROWSE   ▼

The selection methods are as follows:

BROWSE

(Chosen by default.) An item in the list is always selected. Users cannot deselect an item; they can only select a different one. A solid line shows around the last selected item.

SINGLE

Simple select and deselect is permitted. Only one item can be selected at a time. A dashed line surrounds the last selected (or deselected) item.

EXTENDED

An item is always selected and is surrounded by a solid line. Drag select (pressing the mouse button with the pointer over the desired items) extends the selection to cover additional objects. Multiple noncontiguous objects can be selected using <Ctrl>mouse-click. <Shift>left-mouse-button selects all the items between the current item and the last item selected. The -callback is invoked when the mouse button is released.

MULTIPLE

Any number of items can be selected or deselected. A dashed line surrounds the last selected or deselected items. Drag selection is not available but noncontiguous selection is direct (that is, selecting additional items does not deselect previous items). The -callback is invoked when each item is selected.

-rows integer   ▼

Sets the number of character rows displayed in an object to integer.

-scrollBar *boolean*   ▼

If this option is set to false, a vertical scrollbar is displayed only when the number of items in the list exceeds the number of visible items. If set to true, a vertical scrollbar is always displayed. The default is false. Note that to get a horizontal scrollbar to appear, the option -width or -columns must be set. Otherwise, the widget will grow as needed and scrollbars will appear only when the list exceeds the available area.

-topItemPosition *integer*   ▼▲

Sets the position of the item that is at the top of the list.

Inherited Class Options

- Object class
- Geometry class

VtListAddItem

Syntax

VtListAddItem *widgetName* [*options*]

Description

This command adds one or more items to a list.

Options

-item *string*

Sets an item for the list widget.

-itemList *list*

Sets a list of items for the list widget.

-position *integer*

Specifies the list position of the new item. The base position is 1. To indicate the last item on the list, use 0.

VtListDeleteItem

Syntax

VtListDeleteItem *widgetName* [*options*]

Description

This command deletes an item or items from a list.

Options

-all

Deletes the entire list.

-item *string*

Sets an item to delete.

-itemList *list*

>   Sets a list of items to delete.

-position *integer*

>   Sets the position of an item in the list to delete. (The base position is 1. To indicate the last item on the list, use 0.)

-positionList *integer list*

>   Sets a list of positions to delete. The base position is 1. To indicate the last item on the list, use 0.

VtListDeselectItem

Syntax

VtListDeselectItem *widgetName* [*options*]

Description

This command deselects one or more items from a list.

Options

-all

>   Sets the entire list as deselected.

-item *string*

>   Deselects a list item.

-itemList *list*

>   Deselects a list of items.

-notify

>   Calls the select callback.

-position *integer*

>   Sets the position of an item to deselect. The base position is 1. To indicate the last item on the list, use 0.

-positionList *integer list*

>   Sets a list of positions to deselect.

VtListGetItem

Syntax

VtListGetItem *widgetName* [*options*]

Description

This command gets one or more items from a list. The returned value depends on the options to the command.

Options

-all

Returns the entire list.

-position *integer*

Returns the list item at offset *integer*. The base position is 1. To indicate the last item on the list, use 0.

-positionList *integer list*

Specifies a list of item positions to return.

VtListGetSelectedItem

Syntax

VtListGetSelectedItem *widgetName* [*options*]

Description

This command gets the list of selected items from a list. By default, the items are returned by -PositionList.

Options

-byItemList

Specifies that a list of selected items is to be returned. For example:

```
{{item 1} {item 2}}
```

`-byPositionList`

Sets the routine to return items by list position; for example:

```
{1 2}
```

returns items in rows 1 and 2.

VtListSelectItem

Syntax

VtListSelectItem *widgetName* [*options*]

Description

This Vt command selects one or more items in a list.

Options

`-all`

Selects the entire list.

`-item` *string*

Selects item *string* from the list.

`-itemList` *list*

Selects all items in list.

`-notify`

Calls the select callback.

`-position` *integer*

Selects the item at position *integer* in list. The base position is 1. To indicate the last item on the list, use 0.

`-positionList` *integer list*

Sets a list of positions to select.

VtListSetItem

Syntax

VtListSetItem *widgetName* [*options*]

Description

This command sets a list item (indicated by -item or -position) to the value specified by -newItem. To set all items in the list, use -itemList.

Options

-item *string*

Sets the item to change.

-itemList *list*

Sets a list of items to change.

-newItem *string*

Sets the new value to assign to the list item being changed.

-position *integer*

Sets the position of an item to change. The base position is 1. To indicate the last item on the list, use 0.

VtLock

Syntax

VtLock

Description

This Vt command sets the cursor to the watch cursor and locks the application. The application will no longer accept input from the user. New dialogs that are about to pop up are also automatically locked. To unlock the application, see **VtUnLock**. **VtLock** can be called multiple times. Calling **VtUnLock** will free all of the current locks. If you wish only to unlock one layer of the nested locks, use **VtUnLock** -once.

VtMenuBar

Syntax

VtMenuBar *widgetName* [*options*]

Description

This command creates a menu bar. Returns the widget name.

Options

-helpMenuItemList ON_VERSION | ON_CONTEXT | ON_WINDOW |
ON_KEYS | INDEX | TUTORIAL | HELP

　　Sets the default help menu in a menu bar. For example:

　　VtMenuBar $parent.menubar \
　　　　-helpMenuItemList {ON_VERSION ON_CONTEXT}

　　Note that help ON_CONTEXT does not work in character mode.

-spacing *integer*   ▼

　　Sets the spacing between items in a menu bar. Useful for creating toolbars.

Inherited Options

- Object class
- Geometry class

VtMessageDialog

Syntax

VtMessageDialog *widgetName* [*options*]

Description

This command creates a dialog box that contains a message and the default push buttons OK, Cancel, and Help. Returns the widget name of the dialog. All the standard dialog options are also supported. To override the default buttons, the options -ok, -cancel, and -help can be used to specify which buttons go in the dialog. If any one of these options is used, it is assumed that only buttons that have been individually specified or referenced via either a label or a callback option will be put in the dialog.

If the user chooses the OK or Cancel button, the dialog is automatically popped down and destroyed. The -autoHide and -autoDestroy options can be used to override this default behavior.

For example:

```
set msg [VtMessageDialog $but.msg -message "Hi there!" -ok]
VtShow $msg
```

Options

-message *string*

    Sets the text of the message. Use \n to separate lines.

Inherited Class Options

- Dialog class
- Object class
- Geometry class

VtOpen

Syntax

VtOpen class [*options*]

Description

This command establishes a connection to Visual Tcl. An optional second argument is the book name for SCO help books. Returns the application name to be used as a parent for the top form.

Options

-helpBook *bookname*

Specifies the book name to reference for SCO help calls.

VtOptionMenu

Syntax

VtOptionMenu *widgetName* [*options*]

Description

This command creates an option menu widget, which is a menu system component that lets a user select one of several choices. Option menus are created like pulldown menus. First the option menu is created and then it is "filled in" with other widgets. The Label class options are supported so that the option menus can be titled. Returns the option menu widget's name.

For example, to create an option menu with the options dog, cat, and frog:

```
set menu [VtOptionMenu $form.menu -label "Pick one:"]
set but1 [VtPushButton $menu.but1 -label dog]
set but2 [VtPushButton $menu.but2 -label cat]
set but3 [VtPushButton $menu.but3 -label frog]
```

Callbacks can be assigned to the individual widgets that make up the option menu, or a callback can be assigned to the option menu itself. If this is done, callbacks assigned to the option menu children will be overridden, and the option menu callback will be called if any of the children are activated. The child that caused the callback to be called will be passed as callback data.

Options

-callback *cmd*

Sets callback *cmd* as the routine to call when any of the options are activated (by the space bar, <Enter> key, or a single mouse-click). This callback overrides any activation callbacks assigned to children of the option menu.

Additional callback keys
selectedWidget:
    The name of the widget that activated this callback
value:
    The value of the widget that activated this callback

-selectedWidget *widgetName*

>   Specifies the name of the widget that is selected in the option menu.

Inherited Class Options

- Label class
- Object class
- Geometry class

VtPullDown

Syntax

VtPullDown *widgetName* [*options*]

Description

This command creates a pulldown menu. Label resources can be used to title the menu.

Options

-cascadeButton   ▲

>   This flag can be used only with **VtGetValues**. It returns the widget name
>   of the pulldown's cascadeButton. Use this widget to set options such as
>   -font.

-radioBehavior *boolean*   ▼

>   Specifies that the pulldown should act like a radio box. For example, to make
>   a cascade menu within a pulldown:

```
set menubar [ VtMenuBar $form.menubar]
set pm [ VtPulldown $menubar.phonemenu -label "Phone"]
set check [ VtPulldown $pm.check -label "Check"]
set check_yes [ VtPushButton $check.yes -label "Yes"]
set check_no  [ VtPushButton $check.no  -label "No"]
```

>   This creates a menu (Phone) containing the button check, which cascades to
>   another menu that contains the buttons Yes and No.

Inherited Class Options

- Label class
- Object class
- Geometry class

VtPushButton

Syntax

VtPushButton *widgetName* [*options*]

Description

This command creates a push button. Label class options are used to label the button. Returns the push button widget name.

Options

-callback *cmd*

> Sets the callback to call when you press the button.

>> *Additional callback keys*
>> click
>>> Count number of multiclicks pressed inside a button. This is used to detect double- or triple-click events inside a push button.
>> value
>>> Contains the push button's label string.

-armedPixmap *pixmap_file*   ▼

> Sets the pixmap file to use for the armed pixmap. The armed pixmap is displayed when you press a button.

Inherited Class Options

- Label class
- Object class
- Geometry class

VtQuestionDialog

Syntax

VtQuestionDialog *widgetName* [*options*]

Description

This command creates a Message dialog that has a question icon in it. (All the dialog options are available to set up the dialog box.) Returns the widget name.

This dialog box comes up with the default push buttons OK, Cancel, and Help. To override the default buttons, -ok, -cancel, and -help can be used to specify which buttons go in the dialog. If any one of these options is used, it is assumed that only buttons that have been individually specified or referenced via either a label or a callback option will be put in the dialog. If the user chooses either the OK or the Cancel button, the dialog is automatically popped down and destroyed. To override this default, -autoHide and -autoDestroy options can be used.

For example:

```
set msg [VtQuestionDialog $but.msg -message "Are you
sure?"]
VtShow $msg
```

Options

-message string

Sets the text of the message. Use \n to separate lines.

Inherited Class Options

- Dialog class
- Object class
- Geometry class

VtQuitServer

Syntax

VtQuitServer

Description

This command kills all Visual Tcl applications connected to the Visual Tcl server daemon, then kills the daemon. It is provided for development purposes only. This command should not be used routinely to exit an application, because all applications currently using the server will simultaneously die. It returns nothing.

Warning

Visual Tcl applications cannot trap this command; therefore, if an application issues a **VtQuitServer**, all the currently running applications will die without closing files or saving state information. *For SCO OpenServer Release 5 users, if SCOadmin(ADM) or related applications are running, unpredictable system failures may result.*

VtRadioBox

Syntax

VtRadioBox *widgetName* [*options*]

Description

This creates a radio box. Returns the widget name.

Options

-autoSelect *boolean*   ▼

Works only in character mode. If autoSelect is true, buttons within the radio box are automatically selected when traversing to them. The selection follows the focus when moving between radio buttons with the arrow keys. This provides behavior equivalent to the Microsoft Windows radio box. The default is false.

-callback *cmd*

Sets the *cmd* called when a toggle button in the radio box is selected. This overrides any callback set for the contained toggle buttons.

Additional callback keys

selectedWidget	selected toggle button
value	selected toggle button

`-horizontal`   ▼

    Sets the orientation to horizontal.

`-numColumns` *integer*   ▼

    Sets the number of columns of objects to *integer*.

`-spacing` *integer*   ▼

    Sets the spacing between objects inside a row column.

`-value widgetName`   ▼▲

    Turns on the *widgetName* passed in toggle button.

`-vertical`   ▼

    Sets the orientation to vertical.

Inherited Class Options

- Object class
- Geometry class

VtRaiseDialog

Syntax

VtRaiseDialog *widgetName*

Description

This raises the dialog above all others. This works in graphical mode; it is ignored in character mode.

VtRemoveInput

Syntax

VtRemoveInput *fileID*

Description

This command removes the add input command for *fileID*.
Complement: **VtAddInput**

VtRemoveTimeOut

Syntax

VtRemoveTimeOut *timeOutID*

Description

This removes the timeout callback *timeOutID*.
Complement: **VtAddTimeOut**

VtRemoveWorkProc

Syntax

VtRemoveWorkProc *workProcID*

Description

This removes the working procedure *workProcID*.
Complement: **VtAddWorkProc**

VtRowColumn

Syntax

VtRowColumn *widgetName* [*options*]

Description

This command creates a row column widget. Returns the widget name.

Options

-horizontal   ▼

>   Sets the orientation to horizontal.

-numColumns *integer*   ▼

>   Sets the number of columns of objects in a row column, check box, or radio box to *integer*.

-packing NONE | COLUMN | TIGHT   ▼

>   Sets how items contained in a row column widget are packed.
>
>   NONE — No packing is performed. The x and y attributes of each entry are left alone, and the column widget attempts to become large enough to enclose all entries.
>
>   COLUMN — All entries are placed in identically sized boxes. The boxes are based on the largest height and width values of all the children widgets. The value of numColumns determines how many boxes are placed in the major dimension before extending in the minor dimension.
>
>   TIGHT — Given the current orientation (horizontal or vertical), entries are placed one after the other until the row column must wrap. A row column will wrap when there is no room left for a complete child in that dimension. Wrapping occurs by beginning a new row or column in the next available space. Wrapping continues as often as necessary until all of the children are laid out. In the vertical dimension (columns), the boxes are set to the same width; in the horizontal dimension (rows), the boxes are set to the same depth. Each entry's position in the major dimension is left unaltered; its position in the minor dimension is set to the same value as the greatest entry in that particular row or column. The position in the minor dimension of any particular row or column is independent of all other rows or columns.

-spacing *integer*   ▼

>   Sets the spacing between objects inside a row column to *integer*.

-vertical   ▼

>   Sets the orientation to vertical.

Inherited Class Options

- Object class
- Geometry class

VtScale

Syntax

VtScale *widgetName* [*options*]

Description

This command creates a scale that consists of a bar with a graphical representation that shows the current numerical value of the field. Returns the widget name. For example:

VtScale $form.scale -min 0 -max 100 -value 50

Options

-callback *cmd*

Called when the value of scale is changed. The value of the scale at the time of the callback will be passed as part of the callback data. The key to reference is value.

Additional callback keys
value   value of the scale

-horizontal   ▼

Sets the orientation to horizontal.

-length *integer*   ▼

Sets the length of the scale (specified in number of characters) to *integer* characters (in the character environment). In the graphical environment, sets the length of the scale to *integer* multiplied by the maximum font width.

-max integer   ▼▲

Sets the maximum value that a scale can have.

-min integer   ▼▲

Sets the minimum value that a scale can have.

`-readOnly`

>Flag: if set, the slider is disabled.

`-showValue` *boolean*

>When true, the `VtScale`'s value is shown above the scale. The default is true.

`-title` *string*

>Sets the title string displayed at the bottom of the scale.

`-value` *integer*

>Sets the current value (restricted in range from minimum to maximum.)

`-vertical`   ▼

>Sets the orientation to vertical.

Inherited Class Options

- Object class
- Geometry class

VtSelectionDialog

Syntax

VtSelectionDialog *widgetName* [*options*]

Description

This command creates a Selection dialog that contains a set of widgets that allows the user to select an item from a list or to type the item in a text field. The text field is automatically updated to the item selected from the list. All the dialog options are available to this widget. Returns the dialog widget's name.

By default, Selection dialogs have OK, Cancel, and Help buttons. To override the default buttons, the options `-ok`, `-cancel`, and `-help` can be used to specify which buttons go in the dialog. If any one of these options is used, it is assumed that only buttons that have been individually specified or referenced via either a label or a callback option will be put in the dialog.

If the user chooses either the OK or Cancel button, the dialog is automatically popped down and destroyed, and the user's selection is passed as a parameter to the OK callback. To override this default, `-autoHide` and `-autoDestroy` options can be used.

For example, to display a Selection dialog with the choices a, b or c:

```
set sb [VtSelectionDialog $but.sb \
        -itemList {{a} {b} {c}}]
VtShow $sb
```

Options

`-filename` *string*   ▼

Sets a file (named *string*) that contains the list of items. Each line of the file is considered a list item. The full pathname of the file must be specified.

`-itemList` *list*   ▼

Sets the list of items for the selection box.

`-selection` *string*   ▼

Sets the value of the selection in the selection text widget to *string*. The item in the list is not highlighted.

Inherited Class Options

- Object class
- Geometry class
- Dialog class

VtSeparator

Syntax

VtSeparator *widgetName* [*options*]

Description

This creates a separator widget (a horizontal or vertical line). This is typically used to separate other widgets. Returns the separator widget's name. For example, to create a separator that goes from the left to the right side across a form:

```
VtSeparator $form.sep -leftSide FORM -rightSide FORM
```

Options

`-horizontal`   ▼

Sets the orientation to horizontal.

-length *int* ▼

Sets the length of the separator (specified in number of characters) to *int* in character mode. In graphical mode, set the length of the separator to *int* times the maximum font width.

-vertical ▼

Sets the orientation to vertical.

Inherited Class Options

- Object class
- Geometry class

VtSetAppValues

Syntax

VtSetAppValues *widgetName* [*options*]

Description

This command sets the options for the script. *widgetName* is the value returned when **VtOpen** was executed to create the application.

Options

-columnValue AVERAGE | MAXIMUM

Used to determine the number of pixels per character for the -columns option. If AVERAGE, the width of the average character in the font is used. If MAXIMUM, then the width of the largest character in the font is used. The default is AVERAGE. This option has no effect in character mode.

-errorCallback *cmd*

Sets command *cmd* as the procedure to call when an error occurs in a callback. When an error occurs, Visual Tcl will go up the object tree until it finds an error callback to handle the error.

Additional callback keys

callback	Callback that caused the error.
ErrorCode	Return code from Tcl **eval**.
ResultTcl	Result string, the error string.

-versionString *string*   ▼

Sets the version string *string* for a script. This is displayed when "On version" is picked from the help menu.

VtSetFocus

Syntax

VtSetFocus *widgetName* [*options*]

Description

This command sets the focus to an object. If no direction is set, the focus will be set on to *widgetName*. If a direction is set, it is interpreted relative to *widgetName*.

NOTE!   **VtSetFocus** is functional only *after* you have rendered your form/dialog with **VtShow**.

Options

-direction *dir*

where *dir* is one of the following:

DOWN	Move below *widgetName*.
HOME	Go to the first traversable item in *widgetName*'s group.
LEFT	Move to the item to the left of the *widgetName*.
NEXT	Move to the next item in the tab group.
NEXT_TAB_GROUP	Make the next tab group the active tab group.
PREVIOUS_TAB_GROUP	Make the previous tab group the active group.
RIGHT	Move to the right of *widgetName*.
UP	Move to the top of *widgetName*.

VtSetSensitive

Syntax

VtSetSensitive *widgetName* boolean

Description

This command sets the sensitivity of an object. If boolean is set to 0, the object is grayed out but still readable by the user, and the user is unable to traverse to it. The default is 1.

VtSetValues

Syntax

VtSetValues *widgetName* [*options*]

Description

This is used to set the value of a widget option. The option name used is the same option used in widget creation. Only options that have a ▼ symbol next to the option name in the command reference can be set with **VtSetValues**.

Options

Valid options for the particular widget. Supports -xmArgs for passing X resources to the server. For example:

```
set myLabel [VtLabel -label "temporary name"] |
VtSetValues $myLabel -label "Welcome!"
```

The label is relabeled with the name *Welcome!*

VtShow

Syntax

VtShow *widgetName*

Description

This manages (displays) a previously hidden object.

VtShowDialog

Syntax

VtShowDialog *widgetName*

Description

This manages (displays) a previously hidden object. **VtShowDialog** works similarly to **VtShow** but walks up the widget tree to find the dialog to display.

VtText

Syntax

VtText *widgetName* [*options*]

Description

This command creates a text object and returns the widget name. Text fields display text in a box. The text is editable by default, but you can make it read-only. You can create a single line of text or multiple lines. Text fields are useful for displaying text or for fields where the user needs to enter a value.

Options

-callback *cmd*

Sets the callback to call when an <Enter> keypress is received in a single-line text object.

Additional callback keys
value   contents of the text widget

-columns *integer*   ▼

Make the object *integer* number of columns wide. This means that *integer* characters are shown. In the graphical environment, this will make the width of the object *integer* * Max_Charwidth wide.

-filename *string*   ▼

Sets a file (named *string*) whose contents will be displayed in the text widget.

-horizontalScrollBar *boolean*   ▼

Sets whether to include a horizontal scrollbar. If true, a horizontal scrollbar is displayed. The default value is false. This option is ignored in character mode.

`-losingFocusCallback` *cmd*

Sets the command to call when the text widget loses focus. This routine is called regardless of whether the text has changed.

Additional callback keys

`value`   value of the text widget

`-noEcho` ▼

This is a flag: specifies whether or not echoing should be turned off.

`-readOnly`

This is a flag: when set, disables editing of the text widget.

`-rows integer` ▼

Sets the number of character rows displayed in an object.

`-value` *string* ▼▲

Sets the string value of the text.

`-valueChangedCallback` *cmd* ▼

Sets the command called after text is inserted into or deleted from the widget.

Additional callback keys

`value`   value of the object

`-verticalScrollBar` *boolean* ▼

This is a flag: set to true for a vertical scroll bar, otherwise false. The default value is false. This is ignored in character mode.

`-wordWrap`

Sets word wrap on.

Inherited Class Options

- Object class
- Geometry class

VtToggleButton

Syntax

VtToggleButton *widgetName* [*options*]

Description

This command creates a toggle button. The button may be labeled using the standard Label class options. Returns the widget name.

Options

`-callback` *cmd*

>   Sets the callback *cmd* to call when the toggle button is activated.

>   *Additional callback keys*

>   `set`   state of the toggle button

`-set boolean`   ▼▲

>   Sets the state of a toggle button.

`-value` *boolean*   ▼▲

>   Sets whether the state of the toggle is on or off.

>   *Additional callback keys*

>   `set`   Boolean, state of toggle
>   `value`   Boolean, state of toggle

Inherited Class Options

- Object class
- Geometry class
- Label class

VtUnLock

Syntax

VtUnLock [*options*]

Description

This unlocks the application.

Options

`-once`

> Used when the application has nested locks (that is, it has been locked multiple times) to unlock one layer of the nested locks, as opposed to unlocking all the current locks.

Do not do a **VtUnLock** to release the `-autoLock` lock until after you have done a **VtShow** of your secondary form.

VtWarningDialog

Syntax

VtWarningDialog *widgetName* [*options*]

Description

This creates a Message dialog that has a "warning" icon in it. (The standard dialog options are used to configure the dialog box.) Returns the widget name.

This dialog box comes up with the default push buttons OK, Cancel, and Help. To override the default buttons, `-ok`, `-cancel`, and `-help` can be used to specify which buttons go in the dialog. If any one of these options is used, it is assumed that only buttons that have been individually specified or referenced via either a label or a callback option will be put in the dialog.

If the user chooses either the OK or Cancel button, the dialog is automatically popped down and destroyed. Use the `-autoHide` or `-autoDestroy` options to override this default.

For example:

```
set msg [VtWarningDialog $but.msg -message "Warning!"]
VtShow $msg
```

Options

`-message` *string*   ▼▲

> Sets the text of the message. Use \n to separate lines.

Inherited Class Options

- Dialog class
- Object class
- Geometry class

VtWorkingDialog

Syntax

VtWorkingDialog *widgetName* [*options*]

Description

This creates a Message dialog that has a "working" icon in it. Returns the widget name. This dialog box comes up with the default push buttons OK, Cancel, and Help. To override the default buttons, -ok, -cancel, and -help can be used to specify which buttons go in the dialog. If any one of these options is used, it is assumed that only buttons that have been individually specified or referenced via either a label or a callback option will be put in the dialog. The standard dialog options are available to this widget.

If the user chooses either the OK or Cancel button, the dialog is automatically popped down and destroyed. Use the -autoHide or -autoDestroy options to override this default.

For example:

```
set msg [VtWorkingDialog $but.msg \
        -message "Working..."\
        ]
VtShow $msg
```

Options

-message *string*

    Sets the text of the message. Use \n to separate lines.

Inherited Class Options

- Dialog class
- Object class
- Geometry class

Vx Commands

Table 40–1 Vx Commands

Command	Short Description
VxAlignBaseLines	Set top offset of source widget to line up with baseline of target widget
VxAlignedForm	Create vertically aligned widget(s) in a form, return widget name
VxCenterVertically	Set to offset of source widget to line up with center line of target widget
VxCheckBox	Create a check box supporting titles and labels, return widget name
VxComboBox	Create a combo box supporting titles and labels, return widget name
VxEndFormCB	Destroy parent form of widget calling this command
VxGetShortName	Strip parent widgets off widget name, leaving short name
VxGetVar	Get value of variable associated with widget
VxList	Create a list supporting titles and labels, return widget name
VxMenu	Build a menu, given a menu bar and list of items
VxMenuGetButton	Return widget name in a menu created by **VxMenu**

Table 40–1 Vx Commands (cont.)

Command	Short Description
VxOptionMenu	Return option list that contains push buttons for specified options
VxOptionMenuGetSelected	Return label of selected item in an option menu created by **VxOptionMenu**
VxOptionMenuReplaceOptions	Dynamically change specified options in an option menu created by **VxOptionMenu**
VxOptionMenuSetSelected	Set option menu's value to value referring to the label of the selected push button
VxRadioBox	Create a radio box widget supporting titles and labels
VxRowColumn	Create a **VtRowColumn** widget supporting titles and labels
VxSetLeftOffsets	Set left offset of right-aligned widgets
VxSetVar	Set value of variable and associate with specified widget
VxSpinButton	Create a spin button, return widget name of enclosing form widget
VxSpinButtonSetMaxValue	Set upper boundary for a spin button
VxSpinButtonSetMinValue	Set lower boundary for a spin button
VxText	Create a **VtText** widget supporting titles and labels
VxWidgetVarRef	Return reference for per-widget frames variable

VxAlignBaseLines

Syntax

VxAlignBaseLines *targetWidget* *sourceWidget* [*currentOffset*]

Description

Given two widgets that have been created with the source widget connected via -alignTop to the target widget, this sets the top offset of the source widget so that its baseline lines up with the target widget's baseline.

Options

targetWidget

>The widget to which you are aligning.

sourceWidget

>The widget that will be adjusted.

currentOffset

>Any top offset the target widget already has that must be taken into account. This is optional; the default is 0.

VxAlignedForm

Syntax

VxAlignedForm *objectNamStr dataList*

Description

This command creates one or more vertically aligned widgets within a form, with right-justified labels. Each label and widget are in their own form. Their widget names may be retrieved as follows:

```
Form      VxGetVar $name "form$n"
Widget    VxGetVar $name "widget$n"
Label     VxGetVar $name "label$n"
```

Where $name is the name returned by the **VxAlignedForm** call and $n is the position of the widget. The first widget is number 1. For example:

```
set app [VtOpen Demo]
set dlog [VtFormDialog $app.Dialog -title "My Aligned
form"]
set form [VxAlignedForm $dlog.Align \
      { {"Name:" {VtText -columns 15 -value "John Doe"}}
      {"Address:" {VtText -value "123 Hickory Street"}}
      {"Phone Number:" {VtText -value "800-555-1212"}}
```

```
        }]
VtShow $dlog
VtMainLoop
```

Produces a form like this:

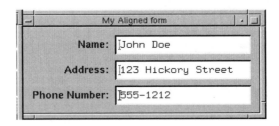

Options

objectNamStr

>   Widget hierarchy of the form.

dataList

>   A list of lists, each containing a label and another list containing the desired widget call and any desired arguments.

VxCenterVertically

Syntax

VxCenterVertically *targetWidget sourceWidget*

Description

Given two widgets that have been created with the *sourceWidget* positioned via -alignTop relative to the *targetWidget*, this sets the top offset of the *sourceWidget* so that the *targetWidget* is in the center.

Options

targetWidget

>   The widget you are centering around.

sourceWidget

>   The widget that will be adjusted.

VxCheckBox

Syntax

VxCheckBox objectNamStr [-title *title*] [-label *label*]
    VtCheckBoxArgs

Description

This command creates a **VtCheckBox**, supporting -title and -label .

Options

objectNamStr

Widget hierarchy of check box.

-title

Creates a form around the check box widget and attaches a label above it. The label is attached to the top side of the form. The check box widget is attached to left, right, and bottom side of the form and also to the bottom side of the label.

-label

Creates a form around the check box widget and attaches a label to the left side of it. The label is attached to the top and bottom of the form. The check box widget is attached to the right, top, and bottom sides of the form.

VtCheckBoxArgs

Any argument(s) legal for **VtCheckBox** options.

To get the *widgetNameStr* of the label or form that is created using this command use **VxGetVar**. For example:

    VxGetVar $widgetNameStr "form"
    VxGetVar $widgetNameStr "label"

VxComboBox

Syntax

VxComboBox *objectNamStr* [-title *title*] [-label *label*]
    VtComboBoxArgs

Description

Creates a **VtComboBox**, supporting -title and -label.

Options

objectNamStr

Widget hierarchy of combo box.

-title

Creates a form around the combo box widget and attaches a label above it. The label is attached to the top side of the form. The combo box widget is attached to left, right, and bottom sides of the form and also to the bottom side of the label.

-label

Creates a form around the Combo box widget and attaches a label to the left side of it. The label is attached to the top and bottom of the form. The combo box widget is attached to the right, top, and bottom sides of the form.

VtComboBoxArgs

Any argument(s) legal for **VtComboBox**.

To get the *widgetNameStr* of the label or form that is created using this command, use **VxGetVar**. For example:

```
VxGetVar $widgetNameStr "form"
VxGetVar $widgetNameStr "label"
```

VxEndFormCB

Syntax

VxEndFormCB

Description

This command is a convenience function for destroying the parent form of the widget by which it was called. This is useful for calls like:

```
set form [VtFormDialog $app.form \
        -ok \
        -okCallback VxEndFormCB]
```

In the above example, when the user presses the OK button, the dialog is destroyed.

VxGetShortName

Syntax

VxGetShortName *widgetNameStr*

Description

Given a widget name, this command strips off all the parent widgets, leaving the short widget name. Returns the stripped widget name.

Options

widgetNameStr
> The widget name to strip.

VxGetVar

Syntax

VxGetVar *widgetNameStr varName*

Description

This command sets the value of the variable associated with the widget.

Options

widgetNameStr
> Name of the widget with which the variable is associated .

varName
> Name of the variable. May be a scalar variable or array reference.

VxList

Syntax

VxList *objectNamStr* [-title *title*] [-label *label*]
   VtListArgs

Description

This command creates a **VtList**, supporting -title and -label.

Options

objectNamStr

   Widget hierarchy of list.

-title

   Creates a form around the list widget and attaches a label above it. The label
   is attached to the top side of the form. The list widget is attached to left, right,
   and bottom sides of the form and also to the bottom side of the label.

-label

   Creates a form around the list widget and attaches a label to the left side of it.
   The label is attached to the top and bottom of the form. The list widget is
   attached to the right, top, and bottom sides of the form.

VtListArgs

   Any argument(s) legal for **VtList**. Returns the widget name of the list
   created.

To get the *widgetNameStr* of the label or form that is created using this command,
use **VxGetVar**. For example:

```
VxGetVar $widgetNameStr "form"
VxGetVar $widgetNameStr "label"
```

VxMenu

Syntax

VxMenu *formDialog MenuBar menuList defaultCB*

Description

This command builds a menu, given a menu bar and a list of items. To create a menu bar on a form dialog, you must specify the form dialog on which to place the menu bar, the widget name of the menu bar, a list of menu item widgets to place on the menu bar, and a default callback (if no callbacks are specified for the menu items). Menu item widgets are buttons; typically, when a button in a menu bar is pressed, its callback creates a menu.

Options

formDialog

>Sets *widgetNameStr* of form dialog.

MenuBar

>Sets *widgetNameStr* of menu bar.

menuList

>Sets menu list from which to build.

defaultCB

>Sets default callback to call if they are not set in *menuList*.

Each item in `menuList` can contain the following indexes:

0. Type: one of pd, hp, cs, bt, or sp.

pd	PullDown
hp	HelpPulldown
cs	CascadeButton
bt	PushButton
sp	Separator

1. Name of the button.
2. Mnemonic.
3. Accelerator.
4. Accelerator string of the button.
5. Callback to associate with the button.
6. If the item is a toggle button, this sets the initial state.

For example:

```
set menuList {
     {pd Phone P}
     {bt Add    A "" "" PhoneMenuAddCB    }
```

```
                        {bt Delete   D "" "" PhoneMenuDeleteCB }
                        {sp}
                        {bt Exit     E "" "" PhoneMenuExitCB   }

                        {pd View V}
                        {bt All      A "" "" ""    }
                        {bt Friends  F "" "" ""    }
                        {bt Enemies  E "" "" ""    }
                        {bt Turkeys  T "" "" ""    }
                }
        set MenuBar [VtMenuBar $form.MenuBar]
        VxMenu $form $MenuBar $menuList defaultCB
```

Use **VxMenuGetButton** to get the reference to a menu item widget; for example:

VxMenuGetButton $dlog "New"

VxMenuGetButton

Syntax

VxMenuGetButton *widgetNameStr buttonLabel*

Description

This command retrieves the widget name of a button in a menu created with **VxMenu**.

Options

widgetNameStr
> Widget name of the menu created by **VxMenu**.

ButtonLabel
> Label of the button to retrieve.

VxOptionMenu

Syntax

VxOptionMenu *objectNamStr label [optionList] defaultCB*
    selection

Description

This command will return the option list that contains push buttons for specified options.

Options

objectNamStr

Widget hierarchy of option menu.

label

Menu label (for example, file name:).

optionList

Tcl list of options (to be used as labels for the push buttons).

defaultCB

Callback to be called when option menu changes.

selection

Option which is initially selected (for example, "one").

VxOptionMenuGetSelected

Syntax

VxOptionMenuGetSelected *widgetNameStr*

Description

This command returns the label of the selected item in an option menu that was created by **VxOptionMenu**.

Options

widgetNameStr

Name of menu returned by **VxOptionMenu**.

VxOptionMenuReplaceOptions

Syntax

VxOptionMenuReplaceOptions *widgetNameStr* [*options*]
    selection

Description

This dynamically changes the options (in an option menu created by **VxOptionMenu**) to the new options passed in.

Options

widgetNameStr

Name of menu returned by **VxOptionMenu**.

selection

Option which is initially selected (for example, "one").

options

Tcl list of options (to be used as labels for the push buttons).

VxOptionMenuSetSelected

Syntax

VxOptionMenuSetSelected *widgetNameStr selection*

Description

This command sets the option menu's value to **selection** where **selection** refers to the label of the selected push button.

Options

widgetNameStr

Name of menu (as returned by **VxOptionMenu**).

selection

Label of option to be selected.

VxRadioBox

Syntax

VxRadioBox *objectNamStr* [*options*] *VtRadioBoxArgs*

Description

This command creates a **VtRadioBox**, supporting -title and -label.

Options

objectNamStr

Widget hierarchy of radio box.

-title *titlestring*

Creates a form around the radio box widget and attaches a label above it. The label is attached to the top side of the form. The radio box widget is attached to left, right, and bottom sides of the form and also to the bottom side of the label.

-label *labelstring*

Creates a form around the radio box widget and attaches a label to the left side of it. The label is attached to the top and bottom of the form. The radio box widget is attached to the right, top, and bottom sides of the form.

VtRadioBoxArgs

Any argument(s) legal for **VtRadioBox**.

To get the *widgetNameStr* of the label or form that is created using this command, use **VxGetVar**. For example:

```
VxGetVar $widgetNameStr "form"
VxGetVar $widgetNameStr "label"
```

VxRowColumn

Syntax

VxRowColumn *objectNamStr* [*options*] *VtRowColumnArgs*

Description

This command creates a **VtRowColumn**, supporting `-title` and `-label`

Options

objectNamStr

Widget hierarchy of row column.

`-title`

Creates a form around the row column widget and attaches a label above it. The label is attached to the top side of the form. The row column widget is attached to left, right, and bottom sides of the form and also to the bottom side of the label.

`-label`

Creates a form around the row column widget and attaches a label to the left side of it. The label is attached to the top and bottom of the form. The row column widget is attached to the right, top, and bottom sides of the form.

VtRowColumnArgs

Any argument(s) legal for **VtRowColumn**.

VxSetLeftOffsets

Syntax

VxSetLeftOffsets *widgetList* [*MOTIFOffset*] [*CHARMOffset*]

Description

Given a list of widgets that have been created with `-%alignRight` relative to the previous label, this command sets the left offset of the first widget so that all the labels fit on the form.

Options

`widgetList`

Sets a list of widgets; the first widget in the list is the one that gets modified.

MOTIFOffset

Sets the graphical environment `leftOffset` possessed by the first widget, which must be taken into account. (This is optional; the default is 0.)

CHARMOffset

Sets the character mode `leftOffset` possessed by the first widget, which must be taken into account. (This is optional; the default is 0.)

To get the *widgetNameStr* of the label or form that is created using this command, use **VxGetVar**. For example:

VxGetVar *$widgetNameStr* "form"
VxGetVar *$widgetNameStr* "label"

VxSetVar

Syntax

VxSetVar *widgetNameStr varName value*

Description

This command sets the value of a variable and associates that variable with the passed-in widget. This is used to store information relevant to the widget (rather than setting a global variable). Returns *value*.

Options

widgetNameStr

Name of the widget with which the variable is associated.

varName

Name of the variable. May be a scalar or array reference.

value

The value assigned to the variable.

VxSpinButton

Syntax

VxSpinButton *objectNamStr* [*options*]

Description

This command creates a spin button called *objectNamStr*, which consists of a text field and two buttons that increase and decrease the numeric value in the text field within upper and lower bounds.

Options

default

The initial default value.

dnOp

Optional operation to perform on *increment* when the Down button is pressed.

increment

Sets how much the value increases or decreases.

lower

The lower boundary value.

overCBA

Callback for when the value goes over the upper bound. If set to "", the package automatically wraps the value around to the lower value.

position

Standard geometry arguments for the text widget.

underCBA

Callback for when the value goes below the lower bound. If set to "", the package automatically wraps the value around to the upper value.

upOp

Optional operation to perform on increment when the Up button is pressed (+ if not present).

upper

>The upper boundary value.

userCBA

>Callback that checks the value of the text widget, or "" for no callback.

width

>The width of the text widget.

Globals

Sblower

>Array of lower boundary values, indexed by widget.

Sbupper

>Array of upper boundary values, indexed by widget.

Returns

The name of the enclosing form widget.

Notes

The returned form widget name is attached to the name of the text widget and row column widget containing the buttons:

>**VxGetVar** $sb text

for the text widget.

>**VxGetVar** $sb rowcol

for the row column widget.

VxSpinButtonSetMaxValue

Syntax

VxSpinButtonSetMaxValue *widgetNameStr upper*

Description

This command sets the upper boundary for a spin button.

Options

widgetNameStr

>   The name of the spin button.

upper

>   The maximum value for the spin button.

Globals

Sbupper

>   Array of upper value boundary values, indexed by instance.

VxSpinButtonSetMinValue

Syntax

VxSpinButtonSetMinValue *widgetNameStr lower*

Description

This command sets the lower boundary for a spin button.

Options

widgetNameStr

>   The name of the spin button.

lower

>   The minimum value for the spin button.

Globals

Sblower

Array of lower value boundary values, indexed by instance.

VxText

Syntax

VxText *objectNamStr* [-title *title*] [-label *label*]
   VtTextArgs

Description

This command creates a text widget supporting -title and -label options.

Options

-title

Creates a form around the text widget and attaches a label above it. The label is attached to the top side of the form. The text widget is attached to left, right, and bottom sides of the form and also to the bottom side of the label.

-label

Creates a form around the text widget and attaches a label to its left side. The label is attached to the top and bottom of the form. The text widget is attached to the right, top, and bottom sides of the form.

VtTextArgs

Any argument(s) legal for **VtText**.

Notes

The widget name of the form and the label, if created, are available from **VxGetVar** under the variable names form and label, respectively.

```
VxGetVar $widgetNameStr "form"
VxGetVar $widgetNameStr "label"
```

VxWidgetVarRef

Syntax

VxWidgetVarRef *widgetNameStr varName*

Description

This command will return a reference for the per-widget variable frames variable. This allows the variable to be passed by reference to other Tcl commands. For example:

array names [**VxWidgetVarRef** my.widget.path data]

Options

widgetNameStr

Name of widget with which the variable is associated.

varName

Name of the variable. May be a scalar or array, but not an element of the array.

Returns

A reference to the variable usable in the current scope.

CD-ROM Instructions

Installing Visual Tcl

If you are running SCO OpenServer Release 5, then you already have SCO Visual Tcl and there is no need to proceed with the following installation instructions.

To install SCO Visual Tcl, do the following:

1. Choose a directory in which to install SCO Visual Tcl. The recommended location is /opt, although you may choose a different location if you wish. Move to this directory by typing:

    ```
    cd /opt
    ```

2. Determine which compressed tar file is the match for your operating system from the following table. Extract the software by typing the associated command.

Platform	You type:
Solaris:	`zcat ./scovt12s.Z | tar xvf -`
SunOS:	`zcat ./scovt12x.Z | tar xvf -`
Intel Solaris:	`zcat ./scovt12i.Z | tar xvf -`
IBM AIX:	`zcat ./scovt12a.Z | tar xvf -`
HP-UX:	`zcat ./scovt12h.Z | tar xvf -`
SGI IRIX:	`zcat ./scovt12m.Z | tar xvf -`
DEC Alpha:	`zcat ./scovt12d.Z | tar xvf -`
Sequent Dynix:	`zcat ./scovt12q.Z | tar xvf -`
SCO UnixWare	`zcat ./scovt12u.Z | tar xvf -`
SCO Open Desktop:	`zcat ./scovt12e.Z | tar xvf -`

If you do not have `zcat`, then type the following sequence:

```
uncompress ./scovt12?.Z
tar xvf ./scovt12?
```

Configuration

When you install SCO Visual Tcl, you should do the following to correctly configure your system, replacing `tcl_dir` with the pathname of the directory in which you installed SCO Visual Tcl:

1. Set the VTCL_HOME environment variable by typing one of the following:

    ```
    Bourne shell: VTCL_HOME=tcl_dir/scovt12<letter> ;
    export VTCL_HOME
    ```

    ```
    C shell:  setenv VTCL_HOME tcl_dir/scovt12<letter>/
    ```

2. The remaining environment variables needed by SCO Visual Tcl can now be set automatically by typing one of the following:

    ```
    Bourne shell: . $VTCL_HOME/share/src/setup/sh-env
    ```

    ```
    C shell:source $VTCL_HOME/share/src/setup/csh-env
    ```

Demo Scripts

Demonstration applets are located in $VTCL_HOME/demo. To run a demonstration applet, do the following:

1. Move to the demo directory by typing the following:

    ```
    cd $VTCL_HOME/demo
    ```

2. Run the appropriate program by typing

    ```
    demo_name
    ```

    or

    ```
    vtcl demo_name
    ```

    replacing `demo_name` with the filename of the demonstration program you wish to run. A browser program is provided to help you use these demonstration programs. To run the browser program type the following:

    ```
    Browser.tcl
    ```

    or

    ```
    vtcl Browser.tcl
    ```

You are presented with a list of demonstration programs. To view one of these programs, click on its name in the list. To run a program, click on the button labeled "Execute...". To quit the browser, click on the Close button.

Files for extending the vtcl interpreter

The Visual Tcl interpreter can be extended with additional functionality written in C. Each port of SCO Visual Tcl includes the three files required in order to link and extend the Tcl interpreter, vtcl.

```
./share/src/vtcl/main.c
./share/include/vtcl.h
./lib/vtcllib.a
```

The method for extending any Tcl interpreter is documented in books such as *Practical Programming in Tcl and Tk* by Brent Welch, Prentice Hall, (1995).

For SCO OpenServer Release 5 users only

The file opensrv.tar contains the main.c, vtcl.h and vtcllib.a files you will need to extend the vtcl interpreter.

The rolodex demonstration application

The distribution for the rolodex example application is contained in the file

```
rolovtcl.tar
```

To extract the distribution, change directory to the place you want to extract the application. For this example, we'll use a fictitious sub-directory in your home environment.

```
cd $HOME/vtcltoys
tar xvf rolovtcl.tar
```

To run the rolodex program, you simply type

```
vtcl main.tcl
```

To run the rolodex program from outside the directory, do the following

1. Copy the file rolo.tcl to a directory in your PATH variable, such as $HOME/bin. Rename it to something like vtrolo.

2. Edit vtrolo so that the first line contains the path name of the Visual Tcl vtcl executable program.

   ```
   #! /bin/vtcl
   ```

3. Then create a UNIX environment variable ROLOENV so that `vtrolo`
    knows where to find its required source files. Unless ROLOENV exists,
    vtrolo will look in your current directory for its companion files.

    ```
    ROLOENV=$HOME/rolodex ; export ROLOENV
    ```

To execute the program, then simply type

```
vtrolo
```

About The Information Refinery, Inc.

The Information Refinery, Inc., or IRI, specializes in the design and implementation of Intranet solutions. IRI assists corporations wishing to take advantage of Intranet products in order to bring the benefits of the Internet to their organizational computing infrastructure. Built upon a foundation of application, network, security and systems management development, IRI distinguishes its services on the basis of commitment to quality, timely delivery, innovation and attention to detail. IRI consulting services include

- Intranet desktop design and construction
- Security design and configuration
- Web server/database design and management
- User and client management

IRI engineers represent over 50 years of combined experience in programming topics ranging from OSF Distributed Computing Environment (DCE) networking to the authoring of papers and books for GUI development. IRI engineers are responsible for the design and implementation of SCO's graphical OSF DCE administration tool, as well as SCO's object-oriented software distribution technology. IRI staff have chaired industry working groups including the X/Open group that defined the XBSA backup services API as well as the Tcl/Tk Conference, Monterey, California 1996.

In its first year of operation, IRI has provided extensive user interface design and networking product development and services to companies such as Cisco Systems and SCO. IRI also coordinated and developed the requirements used by Stanford University for its next-generation distributed computing environment currently under development.

Upcoming Intranet Applications

Leveraging its experience of working with customers trying to apply Internet concepts to the design of Intranet-based solutions, IRI is also developing a suite of Web-based groupware for release in 1997. IRI has developed a technology for enabling on and off-line mobile users to gain the full advantages of Intranet applications that support the same usability that users have grown accustomed to in standard Windows desktop applications. The IRI product will focus on supporting the huge legacy environment of Windows 3.1 users.

Tcl, Tk and Visual Tcl Experts

In addition to its Intranet services, IRI also provides consulting services for the development of graphical user interfaces, network driver development, and technical white paper research and construction, as well as Web server performance measurement. IRI engineers are experts in Tcl-based development including Tk development for Windows and UNIX environments as well as the SCO GUI technology, Visual Tcl. IRI architect, Mark Diekhans, is the co-developer of the TclX Tcl library, covered heavily in this book. IRI developed a Visual Tcl course for Open Learning Center (http://www.openlearning.com). The Visual Tcl Handbook is used as the course text book.

The Information Refinery, Inc.
147 S. River Street, Suite 232,
Santa Cruz, CA 95060
http://www.inforef.com
email:info@inforef.com
408 471 9753
408 471 9754 fax

Index

LICENSE AGREEMENT AND LIMITED WARRANTY

READ THE FOLLOWING TERMS AND CONDITIONS CAREFULLY BEFORE OPENING THIS DISK PACKAGE. THIS LEGAL DOCUMENT IS AN AGREEMENT BETWEEN YOU AND PRENTICE-HALL, INC. (THE "COMPANY"). BY OPENING THIS SEALED DISK PACKAGE, YOU ARE AGREEING TO BE BOUND BY THESE TERMS AND CONDITIONS. IF YOU DO NOT AGREE WITH THESE TERMS AND CONDITIONS, DO NOT OPEN THE DISK PACKAGE. PROMPTLY RETURN THE UNOPENED DISK PACKAGE AND ALL ACCOMPANYING ITEMS TO THE PLACE YOU OBTAINED THEM FOR A FULL REFUND OF ANY SUMS YOU HAVE PAID.

1. **GRANT OF LICENSE:** In consideration of your payment of the license fee, which is part of the price you paid for this product, and your agreement to abide by the terms and conditions of this Agreement, the Company grants to you a nonexclusive right to use and display the copy of the enclosed software program (hereinafter the "SOFTWARE") on a single computer (i.e., with a single CPU) at a single location so long as you comply with the terms of this Agreement. The Company reserves all rights not expressly granted to you under this Agreement.

2. **OWNERSHIP OF SOFTWARE:** You own only the magnetic or physical media (the enclosed disks) on which the SOFTWARE is recorded or fixed, but the Company retains all the rights, title, and ownership to the SOFTWARE recorded on the original disk copy(ies) and all subsequent copies of the SOFTWARE, regardless of the form or media on which the original or other copies may exist. This license is not a sale of the original SOFTWARE or any copy to you.

3. **COPY RESTRICTIONS:** This SOFTWARE and the accompanying printed materials and user manual (the "Documentation") are the subject of copyright. You may not copy the Documentation or the SOFTWARE, except that you may make a single copy of the SOFTWARE for backup or archival purposes only. You may be held legally responsible for any copying or copyright infringement which is caused or encouraged by your failure to abide by the terms of this restriction.

4. **USE RESTRICTIONS:** You may not network the SOFTWARE or otherwise use it on more than one computer or computer terminal at the same time. You may physically transfer the SOFTWARE from one computer to another provided that the SOFTWARE is used on only one computer at a time. You may not distribute copies of the SOFTWARE or Documentation to others. You may not reverse engineer, disassemble, decompile, modify, adapt, translate, or create derivative works based on the SOFTWARE or the Documentation without the prior written consent of the Company.

5. **TRANSFER RESTRICTIONS:** The enclosed SOFTWARE is licensed only to you and may not be transferred to any one else without the prior written consent of the Company. Any unauthorized transfer of the SOFTWARE shall result in the immediate termination of this Agreement.

6. **TERMINATION:** This license is effective until terminated. This license will terminate automatically without notice from the Company and become null and void if you fail to comply with any provisions or limitations of this license. Upon termination, you shall destroy the Documentation and all copies of the SOFTWARE. All provisions of this Agreement as to warranties, limitation of liability, remedies or damages, and our ownership rights shall survive termination.

7. **MISCELLANEOUS:** This Agreement shall be construed in accordance with the laws of the United States of America and the State of New York and shall benefit the Company, its affiliates, and assignees.

8. **LIMITED WARRANTY AND DISCLAIMER OF WARRANTY:** The Company warrants that the SOFTWARE, when properly used in accordance with the Documentation,

will operate in substantial conformity with the description of the SOFTWARE set forth in the Documentation. The Company does not warrant that the SOFTWARE will meet your requirements or that the operation of the SOFTWARE will be uninterrupted or error-free. The Company warrants that the media on which the SOFTWARE is delivered shall be free from defects in materials and workmanship under normal use for a period of thirty (30) days from the date of your purchase. Your only remedy and the Company's only obligation under these limited warranties is, at the Company's option, return of the warranted item for a refund of any amounts paid by you or replacement of the item. Any replacement of SOFTWARE or media under the warranties shall not extend the original warranty period. The limited warranty set forth above shall not apply to any SOFTWARE which the Company determines in good faith has been subject to misuse, neglect, improper installation, repair, alteration, or damage by you. EXCEPT FOR THE EXPRESSED WARRANTIES SET FORTH ABOVE, THE COMPANY DISCLAIMS ALL WARRANTIES, EXPRESS OR IMPLIED, INCLUDING WITHOUT LIMITATION, THE IMPLIED WARRANTIES OF MERCHANTABILITY AND FITNESS FOR A PARTICULAR PURPOSE. EXCEPT FOR THE EXPRESS WARRANTY SET FORTH ABOVE, THE COMPANY DOES NOT WARRANT, GUARANTEE, OR MAKE ANY REPRESENTATION REGARDING THE USE OR THE RESULTS OF THE USE OF THE SOFTWARE IN TERMS OF ITS CORRECTNESS, ACCURACY, RELIABILITY, CURRENTNESS, OR OTHERWISE.

IN NO EVENT, SHALL THE COMPANY OR ITS EMPLOYEES, AGENTS, SUPPLIERS, OR CONTRACTORS BE LIABLE FOR ANY INCIDENTAL, INDIRECT, SPECIAL, OR CONSEQUENTIAL DAMAGES ARISING OUT OF OR IN CONNECTION WITH THE LICENSE GRANTED UNDER THIS AGREEMENT, OR FOR LOSS OF USE, LOSS OF DATA, LOSS OF INCOME OR PROFIT, OR OTHER LOSSES, SUSTAINED AS A RESULT OF INJURY TO ANY PERSON, OR LOSS OF OR DAMAGE TO PROPERTY, OR CLAIMS OF THIRD PARTIES, EVEN IF THE COMPANY OR AN AUTHORIZED REPRESENTATIVE OF THE COMPANY HAS BEEN ADVISED OF THE POSSIBILITY OF SUCH DAMAGES. IN NO EVENT SHALL LIABILITY OF THE COMPANY FOR DAMAGES WITH RESPECT TO THE SOFTWARE EXCEED THE AMOUNTS ACTUALLY PAID BY YOU, IF ANY, FOR THE SOFTWARE.

SOME JURISDICTIONS DO NOT ALLOW THE LIMITATION OF IMPLIED WARRANTIES OR LIABILITY FOR INCIDENTAL, INDIRECT, SPECIAL, OR CONSEQUENTIAL DAMAGES, SO THE ABOVE LIMITATIONS MAY NOT ALWAYS APPLY. THE WARRANTIES IN THIS AGREEMENT GIVE YOU SPECIFIC LEGAL RIGHTS AND YOU MAY ALSO HAVE OTHER RIGHTS WHICH VARY IN ACCORDANCE WITH LOCAL LAW.

ACKNOWLEDGMENT

YOU ACKNOWLEDGE THAT YOU HAVE READ THIS AGREEMENT, UNDERSTAND IT, AND AGREE TO BE BOUND BY ITS TERMS AND CONDITIONS. YOU ALSO AGREE THAT THIS AGREEMENT IS THE COMPLETE AND EXCLUSIVE STATEMENT OF THE AGREEMENT BETWEEN YOU AND THE COMPANY AND SUPERSEDES ALL PROPOSALS OR PRIOR AGREEMENTS, ORAL, OR WRITTEN, AND ANY OTHER COMMUNICATIONS BETWEEN YOU AND THE COMPANY OR ANY REPRESENTATIVE OF THE COMPANY RELATING TO THE SUBJECT MATTER OF THIS AGREEMENT.

Should you have any questions concerning this Agreement or if you wish to contact the Company for any reason, please contact in writing at the address below.

Robin Short
Prentice Hall PTR
One Lake Street
Upper Saddle River, New Jersey 07458